# The Late Foucault

Re-inventing Philosophy as a Way of Life

**Series editors: Keith Ansell-Pearson, Matthew Sharpe, and Michael Ure**

For the most part, academic philosophy is considered a purely theoretical discipline that aims at systematic knowledge; contemporary philosophers do not, as a rule, think that they or their audience will lead better lives by doing philosophy. Recently, however, we have seen a powerful resurgence of interest in the countervailing ancient view that philosophy facilitates human flourishing. Philosophy, Seneca famously stated, teaches us doing, not saying. It aims to transform how we live. This ancient ideal has continually been reinvented from the Renaissance through to late modernity and is now central to contemporary debates about philosophy's role and future.

This series is the first synoptic study of the re-inventions of the idea of philosophy as an ethical pursuit or 'way of life'. Collectively and individually, the books in this series will answer the following questions:

1. How have philosophers re-animated the ancient model of philosophy? How have they revised ancient assumptions, concepts and practices in the light of wider cultural shifts in the modern world? What new ideas of the good life and new arts, exercises, disciplines and consolations have they formulated?
2. Do these re-inventions successfully re-establish the idea that philosophy can transform our lives? What are the standard criticisms of this philosophical ambition and how have they been addressed?
3. What are the implications for these new versions of philosophy as a way of life for contemporary issues that concern the nature of philosophy, its procedures, limits, ends, and its relationship to wider society?

**Other titles in the series:**

*The Selected Writings of Pierre Hadot: Philosophy as Practice,* Pierre Hadot, trans. Matthew Sharpe and Federico Testa

*Effort and Grace: On the Spiritual Exercise of Philosophy,* Simone Kotva

# The Late Foucault

## *Ethical and Political Questions*

Edited by
Marta Faustino and Gianfranco Ferraro

BLOOMSBURY ACADEMIC
LONDON • NEW YORK • OXFORD • NEW DELHI • SYDNEY

BLOOMSBURY ACADEMIC
Bloomsbury Publishing Plc
50 Bedford Square, London, WC1B 3DP, UK
1385 Broadway, New York, NY 10018, USA
29 Earlsfort Terrace, Dublin 2, Ireland

BLOOMSBURY, BLOOMSBURY ACADEMIC and the Diana logo are trademarks of Bloomsbury Publishing Plc

First published in Great Britain 2020
This paperback edition published in 2022

Copyright © Marta Faustino, Gianfranco Ferraro, and Contributors, 2020

Marta Faustino and Gianfranco Ferraro have asserted their right under the Copyright, Designs and Patents Act, 1988, to be identified as Editors of this work.

For legal purposes the Acknowledgements on p. vii constitute an extension of this copyright page.

Series design by Charlotte Daniels
Cover image: Sculpture of Diogenes (© Recebin / Alamy Stock Photo)

All rights reserved. No part of this publication may be reproduced or transmitted in any form or by any means, electronic or mechanical, including photocopying, recording, or any information storage or retrieval system, without prior permission in writing from the publishers.

Bloomsbury Publishing Plc does not have any control over, or responsibility for, any third-party websites referred to or in this book. All internet addresses given in this book were correct at the time of going to press. The author and publisher regret any inconvenience caused if addresses have changed or sites have ceased to exist, but can accept no responsibility for any such changes.

A catalogue record for this book is available from the British Library.

Library of Congress Cataloging-in-Publication Data
Names: Faustino, Marta, editor. | Ferraro, Gianfranco, 1981– editor.
Title: The late Foucault : ethical and political questions / edited by Marta Faustino, Gianfranco Ferraro.
Description: London ; New York : Bloomsbury Academic, 2021. | Series: Re-inventing philosophy as a way of life | Includes bibliographical references and index.
Identifiers: LCCN 2020032076 (print) | LCCN 2020032077 (ebook) | ISBN 9781350134355 (hardback) | ISBN 9781350196773 (paperback) | ISBN 9781350134362 (ebook) | ISBN 9781350134379 (epub)
Subjects: LCSH: Foucault, Michel, 1926-1984.
Classification: LCC B2430.F724 L38 2021 (print) | LCC B2430.F724 (ebook) | DDC 194—dc23
LC record available at https://lccn.loc.gov/2020032076
LC ebook record available at https://lccn.loc.gov/2020032077

ISBN: HB: 978-1-3501-3435-5
PB: 978-1-3501-9677-3
ePDF: 978-1-3501-3436-2
eBook: 978-1-3501-3437-9

Series: Re-inventing Philosophy as a Way of Life

Typeset by RefineCatch Ltd, Bungay, Suffolk

To find out more about our authors and books, visit www.bloomsbury.com and sign up for our newsletters.

# Contents

Acknowledgments — vii

Introduction: Another Word on Foucault's Final Words
*Marta Faustino and Gianfranco Ferraro* — 1

## Part 1  Philosophical Practices, Philosophy as Practice

1. Foucault's Reinvention of Philosophy as a Way of Life: Genealogy as a Spiritual Exercise
*Michael Ure* — 19
2. Self or Cosmos: Foucault *versus* Hadot
*John Sellars* — 37
3. The Great Cycle of the World: Foucault and Hadot on the Cosmic Perspective and the Care of the Self
*Federico Testa* — 53

## Part 2  Care of the Self, Care of Others

4. Foucault According to Stiegler: Technics of the Self
*Amélie Berger Soraruff* — 73
5. Notes Towards a Critical History of Musicalities: Philodemus on the Use of Musical Pleasures and the Care of the Self
*Élise Escalle* — 89
6. Foucault's Ultimate Technology
*Luca Lupo* — 101

## Part 3  Ontology of the Present, Politics of Truth

7. The Care of the Present: On Foucault's Ontological Machine
*Gianfranco Ferraro* — 115
8. Agonistic Truth: The Issue of Power Between the Will to Knowledge and Government by Truth
*Antonio Moretti* — 133
9. From Jurisdiction to Veridiction: The Late Foucault's Shift to Subjectivity
*Laurence Barry* — 149

Part 4  Government of Self, Government of Others

10  Understanding Power Through Governmentality
    *Karim Barakat* — 167
11  On Authority: A Discussion Between Michel Foucault and Hannah Arendt
    *Edgar Straehle* — 183
12  Neoliberal Subjectivity at the Political Frontier
    *Matko Krce-Ivančić* — 197

Part 5  Truth-Telling, Truth-Living

13  Rethinking Confession
    *Andrea Teti* — 215
14  Truth-Telling as Therapeutic Practice: On the Tension Between Psychiatric Subjectivation and Parrhesiastic Self-Cultivation
    *Marta Faustino* — 233
15  Foucault, the Politics of Ourselves, and the Subversive Truth-Telling of Trauma: Survivors as Parrhesiasts
    *Kurt Borg* — 251

List of Contributors — 269
Index — 273

# Acknowledgments

We wish to express our thanks to the Nova Institute of Philosophy (IFILNOVA) for supporting this project in the context of the Art of Living Research Group. We are particularly grateful for its financial support of the 2017 international conference "Government of Self, Government of Others: Ethical and Political Questions in the Late Foucault," from which many of the essays contained in this volume stem. Both the conference and the edition of this book were funded by the FCT (Fundação para a Ciência e Tecnologia).

We are also grateful to Keith Ansell-Pearson, Matthew Sharpe, and Michael Ure for believing in this book and agreeing to include it in the series *Re-inventing Philosophy as a Way of Life*. A special thank you is due to Lucy Russell, Liza Thompson, and the editorial team at Bloomsbury for their interest, patience, and extensive assistance throughout the stages of editing this book. We would also like to acknowledge Carolyn Benson's help with proofreading our own contributions to the volume.

Last but not least, we wish to thank all of the authors who contributed to this volume, the quality of which is due to the excellence of their work. This combination of expertise, personal engagement, and human understanding is extremely rare, and we could not have asked for better partners in producing this work.

# Introduction:
# Another Word on Foucault's Final Words

Marta Faustino and Gianfranco Ferraro

The death of an author never corresponds to his final written words. As Foucault claims in his essay "What Is an Author?," the "relationship between writing and death is ... manifested in the effacement of the writing subject's individual characteristics" (Foucault 1998: 206). After his death, we can only know the writer through "the singularity of his absence"; he must then "assume the role of the dead man in the game of writing" (Foucault 1998: 207). In most cases, this inevitably means that the author is transformed into a victim of his own writing and of third-party decisions about what should or should not be considered part of his "work." Even this, Foucault stresses, is a problematic word. What is the unity that this word designates? What does and does not belong to it? If an author has already disappeared, does everything he once wrote, said, or communicated to others deserve to be published—even if he did not publish it intentionally and explicitly did not want it to be published (posthumously)? If one decides that "everything" should be published, what does "everything" mean, and where does one draw the line? As Foucault himself asks, "how can one define a work amid the millions of traces left by someone after his death?" (Foucault 1998: 207).

Another interconnected problem brought about by an author's death is related to the uses—and often misuses or even abuses—of the words the author leaves behind. How does one seize and evaluate the appropriations (and particularly the misappropriations) of an author's work? There seems to be no escape: after the death of an "author," his "work" begins another life—a life in which it grows and unfolds itself, is expanded, amended and corrected, where it is revised and open to an infinite field of interpretation, commentary, and criticism. All of this occurs in total independence (and sometimes disregard or neglect) of the author, whose words are thus taken, forced, sometimes extorted, often kept in their original context, and brought together in pursuit of the coherence, consistency, and homogeneity demanded by the "author-function" (Foucault 1998: 214–15), or else used as a basis for new and endless possibilities of discourse, in which case the "author function" clearly exceeds his own work (Foucault 1998: 217). The author-person disappears and is rendered a mere function that is "characteristic of the mode of existence, circulation, and functioning of certain discourses within a society" (Foucault 1998: 217). When the author's hand stops writing and his voice can no longer be heard, his name becomes vulnerable and helpless: the paths he had carved out are crossed by a multiplicity of other trails, and the correspondence between the one "who is speaking" and what we receive as his legacy becomes increasingly blurred and dubious. With his death, the author is inevitably exposed to the gaze of the other, rendered completely powerless over the posthumous destiny of his name and work. As Foucault summarizes in the preface to the 1972 edition of the *History of Madness*, it is the final destiny of any book to "disappear without the person who happened to produce it ever being able to claim the right to be its master, and impose what he wished to say, or say what he wanted it to be" (Foucault 2006: xxxviii).

Despite his extreme consciousness and awareness of the vulnerability of the "author" and his efforts to escape the standardized notion of authorship and work—"I am no doubt not the only one who writes in order to have no face. Do not ask who I am and do not ask me to remain the same" (Foucault 2002: 19)—Foucault was far from successful in determining the destiny of his *opus*, and especially the content of his final published words. As is well known, Foucault's early death in 1984 was accompanied by a clear request in his will that none of his works be published posthumously, except for those he had already explicitly authorized.[1] In an incredible act of clairvoyance, Foucault is consistently said to have pleaded to his friends: "Don't pull the Max Brod Kafka-trick on me" (cf. Forrester 2014: 112). However, his posthumous destiny would be tricky and indeed similar to Kafka's. As early as 1997, Gallimard/Seuil began publishing Foucault's lecture courses at the Collège de France (where he held the chair in the History of Systems of Thought from 1970 to 1984), initiating the series out of chronological sequence with *Society Must Be Defended* [*Il faut défendre la société*] (a course held in 1975–6), and concluding it in 2015 with *Penal Theories and Institutions* [*Théories et Institutions pénales*] (a course held in 1971–2).[2] The publications were mainly based on tape recordings made by students with Foucault's consent; as such, the editors could justify their decision to circumvent Foucault's explicit request with the argument that his words had been pronounced in public and, given the existence of authorized audio recordings, that their content had indeed already been public in Foucault's lifetime. The same argument allowed for the publication of other lectures, public conferences, and interviews, such as *L'origine de l'herménéutique de soi, Qu'est-ce que la critique ?, La culture de soi, Discours et vérité, La parrésia* and *Dire vrai sur soi-même* (see Foucault 2013, 2015, 2016, 2017).

A considerably different case, apparently more difficult to justify in the face of Foucault's testamentary request, is the recent publication of the fourth volume of the *History of Sexuality, Les aveux de la chair*, released by Gallimard in 2018 and to date not translated into English. According to Frédéric Gros's preface to this edition, this was a volume that Foucault had clearly planned and prepared for publication. At the time of his death, he was painstakingly amending the typewritten transcription of the manuscript he had already sent to Gallimard; the editors limited their work to correcting the transcription (taking Foucault's own corrections into account), adding missing footnotes, references, and subtitles, translating Greek, Latin, and German quotes, and improving stylistic elements such as punctuation, typos, grammatical mistakes, and the like (Foucault 2018: vii–ix). Although one cannot be completely sure that Foucault would have wanted this book to be published in its current condition, the editors feel they have simply completed Foucault's planned series of volumes of the *History of Sexuality*, sadly interrupted by his sudden death. Be that as it may, the fact is that work on Foucault's unpublished material is ongoing, and we are still far from reaching his final written words.

The decision to circumvent Foucault's clear testamentary (and friendly) request can certainly be reproached from several perspectives—ethical, legal, and juridical. And yet, just as in Kafka's case, it is difficult for readers, critics, and commentators who now have the privilege of accessing some of Foucault's posthumous material not to be grateful for that choice. If this is true for most of the texts, it acquires special relevance when it comes to the final stage of Foucault's thought—the "late Foucault," to which this volume is devoted. Indeed, if his wish had been entirely and literally respected, this late period would be solely represented by the short texts from the 1980s included in *Dits et écrits*, together with the second and third volumes of the *History of Sexuality*—*The Use of Pleasure* [*L'usage des plaisirs*] and *The Care of the Self* [*Le souci de soi*], both published in 1984—which were apparently dramatically disconnected from his previous works, including the first volume of the *History of Sexuality, The Will to Knowledge* [*La volonté de savoir*] (1976).[3] Indeed, whereas the first volume focused on themes Foucault had been developing consistently throughout the 1970s and reflected his genealogical approach to biopolitical institutions, the second and third volumes covered topics that, even though they had been the major focus of Foucault's attention and concern during his last five lecture courses at the Collège de France—from *On the Government of the Living* [*Du gouvernement des vivants*] (1979-80) to *The Courage of Truth* [*Le courage de la vérité*] (1983-4)—were completely unknown to the wider audience, leaving it confused and perplexed by what has been called a surprising "shift" or "turn" in Foucault's thought. What happened to the extremely politicized Foucault of the 1970s? How can we reconcile Foucault's late praise for the technologies of the self and an ethics of care with the inevitably imprisoned and coerced individuals of his previous work on disciplinary and biopolitical power? And how should we interpret Foucault's sudden interest in the ethics of Greco-Roman antiquity?

For some critics and commentators, this ancient or ethical "turn" represented a break in Foucault's thought which eventually made him a representative of individualism, or even neoliberalism.[4] Even today, we have not completely got rid of the idea of a quasi tri-partition in Foucault's thought: a first "archaeological" phase, a second "genealogical" and "biopolitical" one, and a third (final and unfinished) "ethical" or "ancient" one. By making available and understandable the evolution of Foucault's thought during his final years, the complete publication of the lecture courses at the Collège de France allowed not only for general access to a rich and fertile Foucauldian heritage but also for the resolution of tensions, apparent paradoxes, and related misinterpretations of his work as a whole. In short: if the last wishes of Foucault the man had been respected, we would never have had proper access to his final trajectory as an author. This would be a tremendous loss, not only for the universe of readers, scholars, intellectuals, and philosophers who draw on Foucault's work but also, one could say, for the legacy of the very author-function "Foucault."[5]

Given the nature of Foucault's posthumous publications, they must be handled with care, properly distinguished in terms of their importance, put in their specific contexts, and never confused with books published by Foucault. In the lecture courses, for example, Foucault shared his most recent and ongoing research, a sort of work in progress, rather than definitive or final results. As François Ewald and Alessandro Fontana emphasize in the foreword to each of the courses,

> Foucault approached his teaching as a researcher: explorations for a future book as well as the opening up of fields of problematization were formulated as an invitation to possible future researchers. This is why the courses at the Collège de France do not duplicate the published books. They are not sketches for the books even though both books and courses share certain themes. They have their own status. They arise from a specific discursive regime within the set of Foucault's "philosophical activities."
>
> Foucault 2011: xii–xiii

Frédéric Gros comments in the same vein that by listening to—or reading—these lecture courses, "frequently there is the very strong impression of being present at the gestation of a line of research," since "the tone is never dogmatic" (Foucault 2010: 384). Nevertheless, specialized scholarship has used (and perhaps abused) this wave-like revelation of Foucault's previously hidden final train of thought in the persistent attempt to determine and re-determine, time after time, the content, meaning and ultimately the definitive image of Foucault the author on the basis of his successive final publications. Between the first lecture course of the 1980s to be published—*The Hermeneutics of the Subject* [*L'Herméneutique du sujet*] (1981–2) in 2001—and the final course—*Subjectivity and Truth* [*Subjectivité et vérité*] (1980–1) in 2014[6]—there were almost fourteen years of critical commentary. We can thus trace the history of the ways in which Foucault's successive final writings were received, interpreted and integrated into different disciplinary fields and approaches according to the particular perspectives of each of the critics, giving rise to a lively debate that continues today. Over the past two decades, Foucault has thus been many authors labeled in different ways, his author-function being changed, reinterpreted, and reformulated with each new posthumous publication.

Some of the uses and interpretations of Foucault's final words have become particularly famous and influential, to a large extent due to the very authority of the "author-function" of those who produced them. Some of these, such as Gilles Deleuze and Pierre Hadot, interacted with Foucault and exerted their influence on his work at the very time they were also being influenced by it. Their traces are clearly identifiable in Foucault's work, and one might venture to say that certain lines of Foucault's thought would not have existed without them, while the reverse could also be argued. In other cases, such as Giorgio Agamben, Judith Butler, Peter Sloterdijk, Antonio Negri, and Michael Hardt, to name just a few, we see how Foucault's work—and especially his late period—was appropriated, transfigured, and reconfigured, giving rise to new, independent, autonomous, and extremely rich and influential works which, even though they are not identifiable with Foucault's, certainly would never have existed—or, at least, would have been significantly poorer—without Foucault. Scholarly research on Foucault must thus now deal not only with Foucault's "final words" but with the number of words that have been pronounced on them, in an effort to distinguish Foucault from the uses that have been made of him, on the one hand, while promoting and opening up the field of possible future uses, appropriations, and developments of Foucault's legacy, on the other.[7]

It should be noted that this near obsession with Foucault's final words does not seem to fit well with his own struggle against the idea that there could be a final, definitive word or label to describe the meaning of his work once and for all, although the multiple uses, appropriations, and applications that have been made of it is perhaps in line with Foucault's own game with himself as an author. Indeed, one frequently speaks of the multiple uses that have been made of Foucault—but Foucault also made many uses of himself. Throughout his productive life, he constantly played with his name as an author, consistently evading and escaping any general fixing of his words, any final interpretation, any attempt to force on him a specific label or designation that might simply throw him into another black hole in the "history of systems of thought." He was neither (only) a philosopher, nor (only) a historian, nor (only) a sociologist, nor (simply) an intellectual, nor even (merely) a professor: "I don't feel that it is necessary to know exactly what I am. The main interest in life and work is to become someone else that you were not in the beginning" (Foucault and Martin 1988: 9). He equally rejected general classifications of his work that subsume it under basic categories such as "archaeology," "genealogy," or "biopolitics" and instead constantly reworked and redefined the basic concepts and categories with which he and his work would come to be associated or identified. Every time his path risked seeming obvious, he would part ways with it and initiate another unexpected line of research. If his name as an author risked becoming fixed, he would soon trace another life, another genealogy of himself, putting himself to another use and application.[8] As Foucault himself acknowledged, his work is characterized by an endless process of revision, re-working, and self-correction, often permeated by doubt and uncertainty and always open to new understandings and discoveries.[9] In his lifetime, Foucault was already a polemical, controversial, at times confusing and often fashionable author. It is thus not surprising that a similar destiny has accompanied him after his death and that his successive final words continue to replace and relocate the previous ones, making it extremely difficult—and perhaps pointless—to fix the final trajectory of his thought.

This notwithstanding, it is perhaps useful to recall some of Foucault's last pronouncements on himself, not in order to create another rigid fixation or determination of his thought but, quite the contrary, to open up the horizon on which he explicitly wanted his work to be received and ultimately developed and carried through. In an interview from 1982 at the University of Vermont, Foucault described what he considered to be his "role" as follows:

> My role—and that is too emphatic a word—is to show people that they are much freer than they feel, that people accept as truth, as evidence, some themes which have been built up at a certain moment during history, and that this so-called evidence can be criticized and destroyed. To change something in the minds of people—that's the role of an intellectual.
>
> Foucault and Martin 1988: 10[10]

In the same interview, Foucault adds that one of his most important aims was always to show how our most familiar landscapes are not necessary or universal entities but rather a product of very complex political and social processes that have been forgotten (Foucault and Martin 1988: 11). Bringing them to light is both the first step in overcoming them and Foucault's particular contribution in this regard, since, as he explains in another interview from the same period (1984), "philosophy is that which calls into question domination at every level and in every form in which it exists, whether political, economic, sexual, institutional, or what have you" (Foucault 1997a: 300–01). This constant struggle against the present and its multiple forms of coercion, domination, and oppression in order to promote individual freedom and autonomy might be said to characterize Foucault's entire work, even if its explicit formulation, as well as its strong ethical and political significance, only clearly came to the fore in the final period of his thought (cf. Veyne 1993; Veyne 2010: 135). According to François Ewald and Alessandro Fontana, this was an aim that Foucault pursued intensively, not only as a writer but also, and perhaps especially, as a professor, as his courses were never a simple exposition of erudition but were also meant to have a strong performative role in contemporary reality:

> Those who followed his courses were not only held in thrall by the narrative that unfolded week by week and seduced by the rigorous exposition; they also found a perspective on contemporary reality. Michel Foucault's art consisted in using history to cut diagonally through contemporary reality. He could speak of Nietzsche or Aristotle, of expert psychiatric opinion or the Christian pastoral, but those who attended his lectures always took from what he said a perspective on the present and contemporary events. Foucault's specific strength in his courses was the subtle interplay between learned erudition, personal commitment, and work on the event.
>
> Foucault 2011: xv

This constant attempt to directly intervene in the present, which for Foucault could never be accomplished through the mere accumulation and exposition of knowledge, was not disconnected from a certain philosophical attitude or ethos that can equally be said to consistently characterize his practice, especially in his later period. In one of his most self-interpretative and auto-genealogical texts from the final year of his life, "What Is the Enlightenment?" (1984), where Foucault deploys the categories of "ontology of the present" and "critical ontology of ourselves" to his thought, he describes his own philosophical practice in the following terms:

> The critical ontology of ourselves must be considered not, certainly, as a theory, a doctrine, nor even as a permanent body of knowledge that is accumulating; it must be conceived as an attitude, an ethos, a philosophical life in which the critique of what we are is at one and the same time the historical analysis of the limits imposed on us and an experiment with the possibility of going beyond them.
>
> Foucault 1997b: 319

According to the same text, this philosophical ethos is a *"limit-attitude"* which implies "a practical critique that takes the form of a crossing-over" (Foucault 1997b: 315), that is, a historical investigation, both genealogical and archaeological, into the events that constituted us as the subjects of speech, thought, and action that we are today, in order to establish the possibility of transcending those contingent limits and of being, saying, thinking, and doing otherwise. As such, Foucault characterizes the philosophical attitude that is demanded by the critical ontology of ourselves as "a historico-practical test of the limits we may go beyond, and thus as a work carried out by ourselves upon ourselves as free beings" (Foucault 1997b: 315).

This final characterization of his philosophical practice makes clear the strong interconnection and intersection between Foucault's "archaeological" and "genealogical" methods—or, one could say, the consistency of his "archaeo-genealogical" endeavor[11]— adding an ontological component related to the intrinsic connection between a given historical age and the forms of life it determines or enables, combined with a "task" that involves "a work on our limits, that is, a patient labor giving form to our impatience for freedom" (Foucault 1997b: 319).[12] The military vocabulary often used by Foucault in the previous decades ("tactic," "strategic," etc.) already suggested the permeation of his "historical" research with the task he now explicitly formulates: that of directly intervening in the present and in the field of forces that create the present, with a view to overcoming or surpassing them. It is thus not surprising that the "philosophical attitude" he recognizes in the "ontology of the present" or "critical ontology of ourselves" of his last years, deeply influenced by his thorough study of ancient thought and the ethics of care, technologies of the self, and practices of self-transformation, is characterized by the double task of transforming the present through a test and transformation, first and foremost, of oneself.[13] The "work on the limits" and the attribution of form to "our impatience for freedom" is a task that is possible only in the present and through a process of self-transformation directed—one could say, paraphrasing Foucault in his last lecture course—at being *otherwise* and building a world which is *other*.

Indeed, if according to Foucault the Christian tradition had the historical task of transforming the search for a world "which is other" [*un monde autre*] into "another world" [*l'autre monde*] (see Foucault 2011: 247, 319), and of a life which is other into "another life," the opposite task lies before all future readers of and commentators on Foucault's late thought. Now that it has become possible for us to add another word on his final words, it is important to be aware that the only reasonable approach to Foucault's work is not to crystalize those last words but to let them remain infinitely *other* in the endless task of permeating and transforming present lives. This can be achieved only by repeatedly using, applying, and deploying them, letting them tackle our most rooted habits and unfold the many "insides" and "outsides" of our ways of living, while accepting the risk of entering into an archaeology of our practices of living and discovering ourselves, perhaps unexpectedly, as free and autonomous human beings. What is hopefully expected from future commentators and readers— and what we have certainly demanded from ourselves as editors of this volume—is not simply the discovery and offering of *another* word on Foucault's final words, but the ability to allow these words to appear, precisely, as words *which are other*, unraveling a different way of penetrating Foucault's discursive practices and of letting them penetrate our present and our lives, thus transforming them.

\* \* \*

This volume is composed of fifteen essays written by leading scholars from ten different countries on the ethical and political questions at stake in what is generally referred to as "late Foucault." This expression is roughly meant to refer to the period that encompasses the five last lecture courses given by Foucault at the Collège de France, from 1979 to 1984—*On the Government of the Living* (1979–80), *Subjectivity and Truth* (1980–1), *The Hermeneutics of the Subject* (1981–2), *The Government of Self and Others* (1982–3), and *The Courage of Truth* (1983–4)—as well as the second and third volumes of the *History of Sexuality* and the posthumously published fourth volume of the same work, *Les aveux de la chair*. Even though good books on the final stage of Foucault's work are currently available,[14] along with excellent studies on Foucault's ethical and political thought,[15] the recent completion of the publication of Foucault's lecture courses at the Collège de France and the profusion of newly available posthumous material from the same period, together with the liveliness and prodigality of current research and debate in the field, calls for a reappraisal of this final itinerary of Foucault's thought. Indeed, the specific concepts and ideas that Foucault developed during the last years of his productive life—such as the care of the self, governmentality, the ontology of the present, and *parrhēsia*—have important implications for understanding his thought as a whole and provide particularly important tools for reflecting on contemporary ethical and political challenges. They are therefore deserving of a thorough and self-standing treatment.

Our aim is thus to present something of a cartography of the final stage of Foucault's thought, focusing on the key concepts and themes that appear in this phase while at the same time using them to develop a more complex and nuanced approach to his philosophical project as a whole, paying particular attention to the diverse uses and interpretations of Foucault in contemporary philosophy and scholarship. In order to provide a faithful overview of the variety of concerns and perspectives in current scholarship on Foucault, no particular narrative or interpretation was imposed on the authors, and each contributor was given complete freedom to choose his/her own topic, sources and hermeneutic approach. The reader will notice that Foucault's late lecture courses at the Collège de France are no doubt the most recurring source, while the fourth volume of the *History of Sexuality* and the archival material recently made available at France's National Library is still given limited attention. While it is certainly true, as Elden notes, that "with the publication of *Les aveux de la chair* we are entering a new period of Foucault's posthumous reception" (Elden 2018), it is also true that an English translation of this work has yet to be published and that it will take years for it to become fully present and fruitful in the anglophone critical debate on Foucault's work.[16] Given the close continuity of this posthumous book with the work Foucault carried out throughout his lecture courses and the second and third volumes of the *History of Sexuality*, we hope this volume will also provide important tools for reading and engaging with *Les aveux de la chair*, thus supporting a forthcoming new phase in Foucault studies. Our main aim is thus to provide a comprehensive state of the art that simultaneously sheds light on current interpretative trends and encourages new uses and applications of his thought.

The book is divided into five sections, each containing three essays on a specific theme of Foucault's late writings. The aim of each section is to introduce the reader not only to the topic and its role in Foucault's thought, but also to its multiple interpretations, uses, and appropriations in current research.

The first section, "Philosophical Practices, Philosophy as Practice," pays special tribute to the series in which this book is included: "Re-inventing Philosophy as a Way of Life." Indeed, Pierre Hadot's work on ancient philosophy and spiritual practices was one of the most decisive influences in the late period of Foucault's thought, while Foucault's development of notions such as "care of the self" and "technologies of the self" in the second and third volumes of the *History of Sexuality*, and especially in the lecture course *The Hermeneutics of the Subject*, also helped to establish Hadot and the notion of philosophy as a self-transformative practice in current philosophical debates. The three essays contained in this section deal with different aspects of Foucault's reception of Hadot's work and their respective interpretations of ancient philosophy. The first essay, "Foucault's Reinvention of Philosophy as a Way of Life: Genealogy as Spiritual Exercise" by Michael Ure, analyzes the significance of Foucault's studies of antiquity for modern ethics. It examines how Foucault sought to reinvent ancient philosophy in order to develop a contemporary ethics without absolute obligations or sanctions and presents Nietzschean genealogy as Foucault's spiritual exercise. Ure concludes that contemporary subjectivity is partly constituted by a chiastic crossing of the ancient ethics of self-completion and the modern ethics of self-dissolution. The second and third essays discuss Hadot's criticism of Foucault's interpretation of ancient philosophy and put both accounts into perspective. In the second essay, "Self or Cosmos: Foucault *versus* Hadot," John Sellars characterizes both positions as prioritizing either "self" (Foucault) or "cosmos" (Hadot) and assesses their respective strengths and weaknesses. Sellars concludes that the two accounts are more complementary than they are contradictory: while Foucault's account is more plausible when placed within the wider context of his late projects, Hadot's criticisms in part reflect his own background, focused on Neoplatonism. The third essay, "The Great Cycle of the World: Foucault and Hadot on the Cosmic Perspective and the Care of the Self" by Federico Testa, contributes to the debate on the putatively egoistic and disentangled character of Foucauldian ethics in *The Hermeneutics of the Subject* by addressing Pierre Hadot's criticism and offering a political interpretation of the care of the self. After relating the notion of care to the notion of government in Foucault's thought and showing the importance of the cosmos in the care of the self, Testa concludes that what Foucault sees in the perspective of nature is the possibility of a relation to self which is not one of narcissistic self-absorption and moral and political egoism, suggesting that for Foucault it is essentially from ourselves that we must be liberated.

The second section, "Care of the Self, Care of Others," maintains the focus on the central theme of Foucault's lecture course *The Hermeneutics of the Subject*. In this lecture course, Foucault stresses how the notion of *epimeleia heautou* (care of the self) lies at the origins of Western thought and at the center of one of the most ancient and promising ethical frameworks. His focus on the ancient practices of self-constitution, which imply a relation of attention and concern both for oneself and for others, blurs the borders between ethics, politics, and the construction of subjectivity and adds important nuances to his previous views on the subject, power, and government. The essays contained in this part discuss different perspectives opened up by Foucault's focus on the ethics of care. The first essay, "Foucault According to Stiegler: Technics of the Self" by Amélie Berger Soraruff, provides a broad overview of the relevance of the notion of care of the self for Foucault, developing it and contrasting it with the perspective of the French philosopher Bernard Stiegler and his notion of technics. According to Berger Soraruff, while Foucault approaches care from the angle of aesthetics, Stiegler intends to rehabilitate the ancient practice in the current political framework as a means of combatting cultural regression. The two remaining chapters focus on two often neglected topics emerging from Foucault's late lecture course. In Chapter 5, in her essay "Notes Towards a Critical History of 'Musicalities': Philodemus on the Use of Musical Pleasures and the Care of the Self," Élise Escalle draws an interesting connection between "sexual" and "musical" pleasures, using Foucauldian genealogy to show how sexual and musical practices are inseparably and deeply related to the sense of oneself and the practice of self-constitution that lies at the core of the ethics of care. Borrowing from Foucault's late approach to ancient ethics to examine Philodemus' work, Escalle argues that it is possible to find shared historical, cultural and gendered modalities in the "moral problematization" of both "musical" and "sexual" pleasure. Finally, in his essay "Foucault's Ultimate Technology," Luca Lupo relates the practice of the self at stake in the ancient ethics of care with a certain representation of the experience of time, paying special attention to the Stoic technologies and exercises concerning the future (such as the *praemeditatio malorum* and *meditatio mortis*). Emphasizing the connection between the representation of the experience of time and the constitution of subjectivity, Lupo shows how this apparently minor topic in the Foucauldian discourse lies at the very core of his hermeneutics of the subject.

The third section, "Ontology of the Present, Politics of Truth," analyzes both the continuities and the ruptures in the last phase of Foucault's thought. The "ethical turn" that was often attributed to Foucault's late writings on the basis of his shift of attention to Greco-Roman antiquity and the early Christian era is here analyzed and discussed through the prism of two other major topics in Foucault's late texts: the ontology of the present, on the one hand, and the topic of truth, in connection with his lifelong interest in power and the subject, on the other. In the first essay, "The Care of the Present: On Foucault's Ontological Machine," Gianfranco Ferraro stresses how Foucault's research into the notion of "care" is a development of his previous work on disciplinary power and practices, such that the whole hermeneutics of the subject can be interpreted as an original ontological machine. After showing that the "ontology of the present" or "critical ontology of ourselves" with which Foucault characterizes the final stage of this work already permeated his previous archaeological and genealogical approaches, Ferraro argues that the core of Foucault's philosophical practice is a "machine," of which "care" and the "present" are two poles. In the second essay, "Agonistic Truth: The Issue of Power Between the Will to Knowledge and Government by Truth," Antonio Moretti tracks Foucault's references to antiquity throughout his lecture courses at the

Collège de France, underscoring the dynamic connection between power as a productive relationship and truth as an agonistic force. By analyzing within this context the problem of productive power, the relationship between power and knowledge and the issue of how subjectivity is formed, Moretti shows how misleading the notion of an "ancient" or "ethical turn" in Foucault's late thought can be. The third essay, "From Jurisdiction to Veridiction: The Late Foucault's Shift to Subjectivity" by Laurence Barry, contrasts Foucault's approach to truth in the 1981 lectures at Louvain (*Wrong-Doing, Truth-Telling: The Function of Avowal in Justice*) with his previous *Lectures on the Will to Know* (1971–2), in which Foucault had voiced his intention to focus on the effects of a discourse of truth within the discourse of the law. According to Barry, the study of neoliberal governmentality and the focus on the relations between subject and truth led to a reversal in Foucault's thought and to a shift in his approach to truth, whereby "veridiction" rather than jurisdiction became predominant in his approach to contemporary exercises of power.

The fourth section, "Government of Self, Government of Others," is dedicated to Foucault's approach to and engagement with politics, in the broadest sense of the term, in the last phase of his work. Foucault's late focus on the technologies of the self and the modes of interaction between oneself and others adds important nuance to his previous views on the subject, power, and government. Power is no longer exclusively conceived of as a form of control and exclusion but rather approached via the intersection of government and different kinds of techniques, which historically become either forms of government or, on the contrary, forms of not being governed. The essays contained in this section deal with different perspectives opened up by Foucault's late conceptions of power, government and governmentality, putting them in discussion with other relevant authors in current political debates. The first essay, "Understanding Power Through Governmentality" by Karim Barakat, examines the presuppositions behind Foucault's reexamined understanding of power in his later writings and the break with his earlier view of power relations as entirely constitutive of passive and docile subjects. Highlighting Foucault's debt to Kant's analysis of the present, Barakat argues that Foucault's endorsement of a similar view of power serves the purpose of effecting a critique of power. In the second essay, "On Authority: A Discussion Between Michel Foucault and Hannah Arendt," Edgar Straehle focuses on the concept of authority and disentangles it from the notion of power. Drawing on Hannah Arendt's account, Straehle argues that authority should be understood as a kind of power based on recognition, such that whereas power is based on the people in power, authority rests on those who are not in authority. According to Straehle, a similar logic is behind Foucault's concepts of *parrhēsia* and ascendancy, which can thus be deployed to shed light on and rethink the concept of authority. The third essay, "Neoliberal Subjectivity at the Political Frontier" by Matko Krce-Ivančić, deploys Foucault's understanding of the contemporary subject as an entrepreneur of himself and the corresponding view of power in neoliberal governments in order to criticize Laclau's model of emancipation. After demonstrating that the productive character of power is not adequately acknowledged in Laclau's model, Krce-Ivančić critically examines his notion of the political frontier, arguing that this external frontier has failed to take shape due to the emergence of self-entrepreneurial subjectivity. Finally, self-governing is identified as a governmental technology that subverts subversion, preventing Laclau's model from fulfilling its promise of emancipation.

The fifth and final section of the volume, "Truth-Telling, Truth-Living," accompanies the final trajectory of Foucault's thought as expressed in his final lecture course, *The Courage of Truth* (1983–4), where the topic of truth acquires a whole new ethical dimension in the form of the ancient Greek notion of *parrhēsia* and related ways of life. Whereas Foucault devoted the last two years of his life to a thorough study of the notion in ancient Greek texts, the essays contained in this part of the volume aim to contrast this notion with other forms of truth-telling in Foucault's *corpus* and to disclose its significance both to Foucault's thought as a whole and to contemporary ethical and political challenges. The third essay, "Rethinking Confession" by Andrea Teti, brings *parrhēsia* into contact with two other forms of truth-telling, tracing the evolution of Foucault's use of confession (*confession*) and avowal (*aveu*) throughout his work. Teti argues that the two terms refer to two different concepts and that it is analytically useful to make this distinction rather than treating the concepts as interchangeable. In the second essay, "Truth-Telling as Therapeutic Practice: On the Tension Between Psychiatric Subjectivation and Parrhesiastic Self-Cultivation," Marta Faustino evaluates the recent development of psychotherapy from a Foucauldian point of view, discussing the innovation and improvement that contemporary approaches to psychotherapy represent when compared to previous psychiatric approaches, as well as the limits and shortcomings that they must nonetheless overcome if they are to promote the true "politics of ourselves" that Foucault recommended in the last stage of his life. Finally, in "Foucault, the Politics of Ourselves, and the Subversive Truth-Telling of Trauma: Survivors as Parrhesiasts," Kurt Borg elaborates on Foucault's late work on *parrhēsia* to shed light on the ethical and political questions raised by trauma narratives, insofar as survivors are interpreted as parrhesiasts on a possible contemporary interpretation and use of the term. While traumatic self-narration can be co-opted by power in such a way that preferred conceptions of trauma narratives are reinforced, they can also resist such co-option and depoliticization by positively functioning as subversive acts. In this way, Borg argues, narrations of trauma can function as a form of *parrhēsia* by, at a risk to the speaker, courageously uttering truth.

Lisbon, the 25th of March, 2020

## Notes

1 Although ostensibly clear, Foucault's request was in fact open to different interpretations. Pierre Nora argues that the posthumous material was of three different kinds, each of which demanded different treatment: unfinished or abandoned material, which should definitely not be published; the fourth volume of the *History of Sexuality*, which already existed as a manuscript and which Foucault viewed as the most important part of the work (which is why it would be "a heavy responsibility not to publish it"); and the lecture courses at the Collège de France, which have a dubious status because Foucault himself expressed doubt about them. Unlike Nora, Veyne and Dumézil were for the complete publication of the posthumous work. See Eribon (1991: 323–4). In a recent interview,

Daniel Defert, one of Foucault's heirs, explained the process that led him to make the archive available to everyone by selling it to France's National Library: it was a matter of making available Foucault's thought, not his intimacy (see Defert 2012). On this topic, see also Fontana (2018) and Elden (2018).

2   The publication of the courses followed a complex legal fight with Foucault's legatees, which involved not only Gallimard but also the Italian team of Alessandro Fontana and Mauro Bertani, who had published an Italian translation of *Il faut défendre la societé* in 1990 on the basis of tape recordings. The conflict was resolved when the heirs agreed to allow Gallimard/Seuil to publish the complete edition of the courses under the editorial direction of François Ewald and Alessandro Fontana, with the involvement of members of both editorial teams. See Del Vento and Fournel (2007), Fontana (2018), and Elden (2018). In the first months of 2020, the anonymous, "decentralized and non-censable" website "Free Foucault" (https://freefoucault.eth.link) made freely available the tape recordings of all the lecture courses given by Foucault at the Collège de France between 1972 and 1984.

3   On this topic, see Eribon's exhaustive treatment (Eribon 1991: 317–24).

4   On the political interpretations and misinterpretations of Foucault's thought, see Veyne (2010: 135 ff.). See also Elden (2016: 102–11) and Bidet (2014: 155 ff.).

5   In this respect, it is interesting to recall Foucault's own pronouncements regarding the legitimacy of publishing philosophers' posthumous writings in the general introduction to the French edition of Nietzsche's *Complete Works* (Gallimard, 1967), signed together with Gilles Deleuze: "No one can prejudge the form or contents the great book would have had (nor the other forms that Nietzsche would have invented if he had renounced his project). At the most, the reader can dream; even so, he has to be given the means" (Deleuze and Foucault, *cit. in* Eribon 1991: 324).

6   In the English world, the translations appeared in 2005 and 2017, respectively.

7   On the contemporary uses of Foucault, see especially Mayo (2000), Gros (2008), Oulc'hen (2014), and Erlenbusch-Anderson (2018).

8   Foucault portrays others' perceptions of the development of his work in the following way: "'Aren't you sure of what you're saying? Are you going to change yet again, shift your position according to the questions that are put to you, and say that the objections are not really directed at the place from which you are speaking? Are you going to declare yet again that you have never been what you have been reproached with being? Are you already preparing the way out that will enable you in your next book to spring up somewhere else and declare as you're now doing: no, no, I'm not where you are lying in wait for me, but over here, laughing at you?'" (Foucault 2002: 19).

9   See Foucault (1990: 7): "As to those for whom to work hard, to begin and begin again, to attempt and be mistaken, to go back and re-work everything from top to bottom, and still find reason to hesitate from one step to the next—as to those, in short, for whom to work in the midst of uncertainty and apprehension is tantamount to failure, all I can say is that clearly we are not from the same planet" (Foucault 1990: 7). In the same vein, Eribon makes the following comment on the evolution of Foucault's thought: "Clearly, Foucault's project was transformed over the years by the ups and downs of a 'logic of discovery,' in which hesitations and mistakes, bad habits, and moments of repentance played their role, before being overcome and surpassed by new intuitions and new discoveries" (Eribon 1991: 318–19).

10  See also Foucault's definition of philosophical activity in the second volume of the *History of Sexuality: The Use of Pleasure*: "But, then, what is philosophy today—philosophical activity, I mean—if it is not the critical work that thought brings to bear

on itself? In what does it consist, if not in the endeavor to know how and to what extent it might be possible to think differently, instead of legitimating what is already known?" (Foucault 1990: 8–9).
11 On Foucault's "archaeo-genealogical enterprise," see e.g. Han (1998: 205).
12 For an ontological approach to Foucault's work, see Han (1998) and Révél (2015).
13 On this topic, see Eribon (1991: 325–6) and Veyne (2010: 142 ff.).
14 See especially Bernauer and Rasmussen (1988) and Elden (2016). On Foucault's relevance to contemporary issues, see Taylor and Vintges (2004), Galzigna (2008), Binkley and Capetillo (2009), Faubion (2014), Rainsborough (2018).
15 On Foucault's ethics, see for example O'Leary (2002), Lorenzini, Revel and Sforzini (2013), Lorenzini (2015), Lynch (2016) and Olssen (2016). On Foucault and politics, see Kelly (2009, 2014) Bang (2016), and Dean and Villadsen (2016).
16 See, however, the illuminating reviews by Elden (2018), Gefen (2018), and Luxon (2019).

## References

Bang, H. (2016), *Foucault's Political Challenge: From Hegemony to Truth*, Hampshire and New York: Palgrave Macmillan.
Bernauer, J. and D. Rasmussen, eds (1988), *The Final Foucault*, Cambridge and London: The MIT Press.
Bidet, J. (2014), *Foucault avec Marx*, Paris: La Fabrique.
Binkley, S and J. Capetillo, eds (2009), *A Foucault for the 21st Century. Governmentality, Biopolitics and Discipline in the New Millennium*, Newcastle upon Tyne: Cambridge Scholars Publishing.
Dean, M. and K. Villadsen (2016), *State Phobia and Civil Society: The Political Legacy of Michel Foucault*, Stanford, CA: Stanford University Press.
Defert, D. (2012), "Les archives de Foucault ont une histoire politique," *Bibliobs*, 26 November. Available online: https://bibliobs.nouvelobs.com/essais/20121106.OBS8175/daniel-defert-les-archives-de-foucault-ont-une-histoire-politique.html (accessed July 20, 2019).
Del Vento, C. and J.-L. Fournel (2007), "L'édition des cours et les «pistes» de Michel Foucault. Entretiens avec Mauro Bertani, Alessandro Fontana et Michel Senellart," *Laboratoire italien*, 7. Available online: https://laviedesidees.fr/Les-usages-de-Foucault.html (accessed July 30, 2019).
Elden, S. (2016), *Foucault's Last Decade*, Cambridge: Polity.
Elden, S. (2018), "Review: Michel Foucault, *Histoire de la sexualité 4: Les aveux de la chair*," *Theory, Culture & Society*, 35 (7–8): 293–311.
Eribon, D. (1991), *Michel Foucault*, Cambridge: Harvard University Press.
Erlenbusch-Anderson, V. (2018), "Philosophical Practice Following Foucault," *Foucault Studies*, 25: 55–83.
Faubion, J., ed. (2014), *Foucault Now. Current Perspectives in Foucault Studies*, Cambridge and Malden, MA: Polity Press.
Fontana, A. (2018), *Una educazione intellettuale. Saggi su di sé, su Foucault e su altro*, Lucca: La casa USHER.
Forrester, J. (2014), "Foucault's Face: The Personal is the Theoretical," in J. Fabion (ed.), *Foucault Now. Current Perspectives in Foucault Studies*, 225–40, Cambridge: Polity Press.
Foucault, M. (1990), *The Use of Pleasure: Volume 2 of The History of Sexuality*, trans. R. Hurley, New York: Vintage Books.

Foucault, M. (1997a), "The Ethics of the Concern of the Self as a Practice of Freedom," in P. Rabinow (ed.), *The Essential Works of Michel Foucault, 1954–1984, Vol. 1: Ethics. Subjectivity and Truth*, 281–301, New York: The New Press.

Foucault, M. (1997b), "What is Enlightenment?," in P. Rabinow (ed.), *The Essential Works of Michel Foucault, 1954–1984, Vol. 1: Ethics, Subjectivity and Truth*, 303–19, New York: The New Press.

Foucault, M. (1998), "What is an Author?," in J. Faubion (ed.), *The Essential Works of Michel Foucault, 1954–1984, Vol. 2: Aesthetics, Method, and Epistemology*, 205–22, New York: The New Press.

Foucault, M. (2001), *Dits et écrits II, 1976–1988*, Paris: Gallimard.

Foucault, M. (2002), *The Archaeology of Knowledge*, trans. A. M. Sheridan Smith, London: Routledge.

Foucault, M. (2005), *The Hermeneutics of the Subject: Lectures at the Collège de France 1981–1982*, ed. F. Gros, trans. G. Burchell, New York: Palgrave Macmillan.

Foucault, M. (2006), *History of Madness*, ed. J. Khalfa, trans. J. Murphy and J. Khalfa, London: Routledge.

Foucault, M. (2010), *The Government of Self and Others: Lectures at the Collège de France, 1982–1983*, ed. F. Gros, trans. G. Burchell, Basingstoke: Palgrave Macmillan.

Foucault, M. (2011), *The Courage of Truth (The Government of Self and Others II): Lectures at the Collège de France 1983–1984*, ed. F. Gros, trans. G. Burchell, Basingstoke: Palgrave Macmillan.

Foucault, M. (2013), *L'origine de l'herménéutique de soi. Conférences prononcées à Dartmouth College 1980*, Paris: Vrin.

Foucault, M. (2015), *Qu'est-ce que la critique ?* suivi de *La culture de soi*, Paris: Vrin.

Foucault, M. (2016), *Discours et vérité* précédé de *La parrêsia*, Paris: Vrin.

Foucault, M. (2017), *Dire vrai sur soi-même. Conférences prononcées à l'Université Victoria de Toronto 1982*, Paris: Vrin.

Foucault, M. (2018), *Histoire de la sexualité 4: Les aveux de la chair*, Paris: Gallimard.

Foucault, M. and R. Martin (1988), "Truth, Power, Self: An Interview with Michel Foucault," in L. H. Martin, H. Gutman, and P. H. Hutton (eds), *Technologies of the Self: A Seminar with Michel Foucault*, 9–15, Amherst, MA: The University of Massachusetts Press.

Galzigna, M., ed. (2008), *Foucault oggi*, Milan: Feltrinelli.

Gefen A. (2018), "Alexandre Gefen reviews *Les aveux de la chair*," *Critical Inquiry*, August 22. Available online: https://criticalinquiry.uchicago.edu/alexandre_gefen_reviews_les_aveux_de_la_chair/ (accessed March 5, 2020).

Gros, F. (2008), "Les Usages de Foucault," *La vie des idées*, June 13. Available online : https://laviedesidees.fr/Les-usages-de-Foucault.html (accessed July 30, 2019).

Han, B. (1998), *L'ontologie manquée de Michel Foucault*, Grenoble: Millon.

Kelly, M. (2009), *The Political Philosophy of Michel Foucault*, New York: Routledge.

Kelly, M. (2014), *Foucault and Politics: A Critical Introduction*, Edinburgh: Edinburgh University Press.

Lorenzini, D., A. Revel, and A. Sforzini, eds (2013), *Michel Foucault: éthique et vérité: 1980–1984*, Paris: Vrin.

Lorenzini, D. (2015), *Éthique et politique de soi: Foucault, Hadot, Cavell et les techniques de l'ordinaire*, Paris: Vrin, 2015.

Luxon, N. (2019), "*Les aveux de la chair*. Vol. 4 of *L'histoire de la sexualité*," *Contemporary Political Theory*, July 11. Available online: https://link.springer.com/article/10.1057%2Fs41296-019-00333-z (accessed March 5, 2020).

Lynch, R. (2016), *Foucault's Critical Ethics*, New York: Fordham University Press.

Mayo, C. (2000), "The uses of Foucault," *Educational Theory*, 50 (1): 103–16.
O'Leary, T. (2002), *Foucault and the Art of Ethics*, London: Continuum.
Olssen, M. (2016), *Foucault's Ethics: Speaking Truth to Power*, London and New York: Bloomsbury.
Oulc'hen, H., ed. (2014), *Usages de Foucault*, Paris: PUF.
Rainsborough, M. (2018), *Foucault heute. Neue Perspektiven in Philosophie und Kulturwissenschaft,* Bielefeld: Transcript Verlag.
Taylor, D. and K. Vintges, eds (2004), *Feminism and the Final Foucault,* Urbana and Chicago: University of Illinois Press.
Veyne, P. (1993), "The Final Foucault and His Ethics," *Critical Inquiry*, 20 (1): 1–9.
Veyne, P. (2010), *Foucault: His Thought, His Character*, Cambridge: Polity Press.

Part One

# Philosophical Practices, Philosophy as Practice

# 1

# Foucault's Reinvention of Philosophy as a Way of Life: Genealogy as a Spiritual Exercise

Michael Ure

This chapter examines Michel Foucault's research on Greco-Roman philosophy. What is the significance of his "trip" to antiquity for modern ethics? The first section surveys his itinerary. It shows how he challenges conventional histories of philosophy by conceiving ancient philosophies as practices of the self or ways of life rather than simply as theoretical doctrines. Like Ilsetraut and Pierre Hadot, Foucault contributes to modern ethical reflection by rediscovering this ancient philosophy as an ethical work of the self on itself. Ancient philosophy is meant to form rather than merely inform the subject.[1] Foucault adds an important qualification to this claim. Ancient philosophy, he suggests, also invented a new cultural type: *viz.*, the philosophical hero. In doing so, he implies, it sublimated the archaic ideal of a beautiful existence exemplified by Greek heroes like Achilles and Odysseus. Cynicism, he claims, epitomized this ancient philosophical heroism. Foucault shows how ancient Cynics aimed to realize the beauty of invulnerability or sovereignty, but through the new means of living the truth. Cynics, as he conceives them, linked together the beautiful existence and the true life by publically displaying and boldly proclaiming their total sovereignty. Living the truth made the Cynic the true sovereign.

In the second section, I briefly examine why Foucault aims to reinvent philosophy as a way of life. Foucault argues that from roughly the sixteenth century onward, this model of ancient philosophy was practiced only on the margins of academic philosophy. Despite its marginality, he nevertheless claims that ancient philosophy, especially Cynicism and Roman Stoicism, constitutes a decisive moment in the history of thought that is "still significant for our modern mode of being" (Foucault 2005: 9). One of Foucault's central claims about the significance of ancient philosophy is that it may help us address what he sees as a contemporary problem: the absence of a principle of ethics in the context of skepticism about founding our actions on religious decrees or allegedly scientific notions of normality.[2] Foucault, we might say, looks to antiquity to develop a contemporary ethics without absolute obligations or sanctions. This a relatively uncontroversial description of Foucault's late work, even if his ambition of reconstituting the ancient philosophical model remains deeply controversial.[3]

In the final section, however, I question whether Foucault's own philosophical ethos reclaims, as he implies, "the living substance of ancient philosophy" (Foucault 1986: 9). It shows that he conceives Nietzschean genealogy as his own philosophy's "spiritual exercise." Genealogy, as he puts it, aims to introduce discontinuity into our being. This section demonstrates that Foucault's genealogical practice of self-dissolution necessarily opposes the basic goal of ancient ethics: self-sufficiency or sovereignty. Taking this Nietzschean slant on Foucault's philosophical ethos suggests that it does not refashion the ancient practices of the self. Rather, I argue that Foucault's trip to antiquity unintentionally brings to light how contemporary subjectivity is partly constituted by a "chiastic" crossing of the ancient ethics of self-completion and the modern ethics of self-dissolution.

## Philosophical Heroism

Foucault's intellectual histories apply what he calls a genealogical knowledge or effective history, which, as he defines it, "is not made for understanding, but for cutting" (Foucault 1984: 88). "Knowledge," as he explains, "even under the banner of history, does not depend on 'rediscovery', and it emphatically excludes the 'rediscovery of ourselves'. History becomes 'effective' to the degree that it introduces discontinuity into our very being ... 'Effective' history deprives the self of the reassuring stability of life and nature ... It will uproot its traditional foundations and relentlessly disrupt its pretended continuity" (Foucault 1984: 88). Foucault's genealogy lacerates our subjectivity by exposing these ontological discontinuities. In his late works, Foucault applies this genealogical method specifically to the history of ancient philosophy.

In contrast with other major interpretive traditions, by adopting a genealogical approach to the history of philosophy, Foucault aims to show that what counts as "philosophy" is historically variable. In the early 1980s Foucault characterized his overarching research program as the history of "'the games of truth'," through which "being is historically constituted as experience" (Foucault 1986: 6–7). Foucault distinguishes among different philosophical practices in terms of the different relationships they established between truth and subjectivity. Foucault therefore rejects the idea we can treat ancient philosophies as early stages in the progressive development of universal reason, or analyze their arguments as answers to perennial philosophical questions. He eschews what we might broadly call these Hegelian-Marxist and contemporary "analytic" approaches to the history of philosophy. Foucault's goal is to circumscribe the historically specific forms and practices of ancient philosophies rather than seeing them through the lens of these modern models of philosophy.

Following Pierre Hadot, Foucault distinguishes ancient philosophies as practices of the self or as ways of life.[4] Hadot had sought to recapture ancient philosophy "in its original aspect: not as a theoretical construct, but as a method for training people to live and look at the world in a new way. It is an attempt to transform mankind" (Hadot 1995: 107). Foucault affirms Hadot's central claim that "philosophy in antiquity was a spiritual exercise" (Hadot 1995: 104).[5] In his lectures during the 1980s at the Collège de France, he brings into sharp relief how the schools deployed both philosophical doctrines and spiritual exercises as means of giving form to life. Foucault identifies ancient philosophy itself as a kind of bio-technique, or a work ancient philosophers undertook on themselves to transform their own mode of being. As he conceives it, ancient philosophy is a voluntary and deliberate form of self-cultivation; the goal of the ancient philosophical schools is not theoretical knowledge alone, but the transformation or conversion of the self to realize a higher or "other" mode of existence (e.g. Foucault 2011: 244–5, 287). For this reason, he does not formulate a history of philosophical *theories* or *doctrines*, nor does he focus on analyzing the validity of the arguments of ancient logic, physics or ethics. Rather, as he declares, he seeks to sketch "a history of forms, modes, and styles of life, a history of the philosophical life ... as a mode of being and as a form both of ethics and heroism" (Foucault 2011: 210).

We can begin to unpack the significance Foucault attributes to his research for modern ethics by briefly sketching his account of the genesis of this ancient model of philosophy as technology of the self or spiritual exercise. To understand ancient philosophy on its own terms and distinguish it from later models of philosophical practice, he argues, we need to recognize how it recast fundamental aspects of archaic, pre-philosophical culture. Let us briefly consider his account of how ancient philosophy transmuted archaic cultural practices. In *The Hermeneutics of the Subject* (1981–2) lecture series, Foucault argues that we can conceive ancient philosophy as a synthesis of the philosophical goal of delimiting what makes it possible for the subject to access the truth and what he identifies as the "pre-philosophic theme" of "spirituality" (Foucault 2005: 15). How is "spirituality" woven into the fabric of ancient philosophy? Foucault identifies two distinct elements of pre-philosophic "spirituality": (a) the conditions of access to truth and (b) the effects of obtaining truth.

In the first case, he defines spirituality as "the search, practice and experience through which the subject carries out the necessary transformations on himself in order to have access to the truth" (Foucault 2005: 46). Spirituality establishes a particular relationship between truth and subjectivity: *viz.*, "there can be no truth without a conversion or transformation of the subject" (Foucault 2005: 15). "Spirituality," he explains, "postulates that the truth is never given to the subject by right ... [or] by a simple act of knowledge ... that for the subject to have the right of access to the truth he must be changed, transformed, shifted, and become ... other than himself" (Foucault 2005: 15). Ancient philosophy, he claims, took up the archaic practice of "spirituality" by assuming "that a subject could not have access to the truth if he first did not operate upon himself a certain work which would make him susceptible to knowing the truth—a work of purification, conversion of the soul by contemplation of the soul itself" (Foucault 1984: 371). Here Foucault embroiders on Pierre and Ilsetraut Hadot's account of ancient philosophy and its "spiritual exercises."

Both take the view that spiritual exercises or technologies of the self make possible "a profound transformation of the individual's mode of seeing and being. The object of spiritual exercises is precisely to bring about this transformation" (Hadot 1995: 83). "The philosophical act," as Hadot writes, "is not situated merely on the cognitive level, but on that of the self and of being. It is a progress which causes us to *be* more fully and makes us better. It is a conversion which turns our entire life upside down, changing the life of the person who goes through it" (Hadot 1995: 83). According to Ilsetraut Hadot, Stoic philosophy, for example, has two parts: the doctrinal and the paraenetic (or hortatory), including its spiritual exercises. Stoicism requires both parts, as she explains, because it is not enough to know its doctrines: "[o]ne must digest them, assimilate them, let oneself be transformed by them with the help of incessant spiritual exercises" (Hadot 2014: 40). Pierre Hadot quotes the Roman Stoic Seneca to illustrate the conversion required to access the truth: "I feel, my dear Lucilius, that I am being not only reformed but transformed ... I therefore wish to impart to you this sudden change in myself" (Seneca 2001: 25).

We can see in Seneca's depiction of philosophy as a self-transformative practice, the second aspect of spirituality Foucault entwined in ancient philosophy, namely, the self-transfiguration that flows from the ascent to truth. "[S]pirituality," as he explains, "postulates that once access to truth has really been opened up, it produces effects that are, of course, the consequence of the spiritual approach taken in order to achieve this, but which at the same time are something quite different and much more: effects which I will call 'rebound' effects of the truth on the subject" (Foucault 2005: 16). By accessing the truth, ancient subjects did not "merely" acquire knowledge, rather they underwent a profound ontological transformation. As Foucault explains, in the ancient context "the truth enlightens the subject; the truth gives beatitude to the subject; the truth gives tranquility of the soul ... in access to the truth, there is something that fulfils the subject himself, which fulfils or transfigures his very being" (Foucault 2005: 16).

In his final lecture series, *The Courage of Truth* (1983–4), Foucault extends his account of how ancient philosophy transmuted archaic culture. To live philosophically, in the ancient sense, as he conceives it, is to embody truth in a certain style of life. Foucault claims that the Cynics embodied the purest distillation of ancient philosophy insofar as they distinguished themselves precisely by their mode of life rather than by their theoretical discourse (Foucault 2011: 165, 173–4). The Cynics, he suggests, are also paradigmatic of ancient philosophy insofar as they sought to realize the heroic ideal of sovereignty by scandalously living the truth. Cynicism, he claims, expressed ancient philosophy's signature motif: *viz.*, "the philosophical life as heroic life" (Foucault 2011: 210). Let us consider these two points in turn.

In transferring Cynicism from the margins to the center of ancient philosophy Foucault defaces a widespread modern representation of Cynicism as philosophically irrelevant compared with Plato and Aristotle's systematic theoretical discourses.[6] Far from dismissing Cynicism as a marginal, theoretically impoverished ancient school, he sees it as "a sort of essence ... of any possible [ancient] philosophy, the form of philosophical heroism in its most general, rudimentary, and also demanding aspect" (Foucault 2011: 210). While the philosophical mode of life varied across the ancient schools, Cynicism, as a manifestation and act of truth, he asserts, contained the matrix for all these schools. By stripping back theoretical doctrine to the bare minimum and "practicing the scandal of truth in and through one's life," he argues, the Cynic distilled the essence of ancient philosophy as a way of life (Foucault 2011: 174). Cynicism, as he explains, makes "truth itself visible in one's acts, one's body, the way one dresses, and in the way one conducts oneself and lives ... Cynicism makes life, existence, *bios*, what could be called an alethurgy, a manifestation of truth" (Foucault 2011: 172).

Foucault argues that the Cynics are the quintessential ancient philosophers not only because they were almost exclusively practical philosophers who made life a manifestation of truth, but also because in doing so they placed their stamp on a new kind of heroism that circumscribed the whole of ancient philosophy. Foucault conceives this new philosophical heroism as a transmutation of the archaic Greek aesthetics of existence. He argues that Cynicism sublimates the desire for glorious sovereignty that distinguished pre-philosophic heroic culture. Foucault observes that the "aesthetics of existence," the concern for a beautiful existence, was already completely dominant in Homer and Pindar (Foucault 2011: 162). In this pre-Socratic tradition, "the care of the self," he writes, was "governed by the principle of a brilliant and memorable existence" (Foucault 2011: 163). Foucault suggests that ancient philosophy did not replace, but recast the archaic "principle of existence as an oeuvre to be fashioned in all perfection" (Foucault 2011: 163). Following Socrates, he claims, the Cynics "inflected, modified, and re-elaborated" the archaic Greek concern "for a beautiful, striking, memorable existence" (Foucault 2011: 163). What he aims to recover is exactly the relationship between this "beautiful existence and the true life" (Foucault 2011: 163). He describes ancient philosophy's general framework as "the search for a beautiful existence in the form of the truth and the practice of truth-telling" (Foucault 2011: 165).

How should we understand the *aesthetic* element of the art of living Foucault identifies as central to Cynicism (and ancient philosophy as a whole)? Nietzsche gives us a line on Foucault's thinking. "The Greek philosophers," he claimed "went through life feeling secretly that there were far more slaves than one might think—meaning that everybody who was not a philosopher was a slave. Their pride overflowed at the thought that even the most powerful men on earth belonged among their slaves" (Nietzsche 1974: 91).[7] In the context of Foucault analysis of ancient philosophy, the notion of the "aesthetics of existence" encompasses the creation of a specifically noble or sovereign life sharply opposed to an enslaved life. Ancient philosophy, as he sees it, proposes to achieve such a beautiful, noble existence and challenges the dominant Homeric *paideia* for misleading citizens about how to achieve it (see Gouldner 1967).

Foucault's claim that ancient philosophy recalibrated Homer and Pindar's celebration of the archaic and Olympian hero's brilliant and memorable existence entails qualifying the "technical" conception of ancient philosophy's aesthetics of existence (see Sellars' essay in this volume). In the ancient sense of the term, *tekhnē* is a skill or craft like those of rhetoric, medicine or navigation. As Foucault sees it, the Cynics' (and ancient philosophers') art of living certainly required the application of techniques of the self or spiritual exercises. Ancient philosophers deployed techniques of living analogous to those of ordinary, skilled technicians, but they did so only for the sake of shaping a life whose beauty lay in its nobility or sovereignty. Ancient philosophy, as Foucault explains, is one of the aesthetic forms Greco-Roman culture gave to "man's way of being and conducting himself, the aspect his existence reveals to others and himself, the trace also that this existence ... will leave in the memories of others after his death" (Foucault 2011: 162). Foucault's sketch of the way ancient philosophy recalibrated Homeric glory, highlights how the ancient philosophical life was shot through with the heroic, pre-Socratic dream of immortality. On Foucault's view, then, the ancient Cynics made their lives objects of aesthetic elaboration for the sake of creating a life far more exalted than the greatest Greek heroes.[8]

How did the Cynic philosophical life aim to supplant the cultural pre-eminence of archaic Greek heroism? We can see this rivalry between archaic and philosophical heroism in the famous mythical encounter between Diogenes the Cynic and Alexander the Great:

> As he was sunning himself in the Craneion, Alexander stood over him and said, "Ask whatever you wish of me," and he replied, "Stand out of my light."
>
> Hard 2012: 53

Foucault's analysis of this Cynic *khreia* illuminates how ancient philosophy challenged standard Greek conceptions of heroism (Foucault 2011: 275–7). It stages an apocryphal confrontation between symbolic opposites: the greatest political ruler who possesses an insatiable desire for worldly glory and the naked Cynic beggar who finds perfect serenity in his impoverished, bare life. In this celebrated confrontation, as Foucault sees it, we witness an extraordinary role reversal: the true king is not the political king, who enjoys worldly sovereignty, but the philosopher king, who enjoys nothing other than sovereignty over himself. Since through Cynic *askēsis* Diogenes has made himself entirely self-sufficient, he needs nothing from Alexander and can treat him with sublime indifference. Crowned, visible sovereigns like Alexander, as Foucault explains "are only the shadow of true monarchy. The Cynic is the only true king. And at the same time, vis-à-vis kings of the world ... he is the anti-king who shows how hollow, illusory, and precarious the monarchy of kings is" (Foucault 2011: 275). Foucault shows that Diogenes claims the mantle of the true king, and demotes Alexander to a mere shadow of sovereignty, on the grounds that he (Diogenes) alone is entirely self-sufficient. Diogenes claims true sovereignty because unlike Alexander, he exercises sovereignty without depending on anything external; he has defeated his internal enemies, his faults and vices; and he is invulnerable to all reversals of fortune (Foucault 2011: 276–7). By contrast, even the sovereignty of the greatest king is intrinsically vulnerable to external and internal enemies, to misfortune and vice. Alexander is not a true king, but a slave to fortune. Only the Cynic attains unwavering sovereignty or invulnerability. Only philosophy delivers true sovereignty.

## Foucault's Reinvention of Philosophy as a Way of Life

To what end does Foucault recall this ancient model of philosophy as a way of life and rehabilitate the ancient Cynic as the quintessence of its philosophical heroism?

In the first instance, Foucault simply aims to chart and explain its gradual eclipse in modern culture. From antiquity through to the sixteenth century, he maintains, philosophers had continued to address the ancient question: "What is the work which I must effect upon myself so as to be capable and worthy of acceding to the truth?" (Foucault 1984: 371). Though Foucault is wary of identifying a specific moment when philosophy rejected the necessity of practices of self-transformation or spiritual exercises, he nevertheless loosely deploys the phrase "Cartesian moment" to mark this break in the history of the relation between the truth and the subject (Foucault 2005: 14, 17).[9] With Descartes' claim that direct evidence is sufficient to know the truth, and that therefore *any* subject who can see what is self-evident can attain knowledge, modern culture, he argues, largely jettisoned the ancient notion that one must work on the self to get to the truth. "I think the modern age of the history of the truth," as he explains, "begins when knowledge itself and knowledge alone gives access to the truth. That is to say when the philosopher ... or scientist ... can recognize the truth and have access to it in himself and solely through his activity of knowing, without anything else being demanded of him and without him having to change or alter his being as subject" (Foucault 2005: 17).

After this "moment," he claims, for the most part philosophers held that asceticism is not necessary to know the truth. "Knowledge of intellectual knowledge," or knowledge for its own sake, he argues, "gradually limited, overlaid, and finally effaced the 'knowledge of spirituality'" (Foucault 2005: 308). Of course, Foucault recognizes that even with the demise of this ancient conception of the relationship between truth and subjectivity, subjects still needed to satisfy certain conditions to access knowledge, including formal, cultural and "moral" conditions (e.g. a commitment to truth over self-interest). Yet none of these conditions, he observes, concern the transformation of the subject's being, "they only concern the individual in his concrete interest, and not the structure of the subject as such" (Foucault 2005: 18). After the Cartesian moment, he argues, the ancient techniques of the self—purifications, ascetic exercises, conversions and so on—became epistemically superfluous. According to Foucault, therefore, we have arrived at a fundamentally different form of the experience of the relation between the subject and truth. At this point, he argues "the relationship to the self no longer needs to be ascetic to get into relation to the truth ... Thus I can be immoral and know the truth. I believe that this is an idea which, more or less explicitly, was rejected by all previous cultures. Before Descartes one could not be impure, immoral and know the truth" (Foucault 1984: 372). Philosophers now accede to the truth without fundamentally altering their subjectivity and without this acquisition of knowledge producing any ontological transformation, or enlightenment, beatitude, or tranquility. "We can no longer think that access to the truth," as he puts it, "will complete in the subject, like a crowning reward, the work or sacrifice, the price paid to arrive at it" (Foucault 2005: 19). "As such," he explains, "henceforth the truth cannot save the subject" (Foucault 2005: 19).

Foucault recognizes, however, that modern philosophy never completely effaced ancient philosophy. In fact, he draws attention to Schopenhauer and Nietzsche (among others) as illustrative of a nineteenth century European protest against the eclipse of ancient philosophy (Foucault 2005: 251). Schopenhauer and Nietzsche did not conceive the demise of the ancient model of philosophy as a way of life, and the partitioning of truth and transformation as a cognitive gain that properly respects the limits of philosophy. Rather they claimed that this modern severance of truth from transformation, knowledge from spirituality was a historically contingent cultural, institutional and pedagogical shift and one that modern philosophers can and ought to reverse (see Schopenhauer 2014: 149–213; Nietzsche 1985). Drawing on Schopenhauer as his exemplar, Nietzsche waged an untimely campaign against modern academic philosophy precisely for the sake of reviving the model of ancient philosophy as a way of life. "The only critique of philosophy that is possible and that proves something, namely trying to see whether one can live in accordance with it," he asserted, "has never been taught at universities: all that has been taught is a critique of words by means of other words..." (Nietzsche 1985: 187). Nietzsche did not conceive philosophy as a way of life as theoretically bankrupt or historically moribund. Rather he sought to reinvent it. Like Schopenhauer and Nietzsche, Foucault identifies the severance of philosophy from spirituality, truth from transformation, as a theoretical shift, the so-called "Cartesian moment," that became deeply entrenched in philosophical practice partly because of its institutionalization as a university discipline. "When philosophy becomes a teaching profession," as he puts it, "the philosophical life disappears" (Foucault 2011: 211).

However, Nietzsche saw it as his task not simply to explain its demise, but to reclaim philosophy conceived as an art of living (see Ure 2019). Foucault, it seems, also seeks to reconstitute philosophy as practice of self-transformation and he identifies this as plausible option for developing an ethic that does not turn on metaphysical, theological, legal, or scientific claims. He draws a parallel between our struggle to establish an ethics and the situation of the ancients that makes their model of philosophy seem like a viable contemporary option. Ancient citizens, he claims, practiced an "aesthetic of existence" independently of religious dogmas or legal constraints (Foucault 1984: 343). Foucault wonders whether we might reinvent this aesthetics of existence in which rule-following is advocated and practiced for the sake of giving style to one's life. Significantly, he also claims that his own philosophical ethos is continuous with the living substance of ancient philosophy. Yet, as we shall see in the next section, it is far from clear that Foucault's Nietzschean inspired *askēsis* is compatible with ancient practices of the self.[10] On closer inspection, we discover in Foucault's work two discordant, yet equally compelling ethical practices of the self.

## Genealogy as a Spiritual Exercise

How does Foucault's alternative philosophical ethos compare with the ancient practices of the self? We can begin to answer this question by examining his use of the genealogical method as a spiritual exercise. In defining his own philosophical practice, Foucault contrasts it with what he derides as a ludicrous and illegitimate type of "philosophical discourse" that presumes to "dictate to others, to tell them where their truth is and how to find it" with his own reinvented ancient model of a "philosophical exercise," through which the subject works on and changes itself in the game of truth (Foucault 1986: 9). For Foucault, self-transformation is the point and purpose of philosophy, if we assume, as he does, that it is still what it was for the ancients: *viz.*, an *askēsis* or an exercise of oneself in the activity of thought:

> [W]hat is philosophy today ... if it is not the critical work that thought brings to bear on itself? In what does it consist, if not in the endeavor to know how and to what extent it might be possible to think differently instead of legitimating what is already known? ... philosophical discourse ... is entitled to explore what might be changed, in its own thought, through the practice of a knowledge that is foreign to it. The "essay"—which should be understood as the assay or test by which, in the games of truth, one undergoes changes ... is the living substance of philosophy ...
> Foucault 1986: 8–9

Foucault distinguishes between what still remains alive for us in ancient philosophy and what has fallen into desuetude. In modern culture, he seems to assume, the metaphysical aspects of ancient philosophy are dead. Foucault shows no interest in analyzing the validity of the great metaphysical constructions of ancient philosophy like Plato's theory of ideas, Epicurean atoms and the void, and the all-pervading fiery Stoic *pneuma* or *logos*. Yet, he nonetheless asserts that one central element of ancient philosophy remains alive: not its metaphysical beliefs, but its practices of the self. Foucault identifies ancient philosophy's vital element with its foundational premise that one plays the game of truth for the sake of self-transformation.

Foucault defines his genealogical "philosophical exercise" as exemplifying this kind of game of truth. The object of this exercise, as he puts it "was to learn to what extent the effort to think one's own history can free thought from what it silently thinks, and so enable it to think differently" (Foucault 1986: 9). The living substance of ancient philosophy, he implies, continues to flourish precisely in his own genealogical research. In his reinvention of ancient philosophy, Foucault accords genealogy a position analogous to the ancient spiritual exercises of "conversion." Genealogy is Foucault's spiritual exercise.

We can see how through his genealogical exercise he seeks to reinvent the ancient philosophical ethos in a brief, yet remarkable passage in which he declares that he does not conceive the self-transformation that takes place through the practice of "games of truth" as superfluous or irrelevant backstage drama to the main philosophical act. In one of the rare moments that he addresses his readers in the first-person singular, he elaborates his personal motivation for investigating the ancient practices of the self. "It was curiosity," he explains, "the only kind of curiosity ... that is worth acting upon with any degree of obstinacy: not the curiosity that seeks to assimilate what it is proper for it to know, but that which enables one to get free of oneself" (Foucault 1986: 8). After all, he asks rhetorically, "what would be the value of the passion for knowledge if it resulted only in certain amount of knowledgeableness and not ... in the knower's straying afield of himself?" (Foucault 1986: 8). Foucault clearly implies that his own practice of genealogical investigation as a form of "spirituality," the conversion or transformation of the self, and identifies it as an expression of what he calls the passion for knowledge.

What sense can we give to Foucault's strange locution "the passion for knowledge"?[11] His use of this phrase is not incidental or accidental: it alludes to Nietzsche's analysis of the drive to knowledge, which he (Foucault) had directly addressed in a 1971 lecture on Nietzsche (Foucault 2013: 202–19) and his more polished essay from the same year "Nietzsche, Genealogy, History" (Foucault 1984: 76–101). It is worth dwelling on the significance of Foucault's allusion since it illuminates the nature of the conversion of the self that he believes results from the Nietzschean passion for knowledge.

In his 1971 lecture, Foucault observes that Nietzsche distinguished free spirited philosophers as having renounced the happiness that subjects derive from strong, enchanting illusions (see Nietzsche 1997: 184). Instead these free spirits, Nietzsche suggested, pursue knowledge to the point of maliciously violating the basic inclination of our spirit to delight in beautiful appearances (Nietzsche 1996: 141–2). "Knowledge," as he put it, "has in us been transformed into a passion which shrinks at no sacrifice"

(Nietzsche 1997: 184). Nietzsche identifies this passion for knowledge as the source of certain kind of sublimity, which, like all things sublime, constitutes a confrontation with mortal vulnerability. "This will to appearance, to simplification, to mask, to the cloak, in short to the superficial," he asserts, "is *counteracted* by that sublime inclination in the man of knowledge which takes a profound, many sided and thorough view of things and will take such a view: as a kind of cruelty of the intellectual conscience" (Nietzsche 1996: 142).[12] According to Nietzsche, free-spirited philosophers, who sacrifice their own beautiful illusions, do so in the belief that they derive a much higher form of exaltation under the "compulsion and suffering of *this* passion for knowledge" (Nietzsche 1997: 184). In his notes, he implicitly contrasts this heroically sublime willingness to sacrifice oneself in the service of the passion for knowledge with the ancient ethics of knowledge:

> People have warbled on to me about the serene happiness of knowledge—but I have not found it, indeed, I despise it, now I know the bliss of unhappiness of knowledge. Am I ever bored? Always anxious, heart throbbing with expectation or disappointment! I bless this misery, it enriches the world thereby! In doing so, I take the slowest of strides and slurp down these bittersweet delicacies. I no longer want any knowledge without danger: let there always be the treacherous sea or the merciless high mountains around the seeker of knowledge.
>
> Nietzsche 1999: 350–1

In his 1971 lecture Foucault develops the implications of Nietzsche's account of the passion for knowledge for his own account of the relationship between knowledge and subjectivity. Glossing *The Gay Science* §333, Foucault observes how Nietzsche conceives the passion for knowledge as allied "with malice—mockery, contempt, hatred. It does not involve recognizing oneself in things but keeping one's distance from them, protecting oneself from them (by laughing), differentiating oneself by deprecating them (despising), wanting to repulse or destroy them (*detestari*). Murderous, deprecatory, differentiating—knowledge is neither of the order of *homoiōsis*, nor of the good" (Foucault 2013: 204–05). Foucault suggests that this "murderous" knowledge of ourselves does not aim to free us from conventions or contingencies so that we can return to ourselves to pure being. Rather, he claims, we should understand Nietzsche's passion for knowledge as a "malice" specifically "turned also towards *the one* who knows" (Foucault 2013: 205).

In what sense does Nietzsche see the passion for knowledge as an act of cruelty towards oneself? Foucault recounts how Nietzsche identifies the malice of the new passion for knowledge as the will to transgress our heart's desire to affirm, love or worship beautiful appearances or illusions. In this sense, Nietzsche suggests that the knower is an artist of self-cruelty (see Nietzsche 1996: 141). As Foucault understands it, this passion for knowledge is a malicious will to go "behind the surface of things to seek out the secret, to try to extract an essence behind the appearance, a power behind the elusive flickering, a mastery ... But it is also what can recognize that there is still only appearance in this secret finally broken open, that there is no ontological foundation. And that man himself, who knows, is still and always appearance" (Foucault 2013: 205).

Unlike the Christian and modern hermeneutics of desire that Foucault made the object of genealogical analysis in the *History of Sexuality*, this Nietzschean passion for knowledge does not discover an ontological foundation, which one can either liberate or repress, but dissolves every appearance of a stable, permanent self, an ontological foundation. In place of this ontological foundation, Nietzsche's genealogy of the subject identifies irreconcilable discord among competing drives. Unlike Spinoza, Nietzsche discovers nothing divine or "eternally resting in itself" in the subject, only the "*heroism*" we might discover in our "warring depths" (Nietzsche 1974: 262). Nietzsche held that an unconscious war among its drives accounts for most of the subject's activity. Foucault approvingly quotes (in truncated form) this section's penultimate line: "In all knowledge there may be something heroic, but nothing divine" (Foucault 2013: 204).

If, then, we conceive Foucault's genealogical spiritual exercise as an expression of this passion for knowledge, a point, as we saw above, that he deliberately advertises, then this *askēsis* takes on a darker, more problematic appearance than we might otherwise think if we take at face value his suggestion that he revitalizes ancient philosophy. First, as this Nietzschean interpretation makes clear, Foucault conceives his genealogical practice of the self as an exercise of malice towards oneself that is required in order to tear oneself away from oneself. In order to introduce discontinuity into our being, as we noted at the outset, Foucault practices a genealogical exercise that "deprives the self of the reassuring stability of life and nature" (Foucault 1984: 88). Foucault's metaphorical description of the change one undergoes through the exercise of this passion for knowledge pictures the subject as led astray from predictable paths and wandering with no fixed route or known destination. Foucault stresses that for him philosophical curiosity only has value to the extent that it is a work on oneself, and that this practice is not a return to or recovery of oneself, but the paradoxical practice of freeing oneself from oneself. To follow Foucault's metaphor, this *askēsis* cultivates a permanently straying subject.

Foucault's earlier use of Nietzschean language and figures to describe the effects of the passion of knowledge dramatizes this change as a break of the self with itself rather than a return to the self. His description of the passion for knowledge that motivates his genealogical spiritual exercise highlights the "price" the subject pays for playing this particular game of truth. In his earlier analysis of Nietzsche, Foucault suggests that "the murderous relentlessness of knowledge" sets itself against "the welcoming mildness of a phenomenon," or, in other words, against consoling appearances or illusions (Foucault 2013: 206). In this sense, Foucault's exercise entails that the price for playing this game of truth is a type of self-sacrifice. He implies that this exercise introduces permanent discontinuity or discord into our being. If the passion for knowledge relentlessly "murders" all phenomenon or appearances, as he puts it, "this work...is never rewarded with access to being or the essence, but gives rise to new appearances, sets them against one another and beyond one another" (Foucault 2013: 206). What this work on the self discovers beneath appearances is not a permanent, eternally self-sufficient subject, rather it unleashes a war among the drives analogous to the competition for supremacy among heroic warriors.

Foucault's genealogical exercise, as he conceives it, then, entails a "systematic dissociation of identity," which reveals not "a forgotten identity, eager to be reborn," but a complex system of distinct, competing elements (Foucault 1984: 94). "The purpose of history, guided by genealogy," as he puts it, "is not to discover the roots of our identity, but to commit itself to its dissipation" (Foucault 1984: 95). Indeed, following Nietzsche, Foucault suggests that this genealogical exercise not only dissolves the unity of the subject into competing forces and drives, it also risks the destruction of the subject of knowledge. As a genealogical exercise, Foucault maintains, "the will to knowledge does not achieve universal truth; man is not given a serene mastery of nature," rather it "multiplies the risk, creates dangers in every area; it breaks down illusory defenses; it dissolves the unity of the subject; it releases those elements of itself that are devoted to its subversion and destruction" (Foucault 1984: 96). "Knowledge," as he explains this Nietzschean point, "does not slowly detach itself from its empirical roots ... to become pure speculation subject only to the demands of reason; its development is not tied to the constitution of and affirmation of a free subject; rather it creates a progressive enslavement to its instinctive violence" (Foucault 1984: 96). Foucault conceives genealogical exercises as a call "for experimentation on ourselves" that risks the "destruction of the subject who seeks knowledge in the endless deployment of the will to knowledge" (Foucault 1984: 96–7).

We can now begin to take the measure of Foucault's genealogical *askēsis* by seeing how it stands in sharp contrast with the ancient practices of the self. Foucault maintains, as we have seen, that ancient philosophies presuppose that access to the truth "will complete in the subject, like a crowning reward, the work or sacrifice, the price paid to arrive at it" (Foucault 2005: 19), insofar as the truth "fulfils the subject himself ... fulfils or transfigures his very being." Foucault summarizes the Hellenistic and Roman conversion of the self in terms of the idea of the movement towards the self, "the subject must advance towards something that is himself" (Foucault 2005: 248). In Hellenistic and Roman antiquity, Foucault argues, the "self basically appeared as the aim, end of an uncertain and possibly circular journey—the dangerous journey of life" (Foucault 2005: 250). In this context, he writes, "[t]he path towards the self will always be something of an Odyssey" (Foucault 2005: 249). Foucault picks out "this prescriptive figure of the return to the self" as a singular event in the history of Western culture. He identifies this "theme of the return to the self" as what in a "complicated, ambiguous and contradictory way" a whole section of nineteenth century thought sought to reconstitute (Foucault 2005: 251).

By contrast, Foucault's own philosophical *askēsis* does not complete the subject, rather it tears the self from itself without rewarding the subject with access to being or essence. Unlike the ancient philosophies, then, Foucault's *askēsis* has no crowning reward; access to genealogical truth does not grant the subject beatitude or tranquility.

Instead, Foucault generates an ethics of permanent self-dissolution and discord, which he conceives as a condition of freedom. Genealogical diagnosis identifies "virtual fractures" within the self "which open up ... a space of concrete freedom, that is, of possible transformation" (Foucault 1996: 449–50). Through Foucault's philosophical *askēsis* the subject becomes different from itself or goes astray from itself, and does so over and over again. Freedom, as he conceives, is not realized by coming into alignment with nature or the cosmos, the fulfilment of a telos or essence, but through an exercise in the creation or invention of the new. The ethical question is not "How can I model myself on eternal being (e.g. Plato/ neo-Platonism) or live according to nature (e.g. Cynic, Stoic and Epicurean)?" but "[W]hat new game can we invent?" (Foucault 1996: 312).

In Foucault's "philosophical ethos," which he describes as a "*limit-attitude*," freedom is a continuous, infinitely renewable exercise of inventing new norms, and pathology is the inability to transgress the limits of present norms (Foucault 1984: 45) That is to say, Foucault conceives his genealogical critique of the present as an exercise of the self on itself that aims at generating new norms of practice and new modes of living. "It is true," he asserts "that we have to give up the hope of ever acceding to a point of view that could give us access to any complete or definitive knowledge of what may constitute our historical limits. And from this point of view the theoretical and practical experience that we have of our limits and of the possibility of moving beyond them is always limited and determined; thus we are always in the position of beginning anew" (Foucault 1984: 47). Foucault's *askēsis* is a practice of constant self-dissolution in the absence of any eternal horizon (see Ure and Testa 2018).

Taking this Nietzschean slant on Foucault's *askēsis* shows why we should not accept at face value his claim that his genealogical spiritual exercise straightforwardly reconstitutes or transposes the ancient practices of the self. Despite his suggestion that he reclaims the living substance of ancient philosophy, his own genealogical practice of the self radically opposes its ethical goals, broadly conceived. Put simply, by casting the self adrift from any identification with nature, life or being, Foucault's *askēsis* stands in principled opposition to the classical ideal of a transformation of the self that brings it to completion, beatitude or tranquility. Indeed, if we view it through the lens of the Stoic philosophical *askeses*, for example, his model of the work of the self is in fact among the pathologies Stoicism seeks to cure. For Stoic therapy aims at establishing a sovereignty over oneself that abolishes all striving to become other to oneself, and it achieves this composure through extirpating the emotional judgements that place the subject in bondage to chance events. As Pierre Hadot insists, Stoic practices certainly aim to free the subject from conventional identities and their emotional agitations, but they do so only in order to facilitate its identification with universal reason. "Seneca," as Hadot explains, "does not find joy in 'Seneca' but by transcending 'Seneca'; by discovering that there is within him—within all human beings, that is, and within the cosmos itself—a reason which is part of universal reason" (Hadot 1995: 207; also Hadot 2009: 136). If, on the other hand, we fail to achieve this sovereignty, this state of self-completion, Stoics argue, as Foucault himself observes, we must suffer from *stultitia*, a kind of restlessness or irresolution that characterizes the *stultus*, one who "constantly changes his way of life," or changes his "mode of life everyday" (Foucault 2005: 132).

Ironically, Foucault's analysis of the Stoic goal of self-completion and self-sufficiency reveals exactly how his own version of *askēsis*, which makes a virtue of constantly seeking to become other to oneself, is at odds with Stoicism's fundamental normative and therapeutic orientation (Ure 2007). From the Stoic perspective, Foucault's *askēsis* of going astray from oneself is symptomatic of a failure to care for oneself. Foucault himself recognizes that the Roman care of the self was "not a way of marking an essential caesura in the subject" (Foucault 2005: 214). As he observes, the Stoics deployed a series of terms to refer to a break between the self and everything else, but these terms did not refer to a "break of the self *with* the self" (Foucault 2005: 212, *emphasis added*). Foucault's own notion of *askēsis*, in other words, seems to take up the Hellenistic and Stoic conception of philosophy as a work on the self, yet he severs it from its normative ideal of self-sufficiency and the analysis and critique of the emotional pathologies that it seeks to cure. Viewed through the lens of Stoicism, Foucault's celebration of limit experiences that create radical caesuras within the self can only be seen as symptomatic of a failure to understand, analyze and treat the emotional agitations which compel the subject to constantly seek out another place, another time or another self.

However, we do not have to endorse a classical or Hellenistic perspective to recognize the troubling, difficult implications of Foucault's *askēsis*. While Foucault's critics have focused on the alleged normative deficit in his philosophy, even contemporaries who sympathetically defend his ethics recognize its practical and psychological risks. Beatrice Han-Pile, for example, suggests that there is a "threat" in his support for a practice of the self that is an exercise in self-displacement and self-estrangement. Rather than fostering an identification with a set of core features or desires, she suggests, Foucault's *askēsis* is practice of "self-dehiscence" (Han-Pile 2016: 99). She conceives genealogy as an exercise that might cut open and introduce discontinuities within our being, but in doing so risk creating permanent wounds. "In its most radical form," as she explains, "Foucault's conception of critique as practice of the self would prevent identification with any aspect of the self and most likely result in a personality disorder" (Han-Pile 2016: 99).

## Conclusion

How are we to assess the significance of Foucault's reinvention of philosophy as a way of life? In studying ancient Greek and Roman philosophy, Foucault saw himself as continuing a practice "fundamental to Western philosophy": *viz.*, "to examine both the differences that keep us at a remove from a way of thinking in which we recognize our origin, and the proximity that remains in spite of that distance which we never cease to explore" (Foucault 1986: 7). By means of this chiasmus, Foucault suggests that we cannot understand ourselves unless we examine our origins in ancient practices that are both distant and near, familiar and foreign.

This chapter has stressed the ethical distance between Foucault's genealogical spiritual exercise and the ancient practices of the self. Foucault's exercise aims to create radical discontinuities between the self and itself so that it can ceaselessly experiment with new ways of living, whereas the ancient exercises aim to return the self to its true, universal form or being so that it can realize divine self-sufficiency. From the vantage point of the ancient perspective, Foucault's *askēsis* constitutes a pathological dissolution of the subject, while from his perspective, ancient ethics must be an exercise in the stagnation rather than emancipation of the subject.

We have inherited both types of spiritual exercises, exercises of ceaselessly getting free of oneself and of returning to oneself. Foucault's genealogy serves to illuminate this ethical tension between ancient and modern versions of philosophy as a way of life. Because we have inherited these two incompatible practices of the self, we can discover freedom in constant self-dissolution and imprisonment in permanent self-completion, and yet also enslavement in infinite ontological discord and freedom in harmonization with our true nature or being. Nietzsche give us a clear-eyed appraisal of the chiastic structure of our ethical inheritance that Foucault's work exposes. Nietzsche's image of modern free-spirits as akin to Odysseus, but without his hope of returning to Ithaca, beautifully renders the ethical chiasma we must navigate:

> *In the horizon of the infinite*—We have forsaken land and have gone to sea! We have burned our bridges behind us, indeed—we have destroyed the very land behind us! Now, little ship, look out! Besides you lies the ocean: it is true that it does not always roar and from time to time it lies spread out like silk and gold and reveries of goodness. But hours will come when you will realize that it is infinite and that there is nothing more terrible than infinity. Oh, the poor bird that has felt free and now strikes against the walls of this cage! Woe, when homesickness for the land overcomes you, as if there had been more *freedom* there—and there is no longer any "land"!
>
> Nietzsche 1974: 180–1

## Notes

1  I gloss Victor Goldschmidt's statement that the goal of the Platonic dialogue is more to form than to inform, which Hadot used to characterize all of ancient philosophy; see Hadot (2002: 73).

2  Foucault also claims that reconstituting ancient ethics "is an urgent, fundamental and politically indispensable task ..." (Foucault 2005: 252). Here, I bracket his claims about the political significance of reinventing ancient ethics. I discuss this issue in Ure (2020). On the genealogy of normality, see Cryle and Stephens (2017).

3  Bernard Williams' judgement typifies widespread scepticism about revitalising ancient philosophy: "[W]e are surely bound to find the Epicureans too rationalistic, the Sceptic too procedurally obsessed, the Stoics ... too unyieldingly pompous for us to take entirely seriously, not just their therapies, but the idea of them as philosophical therapists" (Williams 1994: 25).

4  Arnold Davidson reports that Foucault indicated that his discussion of the relation between spirituality and philosophy was the fruit of his encounter with the work of Hadot on the tradition of spiritual exercises (Foucault 2005: xxix). Foucault explicitly discusses Hadot in *The Hermeneutics of the Subject* (Foucault 2005: 216–17).

5  To circumscribe ancient philosophy, Foucault occasionally uses Hadot's expression "spiritual exercises" (e.g. Foucault 2005: 292–4; 306–07), or more frequently the cognate term "spirituality" (e.g. Foucault 2005: 15–19, 25–30), though he prefers his own terminology of techniques and technologies of the self. As John Sellars observes, Foucault's own notion of "technologies of the self" shares much in common with Hadot's "spiritual exercises" (see Sellars essay in this volume).

6  In Hegel's commonplace representation, Cynicism is primarily a mode of life, notable only for its crudity and vulgarity (Hegel 2006: 172, 174). "Not much about the Cynics," he opined, "deserves particular notice" (Hegel 2006: 171). Hegel maligns Crates and Hipparchia as "nothing more than swinish beggars, who found their satisfaction in the

insolence which they showed to others. They are worthy of no further consideration in Philosophy" (Hegel 2006: 171, ft. 122). Louisa Shea documents and analyzes heterodox modern rehabilitations of ancient Cynicism from Diderot to Foucault (Shea 2010).

7 "Stoics ... declare that [the sage] alone is free and bad men are slaves ..." (Laertius 1925: 227).

8 Cf. Foucault (1984: 350–1): "What strikes me is the fact that in our society, art has become something which is related only to objects and not to individuals, or to life ... But couldn't everyone's life become a work of art? Why should the lamp or the house be an art object, but not our life? ... From the idea that the self is not given to us, I think that there is only one practical consequence: we have to create ourselves as a work of art." From the perspective of the Homeric and ancient philosophic conception of the art of living, Foucault's thumbnail sketch of a potential contemporary reinvention of the art of living must appear problematic. For Homer, Plato, and Diogenes, the value of the art of living turns not simply on successfully crafting a beautiful existence, but an existence whose beauty resides specifically in its sovereignty or self-sufficiency.

9 Hadot (2002: 263–5) criticizes Foucault's claim that Descartes' philosophy marked a break with these ancient practices. Christopher Davidson suggests that Foucault agrees with Hadot that changes in how the subject knows form key practices of the self in Descartes' *Meditations*, but that Foucault "limits these practices to giving the same subject new capacities for knowing, rather than producing a new subjectivity with a new way of living and being" (Davidson 2005: 139). Davidson therefore agrees with Foucault that Descartes' *Meditations* requires no *ethical* transfiguration of subject as such.

10 On the differences between Nietzsche and Foucault's *askēsis*, see Ure and Testa (2018).

11 On Nietzsche and Foucault's analysis of the passion for knowledge, see Ansell-Pearson (2018).

12 As many commentators observe, Nietzsche struggles to come to terms with the tension between the unconditional will to truth and the need for artistic illusion. I survey this debate in Ure (2019: 208–20).

# References

Ansell-Pearson, K. (2018), "'We Are Experiments': Nietzsche, Foucault, and The Passion for Knowledge," in J. Westfall and A. Rosenberg (eds), *Nietzsche and Foucault: A Critical Encounter*, 79–98, London: Bloomsbury.

Cryle, P. and E. Stephens (2017), *Normality: A Critical Genealogy*, Chicago and London: University of Chicago Press.

Davidson, A. (2005), "Introduction," in *The Hermeneutics of the Subject: Lectures at the Collège de France 1981–1982*, ed. F. Gros, trans. G. Burchell, xix–xxx, New York: Palgrave Macmillan.

Davidson, C. (2015), "Spinoza as an Exemplar of Foucault's Spirituality and Technologies of the Self," *Journal of Early Modern Studies*, 4 (2): 111–46.

Foucault, M. (1984), *The Foucault Reader*, ed. P. Rabinow, New York: Pantheon Books.

Foucault, M. (1986), *The Use of Pleasure: Volume 2 of The History of Sexuality*, trans. R. Hurley, London: Viking.

Foucault, M. (1996), *Foucault Live: Collected Interviews, 1961–1984*, ed. S. Lotringer, trans. L. Hochroth and J. Johnston, New York: Semiotext(e).

Foucault, M. (2005), *The Hermeneutics of the Subject: Lectures at the Collège de France 1981–1982*, ed. F. Gros, trans. G. Burchell, New York: Palgrave Macmillan.
Foucault, M. (2011), *The Courage of Truth (The Government of Self and Others II): Lectures at the Collège de France 1983–1984*, ed. F. Gros, trans. G. Burchell, Basingstoke: Palgrave Macmillan.
Foucault, M. (2013), *Lectures on the Will to Know: Lectures at the Collège de France 1970–1971*, ed. D. Defert, trans. G. Burchell, Basingstoke: Palgrave Macmillan.
Gouldner, A. (1967), *Enter Plato: Classical Greece and The Origins of Social Theory*, New York and London: Basic Books.
Hadot, I. (2014), "Getting to Goodness: Reflections on Chapter 10 of Brad Inwood's Reading Seneca," in J. Wildberger and M. L. Colish (eds), *Seneca Philosophus*, 9–41, Berlin: Walter de Gruyter.
Hadot, P. (1995), *Philosophy as a Way of Life*, ed. A. Davidson, trans. M. Chase, Oxford: Blackwell.
Hadot, P. (2002), *What is Ancient Philosophy?*, trans. M. Chase, Cambridge: Belknap Press.
Hadot, P. (2009), *The Present Alone is Our Happiness: Conversations with Jeannie Carlier & Arnold I. Davidson*, trans. M. Djaballah, Stanford, CA: Stanford University Press.
Han-Pile, B. (2016), "Foucault, Normativity and Critique as a Practice of the Self," *Continental Philosophy Review*, 49: 85–101.
Hard, R. (2012), *Diogenes the Cynic: Sayings and Anecdotes*, trans. R. Hard, Oxford: Oxford University Press.
Hegel, G. W. F. (2006), *Lectures on the History of Philosophy, 1825–1826, Vol. 2 Greek Philosophy*, ed. R. Brown, trans. R. Brown and J. M. Stewart, Oxford: Oxford University Press.
Laertius, D. (1925), *Lives of Eminent Philosophers*, Vol. II, trans. R. D. Hicks, Cambridge: Harvard University Press.
Nietzsche, F. (1974), *The Gay Science*, trans. W. Kaufmann, New York: Vintage Books.
Nietzsche, F. (1985), *Untimely Meditations*, trans. R. J. Hollingdale, Cambridge: Cambridge University Press.
Nietzsche, F. (1996), *Beyond Good and Evil: Prelude to a Philosophy of the Future*, trans. W. Kaufmann, New York: Vintage.
Nietzsche, F. (1997), *Daybreak: Thoughts on the Prejudices of Morality*, trans. R. J. Hollingdale, Cambridge: Cambridge University Press.
Nietzsche, F. (1999), *Kritische Studienausgabe in 15 Bänden*, ed. G. Colli and M. Montinari, vol. 9, Berlin: Walter de Gruyter.
Schopenhauer, A., (2014), "On University Philosophy," in *Parerga and Paralipomena*, ed. S. Roehr and C. Janaway, Cambridge: Cambridge University Press.
Seneca, L. A. (2001), *Epistles*, trans. R. Gummere, Cambridge: Harvard University Press.
Shea, L. (2010), *The Cynic Enlightenment: Diogenes in the Salon*, Baltimore: John Hopkins Press.
Ure, M. (2007), "Senecan Moods: Foucault and Nietzsche on the Art of the Self," *Foucault Studies*, 4: 19–52.
Ure, M. (2019), *The Gay Science: An Introduction*, Cambridge: Cambridge University Press.
Ure, M. (2020), "Stoic Freedom: Political Resistance or Retreat? Foucault and Arendt," in K. Lampe and J. Sholtz (eds), *French and Italian Stoicisms*, London: Bloomsbury.
Ure, M. and F. Testa (2018), "Foucault and Nietzsche: Sisyphus and Dionysus," in J. Westfall and A. Rosenberg (eds), *Nietzsche and Foucault: A Critical Encounter*, 127–49, London, Bloomsbury: 2018.
Williams, B. (1994), "Do Not Disturb: Review of Martha Nussbaum, *Therapy of Desire*," *London Review of Books*, 16 (20): 25–6.

2

# Self or Cosmos:
# Foucault *versus* Hadot

John Sellars

This chapter discusses the relationship between the late work of Michel Foucault and that of his colleague at the Collège de France, Pierre Hadot.[1] Foucault referred to Hadot's work as a key point of reference for his own work on ancient practices of the self, and Hadot recounted that they also spoke on a number of occasions.[2] Arnold Davidson, who knew both men and played a key role in introducing Hadot's work to the English-speaking world, noted that Foucault had been "a careful reader of Hadot's work" (Davidson 1990: 481), and has commented on Foucault's "enthusiasm" for Hadot's work (Davidson 1995: 1). Foucault's interest in what he called "technologies of the self" (*techniques de soi*) drew in part on Hadot's accounts of ancient "spiritual exercises" (*exercices spirituels*). Hadot would later comment on Foucault's use of his work, noting their common ground but also suggesting some distance between them on certain key points, and arguing that in some respects Foucault's account of ancient practices was misleading. In particular, Hadot claimed that Foucault's stress on an aesthetic cultivation of the self placed too much emphasis on the self and downplayed the cosmological aspects of Stoic ethics. This chapter will assess whether Hadot's criticisms of Foucault are fair, and what, if any, criticisms might be raised against Hadot's own stress on dissolution of the self in his accounts of ancient philosophy.

The first section will briefly introduce Foucault's later work and comment on its debt to Hadot. The second section will examine Hadot's criticisms of Foucault's account of ancient practices of self-transformation and outline the contrast between their accounts. The third section will examine Hadot's criticisms and suggest ways in which Foucault's account might be defended, while the conclusion will argue that their accounts might be seen as complementary rather than opposed.

## Foucault's Late Work and its Debt to Hadot

Foucault's later work can be difficult to grasp due to the ways in which his interests shifted and his project developed over a relatively short period of time.[3] By the end of his life, he was effectively working on three inter-related projects that were never fully disentangled from one another. His untimely death in 1984 meant that the second and third volumes of the *History of Sexuality* published that year combine elements of these different projects layered over one another. These three projects were i) a history of sexuality, with a particular focus on shifts in sexual attitudes between pagan antiquity and early Christianity; ii) a genealogy of the modern subject; and iii) an examination of ancient "technologies of the self" associated with the ideas of self-cultivation and "care of the self."[4]

The original plan for the *History of Sexuality* was for a total of six volumes, of which just three were published in Foucault's lifetime (Elden 2016: 62–3); a fourth volume completed before Foucault's death (and at one point intended to be the second volume) has also now been published (Foucault 2018). While that original plan was inevitably cut short by Foucault's illness and death, his focus had already begun to shift away from a narrow focus on sexual attitudes. In the published version of the third volume of his history, *The Care of the Self*, this shift is manifest in the section entitled "The Cultivation of the Self" (Foucault 1984b: 51–85; 1988: 37–68). There he records his interest in what he called an "attitude of severity" towards the self that became prominent in the first two centuries AD and, in particular, a mistrust of pleasures that Foucault took to prefigure and inform early Christian attitudes towards the body. While this was clearly highly relevant to his attempt to map shifts in sexual attitudes, Foucault's concerns quickly broadened into a much wider interest in the ancient idea that one ought to pay attention to oneself.

It was this wider interest in the ancient idea of paying attention to oneself that led Foucault to start to develop a distinct, if related, project focused on the genealogy of the modern subject (see Foucault 2016: 22). Foucault intended that these reflections on the self should become a publication distinct from his *History of Sexuality* (see Foucault 1997: 255), but alas he did not have time to disentangle the two projects before publishing the second and third volumes just before his death. This separate project, focused on the genealogy of the subject, would have examined the origins of the idea that there is some kind of truth about the self that is hidden within and can be uncovered through a hermeneutic process. Foucault had traced this idea, central to the modern notion of the subject, back to the early Church Fathers and in particular to the idea of confession (*aveu*). However, when he went further back to pagan Greco-Roman authors he found something quite different. There he encountered a series of practices concerning the self that, although superficially similar to early Christian confession, had, he thought, a different set of aims. These pagan practices of the self were not intended to uncover a hidden truth about the subject; instead they were processes aimed at the transformation of the self (Foucault 2016: 29–37; also 1997: 276). A key text that Foucault referred to more than once was a passage from Seneca's *De ira*, in which the Roman Stoic describes his own process of self-examination at the end of each day, a practice that had its origins in the Pythagorean tradition:

> The mind must be called to account every day. This was Sextius's practice: when the day was spent and he had retired to his night's rest, he asked his mind, "Which of your ills did you heal today? Which vice did you resist? In what aspect are you better?" Your anger will cease and become more controllable if it knows that every day it must come before a judge. Is there anything finer, then, than this habit of scrutinizing the entire day?[5]

What Foucault found significant about this pagan practice of self-examination was the way in which it was concerned, not with confessing guilt or uncovering hidden truths about oneself, but rather with identifying faults so that one could address them.

This led Foucault to a third, yet inevitably related, project focused primarily on such ancient practices of self-transformation, practices that he often referred to as "technologies of the self" (Foucault 2016: 25; also 1997: 225). It was in this context that Foucault encountered the work of Pierre Hadot. Hadot had begun his career intending to become a Roman Catholic priest, but after a crisis of faith became a respected scholar of Neoplatonism, working on Marius Victorinus and then Plotinus (Hadot 1963, 1993), as well as the interaction between pagan and Christian thought in late antiquity (Hadot 2001: 38–62; 2009: 15–31). Later, he also worked on Roman Stoicism, especially Marcus Aurelius (Hadot 1992, 1998). In the mid 1970s, Hadot wrote an article devoted to the topic of spiritual exercises in ancient philosophy (Hadot 1975–6).[6] Hadot borrowed his title from the Jesuit Ignatius of Loyola, using it to describe a series of ancient practices (such as Seneca's routine of daily self-examination) designed to effect some form of self-transformation. While some commentators have criticized Hadot for anachronistically using an early modern Christian category to describe ancient pagan practices (e.g. Cooper 2012: 402), the notion of an "exercise of the soul" (*askēsis tēs psukhēs*) was already well established in antiquity (Sellars 2003: 110–15). Hadot's account of these ancient practices would prove to be an important influence on Foucault, who referred to Hadot's work a number of times in his later writings,[7] and Foucault's own notion of "technologies of the self" shares much in common with Hadot's "spiritual exercises."

Foucault's interest in these inter-related projects, and especially the third, was announced to the wider world in an interview he gave in English in 1983 (Foucault 1997: 253–80), a year before the publication of the second and third volumes of the *History of Sexuality*. In it he made a number of important, but potentially controversial, claims. Most notably he suggested that ancient ethics was not normative; instead it had an aesthetic aim and was primarily a matter of personal choice (Foucault 1997: 254). While the first part of this claim is not so controversial (cf. Anscombe 1958), the second is certainly more so. He went on to claim that there was also a significant shift in ancient ethics: in the classical Greek period ethics was primarily a *tekhnē*, an art or craft, about how to live well within the context of the *polis*, but later, in the Greco-Roman culture of the first two centuries AD, it became a *tekhnē* of the self, disengaged from society. What had been an aesthetics of life became an aesthetics of the self (Foucault 1997: 260). This led Foucault to some wider reflections (Foucault 1997: 261–2): if the self is not something given, if it is something that must instead be created, then why can it not be a work of art? Further:

> What strikes me is the fact that, in our society, art has become something that is related only to objects and not to individuals or to life. That art is something which is specialized or done by experts who are artists. But couldn't everyone's life become a work of art? Why should the lamp or the house be an art object but not our life?
>
> Foucault 1997: 261

Foucault has been criticized for many of these claims. In the present context one might note a tension between this last idea of self-creation as a work of art and the account he gave in the third volume of the *History of Sexuality* in which "care of the self" is presented as a therapeutics of the soul analogous to medicine for the body (Foucault 1984b: 69–71; 1988: 54–5). In that account there is, albeit implicitly, the idea that care of the self involves returning a diseased soul back to its proper functioning. There are tensions like this one throughout Foucault's late works, reflecting the ways in which three distinct and incomplete projects were never fully disentangled before becoming intertwined in publications that were issued somewhat hastily in the final year of Foucault's life.

## Hadot's Criticisms of Foucault

In discussion with Jeannie Carlier and Arnold Davidson, Hadot remarked that he met Foucault only a few times. Presumably impressed by his work, Foucault encouraged Hadot to submit his candidature to the Collège de France, towards the end of 1980 (Hadot 2001: 215; 2009: 135; also 2002a: 305). They spoke a few times thereafter but never had an extended discussion about their shared interests in ancient philosophy. In the same discussion Hadot summarized what he took to be the principal points of disagreement between their accounts of ancient practices of the self:

> In his descriptions of what he calls the practices of the self, Foucault does not sufficiently valorize the process of becoming aware of belonging to the cosmic Whole, a process that also corresponds to an overcoming of oneself. Finally, I do not think that the ethical model adapted to a modern man can be an aesthetics of existence. I am worried that this may ultimately be no more than a new form of dandyism.
>
> Hadot 2001: 216–17; 2009: 136

According to Hadot, "Seneca finds joy not in Seneca but in Seneca identified with universal reason. One elevates oneself from the level of the self to another, transcendent level" (Hadot 2001: 216–17; 2009: 136). The problem with Foucault's account of ancient philosophy, Hadot claimed, is its excessive attention to the self. It is indeed a great shame that Foucault and Hadot never had an opportunity to sit down and talk through these issues in detail. As Hadot commented elsewhere, "These differences could have provided the substance for a dialogue between us, which, unfortunately, was interrupted all too soon by Foucault's premature death" (Hadot 2002a: 323; 1995b: 206).

Hadot elaborated on these concerns in two short pieces both published after Foucault's death: "Un dialogue interrompu avec Michel Foucault. Convergences et divergences" (first published in Hadot 1987), and "Réflexions sur la notion de «culture de soi»" (Hadot 1989).[8] In the first of these, in which Hadot praises Foucault's "l'extraordinaire présence personnelle et la merveilleuse acuité d'esprit" (Hadot 2002a: 306), points of agreement and divergence are noted. Hadot acknowledges much common ground between Foucault's account of the cultivation of the self (*la culture de soi*) in the third volume of the *History of Sexuality* (Foucault 1984b: 51–85; 1988: 37–68) and his own work on spiritual exercises in ancient philosophy (Hadot 2002a: 306). However, he has reservations about Foucault's notion of an "aesthetics of existence," either as a description of ancient thought or as a model for ethical practice today (Hadot 2002a: 308). Hadot notes that modern notions of aesthetic beauty are quite different from the ancient idea of *kalon*, which encompassed not merely aesthetic but also moral qualities (Hadot 2002a: 308). The idea that one might non-morally add style to one's life in order to turn it into a work of art is, according to Hadot, quite alien to ancient thought. This is one of the reasons why Hadot was suspicious of Foucault's focus on the self. Instead of cultivating the self, Hadot suggests that it would be more appropriate to think in terms of "overcoming the self" (Hadot 2002a: 308). He continues:

> It is not a matter of the construction of a self as a work of art, but on the contrary, of an overcoming of the self, or at least of an exercise by means of which the self is situated in the totality and has an experience of the self as part of this totality.
> Hadot 2002a: 310[9]

While Hadot notes other divergences,[10] these two interconnected points concerning aesthetics and the self appear to be the most significant, and they are developed further in his second essay on Foucault.

Hadot's second essay, "Réflexions sur la notion de «culture de soi»," was first published in 1989, in the proceedings of a conference from 1988 marking the fourth anniversary of Foucault's death. Here he develops his concerns about Foucault's excessive focus on the self. The difference between their positions, Hadot implies, is already evident in Foucault's choices of titles and phrases—"care of the self" (*souci de soi*), "practices of the self" (*pratiques de soi*), "technologies of the self" (*techniques de soi*)—in contrast to Hadot's own "spiritual exercises" (*exercices spirituels*). Hadot's charge against Foucault is that his work is "focused far too much on the 'self', or at least on a specific conception of the self" (Hadot 2002a: 324; 1995b: 207). In particular, Hadot challenges Foucault's interpretation of Seneca (who became one of Foucault's favorite authors). Seneca is not primarily concerned with perfecting and taking joy in himself, Hadot argues, but with "transcending 'Seneca'" (Hadot 2002a: 325; 1995b: 207). Cultivation of the self, for the Stoics, involves transcending the self, cultivating one's inner reason that is a fragment of divine reason: "the goal of Stoic exercises is to go beyond the self, and think and act in unison with universal reason" (Hadot 2002a: 325; 1995b: 207). Hadot goes on to suggest that this was not a failure of comprehension on Foucault's part but rather a deliberate decision to bracket an aspect of ancient thought out of step with modern sensibilities, which was necessary as part of Foucault's attempt to outline an "aesthetics of existence" that could "offer contemporary mankind a model of life" (Hadot 2002a: 325; 1995b: 208). He further suggests that if Foucault had paid more attention to the Epicureans he might have avoided this problem, but even the Epicureans, Hadot argues, were not as focused on the self as Foucault's wider account would have it. A similar problem can be found in Foucault's discussion of "writing the self" (*écriture de soi*) from 1983 (Foucault 1997: 207–22), Hadot claims. In that essay Foucault described a range of ancient forms of writing, all of which he presented as "arts of oneself," as examples of "training of the self by oneself" (Foucault 1997: 207–08). In response Hadot writes:

> The point is not to forge oneself a spiritual identity by writing, but rather to liberate oneself from one's individuality, in order to raise oneself up to universality. It is thus incorrect to speak of "writing the self": not only is it not the case that one "writes oneself," but what is more, it is not the case that writing constitutes the self. Writing, like the other spiritual exercises, *changes the level of the self*, and universalizes it.
>
> Hadot 2002a: 329; 1995b: 210–11

It is worth noting here that Foucault's account drew on a range of Stoic, Platonist, and early Christian sources, and Hadot refers to a similar range of ancient sources as well. For these schools of thought Hadot argues that there is, in effect, a double renunciation of the self. First there is an ascetic moment in which "one frees oneself from exteriority, from personal attachment to exterior objects, and from the pleasures they may provide" (Hadot 2002a: 330; 1995b: 211). This turn inwards is directed towards self-mastery, and on this Hadot and Foucault are in agreement. However, Hadot insists that this move inwards is "inseparably linked" to another move that reconnects the self with the exterior world in a completely new way:

> This is a new way of being-in-the-world, which consists in becoming aware of oneself as a part of nature, and a portion of universal reason. At this point, one no longer lives in the usual, conventional human world, but in the world of nature.
>
> Hadot 1995b: 211

Hadot's principal charge against Foucault, then, is that he "did not sufficiently insist" on this "universalist, cosmic dimension" of ancient thought (Hadot 1995b: 211; also Hadot 2002a: 308, 310). But Hadot's concern was not limited merely to historical accuracy. As we have already seen, Hadot could see that, in part at least, Foucault wanted to draw something from his historical work in order to create an ethical framework for the present day. Hadot's further concern was that an ethics focused on the self would on its own terms be unattractive as an ethical model:

> What I am afraid of is that, by focusing his interpretation too exclusively on the culture of the self, the care of the self, and conversion toward the self—more generally, by defining his ethical model as an aesthetics of existence—M. Foucault is propounding a culture of the self which is *too* aesthetic. In other words, this may be a new form of Dandyism, late twentieth-century style.
>
> Hadot 2002a: 331; 1995b: 211

The contrast is clear: while Hadot is happy to acknowledge a good deal of common ground with Foucault, on this one point there is, in his view, a significant difference between them, both with regard to correctly grasping ancient thought and to what one might take from it and revitalize today. Foucault's work is excessively focused on the self, while Hadot emphasizes the impersonal, universalist, cosmic dimension of ancient practices of self-transformation.

## Analysis of Hadot's Criticisms

Are these criticisms of Foucault justified? Let us begin with the charge of dandyism. Is Foucault right to talk about an ancient "aesthetics of existence" (*esthétique de l'existence*)? In antiquity philosophers, and in particular Stoics, did refer to philosophy as an art of living, a *tekhnē peri ton bion*.[11] In this context *tekhnē* simply means art in the sense of a craft, or a skill. Ancient examples of *tekhnai* would be rhetoric, medicine, navigation, or shoemaking—all examples well known from the early Platonic dialogues. The ancient phrase "the art of living" has no aesthetic overtones. Instead it refers to a practical skill, based on knowledge, as opposed to a mere knack that cannot guarantee consistent results. In this it shares something with skilled craftsmen, but it has little to do with artists in the modern sense of the term. When Foucault wonders whether our lives might become works of art, in the same way that aesthetically attractive objects are works of art (Foucault 1997: 261), it looks as if he has gone well beyond his ancient sources. Taken in these terms, it looks as if Hadot has good grounds to call into question Foucault's notion of an "aesthetics of existence."

It would, however, be unfair to judge Foucault's wider view on the basis of a single passing remark in an interview. In a recent discussion Giorgio Agamben has defended Foucault against Hadot's charge by drawing attention to a number of other texts, including Foucault's 1981–2 lecture course, *The Hermeneutics of the Subject* (Foucault 2001; 2005). One of Hadot's concerns, as we have seen, is the apparent dislocation between the aesthetic and the ethical in Foucault's late work, and the thought that one might follow purely optional rules in order to give style to one's life, seemingly without regard for any moral concerns. But, Agamben notes (Agamben 2016: 97–8), in the lecture course Foucault explicitly warns against reading ancient references to care of the self as a "sort of moral dandyism," insisting that they were the basis of one of "the most austere, strict, and restrictive moralities known in the West" (Foucault 2001: 14; 2005: 12–13). It seems that Foucault was both fully conscious of the danger and explicitly resisted it.

Those lectures were of course not published until 2001, well after Hadot had written his two short essays on Foucault's late work. Perhaps Hadot's judgement was quite reasonable given the texts that were available to him at the time he was writing. However, Agamben insists that the issue was already clear in the second volume of the *History of Sexuality*, published back in 1984 (Agamben 2016: 98–9). There, Foucault outlined his notion of an "aesthetics of existence" by describing it as combining both "rules of conduct" and a certain aesthetic value (Foucault 1984a: 16–17; 1986: 10–11), with a goal that might best be defined as "etho-poetic" (Foucault 1984a: 19; 1986: 13; see also 1997: 209). It is also worth noting that while Foucault does use the phrase "aesthetics of existence," he is primarily concerned with discussing what he calls the "arts of existence" (*arts de l'existence*), which he identifies with "technologies of the self" (Foucault 1984a: 16–17; 1986: 10–11). Taking into account all of these remarks, it seems clear that what Foucault has in mind are arts and techniques precisely in the sense of a *tekhnē*, a craft or skill. Indeed, he goes on to state that his primary concern in volumes two, three, and four of the *History of Sexuality* is with prescriptive texts "whose main object, whatever their form ... is to suggest rules of conduct ... texts written for the purpose of offering rules, opinions, and advice on how to behave as one should" (Foucault 1984a: 18; 1986: 12). From this it seems clear that Foucault did not neglect the ethical dimension of ancient thought.

Agamben's defense of Foucault helps to give us a fuller picture of Foucault's account of ancient ethical practices. However, it is worth noting that when Hadot directed the charge of dandyism at Foucault, he did not say that Foucault had misunderstood the ancient texts; he was more concerned with the attempt to extract something new for today (Hadot 2001: 217; 2009: 136). In that context, Foucault does ask whether we might turn our lives into works of art akin to aesthetic objects (Foucault 1997: 261). For Hadot, then, on this issue the difference is over the foundation for ethics today, not the interpretation of ancient texts. Yet, in the end, Foucault said very little about the idea of a modern aesthetics of the self—just a few passing, and often seemingly contradictory, comments in interviews right at the end of his life.[12]

Closely connected to the charge of dandyism is Foucault's focus on the self. According to Foucault there was a pronounced concern with the self in ancient thought, especially in the Greco-Roman period of the first two centuries AD.[13] For Hadot, by contrast, any such turn inwards was only ever preparatory for a reconnection with something beyond the self. For the ancient Stoics, Hadot stresses the goal of living in harmony with Nature and what he calls the "cosmic dimension" of ancient thought (Hadot 2002a: 330; 1995b: 211). Before pursuing the dispute further, it is perhaps worth pausing for a moment to say a bit more about Hadot's own intellectual background. His early work focused on the interaction between early Christian thought and Neoplatonism, and Neoplatonism remained an important area of work throughout his career. That career began, he told Carlier and Davidson in conversation, with an oceanic experience of oneness with "the Whole" that developed into a fascination with mysticism (Hadot 2001: 23–4, 27–9; 2009: 6, 8–9). Hadot's subsequent book on Plotinus highlights the Neoplatonic claim that one's true self is "not of this world" but nevertheless could be reached by "returning within oneself" (Hadot 1963: 25–6; 1993: 25). For Plotinus,

> The human self is *not* irrevocably separated from its eternal model, as the latter exists within divine Thought. This true self—this self in God—is within ourselves. During certain privileged experiences, which raise the level of our inner tension, we can identify ourselves with it. We then become this eternal self; we are moved by its unutterable beauty, and when we identify ourselves with this self, we identify ourselves with divine Thought itself, within which it is contained.
> 
> Hadot 1963: 28; 1993: 27

The aim in Plotinus's Neoplatonism, then, is not to take care of the self, but to transcend the self, or, to be more precise, to transcend one's everyday sense of self and identify with the divine self. Hadot's spiritual exercises are not concerned with cultivating or taking care of one's everyday self; they are aimed at escaping it.[14]

Neoplatonism and Stoicism are of course quite different philosophies, but Hadot's account of Stoicism also emphasizes this theme of escaping the everyday self. As we have already seen in his criticisms of Foucault, Hadot insists that Seneca takes joy not in being Seneca but in "transcending 'Seneca'" (Hadot 2002a: 325; 1995b: 207), in identifying himself with "universal reason" (Hadot 2001: 216–17; 2009: 136). This idea is also prominent in Hadot's extended study of the Stoic philosopher and emperor Marcus Aurelius:

> The realization of one's self as identical with universal Reason, then, as long as it is accompanied by consent to this will, does not isolate the self like some minuscule island in the universe. On the contrary, it can open the self to all cosmic becoming, insofar as the self raises itself from its limited situation and partial, restricted, and individualistic point of view to a universal and cosmic perspective.
> 
> Hadot 1992: 196–7; 1998: 180–1

While Hadot is quite right to point to this theme within ancient Stoicism, which is especially prominent in Marcus's *Meditations*, there are other themes that are equally important. In the Stoicism of Epictetus, for instance, great emphasis is placed on actions appropriate to the social roles in which one finds oneself.[15] Closely connected to this, as Foucault himself points out (Foucault 2001: 188–91; 2005: 195–8), is taking care of others as well as oneself. Thus, someone who is a parent should embrace the responsibilities that such a role entails, which of course means taking care of their children. Moreover, given that all humans are by nature social beings, taking care of oneself—cultivating the virtues appropriate to a social being—will necessarily involve paying attention to the needs of one's fellow humans. Epictetus is quite explicit that there is nothing antisocial about self-concern; on the contrary, it is essential if we are to develop the virtues necessary to become good ethical agents. He writes:

> This is not mere self-love; such is the nature of the animal man; everything that he does is for himself. Why, even the sun does everything for its own sake, and, for that matter, so does Zeus himself. But when Zeus wishes to be "Rain-bringer," and "Fruit-giver," and "Father of men and of gods," you can see for yourself that he cannot achieve these works, or win these appellations, unless he proves himself useful to the common interest; and in general he has so constituted the nature of the rational animal man, that he can attain nothing of his own proper goods unless he contributes something to the common interest. Hence it follows that it can no longer be regarded as unsocial for a man to do everything for his own sake.[16]

This highlights two key points. The first is that care of the self as understood by Epictetus cannot be disassociated from ethical behavior. Foucault himself explicitly underlined this point:

> The person who takes care of himself properly ... when he has taken care of himself so that when something appears in his representations he knows what he

should and should not do, he will at the same time know how to fulfil his duties as part of the human community.

Foucault 2001: 189; 2005: 197

The second is that while the Stoics stressed our place within the wider context of Nature, they also stressed the need for individual ethical development, aimed at cultivating virtues that shape our inter-personal relationships. Indeed, they identified living in harmony with Nature with a virtuous life.[17] A substantial part of Roman Stoic discourse is concerned with precisely this sort of personal self-cultivation. We can see this in Marcus's *Meditations* alongside his reflections on his place in the cosmos, such as when he reminds himself that he should embrace the work appropriate to a human being, with all the social responsibilities that involves:

> Can't you see the plants, the birds, the ants, the spiders, the bees each doing his own work, helping for their part to adjust a world? And then you refuse to do a man's office and don't make haste to do what is according to your own nature.[18]

Foucault's account of ancient concern with the self is thus well grounded in the Greco-Roman texts with which he became so fascinated. Not only does Hadot's criticism seem potentially unfair, but his own focus on impersonal union with cosmic Nature runs the risk of obscuring this equally important aspect of Stoic ethics.

Foucault also addressed the issue of the relationship between the individual and cosmic self in his *The Hermeneutics of the Subject* lectures, published as has already been noted after the composition of Hadot's two pieces. In a discussion of a passage from Seneca's *Quaestiones naturales*, Foucault writes:

> This flight from ourselves . . . leads us to God, but not in the form of losing oneself in God or of a movement which plunges deep into God, but in the form that allows us to find ourselves again, "*in consortium Dei*": in a sort of co-naturalness or co-functionality with God. That is to say, human reason is of the same nature as divine reason. It has the same properties and the same role and function.

Foucault 2001: 264; 2005: 275

Here, it seems, Foucault fully acknowledges the aspect of Stoicism that Hadot claimed he had neglected. This is akin to Hadot's insistence that Seneca finds joy in "transcending 'Seneca,'" escaping his everyday self in order to reconnect with cosmic, divine Nature. However, Foucault continues with some important qualifications:

> What is involved is not an uprooting from this world into another world. It is not a matter of freeing oneself from one reality in order to arrive at a different reality. It is not a matter of leaving a world of appearances so as finally to reach a sphere of the truth.

Foucault 2001: 264; 2005: 276

In other words, the Stoic connection with Nature is quite different from a Platonic "turning away from this world" (Foucault 2001: 265; 2005: 276). In this particular passage from Seneca's *Quaestiones naturales* (the Preface to Book 1)—but the same applies to many similar passages in the *Meditations* of Marcus Aurelius—one of the main aims is to relocate oneself within a wider cosmic perspective in order to devalue everyday human concerns.[19] As Foucault summarizes:

> Reaching this point enables us to dismiss and exclude all the false values and all the false dealings in which we are caught up, to gauge what we really are on the earth, and to take the measure of our existence—of this existence that is just a point in space and time—and of our smallness.
> 
> Foucault 2001: 266; 2005: 277

Developing such a perspective contributes to the Stoic ethical project insofar as it encourages one not to place value on external possessions and circumstances, which the Stoics deemed to be mere indifferents (*adiaphora*) when compared to virtue (*aretē*).[20] Foucault goes on to stress that, for Seneca, locating oneself within the much wider context of Nature in this way is an essential part of Senecan care of the self: "knowledge of the self and knowledge of nature are not alternatives, therefore; they are absolutely linked to each other" (Foucault 2001: 267; 2005: 278). On Foucault's own account, then, there is no dichotomy between a self-centered care of the self and an impersonal union with cosmic reason; in Stoicism the two go hand in hand. As he put it, "the soul's virtue consists in penetrating the world and not tearing free from it, in exploring the world's secrets rather than turning away towards inner secrets" (Foucault 2001: 269; 2005: 280). This remark alone shows that Foucault's account of ancient practices neither neglected their ethical aspect nor focused narrowly on the self. It seems quite clear, then, that Foucault's account of Stoic ethics avoids many of the charges that have been laid against it. But, to reiterate, all this is to be found in a lecture course published well after Hadot had produced his essays on Foucault's work.

## Conclusion

As we have seen, it is possible to push back against both of Hadot's principal concerns about Foucault's late work. Foucault's account of ancient ethics does not fall into an aestheticized dandyism and its focus on the self is well grounded in the ancient texts. Hadot's doubts about Foucault's focus on the self may simply reflect his own philosophical instincts alongside his scholarly background in Neoplatonism. Yet it would be a mistake to overstate the differences between their positions. As Hadot stressed in both of his short pieces on Foucault's work, there is much common ground between them, with just a few divergences of opinion. But those divergences are not the product of one person getting it right and the other person going wrong; instead they merely reflect differences of emphasis. Foucault's focus on practices of the self, for instance, was entirely appropriate given that one of the central themes in his late work was an attempt to write a history of the subject. Hadot was also quite right to point out that the impersonal dimension within Stoic thought received less emphasis from Foucault, at least in the works he managed to publish before he died. Hadot's remarks,

I suggest, ought to be taken as a supplement to, rather than a rejection of, Foucault's account. Foucault's and Hadot's accounts of ancient practices of self-cultivation and self-transformation ought to be seen as complementary rather than contradictory, each augmenting the other. It is such a shame that, despite knowing each other and being aware of their shared interests, they never found an opportunity to pursue these issues themselves.[21]

## Notes

1. For previous discussions of the relationship between Foucault and Hadot, see Flynn (2005); Wimberly (2009); Irrera (2010); Baudart (2013: 101–25); Lorenzini (2015: 213–18); and Agamben (2016: 95–108).
2. Foucault referred to Hadot in Foucault (1984a: 14, 264; 1986: 8, 271), and in Foucault (1984b: 57; 1988: 243), as well as throughout his 1981–2 lecture course, *The Hermeneutics of the Subject* (Foucault 2001; 2005). Hadot recounts his personal encounters with Foucault in Hadot (2001: 215–17; 2009: 135–6).
3. For a thorough account, see Elden (2016); for a condensed summary, see Sellars (2018: 15–16).
4. It is worth noting that the ideas of self-cultivation and care of the self are potentially quite different. The former implies self-transformation and, on one reading, self-creation. The latter might be taken to imply a pre-existing, true self that must be looked after. On this see Foucault (1997: 261–2), with further discussion below.
5. Seneca, *De ira* 3.36.1-2, in Kaster and Nussbaum (2010). This passage was mentioned by Foucault in his 1979–80 Collège de France lecture course, *On the Government of the Living* (Foucault 2014a: 239–41), his 1980 lectures in Dartmouth and Berkeley (Foucault 2016: 29–30), and his 1981 lectures in Louvain (Foucault 2014b: 97).
6. This article was reprinted in Hadot (1981) (the edition cited by Foucault), which was revised and expanded in 1987; a third edition was issued in 1993 (which I have not seen). I cite from the most recent edition, revised and expanded again, Hadot (2002a: 19–74). It is translated into English in Hadot (1995b: 81–125).
7. See note 2 above.
8. Both texts can be found in Hadot (2002a: 305–11, 323–32). The second is translated in Hadot (1995b: 206–13). The first is due to appear in translation in a volume of Hadot's selected writings currently being prepared by Federico Testa and Matthew Sharpe. It is discussed and quoted at length in Agamben (2016: 95–108); note also the commentary in Baudart (2013: 101–25).
9. This passage is translated into English in Agamben (2016: 96), which I follow here with some emendations. Note that the translation there omits the key phrase "as a work of art" and the pagination given for the original text is incorrect.
10. In Hadot (2001: 216; 2009: 136), he criticizes Foucault's focus on pleasure, especially when discussing the Stoics, and argues that Foucault failed to comprehend the Stoic distinction between joy and pleasure. See also Hadot (2002a: 324–5; 1995b: 207). For further discussion of this dispute, see Irrera (2010). In Hadot (2002a: 310–11; cf. Hadot 1995a: 395–9; 2002b: 263–5), he criticizes Foucault for claiming that Descartes marked a break from these ancient practices, inaugurating a new model of philosophy; Hadot suggests that the break occurred in the early Middle Ages and, in fact, Descartes may be seen as resurrecting ancient practices of the self in his *Meditations*.

11  Foucault used the Greek phrase *teknhē tou biou* (Foucault 1984b: 57; 1988: 43), but this appears nowhere in the surviving ancient texts; see further Sellars (2003: 5).
12  Compare, for instance, Foucault (1997: 256) with Foucault (1997: 294–5). For a very brief discussion, see Sellars (2018: 25–7).
13  Foucault's discussions of the self in ancient thought have generated a huge commentary and a wide range of criticisms, some of which are critically examined in Lorenzini (2015: 203–12).
14  In this context we might also note Hadot's admiration for the philosophy of Henri Bergson (Hadot 1995b: 278), as well as the influence of Bergson on Émile Bréhier, who wrote important works on both Stoicism and Neoplatonism that were regular points of reference for Hadot.
15  See e.g. *Enchiridion* 30, in Oldfather (1925–8).
16  Epictetus, *Dissertationes* 1.19.11–15, in Oldfather (1925–8). Note also *Dissertationes* 2.14.8.
17  See Diogenes Laertius 7.87, in Hicks (1925).
18  Marcus Aurelius, *Meditations* 5.1, in Farquharson (1944).
19  For further discussion of this theme, with examples from a variety of ancient texts, see Hadot (1995b: 238–50).
20  See e.g. Diogenes Laertius 7.102–05, in Hicks (1925).
21  An earlier version of this chapter was read at a workshop in Prato, Italy—*Reinventing Philosophy as a Way of Life*—in July 2018, organized by Michael Ure. I should like to thank all the participants for their comments and discussion, especially Federico Testa, Matthew Sharpe, Matthew Dennis, and Keith Ansell-Pearson.

# References

Agamben, G. (2016), *The Use of Bodies: Homo Sacer IV, 2*, trans. A. Kotsko, Stanford, CA: Stanford University Press.
Anscombe, G. E. M. (1958), "Modern Moral Philosophy," *Philosophy*, 33: 1–16.
Baudart, A. (2013), *Qu'est-ce que la sagesse?*, Paris: Vrin.
Cooper, J. (2012), *Pursuits of Wisdom: Six Ways of Life in Ancient Philosophy from Socrates to Plotinus*, Princeton, NJ: Princeton University Press.
Davidson, A. (1990), "Spiritual Exercises and Ancient Philosophy: An Introduction to Pierre Hadot," *Critical Inquiry*, 16: 475–82.
Davidson, A. (1995), "Introduction: Pierre Hadot and the Spiritual Phenomenon of Ancient Philosophy," in P. Hadot, *Philosophy as a Way of Life*, ed. A. Davidson, 1–45, Oxford: Blackwell.
Elden, S. (2016), *Foucault's Last Decade*, Cambridge: Polity.
Farquharson, A. S. L. (1944), *The Meditations of the Emperor Marcus Antoninus*, 2 vols, Oxford: Clarendon Press.
Flynn, T. (2005), "Philosophy as a Way of Life: Foucault and Hadot," *Philosophy & Social Criticism*, 31 (5–6): 609–22.
Foucault, M. (1984a), *Histoire de la sexualité 2: L'Usage des plaisirs*, Paris: Gallimard.
Foucault, M. (1984b), *Histoire de la sexualité 3: Le souci de soi*, Paris: Gallimard.
Foucault, M. (1986), *The Use of Pleasure: Volume 2 of The History of Sexuality*, trans. R. Hurley, London: Viking.
Foucault, M. (1988), *The Care of the Self: Volume 3 of The History of Sexuality*, trans. R. Hurley, London: Allen Lane The Penguin Press.

Foucault, M. (1997), *The Essential Works of Michel Foucault, 1954-1984, Vol. 1: Ethics, Subjectivity and Truth*, ed. P. Rabinow, trans. R. Hurley, London: Allen Lane / The Penguin Press.

Foucault, M. (2001), *L'herméneutique du sujet: Cours au Collège de France (1981-1982)*, Paris: Gallimard/Seuil.

Foucault, M. (2005), *The Hermeneutics of the Subject: Lectures at the Collège de France 1981-1982*, ed. F. Gros, trans. G. Burchell, New York: Palgrave Macmillan.

Foucault, M. (2014a), *On the Government of the Living: Lectures at the Collège de France 1979-1980*, ed. M. Senellart, trans. G. Burchell, Basingstoke: Palgrave Macmillan.

Foucault, M. (2014b), *Wrong-Doing, Truth-Telling: The Function of Avowal in Justice*, ed. F. Brion and B. Harcourt, trans. S. W. Sawyer, Chicago: University of Chicago Press.

Foucault, M. (2016), *About the Beginning of the Hermeneutics of the Self: Lectures at Dartmouth College, 1980*, ed. H.-P. Fruchaud and D. Lorenzini, trans. G. Burchell, Chicago: The University of Chicago Press.

Foucault, M. (2018), *Histoire de la sexualité 4: Les aveux de la chair*, Paris: Gallimard.

Hadot, P. (1963), *Plotin ou la simplicité du regard*, Paris: Plon.

Hadot, P. (1975-6), "Exercices spirituels," *Annuaire de la 5ᵉ section de l'École Pratique des Hautes Études*, 84: 25-70.

Hadot, P. (1981), *Exercices spirituels et philosophie antique*, Paris: Études Augustiniennes.

Hadot, P. (1987), *Exercices spirituels et philosophie antique*, 2nd ed., Paris: Études Augustiniennes.

Hadot, P. (1989), "Réflexions sur la notion de «culture de soi»," in *Michel Foucault Philosophe: Rencontre Internationale Paris, 9, 10, 11 Janvier 1988*, 261-70, Paris: Éditions du Seuil.

Hadot, P. (1992), *La citadelle intérieure: Introduction aux Pensées de Marc Aurèle*, Paris: Fayard.

Hadot, P. (1993), *Plotinus or The Simplicity of Vision*, trans. M. Chase, Chicago: The University of Chicago Press.

Hadot, P. (1995a), *Qu'est-ce que la philosophie antique?*, Paris: Gallimard.

Hadot, P. (1995b), *Philosophy as a Way of Life*, ed. A. Davidson, trans. M. Chase. Oxford: Blackwell.

Hadot, P. (1998), *The Inner Citadel: The Meditations of Marcus Aurelius*, trans. M. Chase, Cambridge, MA: Harvard University Press.

Hadot, P. (2001), *La philosophie comme manière de vivre: Entretiens avec Jeannie Carlier et Arnold I. Davidson*, Paris: Albin Michel.

Hadot, P. (2002a), *Exercices spirituels et philosophie antique*, Nouvelle édition revue et augmentée, Paris: Albin Michel.

Hadot, P. (2002b), *What is Ancient Philosophy?*, trans. M. Chase, Cambridge MA: Belknap Press.

Hadot, P. (2009), *The Present Alone is Our Happiness: Conversations with Jeannie Carlier and Arnold I. Davidson*, trans. M. Djaballah, Stanford, CA: Stanford University Press.

Hicks, R. D. (1925), *Diogenes Laertius, Lives of Eminent Philosophers*, 2 vols, Cambridge, MA: Harvard University Press.

Irrera, O. (2010), "Pleasure and Transcendence of the Self: Notes on 'a dialogue too soon interrupted' between Michel Foucault and Pierre Hadot," *Philosophy & Social Criticism*, 36 (9): 995-1017.

Kaster, R. A. and M. C. Nussbaum (2010), *Seneca: Anger, Mercy, Revenge*, Chicago: University of Chicago Press.

Oldfather, W. A. (1925-8), *Epictetus, The Discourses as Reported by Arrian, The Manual, and Fragments*, 2 vols, Cambridge, MA: Harvard University Press.

Lorenzini, D. (2015), *Éthique et politique de soi: Foucault, Hadot, Cavell et les techniques de l'ordinaire*, Paris: Vrin.

Sellars, J. (2003), *The Art of Living: The Stoics on the Nature and Function of Philosophy*, Aldershot: Ashgate.

Sellars, J. (2018), "Roman Stoic Mindfulness: An Ancient Technology of the Self," in M. Dennis and S. Werkhoven (eds), *Ethics and Self-Cultivation: Historical and Contemporary Pespectives*, 15–29, New York: Routledge.

Wimberly, C. (2009), "The Joy of Difference: Foucault and Hadot on the Aesthetic and the Universal in Philosophy," *Philosophy Today*, 53 (2): 192–203.

3

# The Great Cycle of the World:
# Foucault and Hadot on the Cosmic Perspective and the Care of the Self

Federico Testa

Foucault's work on the *care of the self* has been criticized for presenting an impoverished image of ethics reduced to self-absorption. Foucault allegedly proposed an "atomized politics of introversion" (McNay 1992: 158), withdrawing from public or collective spheres, taking refuge in moral solitude and aestheticism.[1] Pierre Hadot was one of the first critics to point to apparently significant gaps in Foucault's analyses of ancient philosophies, such as the importance of the human community, as well as the *cosmos* and the cosmologic dimensions of ancient spiritual exercises.

This chapter engages with this line of criticism in two ways. First, it re-situates Foucault's reflection on the self in the context of a political concern. By showing the links between the problematization of *government* and that of *care*, I stress the political significance of the idea of care of the self in the context of Foucault's work on power and governmentality. Second, bearing in mind the definition of the care of the self as "an attitude towards the *self*, *others* and the *world*" (Foucault 2005: 10), I discuss the importance of nature and cosmology in Foucault's reading of ancient philosophical practices in *The Hermeneutics of the Subject*. I will consider Foucault's analysis of the Stoic knowledge of nature and the spiritual exercises it entails, discussing his reading of Seneca's "view from above."

Engaging with Hadot's criticism, I provide textual evidence of the importance that Foucault attributes to the cosmological dimension of the care of the self. To illustrate this, I revisit Foucault's argument according to which it is not through a knowledge of human interiority, but rather through "the great cycle of the world" that it becomes possible for us to accede to ourselves. I then seek to show how Foucault's reading of the Stoics emphasizes an ethical, political and relational understanding of the self. Additionally, I situate Hadot's critique within the context of his own philosophical presuppositions, especially regarding the role of the cosmic dimension in human experience.

## Hadot's Critique

In an interview with Jeannie Carlier and Arnold Davidson, Hadot summarizes his main criticisms to Foucault, formulated in previous texts (see Hadot 2001). These texts could be divided into two groups. The first is characterized by a direct engagement with Foucault, in which Hadot's attempt is to articulate the stakes of "a dialogue too soon interrupted,"[2] presenting convergences and divergences.[3] In the second, a critical assessment of Foucault's work appears in the context of the discussion of themes in ancient philosophy, such as the role of wisdom and the figure of the sage.[4] Here, Hadot uses the reference to Foucault to demonstrate the singularity of his own interpretation, contrasting his view of philosophy as an "exercise of wisdom" to Foucault's idea of philosophy as an "aesthetics of existence."

Hadot's answer to Davidson's question regarding his divergences and criticism to Foucault is structured along four axes. The first is methodological. According to Hadot, Foucault was a philosopher and "a historian of facts and ideas." However, he stresses, Foucault "had not practiced philology" and was not particularly aware of "the problems tied to the translation of ancient texts: the deciphering of manuscripts, the problem of the critical editions and the choices of textual variants" (Hadot 2009: 136). This philological deficit led Foucault to different philosophical positions, but also to "errors of interpretation." The main example would be, according to Hadot, Foucault's projection of the notion of pleasure into Stoic ethics.

This is the second axis of Hadot's critique: "For Foucault, the ethics of the Greco-Roman world is an ethics of the pleasure one takes in oneself" (Hadot 2009: 136). As he explains, Foucault would allegedly have superposed the notions of *voluptas* and *gaudium*, which were clearly distinguished by the Stoics, since they "refused to introduce the principle of pleasure in moral life" (Hadot 2009: 324). Additionally, Hadot's criticism distinguishes the mere "self" (in which, he argues, Foucault sees the source of pleasure) and what he calls "the best part of oneself" (Hadot 2014a: 193)—a difference that, he tells us, Foucault ignored. The notion of a "pleasure one takes in oneself" would express an individualistic way of reading ancient ethics, dissociating it from the relations to society, as well as from the world or the whole of nature. This leads us to the third axis of Hadot's critique.

This criticism concerns what we could call forms of *belonging* and, more specifically, forms in which the individual relates to something that is other than himself, which—in Hadot's view—ultimately transcends himself. These forms of belonging would entail forms of actualizing an anthropological tendency to "*dépassement*" or transcendence of the individual self, a key aspect of Hadot's reading of ancient philosophy, as well as of his personal experience of philosophy.[5] Hadot claims that "in his descriptions of what he calls the 'practices of the self' Foucault does not sufficiently emphasize the process of becoming aware of belonging to the Cosmic whole" (Hadot 2009: 136). Additionally, by emphasizing the self, Foucault's work would express a lack of the awareness of "belonging to the human community."[6]

The fourth critical point concerns the outcomes of Foucault's work and its relation to the present. For Hadot, Foucault's focus on the conversion to the self and the pleasure one takes in oneself would have led him to define ancient ethics as an "aesthetics of existence." This definition, however, extrapolates historical interpretation. Like himself, Hadot claims, Foucault is interested in ancient philosophy as a way to engage with the present and its pressing ethical issues. Their interest in ancient philosophy is not antiquarian but corresponds to an attempt of proposing positive ethical models for the present (Hadot 2009: 307). In this sense, "aesthetics of existence" would be "Foucault's definition of the ethical model that modern man can discover in antiquity," and perhaps the ethics that Foucault subscribed to throughout his life (Hadot 2009: 331). Therefore, Foucault's work on antiquity would propose as a model "a culture of the self which is purely aesthetical" (Hadot 2009: 331).[7] Hadot adds: "I do not think that the ethical model adapted to modern man can be an aesthetics of existence. I am afraid this may ultimately be a new form of dandyism" (Hadot 2009: 136).

These are, in short, the main ways in which Hadot thinks his divergences with Foucault: a philological deficit, a mistaken emphasis on pleasure, the absence of the *other* and the *cosmos* in the technologies of the self and the insufficiency of an "aesthetics of existence" as an ethical model for the present. In this chapter, I look at the third point and the two lines it presents: the importance of the *other* and, particularly, of the *cosmos* for Foucault's analysis of the care of the self. I will focus on Hadot's assertion regarding the absence of an analysis of the relations *self-world* (and therefore, of the importance of ancient physics as a spiritual exercise) in Foucault's research.

## Government, Life, Self

Before reading Foucault's analysis of the "cosmologic perspective" in ancient philosophy, let us take a methodological *detour*. This will allow us to reassess the criticism according to which Foucault's account of the technologies of the self would correspond to a depoliticization, a turn to an aestheticist view of ethics, as well as an alleged "biographical" departure from the political engagement that characterized his trajectory in the 1970s.[8] My contention is that, through this methodological reflection, we can move away from this conception, demonstrating that the notion of "care" emerges in the context of an investigation on power and government. When presenting this reflection, my attempt is to address Hadot's criticism regarding Foucault's lack of consideration of the forms of *belonging* in ancient philosophy. This reflection will serve as a guiding thread in our discussion of the cosmic perspective of the care of the self.

Let us begin by considering the claim according to which the care of the self represents an evasion from the political world. First of all, an attentive reading of Foucault's texts shows that the Hellenistic philosophies in which he situates the care of the self are depicted as fundamentally political, which he stresses in his 1981–2 lectures.[9] This political background also appears in the *Care of the Self*. Quoting Ferguson's *Moral Values in the Ancient World*, Foucault reconstructs the historiographical characterization of the Hellenistic as a period of decline of the city and political life:

> The collapse of the city-state was inescapable.... people felt themselves in the grip of powers which they could not control or even affect ... The philosophies of the Hellenistic Age ... were essentially philosophies of escape, and the principal means of escape lay in the cultivation of autarky.
>
> Ferguson, *cit. in* Foucault 1990: 81

Foucault, however, criticizes this view. For him, the philosophies that emerge in the Hellenistic period are neither the consequence of a world without cities nor a "shelter from the storm" (Foucault 1990: 82). Rather, they responded to a world where politics was intensified and complexified.[10] In this context, there was no opposition between the active life and the "cultivation of the self." The theme of the return to the self implies the concern "to define the principle of a relation to self that will make it possible to set the forms and conditions in which political action, participation in the offices of power, the exercise of a function, will be possible" (Foucault 1990: 86). More important than a series of "withdrawal behaviors" induced by the Hellenistic schools was "in a much more general and essential way, a problematization of political activity" (Foucault 1990: 86).

In fact, Foucault's and Hadot's approaches converge in claiming that it is "erroneous to think of this period as one of decadence" (Hadot 2004: 92–3). Both authors show how the Hellenistic was a "world of cities" and how philosophical activity flourished and developed new forms of relation to politics.

Returning to the criticisms of Foucault's "care of the self," I believe they reflect a tendency to consider the latter as a relatively autonomous issue in Foucault's project, without relating it to the work of the 1970s.[11] By contrast, I contend that we must situate the history of the notion "care of the self" in Foucault's thought in relation to the concepts developed in the conceptual laboratory of 1970s lectures, and the first volume of the *History of Sexuality*. In these works, one finds a line of continuity regarding concern with the political forms of *care* and government of *life*.

Foucault clearly links his works from the 1970s and the 1980s by mobilizing the notions of government and governmentality, which constitute a transversal grid of interpretation that he applies to his project. Thus, reading the idea of care of the self through the lens of the 1970s works, both chronologically and in terms of heuristics, we note that the emergence of the problematics of *care*—of political care—precedes the formulation of the notion of care *of the self*. Political care should be understood as an activity or a set of actions regarding the government of life—or, as Foucault puts it, the government of bodies, of children, of the mad, the sick, of the abnormal subjects (Foucault 2016: 46). As he explains in the *Will to Knowledge*[12] and in the 1975-6 lectures, the nineteenth century saw a displacement in the mechanisms of power from a "right to kill" to a power to "make live and let die" (Foucault 2004: 240–1). "Making live" consists of set of positive technologies for fostering, protecting, and enhancing life or, in a word, a government of living bodies—both the individual body and the collective body of the population. These biopolitical technologies of government mobilized forms of caring for life.[13]

From the perspective of the history of Foucault's thought, it is within this problematization of *government* that we find the emergence of the notion of *care*. The idea of "taking care" understood as a set of operations of government precedes the idea of "taking care of oneself," which is a different and later formulation of an analogous *governmental* concern.[14] The emergence of the latter cannot be conceived independently of the former.

Seen through this prism, the relation to oneself implied in the care of the self is also crucial in terms of our modern political concerns. As Foucault explains in 1982, constituting an ethic of the self "may be an urgent, fundamental, and politically indispensable task, if it is true after all that there is no first or final point of resistance to political power other than in the relationship one has to oneself" (Foucault 2005: 252). In this context, the notion of "aesthetics of existence" appears as a different and voluntary way in which the subject shapes herself, constituting a response to domination (Wimberly 2009: 196). Through this analogy with the artwork, Foucault highlights our "ability to invent and modify norms" (Wimberly 2009: 197), that is to say our position as agents when it comes to the relations to the norms that characterize governmentality. If government mobilizes norms in order to act upon our conducts and define our identity as subjects, then what Foucault referred to through the notion of aesthetics of existence implies an active and voluntary form of relation to norms, different ways of performing and embodying norms, as well as the possibility of creating new norms for shaping one's life.

This crafting of subjectivity is clearly not an aestheticist negation of politics, primarily because, as *Discipline and Punish* shows, one of the main points of application of power, one of its main products and its predominant field of operation, is subjectivity itself.[15] As Foucault explains in 1976, "this means that rather than starting with the subject ... and elements that exist prior to the relationship itself and that can be localized, we begin with the power relationship itself ... showing how actual relations of subjugation manufacture subjects" (Foucault 2004: 45). Therefore, our capacity to reclaim subjectivity as a battlefield in which we engage with existing norms and constitute our own is necessarily a political and polemical activity.

Furthermore, the relevance of the detailed investigation on the care of the self is framed as a "governmental" issue. As Foucault explains:

> [I]f we take the question of power ... situating it in the more general question of governmentality ... understood as a strategic field of power relations in their mobility, transformability and reversibility, then I do not think that a reflection on this notion of governmentality can avoid passing through, theoretically and practically, the element of a subject defined by the relationship from self to self.
> 
> Foucault 2005: 252

As this passage shows, not only is governmentality a particular historical object for Foucault's genealogical studies, but it is also a kind of general intellectual framework for both the analysis of power and the analysis of the care of the self. On different occasions,[16] Foucault shows how the notions of norm, power, and subjectivity integrate the conceptual machine of governmentality. With this in mind, we can situate the research of the 1981-2 lectures in two broader fields. First, the history of the modes of subjectivation, in which we could situate the history of the different relations between truth and subject. The second is the field of governmentality, particularly as we can see it in the philosophies that Foucault analyzes, which are centered on the conception of philosophy "as a general practice of government at every possible level" (Foucault 2005: 135). In short, Foucault sees ancient philosophical practices—the historical support for the formulation of the notion of *care of the self*—through the prism of governmentality. As he explains, "governing, being governed and taking care of oneself form a sequence, a series, whose long and complex history extends up to the establishment of the pastoral power in the Christian Church" (Foucault 2005: 45).

Within this problematization of the forms of governing life, truth plays an important role. Foucault recurrently defines his project on the history of the care of the self as part of a history of the subject–truth relation and of the government of the subject by the truth.[17] In a 1982 lecture, he situates the problematic of the course in relation to the following question: "How is the relationship of truth-telling and practice of the subject established, fixed and defined? Or, more generally, how are *truth-telling* and *governing* (governing oneself and others) linked and connected to each other?" (Foucault 2005: 229). As he explains, the 1981–2 lectures investigate this interaction subject-truth-government within a specific historical period: "I would like to pose this question of the relationship between truth-telling and the government of the subject in ancient thought before Christianity. I would also like to pose it in the form and within the framework of a relationship from self to self" (Foucault 2005: 229–30). The care of the self is also a way to define the forms in which subjects governed themselves, particular ways in which they related to the truth.

Therefore, in Foucault's view, "power relations, governmentality, the government of the self and of others, and the relationship of self to self constitute a chain, a thread" linking ethics and politics (Foucault 2005: 252). Let us illustrate this idea with an image extracted from the material Foucault analyzes: the image of the pilot and of navigation as a general metaphor for government and care.

## Foucault's "Cybernetics"

In February 17, 1982, Foucault discussed the transformation of the notion of care of the self in the Hellenistic period. According to Foucault, "the old requirement to 'care about the self'" was appropriated in the context of the theme of a "conversion to the self," freed from the presuppositions of Platonic philosophy.[18] In this context, Foucault introduces the metaphor of *navigation*, since "the path towards the self will always be something of an Odyssey" (Foucault 2005: 248). Converting to oneself is neither a gesture of self-absorption nor an immediate form of relating to oneself. It is rather a dangerous and complicated journey. Despite the appearances of a movement of interiorization, the metaphor of the *journey* points to a displacement, a movement in the exterior world, where "you encounter unforeseen risks that may throw you off course or even lead you astray" (Foucault 2005: 249).

It is by developing the theme of the conversion to the self as a journey in dangerous seas that Foucault situates the importance of "the art of piloting," the knowledge (*savoir*) or technique presupposed in navigation. Here, the political background of the notion of care of the self becomes clear, since "at least three types of techniques are usually associated with this model of piloting: first, medicine; second, political government; third, the direction and government of oneself" (Foucault 2005: 249).[19] As we have seen, Foucault understood ancient philosophy as a "general art of government." The metaphor of navigation expresses the same principle: one must mobilize a certain technique and a certain knowledge in order to guide oneself through the difficulties of the world; one must govern oneself as a pilot guides his ship and governs his crew.[20] Foucault highlights the figure of the *kubernētēs*, the one who leads the ship, to illustrate the transversal notion of government elaborated in ancient philosophy.[21] The reference to the art of navigation reveals the effort of the ancients to establish a technique of government. Additionally, this figure serves a hermeneutical and analytical tool to connect the analyses of the different practices of the self and the research on political governmentality. Foucault explains:

> I think we could follow the entire history of this metaphor, practically up to the sixteenth century, at which point the definition of the new art of government centered around *raison d'état* will make a radical distinction between government of oneself, medicine and government of others, but not without this image of piloting remaining linked to the activity of government.
>
> Foucault 2005: 250

It is clear how the notion of care of the self emerges as a second step in this genealogy of political care, and how this metaphor of piloting functions as an illustration of the different settings and forms of government that involve government of others and the government of the self. Through the image of the journey associated with it, Foucault shows how, in the context of the "conversion to the self," the self is not already there as if waiting to be known and uncovered; it is rather the aim of the journey of life, a journey that takes place in the world, and in the presence of others.

The metaphor of navigation places this "journey" of conversion to the self in the context of a political concern with governmentality. In the same lecture, Foucault introduces the problem of the knowledge of nature: what sort of knowledge is required for the conversion of the self? What kind of knowledge will allow us to take care of ourselves and navigate the world? For Foucault, it is the knowledge of nature, and therefore, of the exteriority of the world rather than the exegetical knowledge of the secrets of one's interiority. As we will see, in the context of this journey in the world, whose aim is the self, "self-knowledge was not an alternative to the knowledge of nature" (Foucault 2005: 259).

We have seen how the notion of *care* emerges from a political concern and in the context of a political lexicon. The care of the self extends this concern highlighting the ways relate to "oneself, others and the world." With this in mind, we can now engage with two important levels of Hadot's critique, which point to the insufficiency of the notion of culture of the self to account for the relation with the human community and the cosmos. Let us first examine Hadot's conception of what he calls the "cosmic consciousness" and some of its presuppositions.

## Cosmos and Experience in Hadot

Hadot proposes a performative and pragmatic notion of philosophy, defined as an exercise of wisdom. Although one usually identifies ancient philosophy with the discourse concerning its parts (ethics, logic, physics), it cannot be reduced to it. For Hadot, "we shall encounter situations in which philosophical activity continues to be carried out, even though discourse cannot express this activity" (Hadot 2004: 5). Rather than philosophical discourse and a systematic use of language, philosophy is a *single act*, disposition or attitude toward the world.

The notion of *spiritual exercise* opens a field of analysis and interpretation in which philosophy appears as a *lived practice* in each of its parts.[22] This allows Hadot to propose a different history of philosophy, in which, alongside the history of concepts, there would be a *history of philosophical attitudes*. Each philosophy corresponds to an "existential option which demands from the individual a total change of lifestyle, a conversion of one's entire being" (Hadot 2004: 3). Moreover, this history reveals something substantial about human beings, since each of these philosophical attitudes respond to fundamental existential experiences, organized in different philosophical schools. As Hadot explains, in the models of life of the ancient schools, we find "fundamental forms in accordance with which reason may be applied to human existence, and archetypes of the quest for wisdom." He continues: "It is precisely the plurality of ancient schools that is precious. It allows us to compare the consequences of all the various possible fundamental attitudes of reason … Epicureanism and Stoicism, for example, correspond to two opposite but inseparable poles of our inner life …" (Hadot 1995: 273). History would then serve as a sort of stage for the interplay of these fundamental attitudes, the terrain for the instantiation and experimentation of that which is made possible by the poles of our inner life.

Foucault's exploration of ancient philosophical practices aims at revealing a radical contingency dwelling at the core of what we understand as the human subject, undermining universals regarding "human nature," as well as any pretension of founding a philosophical anthropology. Hadot's approach, by contrast, finds in the ancient schools anthropological traits at work, a variety of ways in which universal tendencies are organized, experienced and performed. In a word, the ancient philosophical schools have a historical and anthropological import (Hadot 2014a: 191),[23] and they captured something fundamental of the coordinates of human experience. In this sense, one could read the centrality they assume in Hadot's work in terms of an underlying philosophical anthropology.[24]

In order to organize the quest for wisdom, and enact these anthropological coordinates, each school proposes a series of practices. Hadot thinks that the history of philosophy as a way of living reveals a whole inventory of techniques that can be deployed today. But his approach also changes our perspective on ancient texts. Hadot often stresses that the idea of "philosophy as a way of life" allows us to overcome a series of difficulties and apparent contradictions of ancient texts, by placing them in their context; that is, within the framework of their own "language games."[25] By this Hadot understands the concrete practices, exercises, and institutional settings in which they acquired full meaning for the ancients. Hadot also underlines the importance of looking at how these texts were used, revealing their performative and psychagogical dimensions.

Hadot explores the primacy of *practice* in ancient philosophy as a whole. This means that ethics was not the only part of philosophy that was considered "practical;" the same was valid for logic and physics. Evidently, he argues, there were theoretical discourses on these domains. But he stresses the existence of a lived, practiced logic, as well as a lived physics.[26] The latter is particularly relevant to our discussion regarding the place of the *cosmos* in Hadot's interpretation of ancient philosophy. In lived physics he finds the clearest expression of the cosmologic dimension of philosophy, as well as a site for the experience of the cosmos.

The quest for wisdom was understood as a "way to exist in the world," which should be practiced at each instant, and which should transform one's whole life (Hadot 2002: 290).[27] For Hadot, the way that the philosopher exists "in the world," however, differs from that of the "ordinary man." The latter has lost his contact with world, turning it into a means to his own end (Hadot 2002: 301). The sage, by contrast, is able to break with this utilitarian and interested relationship and experience the world in itself, having the Whole of nature and the world present to his mind. As Hadot explains, "he thinks and acts in a universal perspective. He has the feeling of belonging to a Whole which exceeds [*déborde*] the limits of his individuality" (Hadot 2002: 301). For him, this relation to the Whole, which can be translated as the "contemplation of nature," is central in ancient philosophy. In the Epicurean and Stoic idea of wisdom, he claims, the two fundamental dispositions "of *ataraxia* and *autarkeia* are joined or complemented by a third dimension, that of the 'cosmic consciousness'." In Hadot's words, "the exercise of wisdom implies a cosmic dimension" (Hadot 2002: 301).

This cosmic dimension is central for Hadot's definition of philosophy. This is clear in several of his texts, especially in "Philosophy as a Way of Life." This essay starts with a passage from Philo of Alexandria, describing a person "training for wisdom":

> As their goal is a life of peace and serenity, they contemplate nature and everything found within her: they attentively explore the earth, the sea, the air, the sky ... In thought, they accompany the moon, the sun, and the rotation of the other stars. Their bodies remain on earth, but they give wings to their souls, so that rising into the ether, they may observe the powers that dwell there, as is fitting for those who have truly become citizens of the world.
>
> Hadot 1995: 264

In this passage, Philo presents an image of philosophy in which the relation to the *cosmos* is capital, assuming the form of an exercise of contemplation and an awareness of belonging to the cosmic whole. It presents the therapeutic importance of the knowledge of nature, since through the exploration "of the earth, the sea, the air and the sky," the soul "achieves tranquility." Ascending to the higher realms of ether, the soul contemplates the world from a perspective that goes beyond that of the individual.

Philo's text also illustrates that idea of a lived physics, in which the knowledge of nature is accompanied by an intellectual and spiritual exercise, which follows the movement of the stars; through this exercise, the philosopher places himself in the *cosmos* as "a true citizen of the world." In Hadot's words, "the ancient sage, at each instant, was aware of living in the cosmos, and he placed himself in harmony with the cosmos" (Hadot 1995: 266). Indeed, philosophy implies the of awareness of belonging, as a part, to a Whole, which is infinitely bigger than the particular point that is one's individuality. Hadot defines it as the apperception of oneself as "being part of the cosmos, a dilation of the self in the infinity of universal nature" (Hadot 2002: 291). This, in turn, transfigures the self, which assumes the perspective of this universality;

exceeding one's punctual existence, one accedes to the best part of oneself, which coincides with divine and transcendent reason.[28]

This "cosmic consciousness" was different from a merely discursive knowledge of the universe and astronomic phenomena: it "was the result of a spiritual exercise, which consisted in becoming aware of the place of the individual existence in the great current of the cosmos... *toti se inserens mundo*, in the words of Seneca" (Hadot 1995: 273).

The cosmic consciousness was also important from a political perspective. For Hadot, although the political conceptions differed among the schools, the concern for "having an effect on the city or state, king or emperor, always remained constant" (Hadot 1995: 274). For the Stoics, this concern for politics is connected to an idea of the *cosmos*. They sought a form of wisdom able to harmonize the human community—the reason that is common to human beings—and cosmic reason. From the perspective of the Whole, our individual and "political passions" lose their meaning and their power over us, and so do political structures, such as Empires and borders, and political events such as war and conflicts.[29]

The *cosmos* was also the site of a deeper and mysterious experience. Hadot explains that the *cosmos* is simultaneously the place proper to the human being and the "only sacred place" (Hadot 2014a: 143). It is in this sacred and mysterious place that our existence takes place, inspiring us fear and pleasure. As Hadot writes: "nature and the cosmos are, for our living perception, the infinite horizon of our lives, the enigma of our existence which, as Lucretius said, inspires us *horror et divina voluptas*" (Hadot 1995: 273–4).

According to Matthew Sharpe, Hadot criticized Foucault for his aesthetical approach to ancient ethics. Sharpe, however, shows that Hadot also relied on aesthetical categories to account for this experience of the *cosmos*, constituting what he sees as "an aesthetics of the *monde* or *le Tout*, that is, of Nature as a source of contemplative wonder" (Sharpe 2018: 136).[30] My suggestion is that this "aesthetics" identified by Sharpe has a deeper philosophical import for Hadot.[31] When contemplating the "marvelous presence of the world" (Hadot 2014a: 114) and while being "plunged into the cosmos" (Hadot 2014a: 198),

> we are confronted in an inevitable way with what one could call the ineffable [*indicible*], the terrifying enigma of being-in-the-world [*être-là*], here and now, given over to death, in the immensity of the cosmos. To become conscious of the self and of the existence of the world is a revelation which breaks the security of the habitual and the everyday.
>
> Hadot 2014a: 197

We have seen that the ancient schools had, for Hadot, the merit of embodying the coordinates of fundamental aspects of human experience. I believe the same is valid for the importance that, in Hadot's view, they attribute to the "cosmic consciousness." This experience reveals an anthropological trait related to transcendence, to a form of transcendence of individuality that takes place in the infinity of nature. As he explains, in the experience of the *cosmos* one has the impression that the essence of the human being consists in being beyond himself (Hadot 2014a: 183), or, as he puts it elsewhere, it attests the "the human need for transcendence and infinity" (Hadot 2014a: 112). In this experience, which is ultimately ineffable, one is dissolved into nature, in a relation of fusion, identification and co-presence with the Whole (Hadot 2014a: 115).[32]

Finally, the notion of a cosmic consciousness or of the *cosmos* as the site of an experience of infinity, through which individuals exceed themselves, appears in Hadot's auto-biographical accounts regarding his "conversion to philosophy," where the narration of this experience acquires mystical undertones. The same experience of a "dissolution in nature" and a "marvelous presence of the world" and of the "immensity of the *cosmos*," which Hadot situates in antiquity, seems to be rooted in his own early personal experiences. He narrates:

> Night had fallen. The stars were shining in the immense sky ... I was filled with an anxiety that was both terrifying and delicious, provoked by the sentiment of the presence of the world, or of the Whole, and of me in that world ... I experienced a sentiment of strangeness, of astonishment, and of wonder at being there ... I had the sentiment of being immersed in the world, of being a part of it, the world extending from the smallest blade of grass to the stars. This world was present to me, intensely present. Much later I would discover that this awareness of belonging to the Whole was what Romain Rolland called the "oceanic sentiment." I believe that I have been a philosopher since that time, if by philosophy one means this awareness of existence, of being-in-the-world.
>
> Hadot 2009: 5

Hadot referred this mystical experience of the presence of the world—which later reappears in his readings of ancient philosophy—to Rolland's notion of "oceanic sentiment."[33] In this concept, Hadot finds a nuance of the "wonder before nature," which is the impression of

> being a wave in a limitless ocean, of being part of a mysterious and infinite reality. Michel Hulin, in ... *La Mystique sauvage* ... characterizes this experience as "the sentiment of being present here and now in a world that is itself intensely existing," and also speaks of a "sentiment of an essential co-belonging between myself and the ambient universe." What is capital is the impression of immersion, of dilation of the self in Another to which the self is not foreign, because it belongs to it.
>
> Hadot 2009: 8

Beyond accounts of a conversion to philosophy, these experiences represent a sort of fundamental intuition which, according to Hadot, played an important role in his inner development.[34] Furthermore, he claims that they have "considerably influenced" his "conception of philosophy," since he has "always conceived of philosophy as a transformation of one's perception of the world" (Hadot 2009: 6).

One notes that the way Hadot reads the ancient experience of the *cosmos* is connected to an underlying mysticism—and to his own experience of the "presence of the world" and of being plunged in the immensity and infinity of the world—which refers back to Rolland's "oceanic feeling" (Hulin 1993: 9).

It is true that Hadot attempts at differentiating his own lived experience of the "oceanic sentiment" and the ways in which the ancients cultivated the sentiment of nature and the awareness of belonging to the totality of the world. However, how could one neglect the importance of this fundamental intuition to his understanding of ancient philosophy?

## Foucault on the Knowledge of Nature and the Care of the Self

In the Hellenistic model of conversion to the self, Foucault finds a different modality of knowledge employed in the practice of the self. Differently from what one could think, converting to the self does not mean, in the Hellenistic schools, "constituting oneself as an object and domain of knowledge" (Foucault 2005: 253). Nor would it be "a fundamental and continuous task of knowledge of what we will call the human subject, the human soul, ... the interiority of consciousness" (Foucault 2005: 258). This conversion does not imply a knowledge that would be a rudimentary and early version of the "sciences of the mind" or of psychology. Rather, in the Hellenistic "conversion to oneself," one finds a direct link between knowing nature and taking care of oneself.

In Foucault's analysis, the knowledge of nature appears as a spiritual form of knowledge, whose aim is to transform the subject's being and is therefore *ethopoetic*.[35] This "lived" form of knowledge is relational: it considers "the gods, other men, the *kosmos*" in their inter-relations, and in their relation to us. In his analysis of Epicurean physics or "*phusiologia*," Foucault shows how this knowledge was essentially meant to equip and prepare the subject for the challenges and different circumstances of life, eliminating fears and suffering. As in Hadot's reflections on the ancient "lived physics," the speculative knowledge of nature integrates the repertoire of the practices of the self, as something that changes the subject's *ēthos* and prepares him for situations of adversity. As Foucault explains, "*phusiologia* gives the individual boldness and courage, a kind of intrepidity which enables him to stand firm not only against the many beliefs that others wish to impose on him, but also against life's dangers and the authority of those who want to lay down the law" (Foucault 2005: 240).

It is this spiritual and relational form of the knowledge of nature that will be mobilized in the conversion to the self. It is therefore neither a knowledge of human interiority nor a decipherment or exegesis of the soul, but a "system of speculations about the order of the world" (Foucault 2005: 260). Foucault's main illustration of this comes from Stoicism: he looks both at Seneca's "view from above" and Marcus Aurelius' "infinitesimal view." In the former, the figure of spiritual knowledge employed consists in the subject "stepping back from his place in the world in order to grasp this world as a whole, a world in which he is placed" (Foucault 2005: 289). Marcus Aurelius, on the other hand, describes a "movement of the subject who, starting from the point he occupies in this world," plunges into it, studying it down to its smallest details (Foucault 2005: 289). Although Marcus Aurelius occupies an important place in Foucault's analysis, I will focus on his reading of Seneca. My attempt is to show that, differently from what Hadot thought, the cosmic perspective is a constitutive aspect of Foucault's analysis of the ancient practices of the self, and that an awareness of "belonging to the cosmos" is an important element of the care of the self.

As Foucault explains when analyzing Seneca's texts his aim is to show how the objectives of Stoic ethics are "not only compatible with, but can only be attained … at the cost of the knowledge of nature, that is, at the same time, knowledge of the totality of the word" (Foucault 2005: 266). He adds: "We can only arrive at the self having passed through the great cycle of the world" (Foucault 2005: 266). One must step back from the short-sightedness of one's own individual perspective and attempt to visualize oneself in the place one occupies in the *cosmos*.

In the *Natural Questions,* Seneca proposes to undertake an "immense exploration of the world," Foucault explains, "embracing the sky and earth, the path of the planets, the geography of rivers, the explanation of fire and meteors, etc." (Foucault 2005: 261). For Seneca, this enterprise has an immediate ethical consequence:

> The mind cannot despise colonnades, and ceilings gleaming with ivory, and topiary forests and rivers channeled into houses until it has toured the entire world and until, looking down from on high at the earth—tiny, predominantly covered by sea and, even when it rises above it … —it has said to itself, "This is that pinprick that is carved up among so many nations by sword and fire!"
> 
> Seneca 2010: 137

Rather than historical learning, which narrates "the history of foreign kings and their adventures, exploits" or, in a word, the history of their passions and "suffering, transformed into praise," "it would be much better to overcome and defeat our own passions" (Foucault 2005: 264).[36] Furthermore, historical learning also offers us a false idea of greatness, based on conquest, war and deeds which are meaningless from the point of view of the cosmos. The knowledge of nature, by contrast, would lead us to true greatness, that of seeing the whole of the world and triumphing over one's vices, allowing one to be "free, not by the laws of the city, but by the law of nature" (Foucault 2005: 271).[37] But what characterizes this freedom?

As we have seen, Hadot charged Foucault of overemphasizing the notion of pleasure, claiming that he "made no place for that cosmic consciousness and physics as a spiritual exercise" (Hadot 1995: 24–5). Foucault's analysis of this conception of "freedom by the law of nature" contradicts this claim, for he reads this notion of freedom precisely as a liberation from the self: to flee the servitude to oneself (*effugere servitutem sui*), to no longer be a slave of oneself—which is "the most serious and grave of all servitudes" (Foucault 2005: 272). This idea of freedom shows, as Agamben explained, what "Hadot could not understand" in Foucault's analysis, namely that the care of the self and the dispossession of the self coincide (Agamben 2004: 613).

A sign of this freedom from oneself in Foucault's reading of Seneca is the struggle against pleasure, alongside self-control, steadfastness and serenity in face of adversity, and readiness for dying (Foucault 2005: 272). It is, then, from oneself and from pleasure—more specifically from the "system of obligation-reward, of indebtedness-activity-pleasure" (Foucault 2005: 273) that we must liberate ourselves. In Foucault's reading of Seneca, the knowledge of nature is the very "agency" of this liberation. Let us now briefly examine the four main movements that Foucault attributes to Seneca's approach to nature and the exercise of the "view from above."

Schematically, Foucault describes Seneca's conception of the movement produced by the knowledge of nature in three moments. First, there is a movement of flight: by looking at nature one seeks to break free from oneself, from one's individual and passionate perspective. One, thus, "completes the detachment from one's flaws and vices." This develops into a second movement, leading us to the "source of light," "a movement which plunges deep into God" (we then find ourselves "*in consortium Dei*"). It is in the third movement, which develops the previous two, that the "view from above" takes place. In this third movement, Foucault explains "we rise towards the highest point of this universe (*altum*)," so as to "look down on earth from above." According to Foucault, "this movement which places us at the highest point of the world, will allow us to look down on earth from above. At the very moment that, participating in divine reason, we grasp the secret of nature, we can grasp how small we are" (Foucault 2005: 275–6).

We note that for Foucault the knowledge of nature and the view from above involved in the Stoic "conversion to the self" is the opposite of a movement of self-absorption or interiorization. Rather, it presupposes that we step back from the point we occupy. Instead of "turning away from this world in order to look toward another," as the Platonic or Christian models would propose, it implies an understanding of this world and the exact place we occupy in it—through this relational knowledge, we see "the world to which we belong and, consequently, see ourselves within this world" (Foucault 2005: 276). This cosmic viewpoint which the knowledge of nature makes possible, allows us to see our own "pettiness" as well as the "false and artificial character of everything that seemed good to us before we were freed" (Foucault 2005: 277). Wealth, pleasure, glory appear in their real insignificant proportion. The same is valid for our own individuality; the cosmic viewpoint liberates us from ourselves by showing our limited position and our proportion in the *cosmos*—a "punctual existence in space and time"—while also revealing the relations we entertain with what surrounds us. In Foucault's words, "punctualizing ourselves in the general system of the world" has a "liberating effect" (Foucault 2005: 278). Here, one reaches "the maximum tension between the self as reason ... and the self as individual component" (Foucault 2005: 278), which also allows us a critical detachment from this individual component, contemplating our own existence as linked to a "set of determinations and necessities whose rationality we need to understand" (Foucault 2005: 279). Risking an anachronism, we could say that the cosmic perspective corresponds somehow to a "critique of ideology" and of the "false consciousness" that our short-sighted individual perspective assumes as true, as well as the optical illusions caused by our individual passions and desires regarding the value and dimension of things in the world. In this sense, the view from above "enables us to dismiss and exclude all false values and all false dealings in which we are caught up" (Foucault 2005: 277).

It is important to note that the liberation from oneself and the "sort of dissolution of individuality" (Foucault 2005: 307) that Foucault sees in the cosmic perspective of the care of the self do not carry the fusional and mystical element that we have identified in Hadot's work. The exploration of nature "enables us to grasp ourselves here where we are" (Foucault 2005: 278), in the network of the cosmic events and their complex causal chain. Rather than diving into a mystical experience of the cosmos, in Foucault's view, the contemplation of nature as a spiritual exercise sought "never to lose sight of any of the components that characterize the world in which we exist" as well as "our own situation, in the very spot we occupy" (Foucault 2005: 282). In his analysis of the "lived physics," Hadot also underlined this dimension. Like Foucault, Hadot clearly noted that in Seneca "the contemplation of the physical world complements moral action by showing the full context of human action" (Asmis, Bartsch and Nussbaum in Seneca 2010: xvii). However, Hadot's studies on the ancient relationship to nature bears the signs of the importance he attributed to nature as a site of sacred and transcendent experience, in a word, of the "oceanic feeling." By contrast, Foucault's reading of the cosmic perspective of the care of the self stresses a more systemic, relational and topological perspective, in which one sees oneself within a network of things and events, occupying different positions.

## Conclusion

To conclude, and at the risk of oversimplifying a complex debate, I wish to stress some of the main divergences between Hadot's and Foucault's reading of the cosmologic perspective. As Hadot noted, these divergences ultimately correspond to substantial differences concerning the "philosophical choices" that guide their analyses of ancient philosophy, separating them "beyond" their "points of agreement" (Hadot 1995: 206).

Let us briefly look at their views on the Senecan idea of "plunging into the world." Although Hadot analyzes the element of punctualization and perception of oneself as part of a Whole, his emphasis is on a form of dissolution of the self which would be one of fusion and identification; in this sense, belonging to the cosmic Whole is characterized by an underlying mysticism. Through the cosmic perspective, one can accede to universality and "the wonderful mystery of the presence of the universe" (Hadot 1995: 212). In Foucault's view, the punctualization of the self corresponds to a perception of the *situation* and the *position* of oneself within a network of relations (to persons, things, events). Although underlining the importance of the "partnership with God," Foucault's description of the view from above seems to presuppose a form of belonging to the cosmic network under the lens of immanence. If the underlying tone of Hadot's analysis is mystical, we could say that the underlying tone of Foucault's analysis is political. We have seen how Foucault thought of the conversion to the self in the perspective of government. Moreover, his exploration of the ancient uses of the knowledge of nature appears in the context of an inquiry regarding the form of knowledge necessary for the journey that the conversion to the self constitutes. The sort of knowledge that would help the individual governing himself, situating himself in a field of relations, and navigating the dangerous sea of events is the knowledge of nature.

Finally, for Hadot, the "cosmic consciousness" that played a fundamental role in the ancient schools, alongside *ataraxia* and *autarkeia*, was a way to give form to an anthropological trait and a fundamental human drive for transcendence. For Foucault, on the other hand, the cosmic perspective of the care of the self embodied a contingent and historical form of the relationship between subject and truth, in which the knowledge required for the government of the subject was not the knowledge of the hidden and deep truths of one's interiority, but rather the knowledge of the exteriority of the relations in which one is situated, and which define oneself.

## Notes

1. See Paras (2006) and Welsch (1995).
2. See Hadot (1995: 206), Irrera (2010).
3. See "*Un dialogue interrompu avec Michel Foucault. Convergences et divergences*" (Hadot 2002: 305–12), "*Refléxions sur la notion de 'culture de soi'*" (Hadot 2002: 323–32; 1995: 206–14).
4. See "*La figure du sage dans l'Antiquité gréco-latine*" (Hadot 2014a: 177–98) and "*Le sage et le monde*" (Hadot 2002: 343–60).
5. Hadot's reference for this anthropological discussion is Bernard Groethuysen's *Anthropologie philosophique* (Hadot 1995: 208, 251; 2014a: 193–4).
6. This is a recurrent theme in Hadot's work (see Hadot 1995: 208; 2009: 169–70). For him, these two forms of belonging correspond to self-transcendence in the human being.
7. Wimberly sees in the charges of "dandyism" a reference to Foucault's homosexuality (Wimberly 2009: 202).
8. See Paras (2006: 11–12) and Habermas (1987).
9. This is also the case before the Hellenistic period. In his analysis of Plato's *Alcibiades*, Foucault explains that "this 'oneself' ... must be given a definition which entails ... a knowledge necessary for good government ... This circle, [which goes] from the self as an object of care to knowledge of government as the government of others is ... at the heart ... of this dialogue" (Foucault 2005: 38–9).
10. Regarding this complexification, see Foucault (1990: 82).
11. This is Hadot's case: he reads Foucault's work as a commentary on ancient philosophies and a search for ethical models for the present, disconnecting it from a genealogy of the Western sexuality and the formation of the modern subject of desire.
12. See Foucault (2008: 135–9).
13. See Foucault (2004: 253).
14. Although one could rightly differentiate between the notions of *soin* (biopolitical and medical context) and *souci* (in the context of the arts of living), which are intertwined in the English *care*, I believe that they share a semantic field. Foucault explores this field through the notion of government, but also through the analogies between philosophy and medicine, sharing a *mia chora* (Foucault 1990: 54).
15. See Foucault (1991: 192–4).
16. For example, Foucault (2010: 4).
17. See Foucault (2005: 229).
18. Namely, its connection to a statutory privilege, to a specific age or time in life, and finally, as he later adds, to *recollection*.
19. Or "curing, leading others, and governing oneself" (Foucault 2005: 249).
20. Significant occurrences of this metaphor are found in Plato's *Republic* (for instance, VI, 488b–90a).
21. Indeed, the Latin *gubernator* etymologically derives from *kubernētēs* (Foucault 2005: 267, ft. 7)

22  See Hadot (2014a).
23  Hadot writes: "it seems to me that there are universal and fundamental attitudes of the human being when he searches for wisdom ... there is a universal Stoicism, Epicureanism, Socratism, Pyrrhonism ..." (Hadot 2002: 376).
24  One of the sources of Hadot's insight is Karl Jaspers (Hadot 2002: 301).
25  On the notion of "language games," see Hadot (2014b; 2002: 367–76).
26  Elsewhere, Hadot shows that the distinction of theoretical and practical is intrinsic to each philosophical discipline (Hadot 2014a: 164).
27  Translations of Hadot 2002 and 2014a are by M. Sharpe and F. Testa. They integrate the volume *Philosophy as Practice. Selected Writings of Pierre Hadot* (Bloomsbury, 2020).
28  The theme reappears in Hadot (1995: 207).
29  On this topic, especially on the political differences between Pliny and Seneca regarding the knowledge of the world, see Williams (2012). Williams opposes a Plinian nationalistic Roman-cantered world vision—which is placed at the "center of the imperial world"—to Seneca's cosmic perspective, which looks down from above and despises boundaries (Williams 2012: 42–3). If Pliny's work reflects the Roman imperial expansion, Seneca shows Rome's "relative unimportance as a mere temporal and spatial *punctum*" (Williams 2012: 44).
30  For Sharpe, "Hadot is forced by his ontological agnosticism to draw heavily on aesthetic categories, despite his criticism of Foucault's idea of 'aesthetics of the self'" (Sharpe 2018: 136).
31  Sharpe also suggests "Hadot assigns a key place to *some* substantive conception of the Whole, to which the philosophical self is assimilated," but later emphasizes Hadot's philosophical agnosticism (Sharpe 2018: 130–1).
32  Here, I fully agree with Irrera: "the taxonomic activity of the historian of philosophy, however supported by honest, meticulous and ... philological work, can be performed only starting from the choice of determined theoretical paradigms—in this case, a theory of transcendence—a choice that sublimates into methodological praxis, and finally hides behind the alleged neutrality and non-judgemental character of philological analysis ..." (Irrera 2010: 1008).
33  Hadot's reference is Michel Hulin's *La mystique sauvage*, especially the chapter on Rolland's correspondence with Freud. Hulin's book, however, was published in 1993, and Hadot's effort to frame his experiences of nature through the "*mystique sauvage*" or an "*sentiment océanique*" is retrospective.
34  Hadot says: "This experience dominated my entire life ... Thus, it played an important role in my inner development" (Hadot 2009: 6).
35  As Foucault explains, "*ethopoios* is something that possesses the quality of transforming an individual's mode of being" (Foucault 2005: 237).
36  See Seneca (2010: 25).
37  Seneca (2010: 27).

# References

Agamben, G. and U. Raulff (2004), "An Interview with Giorgio Agamben," *German Law Journal*, 5 (5): 609–14.
Foucault, M. (1990), *The Care of the Self. The History of Sexuality 3*, trans. R. Hurley, London: Penguin.

Foucault, M. (1991), *Discipline and Punish. The Birth of the Prison*, trans. A. Sheridan, London: Penguin.
Foucault, M. (2004), *"Society Must Be Defended": Lectures at the Collège de France, 1975–1976*, ed. M. Bertani and A. Fontana, trans. D. Macey, London: Penguin.
Foucault, M. (2005), *The Hermeneutics of the Subject: Lectures at the Collège de France 1981–1982*, ed. F. Gros, trans. G. Burchell, New York: Palgrave Macmillan.
Foucault, M. (2008), *The Will to Knowledge. History of Sexuality 1*, trans. R. Hurley, Melbourne: Penguin.
Foucault, M. (2010), *The Government of Self and Others: Lectures at the Collège de France, 1982–1983*, ed. F. Gros, trans. G. Burchell, Basingstoke: Palgrave Macmillan.
Foucault, M. (2016), *Abnormal: Lectures at the Collège de France, 1974–1975*, ed. V. Marchetti and A. Salomoni, trans. G. Burchell, London: Verso.
Habermas, J. (1987), *The Philosophical Discourse of Modernity: Twelve Lectures*, trans. F. G. Lawrence, Cambridge: Polity Press.
Hadot, P. (1995), *Philosophy as a Way of Life*, trans. M. Chase, Oxford: Blackwell.
Hadot, P. (2001), *La Philosophie comme manière de vivre. Entretiens avec Jeannie Carlier et Arnold I. Davidson*, Paris: Albin Michel.
Hadot, P. (2002), *Exercices spirituels et philosophie antique*, Paris: Albin Michel.
Hadot, P. (2004), *What is Ancient Philosophy?*, trans. M. Chase, Cambridge: Belknap Press.
Hadot, P. (2009), *The Present Alone is our Happiness*, trans. M. Djaballah, California: Stanford.
Hadot, P. (2014a), *Discours et mode de vie philosophique*, Paris: Belles Lettres.
Hadot, P. (2014b), *Wittgenstein et les limites du langage*. Paris: Vrin.
Hulin, M. (1993), *La mystique sauvage. Aux antipodes de l'esprit*, Paris: PUF.
Irrera, O. (2010), "Pleasure and Transcendence of the Self: Notes on a 'Dialogue too soon Interrupted' between Michel Foucault and Pierre Hadot," *Philosophy & Social Criticism*, 36 (9): 995–1017.
McNay, L. (1992), *Foucault and Feminism. Power, Gender and the Self*, Cambridge: Polity Press.
Paras, E. (2006), *Foucault 2.0: Beyond Power and Knowledge*, New York: Other Press.
Seneca, L. A. (2010), *Natural Questions*, trans. M. Hine, Chicago: Chicago University Press.
Sharpe, M. (2018), "Towards a Phenomenology of Sagesse," *Angelaki*, 23 (2): 125–38.
Welsch, W. (1995), "Estetização e estetização profunda ou: a respeito da atualidade do estético," *PortoArte*, 6 (9): 7–22.
Williams, Gareth D. *The Cosmic Viewpoint: A Study of Seneca's Natural Questions*. Oxford: Oxford University Press, 2012.
Wimberly, C. (2009), "The Joy of Difference. Foucault and Hadot on the Aesthetic and the Universal," *Philosophy Today*, 53 (2): 191–202.

Part Two

# Care of the Self, Care of Others

# 4

# Foucault According to Stiegler: Technics of the Self

## Amélie Berger Soraruff

Foucault's work allegedly took a new turn when he started to explore the ethics of subjectivation. While he views the ancient principle of care as a desirable art of living, Foucault does not clearly elaborate on its political implications and rather defends the arts of the self on an aesthetic level (Foucault 1984a: 350). Moreover, this sudden interest in the subject seems to go against the archaeo-genealogical approach of his earlier investigations (Dews 1989). Indeed, subjectivation seems often to refer in *The Care of the Self* to the reflective elaboration of the self in which the subject is understood as spontaneously free and self-constitutive. It did not take long for Foucault scholars to sense a major difficulty, which is the following: to present the subject as *self*-constitutive is to assume the existence of an originary selfhood. Put otherwise, it is to make the subject the agent of her own creation. As such, this position reactivates the conceptual viability of transcendental subjectivity characteristic of Kant's subject of apperception or Husserl's transcendental ego of consciousness. Yet, as we know, Foucault's archaeo-genealogy had previously problematized transcendental subjectivity by progressively transposing his account of the transcendental into the historical (Han 2002). For Beatrice Han, not only is Foucault reopening the theme of the transcendental in taking subjectivation as a new research focus, but he is even regressing to a "pre-phenomenological account" of transcendental subjectivity in which "the structure of recognition remains an unthematized a priori" (Han 2002: 187). While Han tries her best to resolve the paradoxes that emerge with Foucault's understanding of the creative constitution of the self by the self, she concludes that scholars are left with an impasse in which "the tension between the historical and the a priori repeatedly eroded the courageous project of historicizing the transcendental" (Han 2002: 196). I will argue here that this issue can be resolved, and that in resolving this impasse, one can also clarify the political issues at stake with the ethics of care as an inspirational form of subjectivation.

I propose to read Foucault's work in parallel with that of Bernard Stiegler, known for his three-volume work *Technics and Time*, in which he presents technics as the necessary condition for human existence. In doing so, he comes to terms with the empirico-transcendental divide often at play when one is to describe the conditions of emergence of the subject. Stiegler takes direct inspiration from Foucault when he affirms care as a technique of subjectivation powerful enough to resist the techniques of exploitation which are currently developed by marketing industries (Stiegler 2010: 117–18), hence politicizing what Foucault left in the domain of aesthetics. His philosophy of technics borrows a lot from the phenomenological method, but also flirts with anthropology and sociology. Like Foucault, Stiegler repeats the critical question of Kant in reflecting on the conditions of possibility of knowledge. Like Foucault, he finds himself confronted with the transcendental perspective, which he intends to surpass in technicizing the process of subjectivation. Hence, if Stiegler puts the emphasis on consciousness, the individual, and the necessity of freedom, he nevertheless successfully bypasses the problem of pure transcendentalism in transposing the transcendental onto the empirical basis of technics. To be more precise, Stiegler's key contribution in this case is to claim that consciousness itself is always already technical. As such, the history of technics implies that the history of subjectivity (Stiegler 2009: 2) is at its very core, insofar as the two are concomitant. On a broader level, not only am I arguing that Stiegler offers an interesting response to the major tensions at the core of the autonomous constitution of the self, but that he is also capable, through the resolution of this specific problem, of justifying the political and ethical necessity of care. Indeed, it is because we always exist in the heteronomy of technics, or put more generally, that the empirical always affects the transcendental, that we must develop the right tools to preserve our autonomy as technologies extend their social influence. As such, Stiegler extends Foucault's work, for he demonstrates that taking care of ourselves does not simply mean taking care of our identity or subjectivity, but also of the conditions which form this very subjectivity, conditions which are thoroughly political.

## Between Subjectivation and Subjection

Prior to Han, Deleuze had already argued that subjectivation should be understood in Foucault's work as "derivative from power and knowledge without being dependent on them" (Deleuze 1988: 101). In this respect, Deleuze manages to find a coherence between the early Foucauldian archaeologies of knowledge and the ethics of self-formation, insofar as he views the latter as a folding movement that constitutes the inside from the outside (Deleuze 1988: 97). Phyllis Sutton Morris, for her part, views subjectivation as a self-disciplinary exercise (Morris 1996), whereas Aurelia Armstrong argues that "the project of autonomous self-formation" *emerges* in "the power contexts within which subjects act and think" (Armstrong 2008: 29). Han would not discount these solutions, but the object of her concern lies elsewhere. Subjectivation, she says, is theorized by Foucault on numerous occasions as "a free and reflective activity" (Han 2002: 184). Thus, she is still left with the same difficulty which is that of the ambiguity of the role assigned to consciousness, apprehended as either active and reflective or passive and therefore unreflective. On a broad scale, Han suggests that the phenomenological implications of Foucault's ethics of self-formation lack coherence, for it alternates between a transcendental and a historical account of the subject without being capable of reconciling the two.

Foucault describes subjectivation as "the process through which results the constitution of a subject, or more exactly, of a subjectivity which is obviously only one of the given possibilities of organizing a consciousness of self" (Foucault 1989: 330). For Han, the mention of consciousness is not innocuous. In fact, it is symptomatic of a larger problem, which is that of the impossibility for Foucault to come to terms with the idea of the subject, even though this was the primary intention of his archaeology. She thus reminds us that Foucault was critical of phenomenology for two reasons. The first reason is that of phenomenology's incapacity to formulate an account of the transcendental without a subject (this criticism, she notes, may hold true in the case of Husserl, but significantly less in the case of Sartre or Merleau-Ponty). To be more specific, Foucault sensed that in departing from individual consciousness, phenomenology remained too close to transcendental subjectivity even though it intended to distance itself from pure transcendentalism by positing the necessity for consciousness to reflect on an external object. In that sense, phenomenology could be said to be half empirical and half transcendental; half realist, half idealist. The second reason, Han tells us, is to be found in phenomenology's confusing relationship between the empirical and the transcendental, such that we are caught "in a vicious circle in which the conditions of possibilities are assimilated within that which they were meant to found" (Han 2002: 5). In historicizing the transcendental, Foucault thus intends to succeed where, according to him, phenomenology failed. The irony, as Han emphasizes, is that Foucault goes right back to where he began, for he must deal again with the transcendental in the form "of a free and autonomous self-constitution of the subject" (Han 2002: 196). Han summarizes the main point of contention as follows:

> On the one hand, the subject appears as autonomous, as the source of the problematizations of what he is and as a free actor in the practices through which he transforms himself. On the other, he is shown by the genealogical analyses to be inserted into a set of relations of power and practices that are subjecting to various degrees, and that defines the very conditions of possibility for the constitution of the self.
>
> Han 2002: 172

Yet, Foucault claims that what constitutes the focus of his research is the constitutive relation between the subject and the games of truths (Foucault 1998: 48). He thus suggests that the production of the subject is conditioned by a field of power-knowledge relations. Hence, if *The History of Sexuality* is first intended to study "the modes according to which individuals recognize themselves as sexual subjects," it is insofar as these modes of subjectivation imply the recourse to discipline. This would mean that it is not the subject *per se* that intrigues Foucault, but *how* one turns oneself into a subject; that is, the *process* of subjectivation. As such, Foucault's approach to the subject in his study of Greco-Roman antiquity still presupposes an account of power, that is, a field of relations and a set of practices that conditions the production of the individual. This would work if Foucault's definition of power were consistent. Han reminds us that power is apprehended by Foucault as a structuration and therefore as governmentality. Yet, the concept of governmentality does not refer back to power. Instead, it refers to individuals. She quotes Foucault:

> It is free individuals who try to control, to determine, to delimit the freedom of others and, in order to do that, they dispose of certain instruments to govern others. That rests indeed on freedom, on the relationship of self to self and the relationship to the other ... the notion of governmentality allows one, I believe, to set off the freedom of the subject and the relationship to others, that which constitutes the very matter of ethics.
>
> Foucault 1988: 19–20

Han thus concludes that the problem of subjectivity as the necessary point of reference to understand power and governmentality, far from being resolved, is only exacerbated. Overall, Foucault's ambivalence regarding the role of power in relation to the subject, and vice versa, leaves us uncertain about the priority one should give to one or the other.

In addition, Han explains that if one posits power as the necessary field through which the subject constitutes itself, then subjectivation would correspond to a disciplinary mode of self-constitution, which is that of subjection. There would be nothing wrong with that if subjectivation was not described in the third tome of *The History of Sexuality* as the *voluntary* process through which one becomes subject; hence turning subjection into its negative counterpart insofar as it refers to the eighteenth century's disciplinary forms of self-becoming. Moreover, if we give priority to the theory of power—as does for example Hubert Dreyfus (1994) in finding a correspondence between Heidegger's "being" and Foucault's "power," claiming that what Foucault understood by power resonates with what Heidegger understood by *Dasein* as an opening field of possibilities—we may indeed get rid of the transcendental subject. Yet, we may also turn power into a metaphysical force, as this would serve as the fundament of the subject and the social body in general, which is something Foucault would have likely taken issue with. Indeed, power is, for Foucault, less a force than a network, less a foundation than a relation (Foucault 1997a).

As such, Foucault's analysis of the theme of subjectivation confronts us either with the *aporia* of transcendentalism—which supports subjectivation as the reflective process through which one becomes subject, but contradicts the archaeo-genealogical Foucauldian method—or with the historical account of the process of self-constitution in which the subject remains produced by fields of power, hence contradicting subjectivation as an autonomous activity. Han notes also another difficulty which is going to be crucial for the rest of the argument. If one aims to connect the subject with games of truths in order to present the latter as constitutive of subjectivity, one would sooner or later have to face the externalization of subjectivity. This, she claims, is what Foucault's study of Platonism leads us to:

> The constitution of the self entails a recognition which, by denying individual differences, makes the truth of the subject inseparable from knowledge of the general. Such a recognition introduces a transformation of the very being of the

subject (hence, its "ontological" quality) by means of specific practices—the "techniques of the self."

Han 2002: 178

"Techniques of the self" thus designates the practices that support the becoming-true of the subject. For her, the Platonic approach presents some advantages, but does not resolve the tension she points out between Foucault's half-historical and half-transcendental account of the subject. If on the one hand the Platonic paradigm "reveals the structure of the relationship of recognition as itself a fundamental element of subjectivation," it also "reveals the impossibility of understanding subjectivation exclusively through the solipsistic model of the subject by itself" so that the "agent finds himself *ab initio* confronted with the necessity of finding outside of himself both the universal truth in which he recognizes himself and the techniques that allow him to interiorize it" (Han 2002: 179–80). Read from this angle, one understands why Han does not directly engage with Deleuze. Indeed, the process of subjectivation is, according to Deleuze's reading, "governed by the foldings operating in the ontological as much as the social field" (Deleuze 1988: 116). It is "as if the relations of the outside folded back to create a doubling, allow a relation to oneself to emerge, and constitute an inside which is hollowed out and develops its own unique dimension" (Deleuze 1988: 100). This interpretation suggests that subjectivation derives from the interiorization of the outside. For Han, this remains incompatible with the idea of an autonomous subject who is capable of recognizing itself as subject from within. Hence, the subject appears in Foucault's text as free because of the internal spontaneity of the individual's consciousness (Han 2002: 185). Conversely, if one "reinscribes subjectivation in a set of practices outside the subject," one transforms subjectivation into a passive and unreflective process of self-formation.

Han's suspicion continues when she considers the techniques of self *qua* the study of techniques of domination as a tangible point of departure. Though she acknowledges that the emphasis on the decisive role of external elements would be an interesting way to solve the tension between the transcendental and the historical, this would also run the risk of conflating the history of subjectivity with the history of technique. And Han does not seem particularly interested in following this path, for it only contributes to worsening her problem:

> At first sight, it provides Foucault with the means of deepening and replacing his analyses of the human sciences within the wider context of subjectivation, and seems to confer a greater coherence on his work as a whole; but, in reality, it reproduces and accentuates the first tension between the idealist notion of a fully free constitution of the self by the self, on the one hand, and its genealogical deconstruction, on the other.

Han 2002: 181

In this respect, the *aporia* of the self-constitutive subject along with the larger process of subjectivation inscribed in power relations, cannot be bypassed. She thus concludes that in order to resolve the impasse of his theory of subjectivation, Foucault would either need to renounce the idea of a "conscious and voluntary constitution of the self by the self" or to refine his model of hermeneutic ontology (Han 2002: 185).

## The Technicization of Subjectivation

Foucault has argued that "there is a technology of the constitution of the self" (Foucault 1984a: 369). Yet, Han claims that departing from the exteriority of techniques is not a viable solution, because it accentuates "the idealist notion of a fully free constitution of the self by the self, on the one hand, and its genealogical deconstruction on the other" (Han 2002: 181). Besides, one could answer that starting from techniques, as I am suggesting, instead of power, would only displace the issue. Indeed, far from resolving the paradox of self-constitution and the ambivalence between the transcendental and the empirical, one would simply pass from a metaphysics of power to a metaphysics of technics. In both cases, it denies any transcendence to the subject. If the subject freely constitutes herself, both technics and power appear as a disciplinary threat, which in Han's reading of Foucault is characteristic of subjection (in which the subject is the product of external forces), not subjectivation (in which the subject remains self-determining). Besides, such an approach may not be fully capable of acknowledging the positivity of the *interplay* of forces at work in the emergence of the individual. For Foucault, the relation between individuals and strategies of power remains essential to an understanding of subjectivation, though it inevitably brings a lot of tensions. Han reminds us that Foucault understands power as governmentality, that is, "as an unstable and violent field where the relationships of forces permanently form and dissolve" in a way that, she believes, appears close to Nietzsche (Han 2002: 193). Indeed, Foucault writes that "at the very heart of power relationship" lies an agonism which is both "a reciprocal incitation and struggle," that is, "a permanent provocation" (Foucault 1982: 222).

On this issue, Nietzsche's criticisms of metaphysics taught us that classic metaphysics broke away from the "tragic spirit" insofar as classic metaphysics was not capable of thinking the heterogeneity of forces other than "by opposing good and evil" (Ross 2013: 246), that is, in having recourse to oppositions when the key issue is that of composition. Hence, to posit a metaphysics of power or a metaphysics of technics may jeopardize Foucault's attempt to think the composition of forces at play within the process of subjectivation.

When examining the limits of Foucault's theory of subjectivation, Phyllis Sutton Morris is more inclined than Han to emphasize the technicity of subjectivation. To her, the insertion of the disciplinary model in the theme of subjectivation is not a problem, as she views it as a "deliberate disciplinary technique" in which the spontaneity of the creative activity and the "sharply self-focused discipline" are composing with each other (Morris 1996: 549). Though she does not elaborate further on that, the notion of composition is crucial. She is thus on the right track when connecting the possibility of being both spontaneous and disciplined; free and constrained. The merging of the spontaneity of freedom and disciplinary is precisely what Stiegler will embrace in his reading of Foucault by emphasizing the necessary technical aspect of subjectivation.

While Stiegler is not a Foucault scholar and does not engage with Foucault's aporetic conception of subjectivation, he draws on the work of his predecessor on many occasions. For example, it is by adapting a Foucauldian perspective on biopower (power over the body) that Stiegler is able to model his concept of psychopower (power over consciousness), hence enlarging Foucault's somatic perspective to the realm of psychic life. But Stiegler is also interested in Foucault's ethics of the subject. As I mentioned above, Stiegler puts the emphasis on the technical character of subjectivation. He is particularly inspired by Foucault's reading of the care of the self, which in his view, expresses well the constitutive role of technics in the process of self-formation (Foucault 1984a: 369). Indeed, Foucault has shown through his investigations of care a clear continuity between the intellectual activity of subjectivation and the deployment of *hupomnēmata*, understood literally as memory supports, and more broadly as technologies of the self (Foucault 1997b: 211). But again, it is important to note that Foucault's conception of *hupomnēmata* was restricted to the theme of the art of living, while Stiegler situates it "within a genealogy of technics" (Fuggle 2013: 204).

Yet, to apprehend care as technique—though it could rather be read as an *attitude* that requires the recourse to techniques—is not to misinterpret Foucault. As discussed by Foucault in his series of lectures at the Collège de France in 1981–2, the question that motivates the principle of care is, "which *tekhnē* do I have to use in order to live as well as I ought to live?" (Foucault 1984a: 348) Taking care is a way of life; a code of conduct aimed at self-accomplishment. However, it is *tekhnē* that seems to precede the possibility of subjectivity, precisely because, for Foucault, Greek morality, unlike its Kantian equivalent, cannot be defined *a priori* but only *a posteriori*, through the repetition of actions (Han 2002: 159).

Hence, what captures Foucault's interest is the governance of self through training (*askēsis*), that is, the production of the autonomous subject in the regulatory practice of care. As such, subjectivation is enabled by power-relations and emerges through them. But is Han's problem over? Foucault writes elsewhere:

> It is then a matter of forming and recognizing oneself as the subject of one's own actions, not through a system of signs denoting power over others, but through a relation that depends as little as possible on status and its external forms since this relation is fulfilled in the *sovereignty* that one exercises over oneself.
>
> Foucault 1986: 85

For Han, this understanding of subjectivation as tied to a "conscience" (Foucault 1989: 212) condemns Foucault to repeat what he intended to avoid: the reaffirmation of the Husserlian transcendental subject. But this is not actually fatal if one considers the spontaneity of consciousness as itself derived from the empirical *a posteriori* of technics. This is where Stiegler's technicization of consciousness is useful. While Foucault's work on "the technologies of the self" may have enabled us to reflect on the transformative effects that technics have upon us, Stiegler pushes the Foucauldian influence a little bit further. Instead of viewing technics as mere material supports (*hupomnēmata*), thus reducing these to a receptacle of human activity, Stiegler tries to go beyond this assumption and presents technics as the transcendental condition of the human, hence transposing the conditions of possibility for subjectivity into the field of technics. As I have mentioned, one could accuse Stiegler of turning Foucault's legacy into a metaphysics of technics, that is, of understanding technics as the founding principle of experience and signification. Considering that reservations have been shown earlier regarding the risk of developing a metaphysics of power, to accept Stiegler's move could sound inconsistent. However, Stiegler's account of technics is more sophisticated.

## Between the Transcendental and the Empirical

Foucault has shown that our interactions with technologies of the self "permit individuals to effect by their own means or with the help of others, a certain number of operations on their own bodies and souls, thoughts, conduct, and way of being, so as to transform themselves in order to attain a state of happiness, purity, wisdom, perfection or immortality (Foucault 1998: 18). These technologies can take the form of notebooks or public registers, or refer to any physical or mental exercise aimed at the cultivation of skills and habits. Foucault acknowledges that he "insisted too much on the technology of domination and power" and that he is more interested in developing a "history of how an individual acts upon himself in the technology of self" (Foucault 1998: 19). As interesting as Foucault's approach is for Stiegler, it still presupposes a division between technics and the self that is generated through them; in other words, it still presupposes an antagonism between the empirical and the transcendental. Hence, Stiegler's technicization of the conscious process of subjectivation intends to correct this antagonism. More generally, I argue that Stiegler manages to reconcile the empirical and the transcendental with his argument that technics make experience and signification possible. As such, not only is Stiegler throwing the very transcendental process of self-formation into the political realm, but he is understanding the aesthetics of the self as being always already political, insofar as it depends on its exteriorization in technics.

At this stage, it could be objected that Stiegler is simply following Husserl in giving "empirical contents transcendental value" (Foucault 1994: 248). Insofar as Foucault shows a certain resistance to Husserl, it would only exacerbate the issue. Yet, Stiegler's technicist approach intends to stress how the transcendental *depends* on the empirical (Lewis 2013: 61); he does not transcendentalize the empirical or the reverse.

In Stiegler's vocabulary, technics "encompasses techniques, technology, and the objects produced by these means" (Lewis 2013: 53). The key contribution of his research is to have shown that humans necessarily exist in relation to technics. The latter is characterized by Stiegler as *le défaut qu'il faut* (Howells 2013: 139); it is an absence, not a presence. What makes human beings so specific is their natural deficiency, which however turns out to be the first prosthetic reliance; the default of being is the originary cause of technics. In short, humans are prosthetic beings because they have no essence (Howells 2013). Does that mean that humans are the product of technics? Not exactly. It is this lack of essence that justifies the need for humans to form themselves as subjects; yet, they can only constitute themselves in relation to technics. For Stiegler, the exteriority of technics is constitutive of the human's interiority, but the relationship between the two needs to be clarified. For example, when Phyllis Sutton Morris reflects on Foucault's ethics of the subject, she starts her inquiry as follows:

> If the claim is made that the self forms or creates itself, what or who is it that does the creating? Wouldn't the self already have to exist to be creative, and if the self pre-exists its own creation, how can the self be a product of that creative activity?
> 
> Morris 1996: 537

Yet, to ask "who or what does the creating" is not indicative of the paradox of self-creation: it does not bring to light a lack of coherence in Foucault's work, it simply creates it. For Stiegler, this is not the right way to approach the issue. In the same way Foucault has denied any fundamental substance to the human, Stiegler denies an origin to the human. This means that the question surrounding self-creation does not so much revolve around *who* or *what* does the creating, hence implying the prior existence of an outside constitutive of an inside, but on *how* the creating is done. For Stiegler, the answer lies in the *technogenesis* of the human. By *technogenesis*, inspired by Simondon's concept of *ontogenesis*, Stiegler means that technicity and humanity equally ground each other through the mutual and continuous process of becoming. In this respect, *technogenesis* is what enables Stiegler to give a transcendental account of the emergence of the human through "an empirical account of the emergence of technology" (Lewis 2013: 53). This point is important as it means that subjectivation, as theorized by Stiegler, emphasizes the necessity to think the co-constitution of the inside and the outside, instead of giving priority to one or the other. Not only does Stiegler's position resonates with Deleuze's playful folding of the inside and the outside (Deleuze 1988: 107), he also adopts a tragic discourse in highlighting the compositional character of the process of self-creation.

Overall, Stiegler's approach cannot be qualified as metaphysical, for technics is not foundational but always elusive; it compensates for a lack of foundation. As a former student of Derrida, Stiegler does not simply conflate technics with technical objects, but identifies technics as what his mentor pinpointed as *différance* (Derrida 1982: 7). Simply put, *différance* is the reciprocal coupling of spatial differing and temporal deferring (Stiegler 1998: 139). For both, *différance* is defined as arche-writing. This means that *différance* is an inscriptive process enabling all inscriptive processes. But while Derrida leaves *différance* in the domain of abstraction, Stiegler fixates the principle of *différance* in technics, hence turning Derrida's critique of grammatology into a proto-grammatology (Ross 2013: 249). For Stiegler, technics is the *différantial* process *par excellence*. Thus understood, if we have to speak of the origin of the human, that origin is double: empirical and transcendental. Stephen Barker writes on this issue that "technics is the support for any organic subjectivity, the 'technical synthesis' providing the irreducible empirical base for human agency" (Barker 2013: 267–8). However, that does not mean that technics itself should be understood as a mere entity; instead it is an articulation. This will become more evident with the next point.

Stiegler explains that human beings exteriorize and interiorize themselves in and through technics, thereby continuously transforming and enriching themselves by the means of technical adoption. Again, this echoes Deleuze's interpretation of subjectivation as the "interiorization of the outside" (Deleuze 1988: 98) which, as we have seen, does not fully answer Han's problem which is that of the possibility for the subject to actively reflect on herself. Yet, Judith Butler argues that "to claim that the subject is constituted is not to claim that it is determined" (Benhabib et al. 1995: 46). For her, the subject is ambivalent and cannot be simply reduced to an effect of external forces enacted upon her (Butler 1997: 14). As such, one could simply respond that Han's reading of Foucault is in fact repeating this confusion between constitution and determination and the debate would be over. However, considering that Han tackles the issue of the *conscious* activity of subjectivation, I think that her point needs to be further addressed. The originality of Stiegler's work in relation to Foucault is to suggest that humans are not capable of "achieving transcendental subjectivity" (Lewis 2013: 53), that is, of spontaneously positing themselves as being the founders of their own experience. Instead, humans need technics and are always preceded by them:

> In this way the technical object allows the human being to relate to time while simultaneously anchoring this relation within a history. This goes some way towards explaining why Stiegler describes his work as an *archaeology* of reflexivity.
> Lewis 2013: 54

While Husserl has argued that consciousness is always the consciousness of something, hereby suggesting that the nature of consciousness lies in its intentionality, Stiegler reutilizes Husserl to argue, with the help of the same reasoning, that consciousness is technical, not only because it is formed through the object intended, but because it is always already technically articulated. Hence the point is less empirical than structural (Beardsworth 2013: 210).

Han's reading of Foucault suggests that the recourse to exterior objects necessarily jeopardizes the possibility for autonomy and the possibility for the subject to spontaneously constitute herself. But the autonomy of the self-constituent subject and the heteronomy of technics do not have to be antinomic in Foucault's work. For his part, Stiegler would praise Foucault for having sensed the organizational value of technologies and allowed us to think the significant relationship between the human and the technical field (Stiegler 2010: 122). The Stieglerian move is to posit their necessary concomitance. Hence, Stiegler dismantles the Kantian opposition between autonomy and heteronomy (Stiegler 2015: 16), so that autonomy is no longer a given or the mark of the human, but a skill that must be taught and cultivated. Autonomy, Stiegler argues, emerges in the heteronomy of technics (Stiegler 2015: 16). For Armstrong, Foucault's insight on care suggests the same thing:

> Rather than imagining autonomy as an innate capacity for self-determination or as the achievement of freedom from all forms of social constraint, Foucault holds that it consists in a more modest practice of self-formation which depends on cultivating an "artistic" approach to those codes of conduct, patterns of identification and regulatory norms which are the cultural sources of the self. Thus, the degree of autonomy one enjoys will depend on the extent to which one is able to use these cultural sources of selfhood as resources in one's attempts to

intervene in the formation of one's own identity. Foucauldian autonomy, then, is not opposed to social regulation. Rather, it consists in the struggle to subvert the project of normalization by wresting the power of regulation from the ends of disciplinary control in order to deploy this power in the service of self-creation.

Armstrong 2008: 27

Stiegler's intention is not simply to provoke a confusion between the empirical and the transcendental, but to think about transcendentality in relation to an empirical basis which is that of technics insofar as the technical necessarily *composes* with the human. In other words, they are each other's condition of emergence; both constraining and freeing each other. It means in consequence that the Foucauldian genealogy of the subject, which requires the study of the techniques of the self, does not have to be reduced to a history of techniques, as Han has feared. Instead, as Stiegler's contribution suggests, it is possible to formulate a genealogy of the technical subject. This would neither simply be a history of pure subjectivity nor a history of techniques/technics, but a history of their coevolution.

This said, one has the tools to elaborate with Foucault a coherent politico-technical hermeneutic of the self. Indeed, the deliberate discipline of the relation to oneself does not necessarily rely on a prior consciousness, that is, on the account of something that would be too close to a transcendental subjectivity for Foucault's taste, but on the mutual composition between the technical support and consciousness. As such, Stiegler's examination of the key concepts of care and *hupomnēmata* is the indication that Foucault's work on the technologies of the self gives us all the keys to apprehend the reflective movement of self-constitution as not simply *conditioned* but *enabled* by technics, hence clarifying the status of the individual as an empirico-transcendental doublet (Foucault 1994: 318). On a more significant level, Stiegler extends Foucault's work in being able to identify the political tensions at the core of the aesthetics of the self. Indeed, it is because our existence depends on technics that we must take care of ourselves. And as we will see in the last section, technics can have a harmful effect in the process of self-formation.

## Stiegler's Politics of Care

Foucault shows an interest in care as a technology of the self and argues that it must certainly be something that contemporary societies should take inspiration from (Foucault 1984a: 350). Yet, Stiegler reproaches Foucault for not having seen the political necessity of such techniques of subjectivation (Stiegler 2010: 180). Taking care of oneself is for Stiegler the condition for the reinvention of the human, but it is also a political imperative.

In his article on "Stiegler and Politics," Richard Beardsworth writes that "Stiegler's philosophy of technology has argued for reason and for institution at a moment in critical theory and postmodern debate when there remains a strong and debilitating suspicion of the dominating tendencies of post-Enlightenment reason and its institutions" (Beardsworth 2013: 211). Stiegler's work in *Taking Care of Youth and The*

*Generations* (2010) illustrates well Beardsworth's statement, for in pinpointing the generational malaise individuals are confronted with, Stiegler does indeed favor a return to institutions as guarantors of a healthy political future. This optimism towards institutions is motivated by his reading of Foucault. Indeed, Foucault demonstrated that through apparently repressive structures, institutions enable the production of the individual. Institutions and structures are not necessarily negating, but the conditions for constructing and ordering social relations. Foucault is clear on this issue: "if power were never anything than repressive, if it never did anything but to say no, do you really think one would be brought to obey it?" (Foucault 1984b: 61) Hence, instead of the word "repression," Foucault finally prefers that of "discipline," which encompasses both the productive character of institutional power and its coercive undertones.

However, Foucault was not a defender of institutions and did not see systems of disciplinary powers, such as those that emerged in the eighteenth century, as viable systems of care (Davis 2013). For Stiegler, this is a mistake. On Stiegler's defense of disciplinary institutions, Oliver Davis comments:

> Michel Foucault, in his account of disciplinary power and its institutions in *Discipline and Punish*, is accused by Stiegler of having failed to acknowledge this "positive power of sublimation" ... Foucault failed to see the Third Republic's school system for what it was: a system of care designed to form deep attention on an industrial scale and thereby to make France a mature democracy.
> 
> Davis 2013: 173

For Stiegler, we are currently plunged into a state of intellectual decadence, that is, of social immaturity. To combat this immaturity, we must discipline ourselves. Though his conservative tone may be questionable, and could be the object of strong criticism, to be fully understood it needs to be read in conjunction to his account of psychopower.

New technologies, Stiegler argues, have perverted the process of self-formation (or "individuation," as Stiegler prefers to call it) in short-circuiting the stream of consciousness. In other words, our techno-cultural environment is encouraging practices of desubjectivation insofar as it stimulates "regressive identification processes" and leads to "crowd psychology" (Stiegler 2010: 62). While acknowledging the power of Foucault's work, Stiegler believes that Foucault underestimated the psychological impact of technologies on individuals, for his theory of biopower mostly discusses the issue from a somatic perspective. In this respect, not only is biopower insufficient to describe the disastrous effects of new technologies on the psychic constitution of the individual, but it needs to be refined by the notion of psychopower insofar as it is not the body that constitutes the main political target anymore, but the very structure of consciousness. Psychopower, Stiegler tells us, refers to strategies of power that penetrate the unconscious in order to subvert the aesthetic pleasure of desire in favor of the instant demands of drives. One of the main consequences is that it tends to reduce the individual to the function of consumer. In short-circuiting desire, essential to the process of individuation, the consumerist values spread by the entertainment industries trap individuals in a meaningless existence. The progressive bestialization of the human through consumptive technologies is what Foucault has not considered while elaborating on biopower (Stiegler

2010: 175). According to Stiegler, Foucault has not seen that, as a weapon of psychopower, consumerism destroys minds by penetrating the *id* and unleashing morbid impulses.

As we have seen, consciousness is essential to the process of self-formation. It is the condition of possibility of subjectivation, but as transcendental as it is, it depends on the empirical ground of technics. Hence, the challenge is to reinstall practices of subjectivation at the core of political concern. While for Stiegler this implies an odd return to the institutions of the third Republic, it finally suggests that in order to combat the negative effects of new technologies of the self, one needs to have recourse to their older counterparts. Adopting healthier technologies is indeed the only way to adopt a healthier relationship with oneself.

## Conclusion

Stiegler gives another dimension to Foucault's legacy, for he is able to identify the political implications of care as an art of the self and explicate its utility in the current system of power relations. Yet, it is questionable whether Stiegler's revivification of care in the contemporary socio-technological context is compatible with Foucault's reading of the Greco-Romans. Indeed, while deploring the dislocation of culture, Stiegler believes that taking care of ourselves is not simply desirable, but a duty that demands urgent measures from the state (Stiegler 2010: 175), hence turning what Foucault saw as an art of living into a political imperative and normalizing what was supposed to remain a personal choice (Foucault 1984a: 341). The urgency of Stiegler's thought has been criticized for being dangerous, biased, and almost anti-philosophical (Bennington 1996: 175–6). This sense of urgency should thus be taken into consideration by the unfamiliar reader. Another issue to bear in mind is that Stiegler associates the duty to care with "the nineteenth-century educational apparatuses criticized precisely for their lack of care by Foucault" (Fuggle 2013: 200). As such, one must wonder about the dangers of proposing a disciplinary model of control as an apparatus allegedly designed to free us from control.

## References

Armstrong, A. (2008), "Beyond resistance: A response to Zizek's Critique of Foucault's Subject of Freedom," *Parrhesia*, 5: 19–31.
Barker, S. (2013), "Techno-pharmaco-genealogy," in C. Howells and G. Moore (eds), *Stiegler and Technics*, 259–74, Edinburgh: Edinburgh University Press.
Beardsworth, R. (2013), "Technology and Politics: A Response to Bernard Stiegler," in C. Howells and G. Moore (eds), *Stiegler and Technics*, 208–24, Edinburgh: Edinburgh University Press.
Benhabib, S., J. Butler, D. Cornell and N. Fraser (1995), *Feminist Contentions: A Philosophical Exchange*, New York: Routledge.
Bennington, G. (1996), "Emergencies," *Oxford Literary Review*, 18 (1/2): 175–216.
Butler, J. (1997), *The Psychic Life of Power*, Stanford, CA: Stanford University Press.
Davis. O. (2013), "Desublimation for Education in Democracy," in C. Howells and G. Moore (eds), *Stiegler and Technics*, 165–78, Edinburgh: Edinburgh University Press.

Deleuze, G. (1988), *Foucault*, trans. S. Hand, Minneapolis and London: University of Minnesota Press.
Derrida, J. (1982), *Margins of Philosophy*, trans. Alan Bass, Chicago: University of Chicago Press.
Dews, P. (1989), "The Return of the Subject in Late Foucault," *Radical Philosophy*, 51: 37–41.
Dreyfus, H. (1994), *Being-in-the-World: A Commentary on Heidegger's Sein und Zeit*, Cambridge: MIT Press.
Foucault, M. (1982), "The Subject and Power," in H. L. Dreyfus and P. Rabinow (eds), *Michel Foucault: Beyond Structuralism and Hermeneutics*, 208–26, Chicago: The University of Chicago Press.
Foucault, M. (1984a), "On the Genealogy of Ethics: An Overview of Work in Progress," in P. Rabinow (ed.), *The Foucault Reader*, 340–372, New York: Pantheon Books.
Foucault, M. (1984b), "Truth and Power," in P. Rabinow (ed.), *The Foucault Reader*, 51–75, New York: Pantheon Books.
Foucault, M. (1986), *The Care of the Self: Volume 3 of The History of Sexuality*, trans. R. Hurley, New York: Pantheon Books.
Foucault, M. (1988), "The Ethic of Care for the Self as a Practice of Freedom," in J. Bernauer and D. Rasmussen (eds), *The Final Foucault*, 1–21, Cambridge, MA, and London: The MIT Press.
Foucault, M. (1989), *Foucault Live: Interviews 1966–84*, ed. S. Lotringer, trans. L. Hochroth and J. Johnston, New York: Semiotext(e).
Foucault, M. (1994), *The Order of Things: An Archaeology of the Human Sciences*, New York: Vintage.
Foucault, M. (1997a), "Society Must Be Defended," in P. Rabinow (ed.), *The Essential Works of Michel Foucault, 1954–1984, Vol. 1: Ethics, Subjectivity and Truth*, New York: The New Press.
Foucault, M. (1997b), "Self Writing," in P. Rabinow (ed.), *The Essential Works of Michel Foucault, 1954–1984, Vol. 1: Ethics, Subjectivity and Truth*, New York: The New Press.
Foucault, M. (1998), *The History of Sexuality: The Will to Knowledge*, trans. R. Hurley, London: Penguin.
Fuggle, S. (2013), "Stiegler and Foucault: The Politics of Care and Self Writing," in C. Howells and G. Moore (eds), *Stiegler and Technics*, 192–207, Edinburgh: Edinburgh University Press.
Han, B. (2002), *Foucault's Critical Project: Between the Transcendental and the Historical*, Stanford, CA: Stanford University Press.
Howells, C. (2013), "'Le Défaut d'origine': The Prosthetic Constitution of Love and Desire," in C. Howells and G. Moore (eds), *Stiegler and Technics*, 137–50, Edinburgh: Edinburgh University Press.
Lewis, M. (2013), "Of a Mythical Philosophical Anthropology: The Transcendental and the Empirical in *Technics and Time*," in C. Howells and G. Moore (eds), *Stiegler and Technics*, 53–68, Edinburgh: Edinburgh University Press.
Morris, P. S. (1996), "Self-Creating Selves: Sartre and Foucault," *American Catholic Philosophical Quarterly*, 70 (4): 537–49.
Ross, D. (2013), "Pharmacology and Critique after Deconstruction," in C. Howells and G. Moore (eds), *Stiegler and Technics*, 243–58, Edinburgh: Edinburgh University Press.
Simons, J. (1995), *Foucault and the Political*, London: Routledge.
Stiegler, B. (1998), *Technics and Time: The Fault of Epimetheus*, trans. R. Beardsworth and G. Collins, Stanford, CA: Stanford University Press.

Stiegler, B. (2009), *Technics and Time: Disorientation*, trans. S. Barker, Stanford, CA: Stanford University Press.
Stiegler, B. (2010), *Taking Care of Youth and the Generations*, trans. S. Barker Stanford, CA: Stanford University Press.
Stiegler, B. (2015), "Bernard Stiegler on Automatic Society: As told to Anaïs Nony," *Third Rail Quarterly*, 5: 16–17.

5

# Notes Towards a Critical History of Musicalities: Philodemus on the Use of Musical Pleasures and the Care of the Self

Élise Escalle

In this chapter, I propose to read a few passages of the Epicurean versus Stoic debate in the fourth book of Philodemus of Gadara's philosophical and ethical work *Peri Mousikēs* (Delattre 2007) in the perspective of the late Foucault's inquiry towards the formation during antiquity of what he called "the hermeneutics of the self" (Foucault 2016). By borrowing Foucault's approach to examine Philodemus' work, my aim is to show that it is possible to find shared historical, cultural and gendered modalities in the "moral problematization" (Foucault 1990: 34–7) of both "musical" and "sexual" pleasures. Indeed, and as I hope to demonstrate, these fragmentary discourses may be critically read as part of the genealogies of the modern Western experience of "sexual" and "musical" practices as being deeply related to the sense of oneself as an individual subject, that is to say as part of a Western "history of subjectivity" (Libera 2008). For "musicality," just like "sexuality," is a fairly recent term, which appeared as a keystone in the Western discourses of truth about listening, learning, composing or performing music only when the romantic and post-romantic conceptions of "music" as an autonomous art became hegemonic in Western societies (Brett 2006: 10), the same way "sexuality" emerged as the main conceptual category of an apparatus regulating discourse on "sex" only when "sex" became meaningful in itself and "made it possible to group together, in an artificial unity, anatomical elements, biological functions, conducts, sensations, and pleasures," as Foucault notes in the first volume of *The History of Sexuality* (Foucault 1978: 154).

Yet, if "musical" and "sexual" identities seem to have shared genealogies tying them discursively towards similar processes of autonomy and naturalization, questions still need to be raised about how, to quote Foucault in his introduction to *The Use of Pleasure*, "an 'experience' came to be constituted in modern Western societies ... that caused individuals to recognize themselves as subjects of a 'sexuality'" (Foucault 1990: 4), as well as of a "musicality" (Brett 2006: 11–12). For there seem to be common archaeological distinctions underlying the "will to truth" (Foucault 1981: 56) which allowed both the parallel discursive formalization and the disciplinary reciprocal exclusion of the *scientia sexualis* and the aesthetics of music as a fine art. This enabled, for instance, the formation of psychiatric discourses at the beginning of the twentieth century which drew an intimate connection between pathologized sexual orientations and the notion of unusual and innate musical skills, while securing at the same time what musicologists Elizabeth Wood and Philip Brett described as a "weird dissociation" between homosexuality and academic musical practice within the "cultural mechanism of the closet" (Brett and Wood 2006: 355).

Therefore, by making the epistemological decision to decenter "musicality" from the focus of our interpretation of musical experience, as historian David Halperin, drawing on Foucault's work, famously advised with regards to "sexuality" (Halperin 1989: 271), we might well be able to explore in Philodemus' work how Stoic and Epicurean philosophers of the Hellenistic period discussed the use of musical pleasures as what Foucault proposed to call "technologies of the self" (Foucault 1997b) in order to achieve a good life (*pros to kalōs zēn*), as the stake is defined in the words of Philodemus' self-chosen opponent in the *Peri Mousikēs*, the Stoic Diogenes of Babylon (Delattre 2007: col. 32:35–6).[1] In this framework, I will propose a few hypothesis about how "musical" and "sexual" practices became tightly bounded in an ethical sense of the self, crucial to our Western understandings of what both "sex" and "music" mean. Indeed, and as we shall see, the arguments developed in Philodemus' work never focus on music as an end in itself, but instead nearly exclusively discuss the effects of "musical" activity either as a performer or a listener of *mousikē*—a category much wider than our contemporary Western definition of music, as it simply referred in Greek to the art of the Muses, hence including poetry, but also history and astronomy along with a huge range of danced, vocal and instrumental practices (Delattre 2007: ccxliv–ccl).

Nevertheless, and as we shall see by reading closely some key statements in Philodemus' work, this very signification of *mousikē* came to be harshly disputed towards the end of the Hellenistic period, when the former Greek use of music as a powerful pedagogical and ethical tool central to the *paideia* and ensuring in Plato's terms the acquisition of both a sense of beauty, *eumousia*, and a sense of justice or measure, *eunomia*, was challenged by a new Roman musical context which especially emphasized instrumental performances, partly at the expense of the previously hegemonic vocal genres (Delattre 2007: 279–87). Consequently, philosophers engaged in renewed discussions about the legitimacy and the importance of music among what Foucault proposed to call the "arts of existence" (Foucault 1990: 15–16), focusing especially on whether there could be or not an ethical use of musical sensations in the pursuit of happiness. The answer relied of course heavily on the divergent ontological standpoints held by the main philosophical schools at the time, and their consequential advices about how one should relate or engage in musical practices (Delattre 2007: 91–4).

In this context, the unanimously recommended musical austerity appears to have some complex yet obvious relation with the transformations which occurred simultaneously in discourses about self-moderation and the search for virtue concerning the use of *aphrodisia*, "these pleasurable acts situated in an agonistic field of forces difficult to control," as Foucault defines them (Foucault 1990: 250). This is especially striking in Philodemus' work, which refers to very a wide set of musical practices not only as part of education or domestic leisure, but also as belonging to a lot of different social activities such as rituals, public celebrations, warfare, athletic competitions, symposiums, marriages, and of course theater. All of these practices are being examined in his text through the lens of their effects on the self and an ethical effort of telling the truth about this process (Delattre 2007: ccxlvi–ccxlvii).

In order to show how this problematization precisely occurs, I will first try to describe the very writing practice through which Philodemus conducts his philosophical *askēsis* with respect to music, as it materially commands in his text the terms of his polemic with the Stoics about the use of musical pleasures. Then I will focus on a few aspects of Philodemus' refutation of what Hellenist Andrew D. Barker characterized as the "moral sociology" of music gathered by his Stoic opponent in his book, Diogenes of Babylon, which locates itself at the limit between music and the non-musical—this limit actually being the main object of the Epicurean concern (Barker 2001). Finally, I will attempt to support the conclusion that it is precisely through a discursive move towards what I propose to call a "judgment of the ear" that at the end of the Hellenistic period music tended to become an ambivalent yet unavoidable issue in the emerging hermeneutics of the self—a set of practices within which, as Foucault observes about "sexual" conduct in *The Care of the Self*, "problematization and apprehension go hand in hand" and "inquiry is joined to vigilance" (Foucault 1987: 239).

## The *Hupomnēmata* and the "Moral Problematization" of "Musical" Pleasures

Let us consider first the enunciative modalities of Philodemus' writing about music. In his introduction to his newly reconstructed edition of Philodemus' work published in 2007, Daniel Delattre urges his reader to consider the issue of what he calls a "severe inadequacy" (Delattre 2007: xxvi), according to which the text has often been presented as a philosophical "treatise" in spite of Philodemus himself referring explicitly to his text as belonging to the practice of *hupomnēmata*—a practice Foucault characterized after Plutarch as a form of "*ethopoietic* writing," the aim of which was, in Foucault's terms, "not simply to serve as a memory support" but rather "to capture the already-said, to collect what one has managed to hear or read ... for a purpose that is nothing less than the shaping of the self" (Foucault 1997a: 210–11).

In the precise case of Philodemus' *Peri Mousikēs*, from which only the fourth and last book subsisted as fragments in the library of the so-called "Villa of the Papyri" in Herculaneum after the Vesuvius' eruption (Delattre 2007: lvi–lviii), such an ethical orientation or *telos* involved the framing of its philosophical discourse about musical practices in a rather strict enunciative pattern, inherited from the Epicurean scholarch Zeno of Sidon under the direction of whom Philodemus studied in Athens before leaving for South Italy in around 75 BC (Delattre 2007: xvi–xvii). After a faithful exposition of the adverse claims and views against which one seeks to argue, one had to proceed to a meticulous critical and polemical re-reading of them according to the Epicurean dogma, before summarizing it with definitions in a conclusive statement which enclosed the whole process of recollection (Delattre 2007: xxix–xxx).

Philodemus therefore starts his book with a very precise enumeration of theses and assertions drawn from an important work of the second century BC by the Stoic

Diogenes of Babylon, which is unfortunately lost to us now and thus only known through this very mention of it (col. 1–55). Then he proceeds to a lemma-by-lemma refutation of his opponent's claims, dismissing the conceptions he perceives as misleading according to his own commitment to the doctrine of the Garden (col. 56–140). Finally, he recalls the Epicurean definition of music as a natural but unnecessary pleasure (*phusikē, ouk anankē hēdonē*) in order to reaffirm its contingency for the philosophical form of life which can alone ensure happiness (col. 140–52).

Consequently—and as Foucault noted in his Lecture of March 3, 1982, at the Collège de France—"the *hupomnēmata* are of use to oneself, but you can see also that they may be of use to others" (Foucault 2005: 360). As he composed his work under the protection of the future governor of Macedonia, Lucius Calpurnius Piso Caesonius, who, according to Cicero, adopted the Epicurean doctrine thanks to his teachings and to whom he dedicated numerous epigrams as well (Delattre 2007: xviii), Philodemus was indeed concerned not only with constituting an "equipment of helpful discourses" about music for further Epicurean philosophical discussions and exercising (Foucault 1997a: 210), but also with defending among the Roman Greek-speaking elite at the end of the Republic the doctrine of the Garden itself, which was frequently accused of "rusticity" (*agroikia*) on such matters as the philosopher himself reports in his text (col. 140:14–35). Toward the conclusion of his book, Philodemus repeatedly states that such a reproach was one of his main motivations for writing down his own extensive *hupomnēmata* about music (col. 144:1–6), thus dismissing what could first appear as a performative contradiction in his work, precisely oriented by the assertion that musical practices should have a marginal status among what Foucault would call the "arts of existence" fulfilling the leisure time of a free man (col. 152:29–39).

Yet, as Foucault remarks in his article on "self writing," the *hupomnēmata* "need to be resituated in the context of a tension" according to which the "recollection of the fragmentary *logos*" they perform must deal with the "recognized value of the already-said" (Foucault 1997a: 211). In Philodemus' case, this context refers to a delimited set of authorities on music whose discourses materially function in his text both as a philosophical *corpus* to be contemplated and, in Foucault's terms, as "the very process through which the writer himself constitutes his own identity" (Foucault 1997a: 213). This is especially worth noting as Diogenes of Babylon, Philodemus' self-chosen opponent in the fourth book of his work, unambiguously inscribes his claims about what he calls the "powers" (*dunameis*) of music within a Greek tradition which, since at least Pythagoras and Damon of Athens, saw musical practice as highly contributing to a virtuous life, in so far as its moving and driving capacities are carefully regulated and constrained (Delattre 2007: ccxxxiii–ccxxxv). Indeed, Diogenes first seems to fully agree with Plato's views in his *Republic*, as he draws on his affirmation that music in a proper education harmonizes the soul the way gymnastics does for the body, in so far as musical innovation is carefully controlled and passionate practice consistently rejected.

But whereas for Plato music could give good habits only to the irrational part of the soul, as it was limited to the imitation of virtues and therefore unable to impart any science (Delattre 2007: ccxxxvi–ccxxxvii), Diogenes argues that music also directly triggers ethical dispositions through a process of impulsion (*hormē*), which musical practice and knowledge (*theōria*) precisely aim to rationally master in an appropriate way (col. 13-17). Each melodic line (*melos*) and rhythm (*rhuthmos*) is said to have an obvious kinetic power of its own, that one must control in either performance or listening in order to establish an adequate relation to the self and others (col. 19-20, 41:18-19, 98-100). It is therefore because music by its very nature includes rational and ethical components, "many definitions, systematic distinctions and demonstrations" as well as "affiliated virtues" (*sungeneis aretai*), as Diogenes puts it (col. 18:4-5), that through the knowledge of the different kinds of musical scales (*harmoniai*) and musical instruments (*organa*), musical education might be useful to consolidate the *hēgemonikon*, the ruling "part" of the soul which also ensures its unity (col. 76:28-77:13).

We recognize here the Stoic dogma of the *oikeiōsis*, according to which and in Diogenes' own words "what is strongest in all things is what is proper" (col. 18:6) and "the grounds of our proper dispositions don't come from the outside, but are already within ourselves" (col. 25:3-5). Music is appropriate (*prepon*) to the soul in so far as the soul unified by *logos* operates a rational choice between the affections and representations provoked by musical activity, which is why for the Stoic musical practice prepares boys to the future apprehension of their tasks as free men (Woodward 2009: 39), by helping them to progressively learn how to control and choose among their sensible representations (col. 22-31, 112-13). Consequently, when Diogenes invokes for instance the case of Pythagoras inviting a female *aulos* player to perform a spondaic tune in order to appease drunk young people (col. 42), or the events which reportedly saw the lyric poets Stesichorus and Pindar obtaining in their respective cities reconciliation between adverse factions by the power of their singing (col. 47), what he praises first is the appropriateness of their use of music which prioritized what is divine in musical practice itself, that is to say its rational grounding in the cosmological order of things and not only its mere affective effects which such references are incidentally supposed to demonstrate as well (Barker 2001: 353).

## A "Moral Sociology" of Music *versus* an "Anthropology of Musical Moralities"

Philodemus' *hupomnēmata* thus unfold a double set of constitutive inventories of musical practices, through which the Epicurean effort of telling the truth about the contingency of musical pleasures directly answers Diogenes' own discourse of truth recalling the powers of music in a huge variety of Greek and Hellenistic textual and social sites. Consequently, and in Foucault's terms, the "subjectivation of truth" (Foucault 1997b: 238) about music in Diogenes reported discourse first, and in its detailed critique by Philodemus then, corresponds to two distinct "discursive formations" (Foucault 1972) whose enunciative modalities do not rest upon the same material conditions. This very distinction is indeed being secured by Philodemus himself both as a necessity required by the defense of the integrity of the Epicurean dogma as opposed to its perhaps stronger Stoic counterpart in the historical situation of the end of the Roman Republic, but also as a self-writing constrain resulting from his own engagement of examining all the consequences of this doctrine on music both for himself and for the others (Delattre 2007: 275–87).

Indeed, Philodemus' refutation begins with the affirmation that musical practice is indifferently capable of engendering the best and the worst dispositions (col. 56–85), for it is impossible to educate sensitive perception through *theōria* as Diogenes claims (col. 115–17). Such an affirmation is of course consistent with the Epicurean dogma according to which "every sensation is devoid of reason and incapable of memory," which is precisely why sensations are "standards of truth" (*kritēria tēs alētheias*, Diogenes Laertius 1972: 10.31); but it also matches, as Daniel Delattre notes in his edition, an historical shift in musical practice and listening, which in the Roman world of the first century BC were no longer essential features of the education of a free man (Delattre 2007: 281–82). According to Philodemus, what Diogenes takes to be the specific powers of music are in fact enclosed in the significations transmitted by the poetry it conveys (col. 143:12–43), while the primary sensual and irrational grounding of musical practice makes it definitively closer, in his own terms, "from good cooking and the art of perfumes" (col. 92:1–5),[2] as for him music by nature is devoid of any signification (*asēmanta*, col.143:31–2).

The Epicurean therefore not only dismisses Diogenes reading of Plato through the lens of *oikeiōsis* as both inaccurate and misleading (col. 138:9–35), but also re-reads all the references given by the Stoic in the perspective of a new understanding of *mousikē* (col. 140:14–35). For Philodemus indeed, and quoting his own words, "whoever calls music that which is something else than the poetical genre taken as a whole, by extracting from it bare melodies and rhythm, is acting the right way" (col. 149:39–43). According to the Epicurean, the episodes reported by Diogenes about the lyric poets Stesichorus or Pindar are at least historically doubtful (col. 134:7–21). But nevertheless, they recall the necessity of drawing a distinction within their activity as composers of music (*mousikoi*) on the one hand, and writers or makers of lyrical discourses (*poiētai*) on the other hand, the latter only explaining the ethical effects attributed to the practice of their art in such cases—effects which could have probably been even better achieved without singing (col. 142:16–22, 143:1–39).

Being a "musician" is thus defined by Philodemus after the model of the composer of instrumental music (*kroumatopoios*, col. 140:28, 143:13), a category borrowed from the peripatetic philosopher Aristoxenus which leaves little to no room for the amateur or connoisseur of music described by Diogenes in his claims. This character is indeed mocked by the Epicurean in his refutation under the term *philomousos*, a "musical enthusiast" who mistakes musical pleasures for moral qualities the same way a gourmet would do with his favorite food (col. 115:2). As a result, whereas Diogenes and Philodemus fully agree that music should not be a full-time or a professional occupation and share a common *telos* prioritizing the search for happiness in their consideration of musical pleasures, they nevertheless strongly diverge not only on what Foucault would call the determination of the "ethical substance" of music, but also on the "modes of subjection" and the "form of ethical work" it implies (Foucault 1990: 32).

This has especially interesting consequences if we consider one precise aspect of Diogenes detailed account of the powers of music, namely its relation to *erōs* that the Stoic considers as derived from its being protected by Erato, the Muse of lyric poetry who allowed this very practice to contribute to what Diogenes calls the "virtue of love" (*erōtikē aretē*, col. 43:37–41). According to the Stoic, love and music are affiliated or of the same kind (*sungenes*, col. 39:4) and while the *pathos* they imply might always be a cause of trouble, their divine origin and their very nature authorizes an appropriate and rational use of them both, especially for friendship and benevolence (*philophrosunē*, col. 47:11–22). Diogenes therefore defends the ethical value of a whole series of Greek musical practices of his time, ranging from the *epithalamia* or lyric poems performed in marriage in praise of the bride along with the propitiatory *humenaioi* and sacred songs about fertility (col. 39:1–12, 119:25–41) up to the playing of the *kithara*, the singing and dance by free men during symposiums (col 46:14–28) or the use of specific melodies to appease all kinds of sorrow that might be caused by love (col. 43:29–37).

The discussion about the *aulos* is especially interesting: after the mention of *Ismēnias*, a famous *aulētēs* from the fourth century BC whose melodies were said to be able to summon up the strength of a whole flotilla the same way Orpheus could animate stones with his songs (col. 41:17–28), Diogenes makes it nevertheless clear that its playing should not be recommended to as part of the *paideia*, for it might alter the features of a child's face (col. 41:31–5), a reason already evoked by Aristotle in his *Politics* and that the tradition attributes to Alcibiade's refusal to play this instrument (Delattre 2007: 360). Then, after a few missing lines, the Stoic's demonstration refers to a story he attributes to Pythagoras, in which a girl is invited to play a spondaic tune on the *aulos* for its sobering effects on drunk young men (col. 42:39–45). This musical practice reminds of the risk invoked by Eryximachus in Plato's *Symposium* to send away a female *aulos* player to the *gynaeceum*, as he states that the company is "resolved to force no one to drink more than he wants" (James 2014).[3]

In Philodemus' account of Diogenes' argumentation, this immediately precedes the mention that music fuels the desire of men for women and for boys, possibly engendering for the last a "feminine weakness" (*gunaikismos*, col. 43:14) which was often mocked in the famous comedies of the time (col. 43:14–22). Remarkably enough, this doesn't seem to affect the Stoic's praise of the role of music in the "virtue of love" as long as such a consequence is restricted to its adequate place, that is to say on a theater stage. Melodies can still be the food of love and accompany the drinking in symposiums as long the company behave "in a manner that is no way misplaced" in this situation (col. 46:24–8). Indeed, and because of its close link to *erōs*, music in such a setting is also "appropriate to friendship" (*ekhein de ti kai pros philian oikeion*, col. 47:11–12). Reading Philodemus' refutation, we understand better what is at stake: for him, it is the whole Stoic doctrine of *oikeiōsis* which is misleading when thinking about musical practice (col. 76, 77:1–28) and especially in its relation to *erōs* (col. 130:1–6).

For the Epicurean, to invoke a divine origin of music is already a lie, as according to him it is a "recent art" which is derived from primitive dance (col. 74–5) and not the contrary, as his opponent repeatedly suggests. Music cannot therefore be grounded on a rational piety towards a sacred cosmological order as the Stoic claims, but depends rather on universal sensual feelings which put music in conflict with the ataraxic condition of Gods, among whom it is for Philodemus nevertheless doubtful to count the Muses (col. xx). According to him, Diogenes' praise of their excellence and virginity would be better applied to Artemis or Athena, in so far as Erato's commitment to erotic poetry generally encourages all kinds of lecheries and depraved sexual acts (*lagneiai*, col. 129:24). To quote Philodemus' words, "music has [therefore] not the power to calm down the sorrows of love (*duspraxiai en erōti*), for such a consolation only depends on *logos*—it can only bring distraction and prevent to think, just like drunkenness and sexual pleasures (*aphrodisia*)" (col. 129:1–7). The whole division of Diogenes' "moral sociology" dedicated to the use of music in its relation to *erōs* is thus dismissed at once, according to an anthropological standpoint which sees such practices as derived from what we could call "musical moralities," while the ethical concern of a free man is never supposed to take the form of a subjection to either musical or sexual pleasures, which in such case might have the same distractive and disruptive effects on the self.

Even if we recall, as Foucault remarked in *The History of Sexuality*, that both Diogenes and Philodemus are concerned with "a male ethics which did not try to define a field of conduct and a domain of valid rules … for the two sexes in common [but] was an elaboration of masculine conduct carried out from the viewpoint of men in order to give form to their behavior" (Foucault 1990: 22–3), the gendered modalities of such a discursive shift are still remarkable. Indeed, the Epicurean mocks the distinctions drawn by the Stoic between the melodies sung by women and girls according to their social status (col. 127:38–128:4), and rejects his whole understanding of the relation between *erōs* and music (col. 129:26–44). Philodemus therefore assigns to the whole of "womankind" (*thēleia*) a tendency to relate passively to the sensual pleasures of music and singing (col. 121:9–12), which is precisely the reason why there can't be for him an appropriate "feminine" use of musical pleasure. By contrast, for Diogenes, the notion was meaningful only in relation to its effects on the self, as it was already the case in Plato's *Laws*.[4]

This helps us to understand why the Epicurean repeatedly states that women are by nature more inclined to "licentiousness" (*akolasia*) and "confusion" (*ataxia*), the Bacchic female trances being according to him the best proof of it (col. 121:15–22), against Diogenes' argument that they are first provoked by music itself regardless of its incidental listeners.

In conclusion, I would therefore like to underline that the Stoic and Epicurean forms of musical austerity and control detailed in Philodemus' work confront us to a variable set of differences which, far from being only doctrinal, also concerns practices of truth which are obviously not restricted to the verbal construction of a philosophical and epistemological doxology about music, but also have historical, musical and socio-musical consequences as well. Thus, it is possible to read the Epicurean's *hupomnēmata* as part of a larger philosophical effort to define what I propose to call a "judgment of the ear," which we can trace back to the peripatetic Aristoxenus, who first claimed that musical listening was above all a matter of hearing and mobilizing intelligence—*eis te tēn akoēn kai eis tēn dianoian* (Woodward 2009: 173–90)—and Heraclides Ponticus, who wrote an influential work unfortunately lost to us which aimed to provide an inventory of all musical practices known to him (Delattre 2007: ccxxxix–ccxxx). Such a way of writing, thinking, and exercising in and about music resulted in what Foucault called "disparate discourses" (Foucault 1972) which Diogenes didn't hesitate to explicitly compare to the practice of philosophy itself, according to Philodemus' account of his claims. Given such a context—and as Foucault's notes in his lectures at the Collège de France—the profusion of philosophical works entitled *On Listening* at the end of the

Hellenistic and throughout the imperial Roman period corresponds to the formation of discourses of truth which are completely interlocked with a philosophical inquiry about "true listening" (Foucault 2005). All of these discourses aimed to understand practically what it might mean to listen to the truth in both verbal and musical performances for those seeking happiness, and the nature of the care managed by a self who is precisely defined by an aptitude for self-listening and a distinctive listening attitude toward other.

Here, Diogenes' claim of the primacy of *theōria* as the main criterion to distinguish musicians from non-musicians on the one hand, and Philodemus' assertion of an hermetic distinction between musical and philosophical activity on the background of the universality of sensation on the other hand, both set up the stage for a Western conceptualization of music where the problematization occurring in musical theory will radically diverge from the examination of musical performances and practices. Meanwhile, musical activity will become unavoidable among the sensuous temptations of flesh for early Christian authors, who will soon regard it with the same anxiety and vigilance as those other kind of pleasures with which it was long associated, superposing musical carefulness with the care about one's sexual conduct, as we can see for instance in the Augustinian "confessions of the flesh" and of course in his own work *On Music* (Foucault 2018).

This shift is indeed not fully completed in Philodemus' work, for on the one hand Diogenes' claims about music still praise what the Stoic calls the acquisition of a "skillful sensation" for the well-trained musician (col 34:1–9), and on the other hand Philodemus' own practice of self-writing describes what we might qualify after Foucault as a "parrhesiastic truth" (Foucault 2011: 9) about the use of musical pleasures,[5] in a series of situations that cannot simply be summarized as a uniform set of distractions, for only the *sōphrosunē* is able to discriminate ethically between them once they have been characterized (col. 65:7–13). Thus, and because of the subtlety of such critical and genealogical distinctions, it seems to me that if we are to understand better "how musical is man" (Blacking 1973) according to the Western hermeneutics of the self, we might turn with great interest to what Foucault once proposed to call the "history of the desiring man" (Foucault 1990: 6).

## Notes

1  When referring to Philodemus' work in Daniel Delattre's edition of the text, I will from now on simply indicate the column number and eventually the line quoted from the reconstructed manuscript, separated by a colon (col. xx:xx). When quoting Delattre's introduction and commentaries, I will keep the edition's references with the page numbers in Roman or Arabic numerals (Delattre 2007: xx).

2  As Daniel Delattre underlines in his notes, this association between music and perfumery is recurrent throughout Philodemus' refutation and conclusion in his book (col. 84, 92, 112, 133, and 147).

3  See Plato, *Symposium*, 176e. As Robin James (2014) notes in a recent talk given at DePaul University, "having first decided to be moderate, to not drink to excess, [the company] decides that philosophical conversation is a means to maintaining bodily moderation.

But to avoid excess and to facilitate philosophical conversation, they have to kick out the flute girls because flutes and girls exhibit an unphilosophical, disproportionate relationship between visible embodiment and sonic output ... Women and other non-philosophers, like flutes, have a disproportionate relationship between their speech and their visible bodily structure." Meanwhile, in Pythagoras' story, the female *aulos* player is convoked once the company is *already* drunk, her music being appropriate to this setting according to Diogenes' views.

4   See Plato, *Laws*, 669c–d: "For the Muses would never blunder so far as to assign a feminine tune and gesture to verses composed for men, or to fit the rhythms of captives and slaves to gestures framed for free men, or conversely, after constructing the rhythms and gestures of free men, to assign to the rhythms a tune or verses of an opposite style" (Bury 1968).

5   As Foucault reminds us in his lecture of February 1, 1984, Philodemus is himself the author of a *Peri parrhēsia*, "a large part of which is sadly lost" (Foucault 2011: 7).

# References

Barker, A. D. (2001), "Diogenes of Babylon and Hellenistic Musical Theory," in C. Auvray-Assayas and D. Delattre (eds), *Cicéron et Philodème. La polémique en philosophie*, 353–70, Paris: Éditions Rue d'Ulm.

Blacking, J. (1973), *How Musical is Man?*, Seattle, WA: University of Washington Press.

Brett, P. (2006), "Music, Essentialism, and the Closet," in P. Brett, E. Wood, and G. C. Thomas (eds), *Queering the Pitch. The New Gay and Lesbian Musicology*, 9–26, New York and London: Routledge.

Brett, P. and E. Wood (2006), "Lesbian and Gay Music," in P. Brett, E. Wood, and G. C. Thomas (eds), *Queering the Pitch. The New Gay and Lesbian Musicology*, 351–90, New York and London: Routledge.

Bury, R. D. (1968), *Plato in Twelve Volumes, Vols. 10 & 11*, London: Harvard University Press.

Delattre, D. (2007), *Philodème de Gadara. Sur la musique, Livre IV*, Paris: Les Belles Lettres.

Foucault, M. (1972), *The Archaeology of Knowledge and the Discourse on Language*, trans. A. M. Sheridan Smith, New York: Pantheon Books.

Foucault, M. (1978), *The History of Sexuality. Volume 1: An Introduction*, trans. R. Hurley, New York: Pantheon Books.

Foucault, M. (1981), "The Order of Discourse," trans. I. McLeod, in R. Young (ed.), *Untying the Text: A Post-Structuralist Reader*, 48–78, Boston, London and Henley: Routledge & Kegan Paul.

Foucault, M. (1987), *The History of Sexuality. Volume 3: The Care of the Self*, trans. R. Hurley, New York: Pantheon Books.

Foucault, M. (1990), *The History of Sexuality. Volume 2: The Use of Pleasure*, trans. R. Hurley, New York: Vintage Books.

Foucault, M. (1997a), "Self Writing," in P. Rabinow (ed.), *The Essential Works of Michel Foucault, 1954–1984, Vol. 1: Ethics, Subjectivity and Truth*, 207–22, New York: The New Press.

Foucault, M. (1997b), "Technologies of the Self," in P. Rabinow (ed.), *The Essential Works of Michel Foucault, 1954–1984, Vol. 1: Ethics, Subjectivity and Truth*, 223–52, New York: The New Press.

Foucault, M. (2005), *The Hermeneutics of the Subject: Lectures at the Collège de France 1981–1982*, ed. F. Gros, trans. G. Burchell, New York: Palgrave Macmillan.

Foucault, M. (2011), *The Courage of Truth (The Government of Self and Others II): Lectures at the Collège de France 1983–1984*, ed. F. Gros, trans. G. Burchell, Basingstoke: Palgrave Macmillan.

Foucault, M. (2016), *About the Beginning of the Hermeneutics of the Self: Lectures at Dartmouth College, 1980*, ed. H.-P. Fruchaud and D. Lorenzini, trans. G. Burchell, Chicago: The University of Chicago Press.

Foucault, M. (2018), *Histoire de la sexualité 4: Les aveux de la chair*, Paris: Gallimard.

Halperin, D. M. (1989), "Is there a History of Sexuality?," *History and Theory*, 28 (3): 257–74.

James, R. (2014), "Philosophical Attunements: Flutes & Women in Plato's Symposium," talk given at DePaul University. Available online: https://www.its-her-factory.com/2014/03/philosophical-attunements-flutes-women-in-platos-symposium (accessed May 27, 2018).

Libera, A. (2008), "When Did the Modern Subject Emerge?," *American Catholic Philosophical Quarterly*, 82 (2): 181–220.

Woodward, H. L. (2009), "Diogenes of Babylon: A Stoic on Music and Ethics," MA diss., University College London, London.

# 6

# Foucault's Ultimate Technology[1]

## Luca Lupo

The aim of this chapter is to highlight how the relationship between the subject and time both represents the basis of the practice of the self and constitutes the foundation of another substantive relationship between the subject and truth: one which intersects the relationship between time and truth. It is through the subject's representing time in a certain way, a way which is produced through certain practices of the self, that it is possible to become aware of the value and meaning of one's own existence. This chapter also sets out to emphasize how time and exercises related to the perception of time actually lie at the very core of Foucault's reflection on what he calls "the technologies of the self" in the ancient world, even though—as I will try to show— he does not overtly stress or make explicit their crucial importance to his discourse. Foucault provides a very clear definition of this formula: "technologies of the self" are those kinds of practices "which permit individuals to effect by their own means or with the help of others a certain number of operations on their own bodies and souls, thoughts, conduct, and way of being, so as to transform themselves in order to attain a certain state of happiness, purity, wisdom, perfection, or immortality" (Foucault 1988: 18).

Foucault's lectures take the form of a specific philosophical genre. We must take into account the occasional character of his text: as recalled by Gros in his afterword to the lectures, Foucault's thought takes shape around the texts used in the course of delivering them.[2] The lecture is a kind of philosophical exercise in which Foucault can put into practice his intention of producing dynamic thought:[3] even more than in writing, in the very combination of oral and written forms, in the spontaneous oral communication inspired by his written notes, it is possible to observe the thinking process at the very moment it is generated.

In the lecture we will analyze here, however, there is a certain imbalance between the texts presented by Foucault and his own commentary on them, which is very limited and seems to follow the texts without wandering too far from them.[4] It is as if he were seeking to follow Nietzsche's rule on style, according to which "[i]t is not good manners or clever to deprive one's reader of the most obvious objections. It is very good manners and very clever to leave it to one's reader alone to pronounce the ultimate quintessence of our wisdom" (Nietzsche, *cit. in* Salomé 2001: 78).

In the part of the lecture of March 24, 1982 that I will analyze below, the problem of temporality is introduced by the distinction between tests concerning the truth of what we think and tests concerning the truth of what we are:

> Today I would like to talk about the other series of tests, not those concerning the examination of the truth of what we think (examination of the truth of opinions which accompany representations), but those that test oneself as the subject of truth. Am I really the person who thinks these true things? This is the question to which these exercises must respond. Being the person who thinks these true things, am I the person who acts as someone knowing these true things? What I mean by this expression is: Am I really the ethical subject of the truth I know?
>
> Foucault 2005: 463

In other words, the question the subject is asking himself is: am I embodying the truth I think? We can see how these questions are crucial at all levels of philosophical enquiry: the ontological/gnoseological level (*am* I really the person who *thinks* these true things?), the ethical/gnoseological level (am I the person who *acts* as *someone knowing* these true things?), and in general the ontological/ethical gnoseological level (*am* I really the *ethical subject* of the *truth I know*?).

## "We Should Not Let Ourselves Be Worried About the Future"

The exercises that, according to the Stoics, will help us to follow this advice are: *praemeditatio malorum, meditatio mortis,* and the examination of conscience. The first two are the most closely connected to temporality. The first topic on which Foucault quickly focuses is the ancients' mistrust of the future. Why is this so? The initial reason is that thinking about the future hinders freedom of action because such thinking is conditioning and paralyzing. The second reason is that the ontological status of the future is rather uncertain and even ambiguous, as we will see.

Foucault notes how the notion of "not let[ting] ourselves *be worried about the future*" (Foucault 2005: 464, *emphasis added*) is, from a philosophical point of view, "a fundamental theme in the practice of the self" (Foucault 2005: 464). In other words, the attitude of the subject towards a specific aspect of temporality is crucial to the practice of the self.[5] This relationship takes the form of preoccupation. The future worries us before it occurs. It worries us in the present and occupies the present. Occupying the present, it becomes a hindrance to the possibility of action. The future worries us; hence, it busies us beforehand and does not set us free. Indeed, what actually prompts our worries is *thinking* of the future. Unlike thought of the past, which is viewed positively in the form of the practice of memory, thought of the future makes us worried and is viewed negatively. The antithetical relationship between the future and the past, according to Foucault "is crystallized in the definition of an antinomic relation between *memory* and *thinking about the future*" (Foucault 2005: 464, *emphasis added*).

It is worth noting, incidentally, that Foucault's methodological premises bring to mind the high value that Hellenistic philosophy places on the past. Foucault's epistemology examines the past in order to understand the present (see Gros 2005: 525). This is a matter not of looking to the past as a lifeless object but of doing as the ancients did and employing the past with a view to establishing a general approach to action (to be performed in the present). It is in Foucault's genealogical perspective that we encounter his attitude towards time, especially towards the past. Besides memory, "[t]he other reason why thinking about the future is discredited is, if you like, theoretical, philosophical, and ontological" (Foucault 2005: 464). At this stage, Foucault states the decisive identity of the future and nothingness:

> The future is nothingness: it does not exist, or at any rate not for man. Consequently we can only project on to it an imagination based on nothing. Or else the future pre-exists and, if it pre-exists, it is predetermined, and so we cannot control it. Now what is at stake in the practice of the self is precisely being able to master what one is in the face of what exists or is taking place. That the future is either nothing or predetermined condemns us either to imagination or to impotence. Now the whole art of oneself, the whole art of the care of the self is constructed against these two things.
>
> Foucault 2005: 464–5

The future coincides with nothingness; it simply does not exist. Or alternatively, it pre-exists. If it pre-exists, it is predetermined, and if it is predetermined, it is impossible to control. Thought of the future condemns one to either imagination or impotence. Imagination and impotence appear as two obstacles to *being able to master what one is*. The entire art of the care of the self seems to be built and to grow around the effects of thought of the future, the aim being to neutralize those effects; that is to say, *the entire art of the care of the self revolves around the problem of managing the forms of time*. The future does not exist (at least for man); it is something that *is not* and that *nevertheless* occupies the present. In this lies its ambiguous and paradoxical nature. The future can be and not be *at the same time*. The future is nothingness, yet it produces effects, and in producing them it becomes something. The more encumbering it becomes, the more absent or unreal it appears. While on the one hand the form of the past enhances mastery of the self, on the other the form of the future stands in the way.

## A Hierarchy Based on Perception of Temporality

The contrast between memory and the future has an anthropological counterpart. To that contrast corresponds another, this time between those whose minds are oriented to the past and those who keep their attention on the future. Human attitudes towards time work as a criterion that distinguishes the former from the latter. Indeed, the form of our thoughts determines the form of our lives. More specifically, how we think about time determines how we live. Our attitude towards time, the way we live it, becomes a criterion for choosing a form of living. Our attitude towards time is what gives us our form.

Starting with a quotation from *De Tranquillitate Animi* by Plutarch, Foucault analyzes how our relation to time emerges as a decisive factor in determining the rationality or irrationality of human types, which can be divided into *phronimoi* and *anoētoi*. The *anoētoi* are those who worry about the future, while the *phronimoi* "are clearly in possession of the goods they no longer have, thanks to memory" (Foucault 2005: 465). The *anoētoi* are "those whose position is exactly the opposite of the philosophical position" (Foucault 2005: 465). Hence, the *philosophical* position belongs to those who take the past into consideration and are aware that the problem of time is crucial.

What are the implications of thinking about the future for the lives of these two human types? The *anoētoi*, worrying about the future, do not take care of themselves: "turned towards the future, [the *anoētos*, the *stultus*] cannot grasp the present.⁶ He cannot grasp the present, the actual, that is to say the only thing that is actually real" (Foucault 2005: 465–6). If taking care of oneself means taking care of the present moment, this implies an overlap between being oneself and being in the present moment, between subjective identity and the temporal form of presence: the subject is one who is *present* to himself. To be a subject is to be able to be *in the present*, to be capable of presence. Alongside worrying about the future, our general neglect of the past, an inclination to oblivion, prevents us from assigning the correct value to the present and to ourselves. A second quotation from Plutarch recalls the image of the rope-maker:

> [J]ust as the rope-maker ... lets the donkey feed on the rushes he is plaiting, so for most insensitive and unpleasant people, oblivion seizes their past, devours it, and makes all action, success, pleasant leisure, social life and enjoyment disappear, without allowing life to form a whole in which the past intertwines with the present; as if the man of yesterday were different from the man of today and equally the man of tomorrow not the same as the man of today, forgetting separates them and, in the absence of memory, turns all that happens into nothingness.
>
> Plutarch, *cit. in* Foucault 2005: 466

Not paying attention to the past produces a kind of temporal disaggregation. The image of the rope-maker becomes a metaphor for "the distracted existence of someone who neither pays attention to what he is doing nor to himself" (Foucault 2005: 466). If the future is nothing, men who concentrate their thought on the future reduce their existence to nothingness; they become prisoners of a nihilistic spiral determined by both preoccupation with the future and oblivion with regard to the past. The man of the future is a "man who allows all that happens to be consumed by forgetting ... [he] is incapable of action, incapable of success and incapable of pleasant leisure, of *skholē* (that form of studious activity which is so important in the care of the self)" (Foucault 2005: 466). The men of the future are incapable of *skholē* insofar as they are not equipped with the ability to make proper use of time, which gives it its sense and value. The men of the future are not only "doomed to discontinuity and the flux, they are also doomed to dispossession and emptiness. They are really no longer anything. They exist in nothingness" (Foucault 2005: 467). It is easy to see how contemporary themes resonate in Foucault's choice to turn to the classics,⁷ just as they do in the case of the anthropological profile of the decadent, of the nihilist, from Nietzsche onward.⁸

From this discussion of how *anoētoi* and *phronimoi* experience time, it is clear that a certain orientation towards the form of temporality determines one's way of life.

Simply thinking about time determines one's actions. The theoretical reconfiguration of temporal forms is immediately effective on the ethical-practical level. Thinking differently about time, which is the space, the *khōra*, in which the *ethical* takes its form, has direct consequences for the nature of ethical action. In modifying the structure of time, you also modify the nature of the action taking place. At the same time, however, to think about temporality is to mold it; thinking about temporality is, in turn, a form of "doing," an ethical action. To remain in the prison of the future is to be condemned to be incapable of action.

## *Praemeditatio Malorum*

The Stoic practice of *praemeditatio malorum* (premeditation of misfortunes and evil) should be situated within this theoretical framework, which affirms the primacy of the past and devalues the future. *Praemeditatio malorum* appears as a practice which consists precisely in thinking about future negative events—as an exercise of expectation, and indeed negative expectation. It is a way of thinking and representing time in the form of what is to come. This practice seems to deny the typical ancient mistrust of the future; Foucault engages in showing us the opposite.

Foucault's investigation into the exercise of *praemeditatio malorum* opens with the Epicurean point of view, which is opposed to the Stoic view. From the Epicurean perspective, a present evil is oppressive enough to make space for the thought of a future evil which may never obtain:

> Against this *praemeditatio malorum*, the Epicureans set two other exercises: the *avocatio*, the function of which is to ward off representations or thoughts of misfortune by turning instead to the thought of pleasures, and to the thought of all the pleasures that could come to us some day in life; and then the exercise of *revocatio*, which protects us, rather, and defends us from the misfortunes or so-called evils that may happen to us, by recalling past pleasures.
>
> Foucault 2005: 468

It is possible here to observe the close link between spiritual exercises and temporal form. In the *avocatio* (the representation of possible future pleasures), imagination is used to contain and control negative thoughts that threaten the present; in the *revocatio*, memories are used to avoid possible negative thoughts. Thus, the future and the past are used to contain the negativity and the pain of the present. They are bent to the needs of the present. The exercise appears as an action that is strictly connected to the government of time. Mastery of oneself presents itself as mastery/control of temporal forms.

In the case of the *praemeditatio*, government of oneself appears not only as mastery/control of the future in view of the present but also as containment and control of a specific temporal form, the *exaiphnēs*:[9] a sudden occurrence, the "breaking in" of the event as containing an essential truth about existence. "A man who is *suddenly surprised* by an event," Foucault writes, "is really at risk of finding himself in a weak position if he is not prepared for it and the surprise is great" (Foucault 2005: 469, *emphasis added*). He is a man who

> does not have the discourse-aid available to him, the discourse-recourse that would enable him to react properly, not letting himself be disturbed and remaining master of himself. In the absence of this equipment he will be permeable to the event, so to speak. The event will enter his soul and disturb and affect it, etcetera. Thus he will be in a passive state with regard to the event. We must therefore be prepared for the events that occur, we must be prepared for evils. In letter 91, Seneca says: "The unexpected overwhelms most, and strangeness adds to the weight of misfortune: there is no mortal to whom surprise does not increase the distress."
>
> Foucault 2005: 469

The exercise aims at containing the effects of the breaking in of the unexpected as an expression or manifestation of the smallest portion of time one can conceive of. It is based on the production of a discourse that can be of help at the right moment: the *logos boēthos*. The *logos boēthos* is the paradigmatic expression of thought governing temporality through language. The time to be controlled here by and through language is time in the form of the unexpected. The *praemeditatio* is, furthermore, a representation of the future, a simulation of it, a way of condensing into a single point something that—as Foucault insists—is not the future but rather what Niklas Luhmann would call *the future in the present* (Luhmann 1979: 13). In the *praemeditatio malorum*,

> it is not really thinking about the future. It is much more a case of sealing off the future ... It involves thought systematically nullifying the specific dimensions of the future. For what is at stake is not a future with its different open possibilities. It does not involve a future with the unfolding of time and its uncertainties, or anyway its successive moments. It is not a successive time but a sort of immediate time, gathered up into a point, which must make one consider that all the worst misfortunes of the world, which will happen to you anyway, are already present. They are imminent with regard to the present you are living. You see then that it is not at all a case of thinking about the future that is an exception to the general mistrust of thinking about the future. In reality, within this mistrust, it is a nullification of the future by making everything possible present, if you like, in a sort of present test of thought.
>
> Foucault 2005: 470

Despite Foucault's insistence that it is a matter not of thinking about the future but rather of nullifying the specific form of the future, in the *praemeditatio* you are meant to practice exorcising the future in order to govern temporality. The temporal form of the future places itself at the core of the discourse in as much as it is presented as negative and to be removed. The more urgent the removal of the thought of the future, the greater its presence.

The schematic definition of the *praemeditatio* that Foucault proposes shows that the main purpose of the exercise is to govern that form of temporality that manifests itself as the unexpected future: the *praemeditatio* is actually defined as i) a proof of the worst possibility, and ii) an exercise in thinking both that the worst possible outcome will certainly occur and, above all (and here the emphasis on temporality returns), iii) that the evil will occur *"immediately, very shortly, without delay"* (Foucault 2005: 470, *emphasis added*). Seneca's letter 91 says: "The person who said it only needs a day, an hour or a moment to overturn the greatest Empire of the world has still granted too much time" (Seneca, *cit. in* Foucault 2005: 470). In T. S. Eliot's words: "In a minute there is time / For decisions and revisions which a minute will reverse" (Eliot 1963: 4).

The *praemeditatio* therefore makes possible a "reduction of reality. We do not make the whole of the future present in this way so as to make it more real. Rather it is to make it as least real as possible, or at least to nullify that which could be envisaged as or considered to be an evil in the future" (Foucault 2005: 471). A few lines further, we see how the turning point of this reduction, this nullifying, involves the activity of thought/language on time: "Whatever the evil may be, take its measure in your thought and weigh up your fears: you will certainly see that what frightens you is unimportant and short-lived" (Seneca, *cit. in* Foucault 2005: 471).

## *Meditatio Mortis*

The *meditatio mortis* can be considered a continuation of the *praemeditatio malorum*; it "is fully isomorphous with the presumption, the premeditation of evils" (Foucault 2005: 477). Death is not simply a possible outcome but a necessary event which can occur at any time: it is worth noting that it shares with the future a certain paradoxical nature: it is expected, it is granted, but at the same time it is unpredictable. Yet still, from the point of view of time, death is intertwined with the form of the future: in the imagination of those who do not practice a philosophical way of life, it will happen, but it never belongs to the present. If one makes the unnatural and almost unbearable effort to strip death of its psychological and emotional burdens, conceiving of it only in temporal terms, it can be thought of merely as an *absence, the end of time*.

Foucault is interested in investigating the effects of systematic thinking about death on the form of a life.[10] Such effects modify the forms of time: meditation on death opens up

> the possibility of a certain form of self-awareness, or a certain form of gaze focused on oneself from this point of view of death, or of the actualization of death in our life. In fact, the privileged form of the death meditation in the Stoics is, as you know, the exercise that consists in thinking of death *as present* according to the schema of the *praemeditatio malorum*, and that one is living one's last day.
> 
> Foucault 2005: 478, *emphasis added*

The thought of death as an exercise in making an absent event present transforms the non-philosophical point of view into a philosophical one precisely because, for the non-philosophical form of life, death is never in the present. Among the different forms of time control, Foucault stresses the importance of the metaphor of a day in the practice of the exercises. Life is like a day; a year, a month are like a day. This reduction of the various partitions of time to the time span of a day helps to make what is absent immediately perceivable and concrete; it makes absence itself detectable, reducing the future to the present. The exercise of imagining our entire lives as a single day makes the reduction of temporality possible and temporality easy to grasp:

> This is the exercise of the last day. It does not consist merely in saying to oneself: "Ah! I could die today"; "Ah! Something fatal could well happen to me that I have not foreseen." No, it involves organizing and experiencing our day as if each moment of the day was the moment of the great day of life, and the last moment of the day was the last moment of our existence. Okay, if we succeed in living our day according to this model, then when the day is completed, when we get ready to go to sleep, we can say with joy and a cheerful countenance: "I have lived."
> 
> Foucault 2005: 478

It is noteworthy that the exercise helps to give form to the portion of time represented by a day. The ability to manage the time span of a single day mirrors the ability to manage the time span of a whole life. The thought of death as a form for governing time has a double character: first, it allows us to cast a glance over our lives, on our past, as a whole; second, it prompts us to appreciate the real value of time in our existence: of our past in its entirety as a whole and of the present moment in the singularity of its fatal immediacy:

> This exercise enables us to take a sort of instantaneous view of the present from above; it enables thought to make a cross section of the duration of life, the flow of activities, and the stream of representations. By imagining that the moment or day we are living is the last, we immobilize the present in a snapshot, so to speak. And from this moment, frozen in this interruption by death, the present, the moment or the day will appear in their reality, or rather, in the reality of their value. The value of what I am doing, of what I am thinking, of my activity, will be revealed if I am thinking of it as the last.
> 
> Foucault 2005: 479

If, once again, you strip death of all the psychological and emotional burdens which inevitably accompany it, the representation of death is nothing but the representation of the moment in which time comes to an end and a limited material resource runs out. That very moment makes it possible to look back and thus to become aware of the value of our own existence as a whole:

> The thought of death, then, makes this looking back and evaluative memorization of life possible. Here again you see that thinking of death is not thinking about the future. The exercise, thinking about death, is only a means for taking this cross-section view of life which enables one to grasp the value of the present, or again to carry out the great loop of memorization, by which one totalizes one's life and reveals it as it is. Judgment on the present and evaluation of the past are carried out

in this thought of death, which precisely must not be a thought of the future but rather a thought of myself in the process of dying.

Foucault 2005: 480

Here we see at work the language/thought which acts upon time in the form of memory. Even though Foucault insists that thought of death is not thought of the future, what is nonetheless at stake here is an attempt to control time. Thought of death acts on temporality; its object is temporality, and it is a way of forging temporality itself. Thinking of death as the "end of time," the "absence of time," becomes a means of giving value to time (see Lupo 2018: 54–5). The value of time depends on the moment of death's being the ultimate moment, and thus a unit for measuring the rest of one's lifespan: after one envisions one's myriad accomplishments, the partial endings of the various stages and moments of one's life, death appears as the supreme manifestation of the end of time, its absence, its ultimate depletion as a resource.

A determinate amount, insofar as it is a quantity the availability of which is ontologically limited, has a value: this is the case for the time of human existence. The thought of the limitation of one's lifespan acts on one's actions in the ethical realm, which is the realm of action. But what is it that acts on the meaning of our actions as a modifier? It is the change to our perception of time, the acquired awareness of time as a limited resource: the abandonment of the illusory perception of time as an infinite resource.

## Conclusion

We have seen how in the practice of *praemeditatio malorum* and in the *meditatio mortis* what is at work is what can be defined as a real "technology of time," an expression that can be used in analogy with Foucault's "technology of the self," of which—as should now be clear—it is the culmination. Time and the different ways of governing and controlling it through language/thought seem to be the common thread of these exercises, the final aim of which is a test of the self as a subject of truth: in the case of the *praemeditatio*, the objective is to bring the future back to the present, to be ready and prepared in the face of the unexpected. In the case of the *meditatio mortis*, the aim is to be able to represent to oneself the end of time, to be able to feel the value of one's own time in the present moment, and to experience the time in which one has lived one's whole life from a new perspective.

It is emblematic that consideration of the practices I propose we call "technologies of time" *conclude* the lectures on the hermeneutic of the subject,[11] even if Foucault does not overtly emphasize this connection. The supreme spiritual exercises,[12] the practices of the self *par excellence*, involve thinking about time; more specifically, they aim to give form to time through language in order to gain control of it. Thinking of the end of time sheds light on the meaning of life and thereby on its truth. As Schopenhauer reminds us, "one must comfort oneself with the certainty that one has the truth on one's side ... which once its confederate, time, has united with it, is completely certain of victory, if not today, then tomorrow" (Schopenhauer 2009: 257).

Old age—that stage of life in which the end of time moves closer until it becomes constantly perceptible—is also the stage in which time and truth come together. Precisely, and paradoxically, just when time is coming to an end, the technology of the self reveals itself to the utmost as a "technology of time," disclosing its maximum effectiveness, reaching its peak and attaining its highest goals.[13] As Foucault observes, old age "is not just a chronological stage of life: it is an *ethical form* which is characterized both by independence from everything that does not depend on us, and by the fullness of a relationship to the self in which sovereignty is not exercised as a struggle, but as an enjoyment (*jouissance*)" (Foucault, *cit. in* Gros 2005: 533, *emphasis added*).

In conclusion, while on the one hand Foucault's reflection on the "technology of time" can be interpreted as a *genealogical* step toward the very source of contemporary existential thought on the meaning of death for life (e.g. Heidegger,[14] Jankélévitch), on the other hand Foucauldian recovery of the practical, *performative* role of ancient thought as a tool for combating the contemporary tendency toward nihilism sounds at base like an implicit criticism of resignation to the "primacy of the end"—an attitude which would seem to dominate the philosophical mainstream of our age.

## Notes

1 I dedicate these pages to the memory of Walter Lupi and Emilio Sergio.
2 See Gros (2005: 518): "A new style of teaching is born; Foucault does not expound the results of his work so much as put forward, step by step, and almost hesitantly, the development of a work of research."
3 I am in total agreement with Han, who writes that "in his last texts" Foucault "is no longer the detached observer of the modifications in the conditions of possibility of human knowledge: His discourse has acquired a performative vocation, and is now meant to generate within his readers the very kind of ethical transformation it describes ... Foucault's analysis of Antique spirituality has implicitly acquired a unity of form and meaning in which the description of the aesthetic of existence becomes the operator of ethical transformations. Strikingly, this brings to mind another characteristic of Antiquity, namely the parrhesiastic understanding of the truth" (Han 2007: 202). In this context, what is crucial is the final part of Han's remark on the later Foucault, who, according to her, "spoke in his own name and addressed his readers as a parrhesiast, whose life, personal engagement, and even the manner in which he handled the coming of his own death testified to its authenticity" (Han 2007: 202). Among the often unexciting texts in the recent literature on Foucault, Han's 2007 exemplary contribution stands apart.
4 See Gros (2005: 518): "A major part of the course now consists in a patient reading of selected texts and in a word-by-word commentary on them."
5 Foucault refers—even if briefly—to the importance of this kind of exercise regarding the perception of time in Foucault (1988: 37). There, as here, Foucault does not stress the peculiarity of this exercise as an exercise specifically focused on time.
6 In a previous lesson, Foucault states, significantly, that "the *stultus* ... is someone who does not think of his old age and who does not think of the temporality of his life as having to be orientated by the completion of the self in old age. He is someone who constantly changes his life"; he is "dispersed in time" (Foucault 2005: 132).

7   This turn can be interpreted as an evolution of the "qualified nihilism" for which Foucault himself argues (see Dreyfus and Rabinow 1983: 89), or even the endeavor of a problematic, anti-nihilistic countermovement.
8   On the debate on the relation between Foucault and nihilism, see e.g. Milchman and Rosenberg (2003), Dreyfus and Rabinow (1983), and especially Hicks (2003).
9   This term plays a crucial role in many of Plato's works, for example in the myth of the cave: here, Plato uses it to describe the very moment of the liberation of the prisoner (*Republic*, 515c). A detailed definition of its meaning is given in the *Parmenides*: *exaiphnēs* "seems to indicate a something from which there is a change in one direction or the other. For it does not change from rest while it is still at rest, nor from motion while it is still moving; but there is this strange instantaneous nature, something interposed between" (*Parmenides*, 156d). Moving from Plato to the Christian tradition, a significant use of the word occurs in *Acts*, 22–26, where Paul relates his experience on the road to Damascus. The word represents a *hapax legomenon* in the Gospel: "On that journey as I drew near to Damascus, about noon a great light from the sky suddenly (*exaiphnēs*) shone around me."
10  Such thought, together with its performing effects, assumes a parodic, surreal, exhilarating, but nonetheless meaningful shape in Jaco Van Dormael's movie *The Brand New Testament*, which depicts what it might be like to have clear knowledge of the exact moment one will die. To spite her father, Ea—the ten-year-old daughter of a neurotic and sadistic God who leads a petty-bourgeois life with his family in an apartment in Brussels—steals a file from his computer containing the dates on which every human will die and, as a sort of reversed Prometheus, sends them to everyone via text message (see minute 17').
11  And indeed Foucault's life. See footnote 3 above, especially the final part of the quoted passage from Han (Han 2007: 202).
12  For a detailed discussion of this expression, see Hadot (2002) and Hadot and Hadot (2004). Hadot appreciates Foucault's work on ancient Greek thought and confirms the correspondence between what he calls "spiritual exercises" and Foucault's "practices" or "exercises" of the self; at the same time, however, Hadot feels the need to remark on the significant differences between his and Foucault's positions. For Hadot, Foucault reads too much into the concept of the "self" (see Hadot 1992: 225) and relegates to the background the movement "in which one raises oneself to a higher psychic level; in which one rediscovers another type of exteriorization, another relationship with the exterior, another way of being-in-the-world which consists in being aware of oneself as a part of Nature, as a particle of universal Reason" (Hadot 1992: 230).
13  Foucault speaks of old age as "the center of gravity, the sensitive point of the practice of the self" (Foucault 2005: 92), and of the old man as "the person who is sovereign over himself and who can be entirely satisfied with himself" (Foucault 2005:109). Old age, Foucault stresses, "should not be seen merely as a limit in life, any more than it is to be seen as a phase of diminished life. Old age should be considered, rather, as a goal and as a positive goal of existence" (Foucault 2005: 109). "With regard to our life", old age allows us "to place ourselves in a condition such that we live it as if it is already over" (Foucault 2005: 110). Furthermore, Foucault goes so far as to say that "you have to be old to be a subject" (Foucault 2005: 126). In fact, "there is a privileged relationship between the practice of the self and old age, and so between the practice of the self and life itself, since the practice of the self is at one with or merges with life itself. The objective of the practice of the self therefore is preparation for old age, which appears as a privileged moment of existence and, in truth, as the ideal point of the subject's fulfillment" (Foucault 2005: 126).

14  To the extent that the technologies of the self have as their goal the transformation of the subject through gaining awareness of "being-toward-death," that is, existential awareness of the end of time, they can also be thought of as technologies of time and as intertwined with each other. On the relationship between Heidegger and Foucault, see the classic reading in Dreyfus and Rabinow (1983) and, more recently, Milchman and Rosenberg (2003) and especially Wyschogrod (2003).

# References

Dreyfus, L. H. and P. Rabinow, eds (1983), *Michel Foucault: Beyond Structuralism and Hermeneutics*, Chicago: The University of Chicago Press.
Eliot, T. S. (1963), *Collected Poems 1909–1962*, New York: Harcourt Brace & World.
Foucault, M. (1988), "Technologies of the Self," in L. H. Martin, H. Gutman and P. H. Hutton (eds), *Technologies of the Self: A Seminar with Michel Foucault*, 16–49, London: Tavistock Publications.
Foucault, M. (2005), *The Hermeneutics of the Subject: Lectures at the Collège de France 1981–1982*, ed. F. Gros, trans. G. Burchell, New York: Palgrave Macmillan.
Gros, F. (2005), "Course Context," in M. Foucault, *The Hermeneutics of the Subject: Lectures at the Collège de France 1981–1982*, ed. F. Gros, trans. G. Burchell, 507–50, New York: Palgrave Macmillan.
Hadot, I. and P. Hadot (2004), *Apprendre à philosopher dans l'Antiquité*, Paris: Le Livre de Poche.
Hadot, P. (1992), "Reflections on the Notion of the Cultivation of the Self," in T. J. Armstrong (ed.), *Michel Foucault, Philosopher*, 225–32, Hemel Hempstead: Harvester Wheatsheaf.
Hadot, P. (2002), *Exercices spirituels et philosophie antique*, Paris: Albin Michel.
Han, B. (2007), "The Analytic of Finitude and the History of Subjectivity," in G. Gutting (ed.), *The Cambridge Companion to Foucault*, 176–209, Cambridge: Cambridge University Press.
Hicks, V. S. (2003), "Nietzsche, Heidegger and Foucault. Nihilism and Beyond," in A. Milchman and A. Rosenberg (eds), *Foucault and Heidegger. Critical Encounters*, 74–109, Minneapolis: University of Minnesota Press.
Luhmann, N. (1979), *Trust and Power*, ed. T. Burns and G. Poggi, trans. H. Davies, J. Raffan and K. Rooney, Chichester, New York, Brisbane and Toronto: John Wiley and Sons.
Lupo, L. (2018), *Forme ed etica del tempo in Nietzsche*, Milan-Udine: Mimesis.
Milchman, A. and A. Rosenberg, eds (2003), *Foucault and Heidegger: Critical Encounters*, Minneapolis: University of Minnesota Press.
Salomé, A. L. (2001), *Nietzsche*, trans. S. Mandel, Urbana: University of Illinois Press.
Schopenhauer, A. (2009), "On the Basis of Morals," in A. Schopenhauer, *The Two Fundamental Problems of Ethics*, ed. and trans. C. Janaway, 113–257, Cambridge: Cambridge University Press.
*The Brand New Testament* (2015), [Film] Dir. Jaco Van Dormael, Belgium, France and Luxembourg: Music Box Films.
Wyschogrod, E. (2003), "Heidegger, Foucault, and the Askeses of Self-Transformation," in A. Milchman and A. Rosenberg (eds), *Foucault and Heidegger. Critical Encounters*, 276–94, Minneapolis: University of Minnesota Press.

Part Three

# Ontology of the Present, Politics of Truth

7

# The Care of the Present:
# On Foucault's Ontological Machine

Gianfranco Ferraro[1]

At the same time that Foucault developed his hermeneutics of the subject, which focused on an archaeology of the "care of the self," his research revealed an interest in ontology. He also made clear that this ontological approach to the "present" was in fact, despite appearances, representative of his entire critical, philosophical project. How can we establish a connection between the ontological approach and his research on care, and how can this connection be useful for understanding Foucault's philosophical practice? The notion of a "machine" that is oriented to the present and in turn derived from the request for freedom that stems from this present can help us to understand this connection. In order to make it clear, I will first examine the forms by which Foucault clarifies his ontological inquiry and its connection to his previous archaeological and genealogical methods. Second, I will discuss how this inquiry, despite its apparent incoherence, belongs directly to Foucault's coherent philosophical practice. In particular, I will show how this inquiry is at the same time an archaeology of this practice, a liberating attitude oriented toward the present. I will then explore the connections between Foucault's archaeology of care of the self and of others in antiquity and forms of surveillance in modernity, some of which derived from the former. In this sense, I will show how the practice of care establishes a historical struggle between opposite configurations: those that aim at a form of control, and those that aim at a form of an-archic (literally, without *arkhē*) freedom. Finally, I will show that it is the latter that both informed and inspired Foucault's philosophical attitude of care as critical care of the present.

## An Ontological Inquiry

Readers of the later Foucault's work will be familiar with his references to a "historical ontology of ourselves," a "critical ontology of ourselves," an "ontology of modernity," and an "ontology of the present" and "of present reality" (Foucault 1997a: 315 ff.; 2001b: 1506–07; 2010: 21).[2] For those who were familiar with his previous analyses, this shift was rather unexpected. At the beginning of his career, Foucault had responded to phenomenological approaches by developing—through his "archaeo-genealogical enterprise" (Han 1998: 305)—a deep critique of fundamental transcendentalism and ontology.[3] The resurgence of a discourse on "being" thus prompted a fair amount of disquietude. Since the 1990s, Foucault's ontological approach has been explored by specialists with the goal of situating it within (and reconciling it with) his work as a whole. The progression of the publication of his lectures and writings confirms this possibility and provides a new foundation for appreciating the ontological orientation of his works.

Following Foucault's words, it is possible to approach the peculiarity of this ontology as a questioning of the historical conditions through which, as modern people, we say what we say, see what we see, and act as we act (Foucault 1997a: 315; see Revel 2015: 8). As such, Foucault's ontology can be seen as a hidden thread that runs through his previous approaches, and thus as being inextricably connected to them. In other words, as methods, archaeology and genealogy can be considered two different moments of a "historical ontology," a machine that Foucault would ultimately define as a "critical ontology of ourselves" (Foucault 1997a: 315 ff.) and as an "ontology of the present" (Foucault 2010: 21). Let us recall how Foucault described his archaeology in 1974:

> for me archaeology is the following: a historico-political attempt based not on relations of similarity between past and present, but on relations of continuity and on the possibility of defining the tactical aims of strategies of struggle precisely in terms of this.
>
> Foucault 2001a: 1512, *my translation*[4]

Just a few lines below, he adds that archaeology is "a critical machine, a machine that puts into question certain power relations, a machine that has, or that should have, a liberating function" (Foucault 2001a: 1512, *my translation*).[5] In a similar sense, just two years later—in 1976—Foucault describes the relation between the two historical machines of genealogy and archaeology:

> Genealogy would thus, in relation to the project of inscribing knowledges in the hierarchies of power proper to science, be an enterprise of desubjugating historical knowledges and making them free, that is to say, capable of opposing and fighting against the coercion of a unitary, formal and scientific theoretical discourse ... In short: we could perhaps say that archaeology is the method proper to the analysis of local discursivities thus described, and that genealogy is the tactic that makes use, from the discursivities thus described, of the desubjugated knowledges that emerge from them. This, for the entire project.
>
> Foucault 2001b: 167, *my translation*[6]

Archaeological and genealogical mechanics thus define a sort of "integrated" (not alternative) mechanics, playing a crucial role in the possibility of knowing, transforming and intervening in the present. As Foucault himself would later stress, this very mechanics is to be explicated and amplified through the ontological approach clarified in the lectures of the 1980s. The role of this mechanics belongs indeed on the one hand to a proper ontological question—what are we, we who share this historical age?—and on the other hand to a specific task of "modern" philosophy: a task described by Foucault as an ethos, the specific attitude of philosophy as a critical practice inscribed on the great field of philosophical practices opened up by the Enlightenment.

In 1984, commenting on Kant's answer to the question "What is Enlightenment?," Foucault returns to the meaning of this experimental attitude, which was grounded in Kant and which intersected with his own:

> In that sense this criticism is not transcendental, and its goal is not that of making a metaphysics possible: it is genealogical in its design and archaeological in its method. Archaeological—and not transcendental—in the sense that it will not seek to identify the universal structures of all knowledge [*connaissance*] or of all possible moral action, but will seek to treat the instances of discourse that articulate what we think, say, and do as so many historical events. And this critique will be genealogical in the sense that it will not deduce from the form of what we are what it is impossible for us to do and to know; but it will separate out, from the contingency that has made us what we are, the possibility of no longer being, doing, or thinking what we are, do, or think.
>
> Foucault 1997a: 315–16

According to Foucault, this critical attitude equates to a "critical ontology of ourselves" (Foucault 1997a: 315). Thanks to its archaeo-genealogical mechanics, it can be approached as "a patient labor giving form to our impatience for liberty" (Foucault 1997a: 319). Through his insistence on freedom as a main aim of the critical work of modern philosophy—"I solidly believe in human freedom" (Foucault 2001b: 1512, *my translation*),[7] Foucault would state in an interview from 1984—we can thus observe how Foucault's ontological inquiry inherits aspects of previous epistemological approaches: a continuity that reveals the core of his previous research as also aiming to secure the freedom of forms of living in the present (see Oksala 2005: 182 ff.).

## Self-Genealogy and the Present as an Ontological Field

Within this approach, Foucault manages to situate his own archaeological and genealogical research, as well as his own practice, in the field of the present, considered as the proper ontological object of modern philosophy: "What is philosophy today— philosophical activity, I mean—if it is not the critical work that thought brings to bear on itself?" (Foucault 1985: 9). To understand the working principle of the philosophical machine that Foucault would call "ontological" only at the end of his path, it is necessary to approach not just Foucault's "toolbox" but rather his engagement in tirelessly questioning his own practice. What is at stake is the necessity—not available to us prior to the publication of the complete lectures given at the Collège de France—of applying Foucault's own method to himself, of approaching Foucault not only as a historian of this or that practice or notion but as a genealogist and archaeologist of his own philosophical practice: as an ontologist of himself. The practical form of Foucault's ontology seems in this sense to have been implemented in Foucault's self-genealogy as a philosopher.[8]

Drafts of this self-genealogy are present in his texts on the modern attitude in Kant and Baudelaire from 1984 and in his courses on *The Government of Self and Others* (see Foucault 1997a: 303–19; 2001b: 1498–1507; 2010; 2011). Here, Foucault emphasizes that his ontology of the present derives from the critical attention to the present as a main field of modern philosophical practice that was already evident in the work of certain authors, specifically Kant, Hegel, Nietzsche, Weber, Husserl, Heidegger, Horkheimer, and Habermas (see Foucault 1997a: 303; 2001b: 1507; 2010: 11–21). For these authors, what was at stake was a modern *prosokhē* first reserved for the Enlightenment as a field of contemporary critical practices and of philosophy: as a field of our possible experiences (Foucault 2001b: 1506). For Foucault, what is at stake is the specific way in which philosophical modernity came to question the ethos, the attitude, that characterizes the present, or better, the bystanders involved in the present: in other words, the attitude shared by those who live in a specific historical present. The image, and the paradigm, of this ontology of the present is the basis of the question that lies at the heart of Kant's text on Enlightenment, according to Foucault.

"What is Enlightenment?" asks Kant. Or, as Foucault translates this question: what is this present in which we live? How did we come to be what we are? It is within the framework of this genealogical philosophy that Foucault situates his own philosophical attitude, drawing a line of contiguity connecting the different objects that interested him: an ontological question that has as its basic reference the (utterly modern) problem of what we are in this time that is ours, one that is both a critical question and an attitude—an attitude characterizing a time, or at least a line of research into modernity, having as its direction "the constitution of ourselves as autonomous subjects" (Foucault 1997a: 313).

"Genealogical in its design" and "archaeological in its method" (Foucault 1997a: 315–16), this philosophical attitude is characterized as being "experimental," as aiming to give "new impetus, as far and wide as possible, to the undefined work of freedom" (Foucault 1997a: 316). This ontological attitude must "turn away from all projects that claim to be global or radical" and thus seems to be characterized by being addressed to "partial transformations" (Foucault 1997a: 316):

> I shall thus characterize the philosophical ethos appropriate to the critical ontology of ourselves as a historico-practical test of the limits we may go beyond, and thus as work carried out by ourselves upon ourselves as free beings.
> Foucault 1997a: 316

Philosophical modernity consists specifically in this attitude, the genealogy and archaeology of which Foucault is trying to accomplish. What he views as being characteristic of the modern philosophical attitude is also the main characteristic of his own way of acting philosophically. In this sense, Foucault's ontology can be approached as a real ontology of freedom, an ontology that is at the same time an ethos, the practice of which is a critique of what we are, of the boundaries and the possibilities of removal that produce what we are.

In this sense, the progression of Foucault's research on the ancients never lost sight of the present: it is this present that is the subject of observation and critique, and it is this completely modern attitude that pushes him to take an archaeological and genealogical perspective on ancient practices. Like a game of mirrors, the same attitude that characterizes modernity authorizes the discernment of the "care of the self" as an object of investigation: at the same time, this object is a paradigmatic, ungraspable *arkhē* that allows us to understand the form of the present, the philosophical attitude of modernity. While the ontology of the present functions as a critical attitude, it also functions by making its own archaeology and by discovering the key elements of overtaking the orders of discourse that trap the subject in its own present. We can produce ourselves as "free beings" (Foucault 1997a: 316) only by acting as "free beings," facing what produces us: this is what we can discover by facing our present archaeo-genealogically. This ontology is therefore simultaneously a "practical" strength, one that pushes for a kind of conversion. The place of the *arkhē* is contested by the fact that every *arkhē* we discover brings us once again to ourselves and to our freedom: to take care of this freedom—this freedom of our present form of life, a form which is free precisely because it is present—is in this sense the only *an-arkhē*, the principle without principle governing (it seems to me) the Foucauldian ontological machine.

If the "present," or free beings living in the present, is the object of Foucault's ontology, then the latter clearly presents a form of care: care of the present and care of the self and of others who live in this present. Just as this occurs at the level of the individual, to take care of the present is to be willing and able to exercise critical effort. The image of the ancient forms of *parrhēsia* and modern cynicism—connected by a similar trans-historical way of telling and testifying the truth (see e.g. Foucault 2011: 210–11), and *therefore* of taking care, through the truth, of the self and the other—are two images of an attitude that gives form to freedom through a particular philosophical exercise of it. In this sense, an ontology of the present, a critical ontology of ourselves, refers necessarily to that *prosokhē* on the present, on living creatures, that is the core problem of the history of the "care" that Foucault develops contextually. It can thus be interpreted as the peculiar form of care that is developed by modern philosophy in the form of a critical *askēsis*.

It is in this sense that Foucault's ontological approach appears within the project studying the hermeneutics of the subject launched some years before. If we sketch a line from this final point of the Foucauldian path to the point of departure—the investigation into governmentality, into what allows the subject to let itself be governed and to govern itself—it becomes clear that the following history of the "care of the self"—as a history of the techniques for the creation of subjects through an art of self-government—plays a key role. Foucault's investigation into the art of governing others is thus mirrored by the art of the government of the self: in this sense, the hermeneutics of the self is situated at a crossroads. When his research into the government of the self resulted in research into the government of the self and of others, as Foucault entitled his last two lecture courses, his archaeological investigation into this care—the core of this hermeneutics—revealed the emergence of a "care of the self and others."

## Care of the Self, Care of Others

If the ontological work undertaken by ourselves on ourselves can be connected—as a critical form of taking care of the present—with that history of the practices concerning the "care of oneself" to which Foucault devoted himself in the 1980s, specifically from his lecture courses *Subjectivity and Truth* (1980–1) and *The Hermeneutics of the Subject* (1981–2), to *The Courage of Truth* (1983–4), and the third volume of his *History of Sexuality, The Care of the Self* (1984), Foucault's archaeology of the ancient *epimeleia heautou* must be approached as an ontological matter. Furthermore, taking into account the previous focus on the modern forms of "governmentality," and specifically those forms of care that are revealed by modern forms of "pastoral power," we should also verify how this form of "care" as "surveillance," beyond being the testing ground for Foucault's archaeology, is a testing ground for his ontology.

At this point, we must clarify the genealogy of the notion of "care of the self" (*souci de soi*) within Foucault's thought. The notion of "care" related to the self first occurs in Foucault's texts in the presentation—the *résumé*—of the lectures on *Subjectivity and Truth*, 1980–1 (see Foucault 1997b: 88). Interestingly, Foucault approaches his new investigation's path not by leaving behind his previous interests but rather by transforming them. Beginning with the notion of Alcibiades' "souci de soi-même" (*epimeleia heautou*) Foucault undertakes a history of the care of the self, one that is both an "experience" and a "technique elaborating and transforming that experience" (see Foucault 1997b: 88)—thus a history that follows the same characteristics of Foucault's archaeology and genealogy, already influenced by the concept of "technique" and projected onto the following notion of ontology, *as* a critical experience.

As such, this project is connected to, or located at the crossroads between, two previous themes: a "history of subjectivity" and an "analysis of the forms of 'governmentality'" (see Foucault 1997b: 88). To show how this new history is a part of his project of a history of subjectivity, Foucault recalls his works on madness, illness, the effects of discipline on the constitution of the rational and normal subject, and "the modes of objectification" (see Foucault 1997b: 88) of the subject in the fields of knowledge, language, work, and life. At the same time, he clarifies that the proper aim of the great works with which he was involved for the better part of the 1970s is twofold: on the one hand criticism of conceptions of power, and on the other an analysis of power as the field of "strategic relations" (Foucault 1997b: 88). This latter maintains as its object "the behavior of the other or others" and is defined by the study of institutional fields, social groups, and "different procedures and techniques" (see Foucault 1997b: 88):

> The history of the "care" and "techniques" of the self would thus be a way of doing the history of subjectivity: no longer, however, through the divisions between the mad and the nonmad, the sick and nonsick, delinquents and nondelinquents, nor through the constitution of fields of scientific objectivity giving a place to the living, speaking, laboring subject; but, rather, through the putting in place, and the transformations in our culture, of "relations with oneself," with their technical armature and knowledge effects. And in this way one could take up the question of

governmentality from a different angle: the government of the self by oneself in its articulation with relations with others.

Foucault 1997b: 88

Therefore, the project described above evolves into an in-depth analysis of Foucault's previous projects, particularly his studies on the notion of "governmentality:" a notion which, able "to cover the whole range of practices that constitute, define, organize, and instrumentalize the strategies that individuals in their freedom can use in dealing with each other" (see Foucault 1997d: 300), had already been considered in a text focused on the "technologies of the self" (1982) as "this encounter between the technologies of domination of others and those of the self" (Foucault 1997c: 225).[9]

What appears with the study of the "care of the self" is therefore a further problematization of governmentality: a history of those technologies of the self used by Western subjects to elaborate knowledge of themselves. It is this aim that characterizes twenty-five years of Foucault's research: a history of the forms by which the truth about the subject and the subject of truth were developed, a history of the technologies of self-government and self-emancipation related to truth. This form of "care" is therefore the macro field on which we find these technologies.

At the very beginning of his lecture course *Subjectivity and Truth*, Foucault explains how the two components of the history of subjectivity and of governmentality are related. If the "subject" and the "truth" appear in themselves as empty notions, the real objects of examination are technologies that connect and create them (see Foucault 2017: 10): "What relationship does the subject have to himself when this relationship can or must pass through the promised or imposed discovery of the truth about himself?" (Foucault 2017: 10–11). Finally, Foucault identifies the following problem, on which the developments to come would be focused:

> In what ways is our experience of ourselves formed or transformed by the fact that somewhere in our society there are discourses considered to be true, which circulate and are imposed as true, based on ourselves as subjects?
> Foucault 2017: 12

With this "double-dipping" of the philosophical machine, the problematization of truth, as well as the problematization of subjectivity, belong to the history of the care of the self. The technologies of truth thus belong to the technologies of care: the forms that Foucault would later study within the political and ethical paradigm of *parrhēsia*, of confession, of witnessing truth, would turn out to be merely different perspectives on taking care—and thus establishing subjectivities—through the truth.

On the other hand, it would not be accurate to say that the problem of care—religious and then political—appears in Foucault only as a technology of the self. In turn, governmentality as a crossroad notion derives in Foucault's work directly from his problematization of power as power over life—as bio-power: as the power of taking care, and therefore governing, life. In fact, just a few years before his lecture course *The Hermeneutics of the Subject*, which focused on the practices of the care of the self, Foucault was still working on a "critique of political reason" (Foucault 2002: 298). In the lectures of this period and in a text titled *Omnes et singulatim* ("all and everyone"), Foucault also focused on an investigation into the theme of pastoral power, or the "pastoral technologies" that are applied by the modern state to rationalize its power (see Foucault 2002: 298–325). This form of power, which coincided with the form of the "enlightened" state—Frederick the Great's Prussia or pre- and post-revolutionary France—is a form that exercises itself in a new way and thus creates, through the development of its technologies, a new notion of sovereignty. It is a power that applies much more to the populations that inhabit a given territory than to that territory itself. In this way, what is at stake is more a "population state" than a state defined by land and borders: the sovereign exercises his or her sovereignty as a form of control and protection of individuals, and at the same time as a way of directing the population as a whole. He or she seeks to be legitimated as the chief of a family, as the one who takes care of their family. Therefore, with an inversion of perspective that secularizes and legitimates the state, modern power is born not through a divine sign but rather as a consequence of the "economic" attention given by the sovereign to his subjects. This new kind of state, recognized by Foucault as the direct antecedent of the "providence state," known in Europe after World War II as the "welfare state," is a state in which police science (*Polizeiwissenschaft*), as a form of control, surveillance, and protection of society, gives a form to its subjects.

Can this form of government of others be thought of as a form of "care"? It can be perceived in this way if we consider that this form of power—or art of government—is, as Foucault clarifies, inherited from the Christian theologico-political tradition, which is in turn derived on the one hand from the Hebraic tradition and on the other from the Greeks.

Two characteristics of this form of power are surveillance—pastorship as a power that never ceases to keep vigil over the herd, the "all"—and the practice of confession. Foucault's archaeology of this power recovers "a very strange phenomenon in Greco-Roman civilization, that is, the organization of a link between total obedience, knowledge of oneself, and confession to someone else" (Foucault 2002: 310). In this sense, it is an individualizing power characterized by the personal responsibility of the individual confronting that power:

> [the shepherd] pays attention to them all and scans each one of them. He's got to know his flock as a whole, and in detail. Not only must he know where good pastures are, the season's laws, and the order of things; he must also know each one's particular needs
>
> Foucault 2002: 303

These two practices (surveillance and confession) stress the persistence of a single movement within Foucault's archaeology and reveal how governmentality and the history of the subject are connected. In particular, what Foucault maintains as a point of reference is the intersection between the definition of the field of subjectivity concerning truth, on the one hand, and understanding the rules of conduct through which a subject can have access to its truth and can establish itself as a subject of truth, on the other.

Having left behind his research on the "care of others" (which was at stake in pastoral power), and having approached the individual as a key problem of governmentality, in the first lecture of his course on *The Hermeneutics of the Subject* (identifying the care of the self and the relation of self with oneself as the core of this hermeneutics), Foucault writes:

> the *epimeleia heautou* is an attitude towards the self, others, and the world ... the *epimeleia heautou* is also a certain form of attention, of looking. Being concerned about oneself implies that we look away from the outside to ... I was going to say "inside." Let's leave to one side this word, which you can well imagine raises a host of problems, and just say that we must convert our looking from the outside, from others and the world etc., towards "oneself." The care of the self implies a certain way of attending to what we think and what takes place in our thought. The word *epimeleia* is related to *melete*, which means both exercise and meditation.
>
> Foucault 2005: 10–11

As a form of "attending," the *epimeleia heautou* reveals its proximity to ancient pastorship, a pastorship now turned to the self, we might say. As Foucault clarifies, the care of the self is thus born as a conversion from looking from the "outside" to looking within oneself, although the technique—the "attending," the "taking care"—is quite similar. In this sense, I would affirm that the history of "care" coincides with a true archaeology of the gaze.

The passage from research into the care characteristic of modernity to the care characteristic of antiquity follows the passage from the care of "others" to the care of the self. It would not be long until, in his research on the government of self and others, Foucault would recover the relation between these two poles through a new form of care: indeed, the critical approach to the present through a "critical ontology of ourselves" (Foucault 1997a: 315 ff.), the distant ancestor of which is the philosopher-parrhesiast, giving form to his and others' lives through his courage to tell the truth (see Foucault 2010: 350).

## The Coherence of Incoherence

Foucault's archaeological mechanics functions as a recovery of "gazes" and "turning points" that can be used to develop a critique of the present gaze, to develop a contradiction within the folds of the present. As stressed above, Foucault's investigation into the care of the self was born and developed as an evolution of the project on governmentality. This approach sheds light on a partial answer to the question at the heart of the debate that arose between the publication of the first volume of *The History of Sexuality* in 1976 and the last two volumes in 1984 (thus before the publication of the last courses and many years before the recent publication of the fourth volume, previously projected to be the second one, *Les aveux de la chair* [*The Confessions of the Flesh*]): the question of why, within an ostensibly unified project, Foucault decided to close the first volume by speaking of biopolitics and dedicated the last two to the use of pleasure and the care of the self.¹⁰ In other words, it seems that we find internal coherence along the path connecting, on the one hand, the *mise en forme* of the relation between subjectivity and truth in the first course from the 1980s and the last two courses on *The Government of Self and Others* and, on the other, the problem of the development of his investigation into *parrhēsia* in *The Courage of Truth*—a coherence which can be exemplified by the integration of archaeology and genealogy as historical forms of ontology, by the theoretical passage from governmentality to the hermeneutics of the subject, and finally, by the research into care, first as a form of surveillance, then as a technology of the self, and finally as a critical ontology of the present.

There are two main consequences of this: on the one hand, it would be wrong to speak simply of an "ethical turning" away from Foucault's more political interests of the 1970s. On the other hand, what is at stake here are the notions of *politics* and *ethics*—or at least the two notions of *ethics* and *politics* the modern tradition of which is thought to have been directly inherited from the ancients (cf. Lefebvre 2016).

As happens in the case of the long archaeology of the notion of *parrhēsia*—this same notion appears in both fields, politics and ethics (see e.g. Foucault 2011: 38, 65)— to approach current processes, and finally to arrive at an ontology of subjectivity, is precisely to transform the order of the discourse by placing apparently distant notions at its center. If we wish to interrogate what is at stake in the ways in which politics represents itself and to analyze the relation between its discursive field and what it makes of us, the task is not to recover the political philosophy *strictu sensu* but to recover forms that have yet to be investigated by that tradition. Archaeology is called on to enable the emergence of traces, remains, that allow us to approach with greater certainty the dark side of the moon with regard to the traditions into which we are plunged. The fields of the care and the government of the self are more open, for Foucault, epistemologically and ontologically, than other notions: fields that allow us to delve further into what those notions can still tell us. It is necessary to abandon the notions and horizons that in some sense created us, to understand what we really are.

As Deleuze revealed in a text dedicated to Foucault, the creative element of this practice is identical to its ontological character: it creates *because* it is a critical ontology. It is an *ethopoïetic* technique (see Tallane 2014: 123). In this sense, whereas Deleuze approaches philosophy as a creation of conceptual characters, in Foucault the place of characters is occupied by practices: in other words, the form by which Foucault recovers a paradigm, or a notion, of ancient traditions must be seen as a creation, as a distillation of models and practices.¹¹ The relevance of the archaeological recovery of the *epimeleia heautou* is similar to a true invention of a concept, or perhaps to another attribute of archaeology: that of re-"inventing" or re-"creating" concepts by recovering them in the past, with the aim of connecting remains and traces that cannot be explained in isolation. To give a name to these traces, by recovering them from the past, is itself to modify our paradigmatic horizon, to open another horizon on which they can make sense, and to achieve a meaning that is able to reorganize the discursive order and paradigms into which we are plunged.

What we see in action in Foucault's approach to the care of the self is thus this divergent correspondence between these two perspectives: as if the object of Foucault's research, born in relation to the present, were pushing to give life to a methodological field in which it can have meaning. As a follower of Nietzsche, Foucault's aim was never to achieve abstract scientific neutrality but rather to allow the importance and necessity of the object of his research to come to light.[12]

## The Care of the Present as a Philosophical Task

In Foucault's archaeology of the gaze, the gaze seems to produce its own expression, its own object. The care of the self and of others, the care of the present as a critical ontology of ourselves, thus appears as a practical concept with which we can identify Foucault's critical ontology, his ontology of the present. Some of the ancient technologies of taking care of the self and of ourselves are in this sense paradigmatic, pre-empting figures of the philosophical ethos that would be described by Foucault as a "critical ontology of ourselves."

We can only discover this by applying an archaeological gaze to this attitude: only in this way can we discover how our philosophical attitudes really work, how the concepts and practices that we embody as creatures of modernity, as creatures living in this time and not another, really function. It is within the critique of oneself that the modern agent encounters, in his or her time, an ethos that is equivalent to the ancient *ēthos*.

A critical ontology of the present, archaeo-genealogically examining ancient practices, concerns, for instance, a precise configuration of the relation with time. In this sense, in *The Hermeneutics of the Subject*, we can verify how, almost superficially, Foucault approaches the theme of salvation as a peculiar form of care concerning time. In turn, the theological horizon of salvation is the ancient derivation of the self-finalization that the subject makes of himself through the practice of the care of the self. Salvation, as a form of care of the self, is also a form of care of others. Foucault identifies the notion of salvation as an "operator," one that brings us—at least to a certain point, at which we must continue on our own—to the dimension of the "time of salvation" of the Christian Age. As a technology of government, Christian "care," from which pastoral power would develop in the modern era, also entails a particular, highly consequential relation between the form of being and the form of time.

Let us consider this in more depth. Among the practices of the care of the self, we can stress the direction of consciousness: in the same age in which the direction of consciousness acquires Christian features by leaving to the side its Stoical elements, the pastoral paradigm enters politics as a paradigm of salvation. Surveillance by bishop-shepherds, which replaces surveillance by Christ, the shepherd of all mankind, establishes Christian society as a society waiting for the Second—and increasingly distant—Coming of Christ. In *Omnes et singulatim*, Foucault does not stress this point, but we can underscore how both the development of the political relation *omnes/singulatim* and the form of the direction of Christian consciousness are the distant, parallel traces that secularized modernity would apply in different forms.

The recovery of this ancient moment, in which the "care of the self" becomes a "care of others," traces the development of a technology of time, based on the time of salvation. The time of Christian salvation, as well as the form of the historical time of modernity, opens to a dimension that was completely unknown to the ancient world—that of the time of waiting, of delay. The characteristics identified by Foucault in this notion are therefore twofold: on the one hand, the figure of a boundary, of a crossing through, on the other, the figure of a dramatic event, cutting through time. Nevertheless, according to Foucault these are characteristics that prove that certain ancient religious elements remain present in current, seemingly secular ways of looking at things and that they raise difficulties for understanding the notion of salvation in different terms, such as those of antiquity.

Foucault's archaeological recovery proves, indeed, that seeking safety has a different connotation in the Stoic form of the "care of the self." What is certain is that "the person saved is the person in a state of alert, in a state of resistance and of mastery and sovereignty over the self, enabling him to repel every attack and assault" (Foucault 2005: 184): "Salvation then is an activity, the subject's constant action on himself, which finds its reward in a certain relationship of the subject to himself . . ." (Foucault 2005: 184). Salvation is an agent of the subject itself.

What the archaeology of practices of the care of the self reveals is precisely that the key moment of these practices lies in the transformation of the practices of salvation. The *bios*, life as the way in which the world presents itself to us within our existence, begins to be considered, at a certain moment in antiquity, as an object of transformation: a test object, an object of experimentation, the place in which we can give form to ourselves, an exercise of the self. Here it is possible to encounter what Foucault viewed as the dare at the heart of philosophy, as a "discourse and tradition" (Foucault 2005: 487): the dare of questioning the place in which "the truth of the subject we are" (Foucault 2005: 487) is expressed, and at the same time the dare of situating the world, as the place where one experiments on oneself as an "ethical subject of the truth" (Foucault 2005: 463). In this sense, writes Foucault, Hegel's *Phenomenology of Mind* is the summit of this philosophy, in which it is asked how "a subject of knowledge (*connaissance*) which takes the world as object through a *tekhnē*, and a subject of self-experience which takes this same world, but in the radically different form of the place of its test," can exist (Foucault 2005: 487).

Thus, the long path of the care of the self leads, in Foucault's archaeology, to a place where, by recovering an attitude of pre-Christian salvation, prior to Christian forms of surveillance, such as Stoic nightwatching, an overtaking of modernity as the last territory still placed within a structure of discursive self-legitimacy typical of the Christian era is authorized. At the same time, the same archaeology recovers for the present the ancient attitude of "salvation," which is completely the opposite of the Christian notion of salvation.

It is here, perhaps, that we encounter a crucial meaning of the "critical ontology of ourselves" (Foucault 1997a: 315 ff.), in the form of an ontological machine of "care" detached from the historical machines of metaphysics. This ontological machine opens anew to an unknown threshold of a time that can be understood and that transforms itself within the *ēthos* of the "present people:" people who share a time and the possibility of confronting the world through how they live their truth, of the many who construct this present, in the same way they take care of it, of themselves, and of their words. By recovering the ancient meaning of salvation as a critical care of the present itself, one that for this reason belongs to the history of care, Foucault's ontology of the present is therefore an engine that seeks to move away from the practices of "salvation" that characterized the Christian era, that seeks to move away from the care of a time of delay, to a time concerning the present reality and its "free beings."[13] It refers to care of a present that can only take care of itself.

At this point, what we are facing seems to be a philosophical *machina*, something slightly more complex than what is usually considered to be Foucault's ontological approach. Whereas Han spoke of Foucault's "missed ontology," what we seem to have here is quite the opposite. What was interpreted as a sort of ontological "lack," also due to Foucault's unexpected death, seems to be part of this machine, and indeed its main engine. An ontology that turns on "free beings" (Foucault 1997a: 316) must be a practical attitude that acts as if from a void. As an ontological, archaeo-genealogical, critical machine that stands in contrast to other ontological horizons of the twentieth century, and above all phenomenology—the "subject" does not appear again, not even as a sign—it is an ontology that has as its object its own practices, and thus itself: an ontology of transformation, of overcoming boundaries, and of the unfounded.

Whereas the influence of Heidegger's approach to the question of care as a main question of Western thought is clear in this context, at the same time the an-archic mechanics of Foucault's ontology establishes an answer that is directly connected to Foucault's notion of freedom.[14] In *Being and Time*, Heidegger observed that the expression "care for oneself," following the analogy of taking care and concern, "would be a tautology"—this, because his notion of care "cannot mean a special attitude toward the self" (Heidegger 1996: 180).

> The characterization of care as "being-ahead-of-itself-in-already-being-in"—as being-together-with—makes it clear that this phenomenon, too, is yet structurally *articulated* in itself. But is that not a phenomenal indication that the ontological question must be pursued still further until we can set forth a *still more primordial* phenomenon which ontologically supports the unity and totality of the structural manifold of care?
>
> Heidegger 1996: 183

As an ontological approach, and as a form of "care of the present," Foucault's archaeology does not need to set forth a "*still more primordial* phenomenon"—this, because it finds that the attitude described by the *epimeleia* implies an *ēthos*. Foucault's care is not simply, in this sense, an attribute that tautologically enters into relation with the self but rather precisely what establishes freedom as an ethical ontology. That is, it establishes that freedom requires reflection in order to be a form of ethics: "Freedom is the ontological condition of ethics. But ethics is the considered form that freedom takes when it is informed by reflection" (Foucault 1997d: 284). As with Foucault's use of the "self," the "present" is not something that *needs* care on his view, as if it were something separate from care (see Smith 2015: 137). "Care of the self" is necessarily tautological, as is "care of the present." No practice of the present is possible, ethically or politically, without care, and no care is possible, abstractly, without being plunged in the present. This tautology—the core of Foucault's an-archic ontological machine—is necessary if the aim, in contrast to Heidegger's notion (and according, for instance, to Pareyson's ontology of freedom)[15] is to give form to freedom as a "conscious [*réfléchie*]" (Foucault 1997d: 284) practice performed by people living together in the present.

## Notes

1. This article was written with the financial support of FCT (Fundação para a Ciência e a Tecnologia).
2. On the meaning of "present" (*présent*) and "present reality" (*actualité*), see Revel (2002: 5–6). For an overview of the topic, see Revel (2003), Erozan (2006), Ong-Van-Cung (2013), Raffnsøe, Gudman-Høyer, and Thaning (2016: 455–65).
3. "I would try to take my distance from phenomenology, which was my point of departure. I do not believe in a kind of founding act whereby reason, in its essence, was discovered or established and from which it was subsequently diverted by such-and-such an event. I think, in fact, that reason is self-created, which is why I have tried to analyze forms of rationality: different foundations, different creations, different modifications in which rationalities engender one another, oppose and pursue one another" (Foucault 1998: 442–3).
4. In the original: "Pour moi, l'archéologie, c'est ça: une tentative historico-politique qui ne se fonde pas sur des relations de ressemblance entre le passé et le présent, mais plutôt sur des relations de continuité et sur la possibilité de définir actuellement des objectifs tactiques de stratégies de lutte, précisément en fonction de cela."
5. In the original: "Une machine critique, une machine qui remet en question certaines relations de pouvoir, une machine qui a, ou du moins devrait avoir, une fonction libératrice."
6. In the original: "La généalogie, ce serait donc, par rapport au projet d'une inscription des savoirs dans la hiérarchie du pouvoir propre à la science, une sorte d'entreprise pour désassujettir les savoirs historiques et les rendre libres, c'est-à-dire capables d'opposition et de lutte contre la coercition d'un discours théorique unitaire, formel et scientifique. . . . En deux mots: on pourrait peut-être dire que l'archéologie, ce serait la méthode propre à l'analyse des discursivités locales, et la généalogie, la tactique qui fait jouer à partir des discursivités locales ainsi décrites les savoirs désassujettis qui s'en dégagent. Cela, pour restituer le projet d'ensemble."
7. In the original: "Je crois solidement à la liberté humaine."
8. "Whenever I have tried to carry out a piece of theoretical work, it has been on the basis of my own experience, always in relation to processes I saw taking place around me. It is because I thought I could recognize in the things I saw, in the institutions with which I dealt, in my relations with others, cracks, silent shocks, malfunctionings … that I undertook a particular piece of work, a few fragments of autobiography" (Foucault 1990a: 156). See Eribon (1991: 27–30). For the characterization of Foucault's philosophical practice as "self-modification" and *askēsis* concerning the present, see McGushin (2007: 285), Iftode (2013: 77), Raffnsøe, Thaning and Gudman-Høyer (2018: 12).
9. In this same text, he expresses regret at having focused on techniques of domination and power rather than techniques of self-government and interaction. See Foucault (2016: 26): "having studied the field of government by taking as my point of departure

techniques of domination, I would like in years to come to study government—especially in the field of sexuality—starting from the techniques of the self."

10  For many years, philosophical criticism attempted to grasp the meaning of the Foucauldian turn of the 1980s (see Elden 2017: 205). Further support for my hypothesis regarding the coherent consequentiality of Foucauldian research is provided by the text *Les aveux de la chair* [*Confessions of the Flesh*]. As Gros observes, when Foucault published *The Will to Knowledge* in 1976, he was already refining the connection between confession and Christianity on the basis of his reflections on Christian and modern forms of pastorates, particularly referring to the late Middle Ages and the roots of the Counter-Reformation's rules concerning concupiscence and the direction of conscience. These studies, which were meant to culminate in a book titled *La chair et le corps* [*The Flesh and the Body*], were abandoned in favor of a study focused on the technologies of Early Christianity, a topic of his posthumous book, the publication of which was delayed by Foucault's interest in undertaking his genealogy of antiquity (Foucault 2018: i–xi).

11  I am referring to Deleuze and Guattari's notion of "conceptual personae" (see Deleuze and Guattari 1994: 61–83). Deleuze's interpretation of Foucault follows this approach by making Foucault himself—as he had done in the case of other philosophers—another "conceptual persona" (see Deleuze 1988). Speaking of his archaeological machine, Foucault recalls Deleuze's definition of him as a "poet" (Foucault 2001a: 1512; see Deleuze 1988: 18).

12  In this sense, "a diagnosis of the present is to regain its incontemporaneity" (Raffnsøe, Gudman-Høyer, and Thaning 2016: 465). See also Ong-Van-Cung (2013: 335).

13  A similar necessity is required concerning the recovery of the ancient philosophical care of the self in contrast to the Christian one. Whereas the problem of Western culture was "the positive foundation for the technologies of the self," "[m]aybe our problem is now to discover that the self is nothing else than the historical correlation of the technology built in our history. Maybe the problem is to change those technologies. And in this case, one of the main political problems would be nowadays, in the strict sense of the word, the politics of ourselves" (Foucault 2016: 76). The care of time as an evening-like time, the time between the "not yet" and the "already now," is at the center of Foucault's review of Roger Laporte's novel *La Veille*, from 1963 (Foucault 2015). See Raffnsøe, Thaning, and Gudman-Høyer (2018: 15–18). On this theme, it is also worth mentioning the letter to Rolf Italiaander "Veilleur de la nuit des hommes" (Foucault 2001a: 257–61).

14  In his last interview, Foucault clarifies the crucial role of Heidegger's readings in his thought. See Foucault (1990b: 250). Han identifies the common Kantian origin of phenomenology and Foucault's archaeology. On the "historical ontology of ourselves" projected by Foucault, Han asks whether the hermeneutical ontology is a "more coherent foundation," arguing that the Heideggerian ontology can be read as the *unthought* of Foucault's work (Han 1998: 27). On Heidegger's influence on Foucault, see Han (1998: 305–21), Elden (2002), Rayner (2007), and Milchman and Rosenberg (2013). For a recent, useful approach to the parallelism between the two authors, see Nichols (2014).

15  "Freedom is done; but it is done indeed as freedom. The act by which freedom is done, that is, begins to be, cannot be configured differently from an act by which freedom begins by itself, is initiative" (Pareyson 2000: 16). On freedom as "operational concept," see also Oksala (2005: 208–10).

# References

Deleuze, G. (1988), *Foucault*, trans. S. Hand, Minneapolis and London: University of Minnesota Press.

Deleuze, G. and F. Guattari (1994), *What is Philosophy?*, trans. H. Tomlison and G. Burchell, New York: Columbia University Press.

Elden, S. (2002), *Mapping the Present: Heidegger, Foucault and the Project of a Spatial History*, London and New York: Continuum.

Elden, S. (2017), *Foucault's Last Decade*, Cambridge: Polity Press.

Eribon, D. (1991), *Michel Foucault*, trans. B. Wing, Cambridge, MA: Harvard University Press.

Erozan, B. (2006), "Reflections on Foucault's Concept of Critical Ontology", *Boğaziçi Journal*, 20 (1–2): 115–25.

Foucault, M. (1985), *The Use of Pleasure: Volume 2 of The History of Sexuality*, trans. R. Hurley, New York: Pantheon Books.

Foucault, M. (1986), *The Care of the Self: Volume 3 of The History of Sexuality*, trans. R. Hurley, New York: Pantheon Books.

Foucault, M. (1990a), "Practicing Criticism," in D. Kritzman (ed.), *Politics, Philosophy, Culture. Interviews and Other Writings, 1977–1984*, 152–6, London: Routledge.

Foucault, M. (1990b), "The Return of Morality," in D. Kritzman (ed.), *Politics, Philosophy, Culture. Interviews and Other Writings, 1977–1984*, 242–54, London: Routledge.

Foucault, M. (1997a), "What is Enlightenment?," in P. Rabinow (ed.), *Ethics, Subjectivity and Truth: The Essential Works of Michel Foucault 1954–1984, Vol. 1*, 303–19, New York: The New Press.

Foucault, M. (1997b), "Subjectivity and Truth," in P. Rabinow (ed.), *Ethics, Subjectivity and Truth: The Essential Works of Michel Foucault 1954–1984, Vol. 1*, 87–92, New York: The New Press.

Foucault, M. (1997c), "The Technology of the Self," in P. Rabinow (ed.), *The Essential Works of Michel Foucault, 1954–1984, Vol. 1: Ethics. Subjectivity and Truth*, 223–51, New York: The New Press.

Foucault, M. (1997d), "The Ethics of the Concern of the Self as a Practice of Freedom," in P. Rabinow (ed.), *The Essential Works of Michel Foucault, 1954–1984, Vol. 1: Ethics. Subjectivity and Truth*, 281–301, New York: The New Press.

Foucault, M. (1998), "Structuralism and Post-structuralism," in J. Faubion (ed.), *The Essential Works of Michel Foucault, 1954–1984, Vol. 2: Aesthetics, Method, and Epistemology*, 433–458, New York: The New Press.

Foucault, M. (2001a), *Dits et écrits I* (1954–1975), Paris: Gallimard.

Foucault, M. (2001b), *Dits et écrits II* (1976–1984), Paris: Gallimard.

Foucault, M. (2002), "Omnes et Singulatim: Towards a Critique of Governmental Reason," in J. D. Faubion (ed.), *The Essential Works of Michel Foucault, 1954–1984, Vol. 3: Power*, 298–325, New York: The New Press.

Foucault, M. (2005), *The Hermeneutics of the Subject: Lectures at the Collège de France 1981–1982*, ed. F. Gros, trans. G. Burchell, New York: Palgrave Macmillan.

Foucault, M. (2010), *The Government of Self and Others: Lectures at the Collège de France, 1982–1983*, ed. F. Gros, trans. G. Burchell, Basingstoke: Palgrave Macmillan.

Foucault, M. (2011), *The Courage of Truth (The Government of Self and Others II): Lectures at the Collège de France 1983–1984*, ed. F. Gros, trans. G. Burchell, Basingstoke: Palgrave Macmillan.

Foucault, M. (2015), "Standing Vigil for the Day to Come," trans. E. Woodard and R. Harvey, *Foucault Studies* 19 (1): 217–23.

Foucault, M. (2016), *About the Beginning of the Hermeneutics of the Self: Lectures at Dartmouth College, 1980*, ed. H.-P. Fruchaud and D. Lorenzini, trans. G. Burchell, Chicago: The University of Chicago Press.

Foucault, M. (2017), *Subjectivity and Truth: Lectures at the Collège de France, 1980–1981*, ed. F. Gros, trans. G. Burchell, Basingstoke: Palgrave Macmillan.

Foucault, M. (2018), *Histoire de la sexualité 4: Les aveux de la chair*, Paris: Gallimard.

Han, B. (1998), *L'ontologie manquée de Michel Foucault*, Grenoble: Millon.

Heidegger, M. (1996), *Being and Time*, trans. J. Stambaugh, Albany, NY: State University of New York Press.

Iftode, C. (2013), "Foucault's Idea of Philosophy as 'Care of the Self:' Critical Assessment and Conflicting Metaphilosophical Views," *Procedia*, 71: 76–85.

Lefebvre, A. (2016), *The End of a Line: Care of the Self in Modern Political Thought, Genealogy* 1 (2): 1–14.

McGushin, E. (2007), *Foucault's Askēsis. An Introduction to the Philosophical Life*, Evanston: Northwestern University Press.

Milchman, A. and A. Rosenberg, eds (2013), *Foucault and Heidegger: Critical Encounters*, Minneapolis and London: University of Minnesota Press.

Nichols, R. (2014), *The World of Freedom. Heidegger, Foucault and the Politics of Historical Ontology*, Stanford, CA: Stanford University Press.

Ong-Van-Cung, K. S. (2013), "Histoire et expérience. Foucault et l'ontologie historique de nous-mêmes," in D. Boquet, B. Dufal, and P. Labey (eds), *Une histoire au présent. Les historiens et Michel Foucault*, 333–52, Paris: CNRS.

Oksala, J., (2005), *Foucault on Freedom*, New York: Cambridge University Press.

Pareyson, L. (2000), *Ontologia della libertà. Il male e la sofferenza*, Turin: Einaudi.

Raffnsøe, S., M. Gudman-Høyer, and M. S. Thaning, (2016), *Michel Foucault: A Research Companion*, Basingstoke: Palgrave Macmillan.

Raffnsøe, S., M. Thaning, and M. Gudman-Høyer, (2018), "Foucault and Philosophical Practice," *Foucault Studies*, 25: 8–54.

Rayner, T. (2007), *Foucault's Heidegger: Philosophy and Transformative Experience*, London: Continuum.

Revel, J. (2002), *Le vocabulaire de Foucault*, Paris: Ellipses.

Revel, J. (2003), *Michel Foucault. Un'ontologia dell'attualità*, Cosenza: Rubbettino.

Revel, J. (2015), *Foucault avec Merleau-Ponty. Ontologie politique, présentisme et histoire*, Paris: Vrin.

Smith, D. (2015), "Foucault on Ethics and Subjectivity: 'Care of the Self' and 'Aesthetics of Existence'," *Foucault Studies*, 19: 135–50.

Tallane, J. (2014), "Pour une autre conversion: la spiritualité antique et l'ontologie critique de nous mêmes à partir des derniers cours de Michel Foucault," *Encyclo. Revue de l'ecole doctorale ED 382*, Université Sorbonne Paris Cité: 111–125.

8

# Agonistic Truth:
# The Issue of Power Between the Will to Knowledge and Government by Truth

Antonio Moretti

The publication of *The Use of Pleasure* and *The Care of the Self*, which respectively make up the second and third volumes of the *History of Sexuality*,[1] was upsetting to a considerable number of Foucauldian scholars. Having anticipated an extension of the genealogical inquiry into the *dispositive of sexuality* (*dispositif de sexualité*) introduced in *The Will to Knowledge*, they were instead faced with a sudden and unforeseen account of the *use of pleasure* and the *care of the self* in the ancient Greek, Hellenistic, and Roman philosophy. The sudden death of Michel Foucault left many unanswered questions regarding this shift. What impact did this change of focus from modern Europe to antiquity have on the general coherence of the entire project? Foucault's two previous books, *Discipline and Punish* and *The Will to Knowledge*, had established a precise albeit *in-progress* framework: was the shift from the political analysis of disciplinary societies and nascent biopolitical examinations of the techniques of bodies and populations towards a more *ethical* and *self-focused* approach to be understood as a dismissal, a withdrawal from the political struggles that Foucault had previously embodied, and fostered? These difficulties helped to establish among the readers a general feeling of disconnection between the first and the following two volumes, which led to philosophical and conceptual disappointment: the recognition of an alleged (and oft-quoted) *ethical* or *ancient turn* in Foucault's thought.

In 2008, the Italian philosopher and epistemologist of psychiatry Mario Galzigna edited a collection of essays titled *Foucault, oggi* [*Foucault, today*], which provided an overall glimpse of the state of the art on the political and cultural reception of Foucault almost twenty-five years after his death. Among the contributors, Mario Vegetti, a well-known historian of ancient philosophy, voiced his concern regarding the "turn" in Foucault's trajectory in the light of the publication of *The Hermeneutics of the Subject* (Foucault 2005). Vegetti maintained that what he called "the 1980 turn" (Vegetti 2008: 150–62) left a deep sense of sorrow in every scholar interested in studying ancient philosophy according to Foucault's archaeological and genealogical method, precisely due to the extensive changes undergone by that methodology. Furthermore, he not only *reproached* Foucault for the betrayal of the method but insisted that the *results of* and *reasons for* the alleged ancient turn should be disapproved of as well. In his view, not only had Foucault selected his source material through the extremely narrow lens of the "care of the self," leaving many notable elements of ancient philosophy out of his consideration, but—even in this specific field—Vegetti could not make sense of the arbitrary exclusion of Plato's *Republic*, the quintessential locus of the theory of the soul and its relation to politics. Moreover, Aristotle was apparently nowhere to be found in Foucault's account:

> Basically, the entirety of Aristotle and the Aristotelian tradition was left to the side. This omission allowed Foucault to hold modernity responsible for the scission between ethics and truth—between the construction of the moral subject and access to knowledge—which is instead clearly rooted in Aristotelianism. This also allowed him to portray "the whole of ancient thought" as "a long movement from memory to meditation."
>
> Vegetti 2008: 150–55, quoting Foucault 2005: 460

Vegetti's accusation is clear: in his attempt to study antiquity, Foucault violated the assumptions of both archaeology and genealogy. His critique relies on the concepts of *archaeology* and *genealogy* elaborated by Foucault during the 1960s and early 70s, such as in *The Order of Things*, *The Archaeology of Knowledge*, and in the essay "Nietzsche, Genealogy, History," before Foucault tied his historical project to an overall critical enterprise defined as *historical ontology of ourselves*, as he affirmed in 1980 (Foucault 1997b). In *The Archaeology of Knowledge*, however, Foucault underscored different aspects of archaeology as a method, namely that systems of thought and knowledge (epistemes or discursive formations, in Foucault's terminology) are governed by rules operating beyond (or beneath) the level of consciousness, a level that bypasses and comprehends individual subjects' intentionality. These rules define a field of conceptual possibility in a given domain and period. Therefore, archaeology allowed Foucault to put forth a practice of historiography that displaced the relevance of the usual objects of history (the *books*, the *authors*), in favor of the bureaucratic, material level of what *has been said*, the *archive*. Likewise, Foucault elaborated the concept of genealogy evoking Nietzsche's genealogy of morals, aiming to contrast the multifaceted, trivial, and inglorious origins of historical objects with the presumption of a linear grand scheme suggested by progressive history. Genealogical analyses aim to show that any given system of thought is grounded in the struggle between multiple forces acting throughout history—and is therefore contingent (let alone inevitable). Compared to these previous statements and methodology, Vegetti maintains that Foucault, in his inquiry into antiquity, overlooked the bureaucratic, impersonal, and *archive-oriented* approach and instead faced authors in their subjective intentionality. Therefore, stating that "from Plato to Saint Augustine there was this movement from memory to meditation" (Foucault 2005: 461), he took historical continuity for granted, dismissing the methodological rule of structural discontinuity between systems of speech and the corresponding systems of power. Despite acknowledging the impossibility of bringing to life an "ancient" version of *History of Madness* (Foucault 2006a) or *Pierre Rivière* (Foucault 1982) due to a lack of the same type of archive material, Vegetti underlines the extent to which Foucault overlooked the huge amount of material that Roman law and ancient medicine (in its interactions with the justice system) could have provided him as part of a proper genealogical and archaeological study.

However, it will become increasingly difficult to thoughtlessly accept the *topos* of an "ancient turn:" it is becoming increasingly clear that this interpretation suffers from a sort of *teleological* bias (as it consistently treats the last years of Foucault's research as the completion, the fulfilment, of a path we must make sense of). Nevertheless, this idea is far from having disappeared, and remains a key topic in school textbooks, for instance.

In fact, we are currently facing an utterly different perspective, one that led the French sociologist and Foucault's biographer Didier Eribon to exclaim, in the preface to the third edition of his *Michel Foucault*, "How much has Foucault himself changed in the last years!" (Eribon 2011: vii). The progressive issuing of interviews and the short essays and lectures—such as the majestic collection of the *Dits et écrits*, the entirety of which was unavailable to first-generation Foucauldian scholars—as well as the complete publication of the lecture courses at the Collège de France, and, ultimately, the recent publication of *Les aveux de la chair*, the unfinished version of the fourth volume of the *History of Sexuality* written between 1980 and 1982, provide us with the instruments and material we need to challenge and ultimately revise this paradigm, allowing us to look at the eight years that divide the allegedly *political* Foucault from the so-called *ethical* one from a radically different perspective. We are indeed facing unexpected cohesion, less related to the topics Foucault addresses or the means he uses than to the questions exposed in his research: questions regarding the perpetual and inextricable relationship between truth, power and subjectivity. The aim of this essay is to provide a short account of this perpetual questioning, which links Foucault's inquiry to ancient Greece and the problem of subjectivity through the thread of truth.

This is why Vegetti's critique is relevant: on the one hand, although it did not benefit from the sources available today—such as the crucial lectures on *Truth and Juridical Forms* (Foucault 2000) and *About the Beginning of the Hermeneutics of the Self* (Foucault 2016)—and although it succumbs to the bias of the "ancient turn," it comes very close to the point. Vegetti makes an observation that is interesting and worthy of examination insofar as he highlights Foucault's dismissal of the bureaucratic level of the discourse in order to embrace a more direct account of the authors of ancient philosophy in their function as authors and authorities. On the other hand, however, we must make several remarks directly linked to our topic. First, Foucault opened his permanent work-in-progress at the Collège de France by dealing mainly with ancient Greece—more precisely, with certain aspects of Greek philosophy, theater, and juridical institutions, questioning the relationship, established among them, between the will to know, the will to truth, and the role they play in enabling a certain path for relationships of power. Furthermore, Foucault accomplished his aim specifically by starting from the alleged "empty space of Aristotle" identified by Vegetti.[2] Therefore—leaving behind the lens of the so-called "turn" and at the same time trying to avoid any sort of continuity—I aim to establish a connection between the former and the latter Foucauldian references of antiquity, underscoring the dynamic connection between power as a productive relationship and truth as a polemical and agonistic force. I will focus on three main occurrences. First, I will consider the distinction drawn by Foucault in the *Lectures on the Will to Know* between an Aristotelian and a Nietzschean paradigm of truth. Second, I will follow the lines of this distinction, echoed in the "little history of truth" in *Psychiatric Power*. Third, I will tackle *On the Government of the Living*, where Foucault seems to reconnect some of the threads he followed in his previous years at the Collège de France, joining together the problem of productive power, the relationship between power and knowledge, and the issue of how subjectivity is formed in the investigation of the "government of men through the manifestation of truth in the form of subjectivity" (Foucault 2014: 80).

## *Lectures on the Will to Know*: Polemic Truth

Foucault dedicated his first course at the Collège de France (1970–1) to investigating the origin of the "will to know." This inquiry begins with a disarmingly straightforward acknowledgement: the involvement of a direct and unquestioned relationship between will and knowledge and between knowledge and truth in the Western philosophical tradition. The question is: what is the strategic function of the argument that proclaims every human being's natural and undisputed tendency towards knowledge? Why has truth always been portrayed as being *powerless*, i.e. free from connections to power, insofar as it is considered *disinterested*? As a declaration of intent, Foucault states that the game he would like to play will involve seeing

> [w]hether the will to truth is not as profoundly historical as any other system of exclusion; whether it is not as arbitrary in its roots as they are; whether it is not as modifiable as they are in the course of history; whether like them it is not dependent upon and constantly reactivated by a whole institutional network; and whether it does not form a system of constraint which is exercised not only on other discourses, but on a whole series of other practices. In short, it is a matter of seeing what real struggles and relations of domination are involved in the will to truth.
> 
> Foucault 2013: 2

Taking this topic into account, Foucault recommends undertaking a *sort of genealogy* of philosophical speech, starting from the inception of its systematization in ancient Greece, thus putting forth one of the most effective means of identifying both the tactics and the strategies through which philosophy has tried, throughout history, to connect desire, knowledge, and truth. For this reason, Foucault begins his work with what he considers the most crucial moment of this intersection, the first book of Aristotle's *Metaphysics*, focusing his attention on the *incipit*:

> All men by nature desire to know. An indication of this is the delight we take in our senses; for even apart from their usefulness they are loved for themselves; and above all others the sense of sight. For not only with a view to action, but even when we are not going to do anything, we prefer seeing (one might say) to everything else. The reason is that this, most of all the senses, makes us know and brings to light many differences between things.
> 
> Aristotle 2012

According to Foucault, this passage is vital to understanding some of the unquestioned assumptions of the Western philosophical tradition: the existence of a desire to know, the universality of this desire (because of its innate presence in every human being), and its naturalness. Foucault observes that Aristotle's supposedly neutral enthymeme actually implies three moves "that maybe cannot be completely superimposed on the move that allows one to descend quite simply from the general to the particular" (Foucault 2013: 7). In this way, first, there is a move from knowledge to sensation; second, the natural desire to know is linked to the pleasure of the sensation in itself, thus inscribing in nature the non-utility of the sensation; last but not least, there is the move from desire to pleasure. Foucault maintains that Aristotle aims to establish a continuity between the simple pleasure of the sensation and what he perceives as the most noble and complete form of knowledge, i.e. philosophy. This uninterrupted continuity implies "that knowledge (*savoir*) and desire are not in two different places, possessed by two subjects or two powers, but that the one who desires knowledge is already the one who possesses it or is capable of possessing it; and it is without violence, appropriation, and struggle" (Foucault 2013: 16). In other words, Foucault intends to underscore the extent to which the Aristotelian paradigm of knowledge must assume the existence of truth and its specific role in ensuring the passage from desire to knowledge. Truth plays a key role because it ensures, through the connection of these two elements, the identity and unity of the subject, who must simply actualize his or her own nature to obtain the truth—along with the permanence, the stability of the object—which lies idle, waiting to be *found*. One could say that we are still facing the perpetuation of the myth of the *uselessness* and *powerlessness* of truth.

Foucault opposes this *Aristotelian paradigm* to another approach to the relationship between will, truth and knowledge, maintaining the possibility of finding in Nietzsche the philosopher who would unleash a radical critique of the unquestioned pattern of desire's natural tendency towards truth. Relying heavily on Nietzsche's early writings, from *On Truth and Lies in a Nonmoral Sense* to certain chapters of *The Gay Science*, Foucault aims to open up the possibility of historical inquiry into the *pudenda origo* of truth, an origin—or better, *emergence*[3]—that has less to do with contemplation and tendencies than with *struggle* and *violence*.[4] In Foucault's opinion, however, in his attempt to overstep the bounds of knowledge and move *beyond* it, Nietzsche is susceptible to a Kantian objection: "Either what we say about knowledge is true, but this can only be from within knowledge, or we speak outside of knowledge, but then nothing allows us to assert that what we say is true" (Foucault 2013: 26). There is only one way out of this dilemma: to negate the co-implication of truth and knowledge. Whereas Kant postulated both inaccessible truth and limited knowledge, Foucault—through an anti-Heideggerian reinterpretation of the relationship between knowledge, truth, and will—"doesn't place Nietzsche at the summit of the Western philosophical tradition, along a continuous line ideally connecting Aristotle, Descartes and Kant (as Heidegger did), but rather on an alternative route where Nietzsche showed the fundamental *dis-implication* of truth and knowledge" (Irrera 2015: 46).

If there is no natural link between truth, will, and knowledge, what is the relationship between will and truth? According to Foucault, the Western philosophical tradition prefers to define their connection in terms of their mutual articulation through *freedom*: it is because truth is free from all constraints that we can affirm that it is indeed true; it is because the will freely makes room for truth—thus putting aside its own specific interests—that a subject can claim to have achieved truth. These are the coordinates of a paradigm of knowledge as *adæquatio rei et intellectus*.

This articulation is nothing more than the historical and cultural outcome of the Aristotelian paradigm, however, a "regime of speech" which takes for granted the natural human disposition towards knowledge. Yet this is merely a falsehood and an illusion, as Nietzsche states—a peculiar kind of falsehood that helps humans to cope with a world otherwise ruled by chaos. This is why he instead situates *violence, compulsion* and *domination* as the pivotal point between will and truth:

> In *The Gay Science*, Nietzsche defines a completely different set of relations:
>
> —knowledge is an "invention" behind which there is something altogether different from it: an interplay of instincts, impulses, desires, fear, will to appropriation. Knowledge appears on the stage where these battle with each other;
> —it does not come about as the effect of their harmony, of their happy equilibrium, but of their hatred, of their dubious and provisional compromise, of a fragile pact which they are always ready to betray. It is not a permanent faculty but an event, or at least a series of events;
> —it is always servile, dependent, interested (not in itself, but in what is liable to interest the instinct or instincts which dominate it);
> —and if it passes itself off as knowledge of the truth, this is because it produces the truth through the action of a primary and always renewed falsification that posits the distinction between true and false.
>
> Foucault 2013: 227

Nietzschean critique emphasizes that there is no such thing as a *Hyperuranion*: "truth is a thing of this world: it is produced only by virtue of multiple forms of constraint" (Foucault 1980: 131). Truth "isn't outside power, or lacking in power: contrary to a myth whose history and functions would repay further study, truth isn't the reward of free spirits, the child of protracted solitude, nor the privilege of those who have succeeded in liberating themselves" (Foucault 1980: 131), but it is considered an invention as much as knowledge is. Therefore, there is no natural desire for truth: both truth and knowledge are the outcome of restriction and constraint; they both emerge as the results of specific historical-political conflicts, aiming to dominate and prevail. Thus, there is no truth without a will to foster it. Knowledge is not *intelligere* but rather—in Nietzsche's subversion of the Spinozian motto—*ridere, lugere,* and *detestari*.[5] The *useless* truths of philosophy, the *disinterested* knowledge that observes without judging, are nothing more than detours of "the most arrogant and the most mendacious moment in 'world history'" (Nietzsche 1990: 79). Knowledge has no origin; it has only a history. There is no *singular* truth as the outcome of the implementation of a method, as the application of formal rules, but only the space of knowledge, opened by the mutual interplay of agonistic truths.

What is left of the theory of knowledge once the Nietzschean hammer has been put to one side, and what benefit can Foucault take from appropriating the theoretical model of truth as a struggle among forces? For the French philosopher, this *completely different set of relations* allows us:

—to speak of sign and interpretation, of their inseparability, without reference to a phenomenology;
—to speak of signs without reference to any "structuralism";
—to speak of interpretation without reference to an original subject;
—to connect up analyses of systems of signs with the analysis of forms of violence and domination;
—to think knowledge as an historical process before any problematic of the truth, and more fundamentally than in the subject-object relation.

Foucault 2013: 213–14

Neither Nietzsche nor Foucault aims to negate the idea of truth *qua* truth; rather, they aim to underline its *event*-like character and the fact of its *production*, outlining an *agonistic*—rather than *indifferent* and *useless*—form of truth. Most importantly, this approach to truth makes it possible to put forth a history of knowledge, a history of truth that, far from being the progressive unveiling of a *telos* or the search for a long-lost *origin*, is a history of the production of truth in the actual struggles among the forces that attempt to seize it, in the becoming of practices that shape knowledge and in the practical effects of truth: the possibility of historical research as genealogy.

In the idea of truth as the consequence of agonistic forces battling for a portion of reality, it is possible to appreciate the great extent to which Deleuzian theses—such as the pivotal "theory of forces" outlined in *Nietzsche and Philosophy*—influenced Foucault's thought in the beginning of the 1970s. Kevin Thompson, for instance, suggests that Deleuzian theses shaped the very form of the genealogical method (Thompson 2016). The hypothesis of a Deleuzian influence gains even more credit in light of the fact that, throughout the lecture courses, the idea of the production of truth takes into account another major Deleuzian concept: the concept of "event". We find this concept at the core of Foucault's "little history of truth" in the course on *Psychiatric Power* (Foucault 2006b: 235), suggesting once again that two different series of truth have been expounded by Western philosophy. The first overlaps perfectly with the description of the aforementioned Aristotelian paradigm in the *Lectures on the Will to Know* and relies on the idea that truth is to be found everywhere as a product of the meticulous application of methodological rules: this is what Foucault defines as "truth-demonstration" (Foucault 2006b: 238). On the other hand, we have the "truth-event" (Foucault 2006b: 234), corresponding to the Nietzschean paradigm, a truth that can only be produced or provoked but never *found*, that has its own history of propitious timing, a geography of befitting places, a cohort of suitable mentors. This implies the idea that truth needs to be achieved beyond the simple actualization of human nature or through the safe path of a method, i.e. that it demands a *strategy*.

## Submitting to Truth

The idea of truth as an agonistic, polemic and *strategic* instance appears to be what holds together, on the one hand, Foucault's inquiry into the problem of productive power during the early 1970s—a power that produces bodies, knowledge and subjectivities through mechanisms of *disciplinarization*—and, on the other, the slow shift towards the concept of *government* as the *conduct of conducts*, as the capacity to "structure the possible field of actions of others" (Foucault 1983b: 221). In fact, the concept of government revolves closely around the three *axes* of Foucauldian reflection, placing both the epistemological and the ethical question center stage, alongside the political question. It is therefore of paramount importance to address the role that concept plays starting from *On the Government of the Living*.[6]

The 1979–80 lecture course is, for many reasons, strategically fundamental to understanding how the issue of truth is deeply intertwined with the problem of power and of the self and, at the same time, to showing once and for all that where there is supposed to have been be a "turn" (ethical or ancient), there is rather the deepening of a decade-long study pointing towards the co-implication of productive power, agonistic truth, and moldable subjectivity (by oneself or others). In the first lecture, Foucault declares his intention to re-center his research around the question of the articulation of the exercise of power and the manifestation of truth, stating that it is "very difficult to find an example of a power that is exercised without being accompanied, in one way or another, by a manifestation of truth." He adds that "we could call 'alethurgy' the manifestation of truth as the set of possible verbal or non-verbal procedures by which one brings to light what is laid down as true as opposed to false, hidden, inexpressible, unforeseeable, or forgotten, and say that there is no exercise of power without something like an alethurgy" (Foucault 2014: 4, 7). Moreover, Foucault now prefers to use the terms "government" and "governmentality" instead of the more generic "exercise of power"— above all, to underline the achievements of his inquiry into microphysical relationships of productive power, the terms of which do not pre-exist the relationship itself. These terms are carefully chosen by Foucault to reactivate on a larger scale his inquiry into the techniques of confession and spiritual direction stemming from the Council of Trent, techniques that he had begun to address at least since the lecture course on the *Abnormal* (Foucault 2004), investigating their importance to judiciary power and then considering them through the lens of *pastoral power*, the complex system of institutions, values and techniques, specific to the Catholic Church, that put forth the framework of power conceived as a form of *conduct of conducts*, exemplary in 1978, both in *Security, Territory, Population* (Foucault 2007) and in the conference on enlightenment and critique at the Societé Française de Philosophie (Foucault 1997a). Reactivating the analysis of *pastoral power*, Foucault's intention is to study the relationship between the government of the conduct of human beings and the associated manifestation of truth. This is what Foucault defines as the "government of men through the manifestation of truth in the form of subjectivity" (Foucault 2014: 80).

In the previous two courses, Foucault examined genealogy, structure, and contemporary political forms of the relationship of government, insofar as it is exercised as an efficient means to ensure the deployment of a *rationality* of government.

The 1980 course, however, pivots on the idea that alethurgical acts were intertwined with the relationship of government all along the history of pastoral power, long before the modern and contemporary forms of the rationality of government posited what we might call a rule of efficiency. In other words, Foucault reaches back—once again—to antiquity and early Christianity to demonstrate that even then one could not "direct men without carrying out operations in the domain of truth, and operations that are always in excess of what is useful and necessary to govern in an effective way" (Foucault 2014: 17).

Insofar as government is a relationship in which truth is used as a means—among others—to structure one's possible field of action, it is clear that governing is tantamount to taking charge of one's *ēthos*, i.e. one's own way of conducting oneself (Irrera 2014; Marzocca 2016). Therefore, the truth *qua* truth is never neutral in a relationship of government since it is both the means of, and what is at stake in, that relationship (with oneself or others): here again, it is an *agonistic* truth as an historical conglomeration of verbal and non-verbal practices that determines individuals' obligations concerning the procedures of manifestation of truth. The historical, cultural, social, and institutional conditions under which said obligations are shaped constitute what Foucault calls a "regime of truth." Foucault had already used this term in June 1976, during the well-known *entretien* with Alessandro Fontana and Pasquale Pasquino, when he stated:

> Truth is a thing of this world: it is produced only by virtue of multiple forms of constraint. And it induces regular effects of power. Each society has its *regime of truth*, its "general politics" of truth: that is, the types of discourse which it accepts and makes function as true; the mechanisms and instances which enable one to distinguish true and false statements, the means by which each is sanctioned; the techniques and procedures accorded value in the acquisition of truth; the status of those who are charged with saying what counts as true.
> 
> Foucault 1980: 131

Even then, Foucault referred to constraints from which truth is born and that, in turn, it puts into place. In the 1980 course, however, Foucault asks why one should add the ideas of constraint and obligation to the notion of manifestation of truth, echoing *ex negativo* the argumentation on the Aristotelian paradigm featured in *Lectures on the Will to Know*.

Foucault argues with himself, stating that one can say that, insofar as one is compelled to declare something as true, one is coping with something *that is not the actual truth* (Foucault 2014: 94–5). This is because, according to the Aristotelian paradigm and truth-demonstration, as long as the truth is really true, it does not require anything but itself to be recognized and accepted as such. Therefore, a regime of truth appears to be a contradiction in terms and, rigorously speaking, one must admit that something—a supplement of coercive force of some sort—must have been added to the intrinsic rules of manifestation of truth. If this is the case, it must be something the truth of which cannot be demonstrated, thus confronting one with the "*coercion of the non-true*, or the coercion and constraint of the unverifiable" (Foucault

2014: 95). After all, if it were true, if it were the *true truth*, it would be self-sufficient and self-evident, not coercing and coerced. In the wake of the Aristotelian paradigm, truth should never stand with power and should instead flow freely toward the good will of the subject.

These objections raised by Foucault are clearly nothing more than expressions of the *internal* point of view of our contemporary regime of truth, the view that has been hegemonized by truth-demonstration as self-transparent and self-evident and by the assumption of the natural co-implication of truth, will, and freedom. According to this paradigm, there cannot be anything else coercing one to accept the veracity of the truth beyond the truth itself. Yet if this kind of objection is insufficient, it is precisely because it fails to take into account the systems of constraints that are *external* to the individual *game of truth*. If one attempts to consider these external bonds, what would the acceptance of something as true mean? In Foucault's words:

> In the most rigorously constructed arguments imaginable, even in the event of something being recognized as self-evident, there is always, and it is always necessary to assume, a certain assertion that does not belong to the logical realm of observation or deduction, in other words, an assertion that does not belong exactly to the realm of the true or false, that is rather a sort of commitment, a sort of profession. In all reasoning there is always this assertion that consists in saying: if it is true, then I will submit; it is true, *therefore* I submit; it is true, therefore I am bound. But this "therefore" of the "it is true, therefore I submit; it is true, therefore I am bound," is not a logical "therefore," it cannot rest on any self-evidence, nor is it univocal moreover. If in a certain number of cases, in a certain number of games of truth, like precisely the logic of the sciences, this "therefore" goes so much without saying that it is as if it is transparent and we do not notice its presence, it nevertheless remains the case that standing back a bit, and when we take science as precisely an historical phenomenon, the "it is true, therefore I submit" becomes much more enigmatic, much more obscure. This "therefore" that links the "it is true" and the "I submit," or which gives the truth the right to say: you are forced to accept me because I am the truth — in this "therefore", this "you are forced", "you are obliged", "you have to submit", in this "you have to" of the truth, there is something that does not arise from the truth itself in its structure and content.
>
> Foucault 2014: 96–7

Truth has effects of power that are neither inscribed in its own nature nor logically inferable from truth itself. The "therefore" emphasized in Foucault's manuscript represents the same logical connection as in Descartes' "*cogito ergo sum*" [*I think, therefore I am*]. Descartes' "therefore," which ties the "I think" to the "I am," is grounded in logic and may even be considered "theoretically unanswerable;" yet behind it lies another implicit "therefore" that is indeed that of the "profession," which claims *it is true, therefore I submit*: "The explicit 'therefore' of Descartes is that of truth that has no other origin than itself and its intrinsic force, but under this explicit 'therefore' is another implicit 'therefore'. This is of a regime of truth that is not reduced to the intrinsic character of truth. It is the acceptance of a certain regime of truth" (Foucault

2014: 98)—meaning that there is no logical necessity whatsoever underpinning the implicit "therefore." It represents the surplus of power, the ethical and political effects of a certain regime of truth put into place and carried along by truth, insofar as it has been, since its inception, a conglomeration of forces, practices, instincts, and so forth.

These two dimensions—implicit and explicit obligation, external and internal argumentation—are not to be confused. On the one hand, truth is always *index sui*, an indicator of itself: in a given "game of truth," the "intrinsic rules of manifestation of truth" are the only means of *partage* between truth and falsity. On the other hand,

> this does not mean that the truth is *rex sui*, that the truth is *lex sui*, that the truth is *judex sui*. That is to say, the truth is not creator and holder of the rights it exercises over men, of the obligations the latter have towards it, and of the effects they expect from these obligations when and insofar as they are fulfilled. In other words, it is not the truth that so to speak administers its own empire, that judges and sanctions those who obey or disobey it. It is not true that the truth constrains only by truth.
> 
> Foucault 2014: 96

Truth is an indicator of itself only in a given game of truth, if that game of truth stands for the criteria, the processes, and the rules of the *partage* between truth and falsity from the point of view of their formal rules, regardless of the actual implication of given participants. In a game of truth, the "implicit therefore" is completely irrelevant and systematically tends to become transparent—according to the "truth-demonstration" paradigm of self-evidence—even though it is still utterly unprovable and impossible to ground in further truths or evidence. Daniele Lorenzini summarizes the question as follows:

> [Foucault] [n]ever intended to deny that … the rules of each game of truth autonomously define, *in that game*, the *partage* between truth and falsity. Nevertheless, the rules themselves are not autonomous: on the contrary, they are the outcome of a historical, social and cultural production. What Foucault claims to be currently at stake from a political perspective is underlining not the autonomy of the game of truth's *internal* point of view (which is, after all, entirely abstract), but rather the *heteronomy* of the regime of truth's *external* point of view. To sum this up in an adage, I would say that according to Foucault there is no game of truth without a regime of truth.
> 
> Lorenzini 2012: 395–6

There is no such thing as a "pure" game of truth, since every game is always tied to a regime that determines the obligation of each involved individual to accept (more or less voluntarily, more or less consciously) the power of the "therefore" that binds the "it is true"—determined by the rules of the game of truth—to the "I submit" of subjectivity, thus becoming a specific subject of the given regime of truth.

A regime of truth is therefore the twine that wraps and coerces individuals to perform certain "acts of truth," while at the same time establishing how these "acts" must be performed. In this sense, and insofar as a regime of truth constitutes the insertion of games of truth in actual practices, it constitutes the condition of possibility of the "government of men by the means of truth." Thus, the issue of the "implicit therefore" and of the nature of the specific form of a regime of truth are not questions of logic; rather, they represent both "a fundamental historical-cultural problem" and, as such, an ethical and political issue. On the one hand, the effects of "the force of truth" are put forth by the surplus of force exercised by the regime of truth, i.e. the tactics and strategies employed in a given society to manage the partitions and effects of truth; on the other, only by undertaking a genealogy of regimes of truth will it be possible to pinpoint and eventually subvert the means and ends of a government by the means of truth. Hence, the main goal of a genealogy of the force of truth will be to pinpoint and historicize the various regimes of knowledge (*savoir*) in a given society, where a regime of knowledge is "the point where a political regime of obligations and constraints and this particular regime of obligations and constraints that is the regime of truth are articulated" (Foucault 2014: 102). Through the idea of a "regime of truth," Foucault suggests that we put aside the issue of *Truth* with a capital "T" (whatever its nature may be) as an autonomous question and pose a more precise and urgent problem, from the political point of view: the problem of the relationship between the manifestation of truth, the government of human beings and the constitution of subjectivities.

## Conclusion

This brief overview has aimed to show how misleading the category of an "ancient" or "ethical turn" can be—in the light of new sources—when it comes to making sense of Foucault's (late) thought. While finding continuity in the ever-changing scenario that was his philosophical path was neither my intention nor my goal, there is no doubt that the relationship Foucault entertained with both truth and power dates back at least to the early 1970s and that, at the same time, he reached back to antiquity at several disparate moments to cope with one of the main questions that constituted a sort of *basso continuo* for over a decade of his research: how is power exercised, and how does it relate to subjects insofar as it produces knowledge and induces pleasure?

To sum up the results of this chapter, it is possible to maintain that truth is tied to the issue of force and power in a threefold knot: 1) truth is an object of dispute (it is therefore *political*: it is something one fights for, it is the outcome of disharmony and struggle); 2) truth is the battlefield (it is therefore polemic, *agonistic*: it is the "place" where the struggle occurs, the "site of the confrontation," the "field" where the forces fight among themselves); and 3) truth is the instrument in the fight (it is heuristic and *strategic*: it is something to fight with, i.e. the surplus of power capable of producing the ethical and political effect of subjection and subjectivation). In this sense, the issues Foucault addressed in his final years—the problems of *parrhēsia* and the "courage of truth" (Foucault 2011)—can be interpreted as a declaration of war first on the regime of truth of the "hermeneutics of the self," where the aim is to put forth a completely different way to speak candidly and to "say-everything" utterly free of the incessant labor of interpretation of *arcana conscientiae*; second on the paradigm of self-transparent truth, corresponding to a power that perceives itself as "going without saying" (Foucault 2014: 77); and third on the "uselessness" of truth, insofar as *parrhēsia* (Foucault 1986) is an aggressive truth, which means "telling the truth so that it might be *attackable*"[7] (Foucault 1996: 261), i.e. speaking the truth of the actual practices tying a certain game of truth to its corresponding regime in order for them to be disarticulated and ultimately subverted.

In conclusion, rather than considering Foucault a nihilist or an irrationalist because of his conception of truth, we can say that he puts forth a *non-naïve* conception of truth. Taking into account the *pudenda origo* of truth, its *invention* and the effects of power that this concept puts in place, a non-naïve conception of truth—far from taking it for granted or conceiving it as an eternal and self-transparent entity—aims to take *responsibility* for the strategic battlefield represented by truth. On the one hand, one must distance oneself from each and every unquestioned effect of power put in place by truth. Therefore, the first move step should always be to ask the genealogical question: who is speaking? Whose truth is this, and why is it asking me to submit? On the other hand, one must produce truths able to speak the truth about the current configurations of systems of power, shedding light on the structure of the regimes of truth. Since it is impossible *not* to play the game of truth, one should play it by telling the truth in such a way that it may be attackable—playing the game and attempting to change the rules at the same time.

Ultimately, we should probably stick to one of the "rules" outlined by Foucault when he defined *Anti-Oedipus* as an "introduction to the non-fascist life": "Do not use thought to ground a political practice in Truth; nor political action to discredit, as mere speculation, a line of thought. Use political practice as an intensifier of thought, and analysis as a multiplier of the forms and domains for the intervention of political action" (Foucault 1983a: xiv).

## Notes

1  Both texts were issued in 1984, eight years after the publication of the first volume, diverging considerably from the original 1976 project.
2  Considering the entirety of Foucault's courses, Aristotle is far from constituting an "empty space," appearing at least twice in a significant way: in the 1970 course (*Lectures on the Will to Know*, Book I of the *Metaphysics*) and in the last course in 1984 (*The Courage of Truth*, where Foucault addresses the *Nicomachean Ethics* in the first lecture).
3  See Foucault (1978).
4  For an (albeit partial) attempt to underline Foucault's limited reading of Nietzsche, see Bouveresse (2016). For a critique of Bouveresse's position, see Lorenzini (2017: 5–19). For two interesting accounts of the usage of Nietzsche's thought in the early Foucault, see Patton (2018) and Schrift (2018).
5  See *The Gay Science*, §333: "*The meaning of knowing. Non ridere, non lugere, neque detestari, sed intelligere!* says Spinoza simply and sublimely, as is his wont. Yet in the last analysis, what else is this *intelligere* than the form in which we come to feel the other three at once? One result of the different and mutually opposed desires to laugh, lament, and curse? Before knowledge is possible. each of these instincts must first have presented its one-sided view of the thing or event; after this comes the fight of these one-sided

views, and occasionally this results in a mean, one grows calm, one finds all three sides right, and there is a kind of justice and a contract; for by virtue of justice and a contract all these instincts can maintain their existence and assert their rights against each other. Since only the last scenes of reconciliation and the final accounting at the end of this long process rise to our consciousness, we suppose that *intelligere* must be something conciliatory, just, and good—something that stands essentially opposed to the instincts, while it is actually nothing but a *certain behavior of the instincts toward one another*" (Nietzsche 1974: 261). The Spinozian sentence is from *Tractatus Politicus*, I, §4.

6 For the sake of concision, it is beyond the scope of this essay to address the genealogy of the concept of government in the years and courses immediately preceding *On the Government of the Living*.

7 The translation has been modified. Since the original French reads "Dire la vérité pour qu'elle soit *attaquable*," it is simply not possible to express it as "telling the truth so that it might be *acceptable*," as the English translation has it.

# References

Aristotle (2012), *Aristotle's* Metaphysics *Alpha*, ed. C. Steel, Oxford: Oxford University Press.

Bouveresse, J. (2016), *Nietzsche contre Foucault. Sur la vérité, la connaissance et le pouvoir*, Marseille: Agone.

Deleuze, G. (1983), *Nietzsche and Philosophy*, trans. H Tomlinson, New York: Columbia University Press.

Eribon, D. (2011), *Michel Foucault*, Paris: Flammarion.

Foucault, M. (1977), *Discipline and Punish: The Birth of the Prison*, trans. A. Sheridan, New York: Random House.

Foucault, M. (1978), "Nietzsche, Genealogy, History," in J. Richardson and B. Leiter (eds), *Nietzsche*, 139-64, Oxford: Oxford University Press.

Foucault, M. (1980), "Truth and Power," in C. Gordon (ed.), *Power/Knowledge: Selected Interviews and Other Writings, 1972–1977*, 109-33, New York: Pantheon Books.

Foucault, M., ed. (1982), *I, Pierre Rivière, Having Slaughtered My Mother, My Sister, and My Brother: A Case of Parricide in the 19th Century*, trans. F. Jellinek, Lincoln: University of Nebraska Press.

Foucault, M. (1983a), "Preface," in G. Deleuze and F. Guattari, *Anti-Oedipus*, xi–xiv, Minneapolis: University of Minnesota Press.

Foucault, M. (1983b), "The Subject and Power," in H. L. Dreyfus and P. Rabinow (eds), *Michel Foucault: Beyond Structuralism and Hermeneutics*, 2nd ed., 208-26, Chicago: The University of Chicago Press.

Foucault, M. (1985), *The Use of Pleasure: Volume 2 of The History of Sexuality*, trans. R. Hurley, New York: Vintage Books.

Foucault, M. (1986), *The Care of the Self: Volume 3 of The History of Sexuality*, trans. R. Hurley, New York: Vintage Books.

Foucault, M. (1996), "Clarifications on the Question of Power," in S. Lotringer (ed.), *Foucault Live: Interviews 1966–84*, 255-63, New York: Semiotext(e).

Foucault, M. (1997a), "What is Enlightenment?," in P. Rabinow (ed.), *The Essential Works of Michel Foucault, 1954–1984, Vol. 1: Ethics, Subjectivity and Truth*, 303-19, New York: The New Press.

Foucault, M. (1997b), "What is Critique?," in S. Lotringer and L. Hochroth (eds), *The Politics of Truth*, 23-82, New York: Semiotext(e).

Foucault, M. (1998), *The Will to Knowledge: The History of Sexuality, Volume 1*, trans. R. Hurley, London: Penguin Books.
Foucault, M. (2000), "Truth and Juridical Forms," in J. D. Faubion (ed.), *The Essential Works of Michel Foucault, 1954–1984, Vol. 3: Power*, 1–89, London: Penguin Books.
Foucault, M. (2002a), *The Order of Things: An Archaeology of the Human Sciences*, London: Routledge.
Foucault, M. (2002b), *The Archaeology of Knowledge*, trans. A. M. Sheridan Smith, London: Routledge.
Foucault, M. (2004), *Abnormal: Lectures at the Collège de France, 1974–1975*, ed. V. Marchetti and A. Salomoni, trans. G. Burchell, New York: Picador.
Foucault, M. (2005), *The Hermeneutics of the Subject: Lectures at the Collège de France 1981–1982*, ed. F. Gros, trans. G. Burchell, New York: Picador.
Foucault, M. (2006a), *History of Madness*, ed. J. Khalfa, trans. J. Murphy and J. Khalfa, London: Routledge.
Foucault, M. (2006b), *Psychiatric Power: Lectures at the Collège de France 1973–1974*, ed. J. Lagrange, trans. G. Burchell, Basingstoke: Palgrave Macmillan.
Foucault, M. (2007), *Security, Territory, Population: Lectures at the Collège de France 1977–1978*, ed. F. Gros, trans. G. Burchell, Basingstoke: Palgrave Macmillan.
Foucault, M. (2010), *The Government of Self and Others: Lectures at the Collège de France, 1982–1983*, ed. F. Gros, trans. G. Burchell, Basingstoke: Palgrave Macmillan.
Foucault, M. (2011), *The Courage of Truth (The Government of Self and Others II): Lectures at the Collège de France 1983–1984*, ed. F. Gros, trans. G. Burchell, Basingstoke: Palgrave Macmillan.
Foucault, M. (2013), *Lectures on the Will to Know: Lectures at the Collège de France 1970–1971*, ed. D. Defert, trans. G. Burchell, Basingstoke: Palgrave Macmillan.
Foucault, M. (2014), *On the Government of the Living: Lectures at the Collège de France 1979–1980*, ed. M. Senellart, trans. G. Burchell, Basingstoke: Palgrave Macmillan.
Foucault, M. (2016), *About the Beginning of the Hermeneutics of the Self: Lectures at Dartmouth College, 1980*, ed. H.-P. Fruchaud and D. Lorenzini, trans. G. Burchell, Chicago: The University of Chicago Press.
Foucault, M. (2018), *Histoire de la sexualité 4: Les aveux de la chair*, Paris: Gallimard.
Irrera, O. (2014), "La verità come forza. Dir-vero, potere e soggettività nell'ultimo Foucault," in G. Brindisi (ed.), *Foucault e le genealogie del dir-vero*, 33–57, Naples: Cronopio.
Irrera, O. (2015), "Michel Foucault e la critica dell'ideologia nei Corsi al Collège de France," in P. B. Vernaglione (ed.), *Michel Foucault. Genealogie del presente*, 59–85, Castel San Pietro Romano: manifestolibri.
Lorenzini, D. (2012), "Foucault, il cristianesimo e la genealogia dei regimi di verità," in *Iride*, XXV (66), 391–401, Bologna: Società Editrice il Mulino.
Lorenzini, D. (2017), *La Force du Vrai. De Foucault à Austin*, Lormont: Le Bord de l'Eau.
Marzocca, O. (2016), *Foucault ingovernabile. Dal bios all'ethos*, Sesto San Giovanni: Meltemi.
Nietzsche, F. (1974), *The Gay Science*, trans. W. Kaufmann, New York: Vintage Books.
Nietzsche, F. (1990), "On Truth and Lies in a Nonmoral Sense," in D. Breazeale (ed.), *Philosophy and Truth: Selections from Nietzsche's Notebooks of the early 1870s*, 79–91, New Jersey and London: Humanities Press.
Patton, P. (2018), "Foucault, Nietzsche and the History of Truth," in A. Rosenberg and J. Westfall (eds), *Foucault and Nietzsche: A Critical Encounter*, London: Bloomsbury.
Schrift, A. (2018), "Nietzsche and Foucault's 'Will to Know'," in A. Rosenberg and J. Westfall (eds), *Foucault and Nietzsche: A Critical Encounter*, London: Bloomsbury.

Thompson, K. (2016), "Foucault and the 'Image of Thought': Archaeology, Genealogy, and the Impetus of Trascendental Empiricism," in N. Morar, T. Nail and D. W. Smith (eds), *Between Deleuze and Foucault*, 200–11, Edinburgh: Edinburgh University Press.

Vegetti, M. (2008), "*L'ermeneutica del soggetto*. Foucault, gli antichi e noi," in M. Galzigna (ed.), *Foucault, oggi*, 150–62, Milan: Feltrinelli.

9

# From Jurisdiction to Veridiction: The Late Foucault's Shift to Subjectivity

Laurence Barry

The "late Foucault" was, for a long time, an enigma. After the publication of the first volume of the *History of Sexuality* in 1976, in which he announced a series of books that never appeared, Foucault remained silent for eight long years. And then, a couple of weeks before his untimely death, two books were released, formally as the second and third volumes of the *History*. But these new volumes had nothing to do with the first, except for their title: the first volume dealt with the modern era and mechanisms of power, whereas the last two books dealt with the Ancient Greek period and the care of the self.

How and why did Foucault shift his interest from power to subjectivity? Some of the interviews and articles published between 1976 and 1984 contain elements of this evolution in his thinking (see for instance Foucault 1997a, 1997b). But it was only the publication of the lectures at the Collège de France that has made it possible to fully follow Foucault's train of thought during this period. My purpose here is to demonstrate the crucial impact of the lectures on liberal and neoliberal governmentality in 1978 and 1979 on the shift from analyses of power to analyses of subjectivity.

In one of his first lectures at the Collège de France in 1970, *Lectures on the Will to Know*, Foucault outlines the general framework of his future studies and explains that "the aim of the research will be to identify the function and assess *the effect of a discourse of truth in the discourse of law*" (Foucault 2013: 2, emphasis added). His studying of neoliberal governmentality, however, led, I suggest, to a reversal in his thought: in the contemporary exercise of power, the dimension of "veridiction"—the discourse of truth—was identified as becoming predominant over jurisdiction, the discourse of the law.[1] One might even argue that the discourse of the law is *just one historical instance of the discourse of truth*. Consequently, Foucault revises his first description of modern power as discipline exercised on docile bodies: governmentality, the "way one conducts the conduct of men" (Foucault 2008: 186), implies subjects acting on their own. I suggest that in order to better comprehend the nature of the constraints imposed by neoliberal governmentality, Foucault turns to the relations between subject and truth.

Much has been written on subjectivation and truth-telling.[2] However, little attention has been given to the interplay between the notions of veridiction and jurisdiction, to which Foucault turns repeatedly in his texts. I suggest that analyzing this interplay will shed light on why the study of neoliberal government led Foucault to consider that antique processes of subjectivation bore relevance to the understanding of Western societies.

The shift from jurisdiction to veridiction implies first a renewed approach to truth. In the first 1980 lecture, Foucault indeed insists that his move from the concept of power to that of governmentality entails a shift from power/knowledge to the more general notion of "government *by the truth*" (Foucault 2014a: 12), further linked in the remainder of the lectures to processes of subjectivation. The veering of Foucault's interest toward subjectivity in the 1980s can be illustrated by comparing two readings of Homer's text on the judgment between Menelaus and Antilochus. The first reading is in the 1971 lectures at the Collège, which I will analyze in the first part of the paper; the second is in the 1981 lectures at Louvain, to which I will refer in the concluding part. In the middle section, I will try to show how between those two readings, the 1978 and 1979 lectures on neoliberal governmentality triggered a shift in Foucault's analysis of modern power that implied giving veridiction precedence over jurisdiction.

## Power/Knowledge and the First Reading of Homer (1970–1)

The analysis of the relations between power and knowledge started with the 1970–1 lectures entitled *Lessons on the Will to Know*, where Foucault studies texts of Nietzsche and questions knowledge as *connaissance*.[3] These lectures indeed frame the power/knowledge analyses that followed since they claim that the truth imposed by knowledge as *connaissance* imply specific mechanisms of power, exclusion and domination (Beistegui 2014). For Lorenzini, Foucault does not offer an alternative conceptualization of truth, but shows that the objective truth under the assumption of knowledge as *connaissance* should be seen as one form of the archaic modes of the truth, shaped in the dreadful and unpredictable will of the gods (Lorenzini 2016). While this claim suits Foucault's later conception of truth, as will be shown in the last part, I suggest that in the 1970–1 lectures he does contrapose two distinct forms of truth, one masking the other; behind the so-called objective, scientific split between true and false, there is always a struggle and the imposition of a will (Foucault 2013: 202–08). To demonstrate that truth is an arbitrary and sheer force, in these lectures, Foucault refers to Homer's text on the judgment between Menelaus and Antilochus for the first time, in the terms exposed below.

In a race between warriors, Antilochus uses a stratagem to pass another competitor, Menelaus. Menelaus appeals against the result. He offers Antilochus to take the "purgatory oath." In the archaic procedure, if Antilochus accepts, he puts himself in the hands of the gods: "The truth is not what one says . . . It is what one confronts, what one does or does not accept to face up to. It is the formidable force to which one surrenders" (Foucault 2013: 75). The gods themselves are not bound by truth, and the punishment of the one who takes a false oath is neither necessary nor immediate. "Nothing is said about what will happen to the person who swears after the test of the oath; we know only that he is in the hands of the gods, that they may punish him or his descendants" (Foucault 2013: 76). Archaic justice is therefore presented in the 1970–1 lectures in the form of a contest, whose result is completely arbitrary. Foucault concludes his reading by stating that in Homer's episode, truth itself is the result of a fourfold confrontation: the initial confrontation in the race; the contestation of the results of the race by Menelaus; the latter's challenging of Antilochus to take an oath; and the final confrontation with the gods.

Both in 1971 and in 1981, Foucault quotes the work of Gernet as the source of his reading. However, Gernet concludes his own study of the Antilochus and Menelaus episode with the remark that what defines negatively the pre-law (*pré-droit*) in Greece is that the judicial decision is *not based on truth:* "In this case, there is not even a sentence; the contest between the adversaries is decided simply through the process of proof (*épreuve*)" (Gernet 1982: 95, *my translation*). Gernet speaks less of two kinds of truth than of two kinds of right, one of which is devoid of a reference to objective truth. Furthermore, Gernet explicitly rejects the contention that archaic justice was based on an arbitrary and violent confrontation between two parties. On the contrary, he insists that the ritual itself, and not brutal force, produces the justice's efficacy (Gernet 1982: 64–5).

By contrast, Foucault in 1971, and in the following years, challenges the common understanding of truth and knowledge as *connaissance*—the Aristotelian model—with the aid of a Nietzschean one: behind the mask of *connaissance*, one finds the will to knowledge and the instincts aiming at domination and control (Foucault 2013: 17, 197–8, 209). In archaic times, the truth is not something waiting outside to be discovered as the order of the world. Instead, truth is something that happens arbitrarily as a dreadful event, as a lightning or a thunder (Foucault 2013: 116–17, 203–04).

The 1970–1 lectures are designed to show how the discourse of truth as we know it imposed itself historically, while masking the arbitrary distribution of wealth and power in archaic times (Foucault 2013: 193). Continuing his studies of different legal systems the following year, Foucault insists that in a system regulated by "proof" (*l'épreuve*), the issue is one of peace and victory (i.e., a vocabulary of war) and not one of demonstration and truth (Foucault 2015: 129).[4] The founding of the *polis* on law, money and religion meant also establishing a new order based on truth as purity, where the impure was excluded and truth had to be *known*.

After the 1970–1 lectures and until roughly 1979, Foucault continued to follow this approach. Focusing on the modern exercise of power, he aimed to indicate its entanglement with knowledge and to question one of the basic credos of modernity: that knowledge is situated in a field devoid of power relations and that it would bring about emancipation. For Foucault, knowledge is not *connaissance*—the discovery of an objective and scientific reality unveiled in discourse—but *savoir*, that is always involved in struggles and power relations; power is always "founded on a discourse of truth" (Foucault 2013: 193).[5]

## From Jurisdiction . . .

In 1978, right after the first series of lectures on liberal governmentality ended, Foucault defines his work as the analysis of "regimes of practices" (Foucault 1997c: 225). In his words, the analysis refers to "*programs of conduct* that have both a prescriptive effect regarding what has to be done (effects of *jurisdiction*) and codifying effects regarding what has *to be known* (effects of *veridiction*)" (Foucault 1997c: 225, *emphasis added*). The two axes of jurisdiction and veridiction can easily be associated with power and knowledge: power as the prescription for a conduct, and knowledge as "the correlative formation of domains and objects and of the verifiable, falsifiable discourses that bear on them" (Foucault 1997c: 237). Yet, in the course of the study of modern governmentality, both terms shift and take on a new meaning. In this part I aim to follow this shift and show why veridiction and subjectivity finally take precedence over jurisdiction in the inquiries of the late Foucault.

Up to the 1978 lectures, Foucault discussed jurisdiction in terms of two distinct poles: on the one hand, there is law as the "will of the king" or the expression of the authority of the sovereign, also sometimes coined "the juridical" (Foucault 1978: 144; 1995: 47–50; see also Ewald 1990: 138–61); on the other hand, there is the norm of modern disciplinary power, which Foucault sees as slowly replacing the former jurisdiction. He thus claims in *The History of Sexuality I* that we are facing a "juridical regression" (Foucault 1978: 144).

In the 1978 lectures, Foucault takes two further steps in the analysis. First, he recognizes that the disciplinary norm and the sovereign law had more in common than originally stated. In a 1977 interview, he had already admitted that his analysis "was still too much imprisoned in the juridical model of power" (Foucault 2001a: 234, *my translation*). In the lectures, he explains that both law and norm determine what is permitted and forbidden but in opposite ways. The sovereign law determines what is forbidden and permits whatever is left unsaid; the disciplinary norm, by contrast, codifies precisely what must be done, while all that is left unstated is prohibited (Foucault 2009: 45–6).

Second, Foucault distinguishes now between the law and disciplinary norm on the one hand, and the statistical norm on the other. The statistical norm escapes the dichotomy between permitted and forbidden. It takes a distance from what is desirable, and instead tries to work within the reality of "things as they are." Both the law and the disciplinary norm impose an arbitrary and sovereign will on the subject. The statistical norm, by contrast, has no prescriptive dimension with regard to the conduct of the individual. It accepts any of the phenomena as natural and integrates them as part of the statistical distribution of behaviors (Foucault 2009: 62–3).

It is thus possible to extend the "regression of the juridical," as defined by Foucault in *The History of Sexuality I* and to argue that in the neoliberal order, the statistical norm takes precedence over the disciplinary one. While the disciplinary norm still functions as a law (by being prescriptive), the statistical norm—originally seen by Foucault as complementary to the disciplinary norm in the exercise of modern power—is a norm of *regulation* (Foucault 1978: 145–6).

The nature of the law is also at the heart of Foucault's analyses in the 1979 lectures on neoliberal governmentality. More precisely, the first lesson is devoted to showing how liberalism as a modern mode of government implied a redefinition of the nature of the law. At the time of *Raison d'État*, power was exercised within the kingdom through the unlimited action of the police. The only limit placed upon this action originated from external jurisdiction formalized in the Natural Law. Surprisingly, Foucault shifts the meaning of the "juridical," which in this case is not the will of the king but rather the natural rights and the principles of the social contract, that both limit the sovereign power (Foucault 2008: 11–13).[6]

With the advent of liberalism, the rules and limits of power fundamentally change and are now derived from the knowledge of political economy; they are thus codified along the true/false dichotomy rather than the allowed/forbidden one (Foucault 2008: 18). The function of the law therefore changes for both the governors and the governed. Indeed, if to govern is "to structure the possible field of action of others" (Foucault 1982: 221), then the law becomes the main tool to build such a structure. Yet, it is strikingly different from the will of the king: the laws now function to regulate the environment in which the individuals are expected to make rational decisions. Foucault insists that:

> It is necessary to change the conception of law, or at least elucidate its function. In other words, not confuse its form (*which is always to prohibit and constrain*) and its function, which must be that of *rule of the game*. The law is that which must favor the game, ... enterprises, initiatives, changes.
>
> Foucault 2008: 260, *emphasis added*

In the summary of the 1979 lectures, Foucault claims that liberalism found in law a useful tool "because the law defines forms of general intervention *excluding particular, individual, and exceptional measures*, and because participation of the governed in drawing up the law in a parliamentary system is the most effective system of governmental economy" (Foucault 2008: 321, *emphasis added*). Foucault immediately adds that this does not mean that democracy and the rule of law were necessarily liberal, nor that liberalism was always democratic. Yet this statement is still remarkable when compared to the texts dating back to the early 1970s. Instead of the sovereign law as prohibiting and the disciplinary code as prescribing behavior—both applied at the level of the individual *body*[7]—Foucault sees the liberal rule of law as having precisely the opposite characteristics, i.e., excluding intervention at the level of the individual.

In this description of the rule of law, one finds it difficult to recognize any form of physical constraint. However, the possibility that the modern subject might be an "atom of freedom" (Foucault 2008: 271) in the game defined by liberal law is rejected by Foucault. Indeed, he rhetorically asks at the end of a long and fascinating unread passage whether "this means that we are dealing with natural subjects?" (Foucault 2008: 261). In the next lesson, Foucault gives a clear and negative answer to this question, explaining: "*Homo oeconomicus* is someone who is eminently governable" (Foucault 2008: 270).

I would suggest that in the following years, Foucault tried to grasp precisely the modes of constitution of this specific subjectivity that functions without the constraint of a prescriptive jurisdiction, and yet allows the exercise of power as neoliberal governmentality as its counterpart.

This might well be the major implication of the conceptualization of power in terms of government: "In effect, what defines a relationship of power is that it is a mode of action *which does not act directly and immediately on others*. Instead, it acts *upon their actions: an action upon an action*" (Foucault 1982: 220, *emphasis added*). The disciplines as described in *Discipline and Punish* are still very close, perhaps too close, to a mode of power acting directly on people. Government as the conduct of conducts in contradistinction to the discipline of the bodies operates differently:

> A relationship of violence acts upon *a body* or upon things; it forces, it bends ... it destroys ... A power relationship can only be articulated on the basis of two elements which are each indispensable if it is really to be a power relationship: that "the other" (the one over whom power is exercised) *be thoroughly recognized and maintained to the very end as a person who acts.*
>
> Foucault 1982: 220, *emphasis added*

In his studies of neoliberal governmentality, Foucault hints that the action upon actions, unlike discipline or sovereign power, is obtained not by way of jurisdiction but through veridiction. In the first lesson of the 1979 lectures, Foucault indeed insists that liberalism should be looked upon as a practice regulated by a veridiction, as if the jurisdiction dimension did not exist at all: "instead of coming up against limits formalized by a jurisdiction, it gives itself *intrinsic limits* formulated in terms of veridiction" (Foucault 2008: 21, *emphasis added*). Would this mean that the code of conducts has been absorbed, so to speak, into the heart of knowledge and political economy? Obviously not; yet, what kind of acts do neoliberal subjects do, that maintain them as subjects of power?

## ... To Veridiction

Up until 1979, the veridiction axis that constitutes one of the two axes of the regime of practices is readily identified as knowledge in the sense of *savoir*, or the field where "verifiable, falsifiable discourses" take place (Foucault 1997c: 237). Foucault easily identifies the type of veridiction associated with liberalism: it is political economy and the forms of knowledge based on statistics and economics that he analyzed in the 1978 lectures. In 1979, he insists that the market becomes a place of validation, a place of "verification-falsification" for the practice of government (Foucault 2008: 32). Yet just as the juridical changed in form and is no longer the dichotomous split between the allowed and the forbidden, so does veridiction shift away from knowledge as the distribution of true and false propositions.

Foucault indeed describes the process through which the market, as well as the asylum or the prison, became places of veridiction, after having been historically places of jurisdiction. He then states the following:

> A certain practice of veridiction was formed and developed in these penal institutions that were fundamentally linked to a jurisdictional practice, and this veridictional practice—supported, of course, by criminology, psychology, and so on, *but this is not what is essential* —began to install the veridictional question at

the very heart of modern penal practice, even to the extent of creating difficulties for its jurisdiction, which was the question of truth addressed to the criminal: Who are you?

Foucault 2008: 34, *emphasis added*

Foucault seems to have abandoned here the epistemological domain of knowledge-*savoir per se*. Indeed, "veridiction" does not refer to the content of the human sciences (criminology or psychology) nor to political economy as a new field of knowledge. In other words, it does not refer to the split between true and false within the exercise of power ("this is not what is essential"). Rather, what becomes important in these sciences, or in their practice is veridiction as an act of truth, as truth-telling; veridiction is indeed redefined above *as the truth as told* by the individual.[8]

Interestingly, in the 1975 lectures, the emergence of the normal, rational individual (as opposed to the abnormal one) in the practices of justice in the course of the nineteenth century, was shown to imply such a veridiction. Since, according to French law, only the mentally healthy could be judged, a definition of "normal" individuals was called-for. Motivated by their interests, "normal" individuals were defined as those who were able to give meaning and reasons for their own actions. Foucault explains further that some of the major problems for criminal psychiatry in the nineteenth century were posed by "motiveless acts committed by a subject endowed with reason" (Foucault 2003: 117), acts performed by individuals who were obviously not mad, but had neither subjective nor objective motives for their crimes.[9]

The necessity to explain those acts led in fact to the incorporation of psychiatric experts within the judicial system. This had two consequences. First, the psychiatrists invented "instinct" as a concept with a "regulated use within a discursive formation" to explain acts that lacked a motive (Foucault 2003: 131; 1978: 153; 2001b: 322–3). Later in the nineteenth century, sexual instincts were codified as an alternative to the logic of interest, under the internal "economy of pleasure" (Foucault 2003: 311).[10] Second, the penal system where the "abnormal" appeared, was also the site for the emergence of a new veridiction: it no longer centered on the imputation of the crime but on "criminal subjectivity." The judgment was based on the avowal of the individual, but this avowal did not concern the admission of what one *did*, but what one *is*. The liberal subject is thus a subject formed in the expectation that he is able to tell the truth about himself, to express his interests and desires, sexual or others (Foucault 2014b: 223–9). There is, therefore, a strong association between the emergence of the "rational individual," the *homo oeconomicus* (who is "governed through economic principles") and his capacity to give reasons for his acts.

These acts of truth are the subject matter of the lectures starting in the 1980s: veridictions—or forms of "truth-telling"—*as government*, in different historical periods. The 1980 lectures are focused on "the government of men through the manifestation of truth in the form of subjectivity," and link, for the first time, government, truth, and subjectivity. Foucault further explains that he is interested in "acts of truth," where truth is manifested *through* a subject, who appears either as the operator, the witness or as the object of this truth (Foucault 2014a: 81–5). He first discards the acts of truth in the form of acts of faith since the truth at stake is a revealed and dogmatic truth (Foucault 2014a:

85; see also Foucault 2014b: 188). He wants instead to focus on those specific acts where the subject tells the truth *about himself*, as in the act of confession (or in the judicial avowal). These are *reflexive* acts of truth, where the subject is *at the same time* the operator, the witness and the object of truth. They are very different from acts of faith since the act of truth "is not at all a matter of adhering to a content of truth, but of exploring individual secrets, and of exploring them endlessly" (Foucault 2014a: 84).

The practice of confession was already dealt with by Foucault in the 1975 lectures, in 1976's *The History of Sexuality I* and again in the 1978 lectures, all showing the specificity of the Christian direction of conscience. It consists in "starting from oneself, [to] extract and produce a truth which binds one to the person who directs one's conscience" (Foucault 2009: 183). The 1980 lectures come back to pastoral power, yet what is being discussed now is Christianity as *an example* of power exercised through the establishment of a relationship of self to truth. This relationship appears in different forms in different periods, and early Christianity is just one of those periods.

Besides the above-mentioned differences between acts of faith and reflexive acts of truth, Foucault clearly identifies here acts of truth and "the point of subjectivation." Government asks of individuals certain acts of truth, by which they constitute themselves as subjects of a certain exercise of power. This actually seems to be the heart of the art of government:

> We have now more or less tightened up the problem: why and how does the exercise of power in our society, the exercise of power as government of men, demand not only acts of obedience and submission, but truth acts in which individuals who are subjects in the power relationship are also subjects as actors, spectator, witnesses, or objects in manifestation of truth procedures?
> 
> Foucault 2014a: 82

If power solely asked for obedience and submission, then it would function in the mode of discipline. As mentioned above, Foucault understands that in contrast to what he stated in *Discipline and Punish*, power does not function by the imposition of force on bodies. Rather, it functions by recognizing and maintaining individuals as "*persons who act*" and acts of truth are one such form of action. In 1980, Foucault is interested in the reflexive form of acts of truth—the act of avowal—to which he accorded genealogical importance. The disciplinary regime, creating subjugated subjects under the scrutiny of the human sciences, is now subsumed under a more general investigation of the subjectivity implied by each mode of government. In 1980, for instance, Foucault states that he intends to analyze the type of government in early Christianity that "does not just require one to obey [along the prescriptive axis of jurisdiction] but also to manifest what one *is* by stating it [in a veridiction]" (Foucault 2014a: 321).

The analysis of government turns therefore into an analysis of the relations between the subject and truth. It seems that the modes of constitution of the subject *through* veridiction become central to the analysis, following the understanding that in the current neoliberal exercise of power, the role of the law is to determine the rules of the game and does not imply any action or any physical constraint on the individual body.

The social constraint thus has to be found not in the prescription of the sovereign law or the disciplinary norm, but elsewhere. If the subject is still constituted within the mechanisms of power, this subjection needs to have other sources. It is for this reason, I suggest, that Foucault turns to acts of truth as a form of obligation on the self.

While Foucault arrived at the issue of acts of truth and modes of subjectivation via the analysis of liberal governmentality, it is the concept of government in general as the conduct of conducts, and not solely its liberal form, which in the 1980s is associated with truth. Government always implies a relation to the self: "the reflection on this notion of governmentality cannot avoid passing through, theoretically and practically, the element of a subject defined by the relationship of self to the self" (Foucault 2005: 252).[11]

## The Second Reading of Homer (1981)

In a series of lectures given at the University of Louvain in 1981, Foucault weaves together fascinatingly elements from the 1970–1 lectures on archaic truth and justice, reflection on the disciplinary psychiatric power he studied in 1974 and 1975, and his most recent inquiries on subjectivity and confession. His stated aim is to do "a political and an institutional ethnology of truth-telling," which gives an account of the practice of avowal in judicial procedures over time, including our own (Foucault 2014b: 28). Interestingly, he goes on to say that he intends to study the relationships between "what Georges Dumézil called 'truthful speech' . . . veridiction, and that other form of speech one might call speech of justice . . . Veridiction and jurisdiction." One should note that jurisdiction here is not exactly the prescription of a code, but rather the judicial sentence that says "what is just and *what has to be done* [in order] for justice to be established or restored" (Foucault 2014b: 28, *emphasis added*). Dealing with archaic Greece, the first two lessons seem to illustrate the shift from the 1970–1 lectures, and to provide Foucault with an opportunity to revise his original reading of the episode between Menelaus and Antilochus. Most probably, returning to this text was not a coincidence, and it is therefore interesting to trace the manner in which he adjusts this re-reading to his new concerns.

First, as in 1971 lecture, the race and the judicial procedure are seen as part of a sequence, i.e., the oath is the continuation of the confrontation that started with the race: "there is a continuity between the *agon* and the judicial" (Foucault 2014b: 37). But in 1981, Foucault says that the race itself is *not* a sportive confrontation of heroes, with unpredictable results. In fact, he contends the opposite: the race is a ceremony where the existing order, the hierarchy between the heroes is made visible, as "the visible ceremony *of a truth already visible*" (Foucault 2014b: 39, *emphasis added*).

This completely overturns the 1971 interpretation of the race. Indeed, as presented in the 1970–1 lectures, the tragic truth of archaic Greece could never have coincided with order and hierarchy. Truth was supposed to be unpredictable, the same way that the winner of the race is not known in advance. However, in 1981 Foucault specifically indicates that this is not the case. The race, in fact, is supposed to be "the liturgical unfolding of a truth *already known*" (Foucault 2014b: 39, *emphasis added*). The maneuver of Antilochus actually disturbs a well-ordered ceremony, where *truth as order* is supposed to be exposed. Indeed, when reaching Menelaus at a point in the road where only one could pass, Antilochus should have shown his respect for the best warrior, and let Menelaus pass first. Instead, he confronts him and passes first; here the contest does not reveal the truth, it *masks* it (Foucault 2014b: 39)! Truth is not *created* in the confrontation; it is only expected to become manifest, as something that existed *prior* to the race. Antilochus did wrong by disturbing the manifestation of truth as "the order of reality" (Foucault 2014b: 42).[12]

Foucault seems therefore to abandon his 1971 Nietzschean interpretation of truth as an event or a lightning. The distinction between two different types of truth—the scientific split between true and false and the tragic dreadful truth of the Ancients—characteristic of the analysis of power/knowledge, now becomes irrelevant: "science, objective knowledge (*connaissance*) is *only one possible case of all these forms by which truth can be manifested*" (Foucault 2014a: 7, *emphasis added*). Indeed, in 1981 the quasi-avowal of Antilochus is not about the recognition of factual evidence (as opposed to the lightning); it is about letting truth be manifested (Foucault 2014b: 39).

This manifestation of truth, the *alethurgie*,[13] is henceforth Foucault's central preoccupation. It is defined as "the set of possible verbal or non-verbal procedures by which one brings to light what is laid down as true as opposed to false, *hidden, inexpressible, unforeseeable, or forgotten*" (Foucault 2014a: 7, *emphasis added*): all of these are opposed to "what is true." True is opposed to false (as in the scientific/ rational approach) the same way that it is opposed to the hidden or the dreadful (as in the archaic/ mythological one). The form of the *alethurgie* or the truth act, as much as truth itself, is thus historically and culturally determined. When Antilochus renounces the taking of the oath, he demonstrates that he recognizes and accepts the existing hierarchy between the protagonists: it is "the renunciation of what had for a moment *veiled the truth and the true brilliance of the heroes*" (Foucault 2014b: 43, *emphasis added*). This manifestation of truth, in archaic time, respects the structure of society: "the avowal consists in restoring, within an agonistic structure, the forms in which the truth of their strength was supposed to ritually appear" (Foucault 2014b: 42). We are thus in a veridiction process, a truth-telling, which is adjusted to the society in which it takes place. The discourse of the law, the jurisdiction, is now presented as an instance of veridiction.[14]

The power—effect of (modern) knowledge as the setting of the rules of true and false that was the focus of Foucault in the 1970s, has thus turned into a much larger issue—the way in which a subject binds himself to a manifestation of truth, an *alethurgie* as an act of truth, whatever the type of truth at stake. Foucault intends at this point to study the "power of the truth" on the subject (Foucault 2014a: 101). Interestingly enough, in his criticism of Foucault's power/knowledge entanglement Habermas challenges Foucault because he "abruptly reverses power's truth dependency into the power-dependency of truth" (Habermas 1990: 274). Foucault seems here to agree with Habermas on "power's truth dependency" and to hold that power resides in the manifestation of truth. The point though, as I have tried to show here, is that Foucault does not assume that "truth" is objectively valid. This significantly changes the meaning of Habermas' assertion.

## Conclusion

In the introductory lesson of the 1980 lectures, Foucault states that his aim is now to study the fundamental link between power and truth:

> It is often said that, in the final analysis, there is something like a kernel of violence behind all relations of power and that if one were to strip the power of its showy garb one would find the naked game of life and death. Maybe. But can there be power without showy garb? ... Can there be an exercise of power without a ring of truth, without an alethurgic circle that turns around it and accompanies it?
> Foucault 2014a: 17

While the "undressing" of power, for the sake of exposing its violence on the bodies might well have characterized Foucault's project up until 1976, from then on he moves to a new topic of interest: the ways in which power is exercised in terms of truth. He also insists that *any* form of government, from the most ancient to the most recent, including the government of self or government of others, is always an *alethurgie*, a manifestation of truth:

> For the link between manifestation of truth and exercise of power to be made, we don't have to wait for the constitution of these new, modern relations between the art of government and, let's say, political, economic, and social rationality. The link between exercise of power and manifestation of truth is much older and exists at a much deeper level.
> Foucault 2014a: 17

Interestingly enough, at the very end, Foucault returns to the two axes of jurisdiction and veridiction for the government of people, but in a different formulation. In the introduction to *The Use of Pleasure*, the issue in question is morality, with the code of conduct, namely, jurisdiction, and with what Foucault now terms "the forms of subjectivation," instead of veridiction. Different moral practices could emphasize either one axis or the other. The Christian penitence system of the thirteenth century focused almost all its effort on the juridical side, developing a very strict code of conduct (Foucault 1990: 29–30; see also 2014a: 211; 2014b: 174–82). At the other end of the spectrum, the "moral conceptions in Greek and Greco-Roman antiquity were much more oriented toward practices of the self and the question of *askesis*" (Foucault 1990: 30).

The "turn to the Greeks," therefore, might well be explained by the fact that with some similarity to neoliberal governmentality and the accompanied "regression of the juridical," in Greco-Roman antiquity, the conduct of conducts was not obtained by sovereign law, nor by the norm of discipline. Rather, it was obtained by forms of veridiction:

> I wonder if our problem nowadays is not in a way similar [to that of the Greeks] since most of us no longer believe that ethics is founded on religion, *nor do we want a legal system to intervene in our moral, personal, private life.*
> Foucault 1997a: 255

From the perspective of our contemporary governmentality, this position calls on us to draw two conclusions. First, one should reconsider our neoliberal order and the acts of truth it demands of its subjects. Indeed, the confession practices and the avowal in the judicial system described by Foucault in 1980 and 1981 seem to have overflowed and turned into a generalized exhibition of the self on social media (Harcourt 2015: 99). Others speak of a "publicity culture," where people are expected to and rewarded for "displaying themselves in an easily-consumed public way" (Marwick and boyd 2011: 119). This further leads to a second question concerning the nature of truth itself; social media algorithms are indeed tuned to promote posts based on their potential virality, with no or little concern for their veracity. As Zuboff puts it: "Google is 'formally indifferent' to what its users *say or do*, as long as they say it and do it in ways that Google can capture and convert into data" (Zuboff 2015: 79). The current digital power's *alethurgie*, so to speak, might therefore be deeply linked to the fake news it propels.

## Notes

1. The term "veridiction" is Foucault's creation. It is a neologism that results from the combination of the Latin root *veri* for truth, and diction for speaking, pronouncing, or telling. It captures best this notion of truth-telling (see Becker et al. 2012: 5, ft. 9).
2. See for instance Harrer (2005), Landry (2009), Butler (2016), and Lorenzini (2016).
3. The distinction between knowledge as "*savoir*" and knowledge as "*connaissance*" is first introduced in *The Archaeology of Knowledge* (Foucault 1972: 15, ft. 2; 183). The distinction is also one of the main objects of inquiry of the 1970–1 lectures. See, for instance, in the first lesson: "Let us say that we will call knowledge-*connaissance* the system that allows desire and knowledge-*savoir* to be given a prior unity, reciprocal belonging, and a co-naturalness. And we will call knowledge-*savoir* that which we need to drag from the interiority of knowledge-*connaissance in order to rediscover in it the object of a willing, the end of a desire, the instrument of a domination, the stake of a struggle*" (Foucault 2013: 17, *emphasis added*).
4. In addition, Defert (2011: 259) reminds us that in his interpretation of the split between archaic and classic Greece forms of truth, Foucault was also clearly influenced by the work of Detienne, who claims that the "true" in archaic times was not opposed to the "false;" "the only significant opposition was between *Aletheia* and *Lethe*" (Detienne 1994: 69–70).
5. For Defert, in the 1970–1 lessons and onward, Foucault is actually conducting "a genealogy"—in a Nietzschean mode—but a genealogy of knowledge rather than morals (Defert 2011: 260).
6. Actually Foucault distinguishes for the first time the "juridical" from the will of the king and presents the Natural Law as a counter-conduct in a conference that follows the end of the 1978 lectures (see Foucault 1996).
7. In *Discipline and Punish*, Foucault depicted the public execution and torture of the convicted person as "justice as the physical, material and awesome force of the sovereign" (Foucault 1995: 50).
8. It can be argued that the importance of truth-telling was already highlighted, albeit with regard to sexuality, in *The History of Sexuality*. Davidson, for instance, shows that when

tackling the repressive hypothesis, Foucault rejects the juridical model of power and proposes instead a mechanism that puts "the discursive ritual of confession" at the center (Davidson 2016: 58). Yet, the notion of "subjectivation" is absent from this text; saying the truth about one's sexuality is not (yet) the active constitution of a subject in relation to truth, but the production of a subjected subject within the sexual apparatus. With regard to the important shift from subjectivity to subjectivation in Foucault's late inquiries, see also Revel (2016).

9   Beistegui (2016) further shows that the physiocrats were the first to understand that desires should not be opposed but governed; with the advent of liberal governmentality, a distinction was thus made between licit desires (interests) and illicit ones (instincts).

10  Strikingly, Foucault's claim that "instincts" are social/cultural constructions constitutes a major departure from the Nietzschean lessons of 1971 (see Butler 1989: 604–05).

11  In the lectures at Dartmouth in 1980, government is presented as the point of encounter between the technique of the self ("how the self constitutes himself") and the way this technique is integrated into structures of coercion: "The contact point, where the individuals are driven by others is tied to the way they conduct themselves, is what we can call, I think, government ... *Governing people is not a way to force people to do* what the governor wants; it is always a versatile equilibrium ... between techniques which assure coercion and processes *through which the self is constructed or modified by himself* ... I insisted too much on techniques of domination. Discipline is only one aspect of the art of governing people" (Foucault 1993: 203–04, *emphasis added*).

12  This contradicts almost point for point the lesson of February 17, 1971: Homeric justice in the contest is precisely *not* in accordance with the order of the world (see Foucault 2013: 116–17).

13  According to Senellart (2012: 325), Foucault created the word, therefore I kept the French orthography. In the lecture, Foucault explains that it is developed from the Greek "alethourges," the veridical (Foucault 2014a: 7).

14  Similarly, in *Confessions of the Flesh*, Foucault describes David's avowal as a veridiction that includes the constitutive elements of a judicial procedure (Foucault 2018: 399).

## References

Becker, G. S., F. Ewald, and B. E. Harcourt (2012), "Becker on Ewald on Foucault on Becker: American Neoliberalism and Michel Foucault's 1979 'Birth of Biopolitics' Lectures," *Coase-Sandor Institute for Law & Economics,* Working Paper No. 614.

Beistegui, M. (2014), "The Subject of Truth: On Foucault's *Lectures on the Will to Know*," *Quadranti: Rivista Internazionale di Filosofia Contemporanea*, 2 (1): 80–99.

Beistegui, M. (2016), "The Government of Desire: A Genealogical Perspective," *Journal of the British Society for Phenomenology*, 47 (2): 190–203.

Butler, J. (1989), "Foucault and the Paradox of Bodily Inscriptions," *Praxis International*, 11: 601–07.

Butler, J. (2016), "Wrong-Doing, Truth-Telling. The Case of Sexual Avowal," in L. Cremonesi, O. Irrera, D. Lorenzini, and M. Tazzioli (eds), *Foucault and the Making of Subjects*, 77–93, London: Rowman & Littlefield.

Davidson, A. (2016), "From Subjection to Subjectivation—Michel Foucault and the History of Sexuality," in L. Cremonesi, O. Irrera, D. Lorenzini, and M. Tazzioli (eds), *Foucault and the Making of Subjects*, 55–62, London: Rowman & Littlefield.

Defert, D. (2011), "Situation du Cours," in M. Foucault, *Leçons sur la volonté de savoir: Cours au Collège de France, 1970–1971,* ed. F. Ewald, A. Fontana, and D. Defert, 255–79, Paris: Gallimard/Seuil.
Detienne, M. (1994), *Les Maîtres de Vérité dans la Grèce Archaïque,* Paris: Pocket.
Ewald, F. (1990), "Norms, Discipline and the Law," *Representation,* 30: 138–61.
Foucault M. (1972), *The Archaeology of Knowledge and the Discourse on Language,* trans. A. M. Sheridan Smith, New York: Pantheon Books.
Foucault, M. (1978), *The History of Sexuality. Volume 1: An Introduction,* trans. R. Hurley, New York: Pantheon Books.
Foucault, M. (1982), "The Subject and Power," in H. L. Dreyfus and P. Rabinow (eds), *Michel Foucault: Beyond Structuralism and Hermeneutics,* 208–26, Chicago: The University of Chicago Press.
Foucault, M. (1990), *The Use of Pleasure: Volume 2 of The History of Sexuality,* trans. R. Hurley, New York: Vintage Books.
Foucault, M. (1993), "About the Beginning of the Hermeneutics of the Self: Two Lectures at Dartmouth," *Political Theory,* 21 (2): 198–227.
Foucault, M. (1995), *Discipline and Punish. The Birth of the Prison,* trans. A. Sheridan, New York: Vintage Books.
Foucault, M. (1996), "What is Critique?," in J. Schmidt (ed.), *What is Enlightenment? Eighteenth-Century Questions and Twentieth Century Answers,* 23–61, Berkeley: University of California Press.
Foucault, M. (1997a), "On the Genealogy of Ethics: an Overview of Work in Progress," in P. Rabinow (ed.), *The Essential Works of Michel Foucault, 1954–1984, Vol. 1: Ethics, Subjectivity and Truth,* 253–80, New York: The New Press.
Foucault, M. (1997b), "The Ethics of the Concern of the Self as a Practice of Freedom," in P. Rabinow (ed.), *The Essential Works of Michel Foucault, 1954–1984, Vol. 1: Ethics, Subjectivity and Truth,* 281–302, New York: The New Press.
Foucault, M. (1997c), "Question of Method," in P. Rabinow (ed.), *The Essential Works of Michel Foucault, 1954–1984, Vol. 1: Ethics, Subjectivity and Truth,* 223–38, New York: The New Press.
Foucault, M. (2001a), "Les rapports de pouvoir passent à l'intérieur des corps," *Dits et écrits* II, ed. D. Defert and F. Ewald, 228–36, Paris: Gallimard.
Foucault, M. (2001b), "Le jeu de Michel Foucault," *Dits et écrits* II, ed. D. Defert and F. Ewald, 298–329, Paris: Gallimard.
Foucault, M. (2003), *Abnormal: Lectures at the Collège de France, 1974–1975,* ed. V. Marchetti and A. Salomoni, trans. G. Burchell, London: Verso.
Foucault, M. (2005), *The Hermeneutics of the Subject: Lectures at the Collège de France 1981–1982,* ed. F. Gros, trans. G. Burchell, New York: Palgrave Macmillan.
Foucault, M. (2008), *The Birth of Biopolitics: Lectures at the Collège de France 1978–1979,* ed. M. Senellart, trans. G. Burchell, Basingstoke: Palgrave Macmillan.
Foucault, M. (2009), *Security, Territory, Population: Lectures at the Collège de France 1977–1978,* ed. M. Senellart, trans. G. Burchell, Basingstoke: Palgrave Macmillan.
Foucault, M. (2013), *Lectures on the Will to Know: Lectures at the Collège de France 1970–1971,* ed. D. Defert, trans. G. Burchell, Basingstoke: Palgrave Macmillan.
Foucault, M. (2014a), *On the Government of the Living: Lectures at the Collège de France 1979–1980,* ed. M. Senellart, trans. G. Burchell, Basingstoke: Palgrave Macmillan.
Foucault, M. (2014b), *Wrong-Doing, Truth-Telling: The Function of Avowal in Justice,* ed. F. Brion and B. Harcourt, trans. S. W. Sawyer, Chicago: University of Chicago Press.

Foucault, M. (2015), *Théories et institutions pénales: Cours au Collège de France 1971-1972*, ed. F. Ewald, A. Fontana, B. Harcourt, E. Basso, C. Doron and D. Defert, Paris: Gallimard/Seuil.

Foucault, M. (2018), *Histoire de la sexualité 4: Les aveux de la chair*, Paris: Gallimard.

Gernet, L. (1990), *Droit et institutions en Grèce antique,* Paris: Flammarion.

Habermas, J. (1990), *The Philosophical Discourse of Modernity,* Cambridge: MIT Press.

Harcourt, B. E. (2015), *Exposed,* Harvard: Harvard University Press.

Harrer, S. (2005), "The Theme of Subjectivity in Foucault's Lecture Series *L'Herméneutique du Sujet*," *Foucault Studies,* 2: 75-96.

Landry, J.-M. (2009), "Confession, Obedience, and Subjectivity: Michel Foucault's Unpublished Lectures—*On the Government of the Living*," *Telos,* 146: 111-23.

Lorenzini, D. (2016), "Foucault, Regimes of Truth and the Making of the Subject," in L. Cremonesi, O. Irrera, D. Lorenzini, and M. Tazzioli (eds), *Foucault and the Making of Subjects*, 63-75, London: Rowman & Littlefield.

Marwick A. E. and d. boyd (2011), "I Tweet Honestly, I Tweet Passionately: Twitter Users, Context Collapse, and the Imagined Audience," *New Media & Society,* 13 (1): 114-33.

Revel, J. (2016), "Between Politics and Ethics—The Question of Subjectivation," in L. Cremonesi, O. Irrera, D. Lorenzini, and M. Tazzioli (eds), *Foucault and the Making of Subjects*, 163-73, London: Rowman & Littlefield.

Senellart, M. (2012), "Situation du Cours," in M. Foucault, *Du gouvernement des vivants: Cours au Collège de France 1979-1980,* ed. F. Ewald, A. Fontana and M. Senellart, 321-50, Paris: Gallimard/Seuil.

Zuboff, S. (2015), "Big Other: Surveillance Capitalism and the Prospects of an Information Civilization," *Journal of Information Technology,* 30: 75-89.

Part Four

# Government of Self, Government of Others

# 10

# Understanding Power Through Governmentality

## Karim Barakat

In 1984, Foucault began to characterize himself as a Kantian, which raised interpretational problems for several commentators who have attempted to put forward a coherent account of Foucault's genealogical exposition in relation to Kant.[1] Most prominent is Beatrice Han-Pile's criticism, which has characterized Foucault's work as alternating between the transcendental and the empirical without being able to reconcile the two. According to Han-Pile, Foucault introduces a "transcendental history" of specific forms of knowledge, which is void of a proper transcendental grounding for the historical empiricism to which he is committed (Han 2002). Nonetheless, whether Foucault retains the transcendental element in his critique is a contentious matter. I argue in this chapter that we can understand Foucault's work as empirically concerned with determining conditions of possibility that are historical and contingent rather than universal and necessary. This makes Foucauldian critique immanent and allows for recognizing Foucault's methodological commitments as broadly Kantian. I argue that, following Kant, Foucault disposes of metaphysical dependencies by defining conditions that make knowledge possible. This reading of Foucault emerges primarily from focusing on his empirical method coupled with the justifications that can be offered for his historical nominalism. I thus argue that by taking Kant's critique of metaphysics as a basis, we can justify Foucault's historical method on Kantian grounds by recognizing that it deals with the question of conditions of possibility. Though this raises the issue of whether we can incorporate the notion of the historical *a priori* Foucault employs in his archaeological work into a Kantian framework, I will be setting aside Foucault's early work and will focus mainly on his genealogical method.[2] Foucault, consequently, offers a post-Kantian account of politics that relies on a historical basis instead of a metaphysical one.

## Foucault's Kantian Method

Situating Foucault within the Kantian dichotomy of transcendental and empirical has thus far proven to be challenging. For instance, in *The Politics of Ourselves*, Amy Allen rightly argues that for Foucault, critique must be understood as immanent. This is primarily the product of recognizing that Foucault does not eliminate the notion of the subject altogether, but merely eliminates the transcendental subject and thus institutes a critique of critique. On Allen's reading, Foucault both endorses the Kantian project and seeks to develop it further by ridding it of the transcendental element. He thus transforms rather than rejects Kant's project, by exposing the role of the historical and social in the constitution of subjectivity. This critique of critique is not only to be understood as a critique of Kant, but also a critique in the Kantian sense, namely, one that specifies the "conditions and limits of possibility of that which Kant himself took as his own starting point, namely the transcendental subject" (Allen 2007: 35). For Allen, however, Foucauldian critique remains partly transcendental, as it is concerned with specifying *necessary* conditions of possibility for the thinking subject. Though the conditions themselves are historical and contingent, their actualization is necessary to render forms of subjectivity possible. According to Allen, therefore, these are necessary though not sufficient conditions. Yet this does not qualify to be a fully transcendental critique, as it is rooted in contingent historical processes rather than in necessary conditions (Allen 2007: 35).

I hold that labeling the conditions of possibility Foucault identifies as necessary is problematic for two reasons. First, on textual grounds, Foucault repeatedly and explicitly rejects the introduction of necessary conditions, and consequently transcendental conditions.[3] Moreover, conditions of possibility need not be thought of as necessary conditions. For instance, the conditions for the emergence of sexuality as a field where disciplinary and biopolitical mechanisms intersect have made sexuality possible, but different historical conditions may have also produced the same form of subjectivity. Allen recognizes the contingency of the appearance of these conditions, but takes them to be necessary for the specific problematization at hand. Yet given Foucault's continuous attempt to recast necessity in terms of contingency, this ascribes to Foucault a position from which he often distances himself. The appearance of a discursive framework can make a domain possible, but by no means is it the only framework that could produce the domain. Consequently, Foucault recognizes that though sexuality may arise out of different historical conditions, it may still fulfill similar social roles. Thus, the conditions of possibility to which Foucault is committed cannot be understood as necessary but should be recognized as sufficient.[4]

Colin Koopman, alternatively, argues that whereas the phenomenological tradition attempted to reconcile Kant's transcendental philosophy with a historical inquiry, Foucault disposes of the transcendental altogether (Koopman 2010: 101). Foucault thus incorporates into his work Kant's notion of critique, where critique is not concerned with universal or necessary conditions, but with historical conditions, rendering his critique immanent (Koopman 2010: 108). Koopman accepts Johanna Oksala's reading of Foucault as refusing to begin with a cogito or subject and locates instead the core of Foucault's critique in problematization. Problematization becomes "a stable conceptual matrix" that allows for shedding light on the "emergence of hybrid networks of problems we can come to recognize ... as contingent complexes rather than necessary givens" (Koopman 2010: 110). Thus, the contingent and local analysis of problematization replaces the transcendental approach Kant had undertaken. Koopman thus introduces a distinction between "critical conditions of possibility," which are neither universal nor necessary, and "transcendental conditions of possibility."

On Koopman's account, the former are what Foucault endorses through his local genealogical analysis. These conditions define the "limits" of knowledge under a specific historical period (Koopman 2010: 115).

Koopman presents an interesting link to Kant, yet as Colin McQuillan argues, this reading of Foucault's work casts doubt on the Kantian aspect of Foucault's critique. To begin with, McQuillan points out that Kant took all critique to be transcendental. This raises the question of whether we can maintain any form of Kantian critique once we dispose of the universal scope and necessary modality of the conditions Foucault specifies. More importantly, McQuillan identifies a significant difference between the Kantian and Foucauldian projects. Whereas Kant was interested in defining the limits of reason and thus confining its legitimate use to ward off dogmatism, Foucault is explicitly concerned with transgression, or with "crossing over" (McQuillan 2010: 154). Kant had argued that reason must renounce exceeding its own limits, while Foucault's main aim is to undo those limits by unmasking them as neither universal nor necessary, but contingent and thus subject to change.

We are, thus, left with the problem of reading Foucault as rejecting transcendental philosophy while maintaining a Kantian element to his critique. In order to account for this position, Christina Hendricks offers an interesting interpretation of Foucault's reading of Kant in *The Government of Self and Others*. In those lectures, Foucault notes that we find two threads that develop out of Kant. The first is concerned with the "analytic of truth," a transcendental approach that raises the question of the conditions of possibility of true knowledge. The second pertains to what Foucault terms an "ontology of the present" or an "ontology of ourselves" stemming from Kant's commitments in his two essays "What is Enlightenment?" and "What is Revolution?". For Hendricks, whereas an analytics of truth is concerned with limits, an ontology of ourselves opens the space for transgression. On this view, Foucault identifies in Kant's "What is Enlightenment?" essay a legitimate move towards crossing limits through raising the question of the present (Hendricks 2008: 361–2).

Under Foucault's reading, having determined the limits of reason in the first *Critique*, Kant introduces a normative demand of daring to liberate oneself from the condition of nonage (Kant 1991). Hendricks reads in Foucault's Kant the identification of contingent limits pertaining to a contemporary problem (Hendricks 2008: 362). Kant, thus, was concerned with identifying the status of the stifling of the free use of reason in Prussia, and as a result of recognizing it as a contingent limit, urges for transforming it. Kant's approach comes through critique and argument, by primarily introducing the distinction between the public and private use of reason, and thus marking separate uses of reason, which renders obedience and autonomous rational thinking compatible.

For Hendricks, this is a mark of the attitude of modernity that Foucault identifies in his essay on the Enlightenment, where the critic locates something in the present and attempts to transform it. The critic does not stand outside of it in a historically neutral position. In a similar manner, through aligning himself with Kant's project, Foucault does not assume a metahistorical perspective that gives him access to an objective view of history, but locates himself in a present moment, and initiates transformations from within (Hendricks 2008: 364). This sheds light on the advantage that Foucault's analysis provides with respect to critique. Given the conclusions of Foucault's methodological commitments in terms of how we understand history, critique must follow from within a specific historical power-knowledge regime. It is in this sense that Foucault's critique can be understood as immanent rather than transcendental. Historical analysis becomes a tool for transgression by locating historically contingent limits that have been considered to be self-evident, universal, and necessary limits. But this could only follow from aligning oneself with a historical tradition, one that allows for historicizing the present. Consequently, whereas Foucault does not specify the direction which critique should take, he provides the theoretical means to effect transformations on present conditions. The question that follows pertains to the role the empirical side in Foucault's work plays, an issue I will address in the next section.

## Nominalism and Empiricism in Foucault's Work

Foucault's relation to Kant opens up the space for the broader question of the method he endorses in his work pertaining to the genealogy of governmentality. Whether Foucault has been consistent in method throughout his work is questionable, but it is crucial to note that apparent inconsistencies can be traced to changes in his view that ultimately rest on empirical grounds. I will not be concerned here with putting forward a coherent reading of method across all of Foucault's work. Though the question of "conditions of possibility" is abundant in Foucault's archaeologies, rendering that work consistent with a genealogical approach is not straightforward and raises problems that I will set aside for my purposes. This includes, but is not limited to, Foucault's early commitment to the historical *a priori* in his archaeologies.[5] It is crucial, however, to note that Foucault retains the question of the conditions of possibility in his genealogical work. This is most explicitly specified in his 1978–9 lectures *The Birth of Biopolitics*, where Foucault maintains that "critique would consist in determining under what conditions and with what effects a veridiction is exercised." Foucault continues to state, "the problem is to bring to light the *conditions* that had to be met for it to be *possible* to hold a discourse on madness ... that can be true or false according to the rules of medicine, say, or of confession, psychology, or psychoanalysis" (Foucault 2008: 36, *emphasis added*).

To clarify the empirical aspect of Foucault's work, Koopman emphasizes Foucault's concern with conditions of possibility as opposed to Hume's empiricism. According to Koopman, Humean empiricism searches for conditions of actuality, understood in terms of causal conditions.[6] Locating conditions of possibility, alternatively, does not introduce any kind of necessary causation (Koopman 2010: 119). The shift to genealogy, then, should not be seen as a complete break with the archaeological work. Instead, it offers a different approach in order to deal with specific problems identified in archaeology. As Koopman shows, Foucault maintains the question of conditions of possibility in his genealogical work, which becomes crystallized in the focus on problematizations. While archaeology specifies conditions that make discourses possible, it does not engage change and mobility and cannot account for periods of transition between epistemes. This is why conditions of possibility end up being inexplicably transient. These gaps, however, remain inaccessible under an archaeological approach and, as Koopman argues, this necessitates a shift to genealogy (Koopman 2010: 114).

Attributing an empiricism to Foucault can be justified by appealing to a strong form of nominalism. In *The Birth of Biopolitics*, Foucault begins by methodologically assuming that universals do not exist (Foucault 2008: 3). This marks a development of the nominalist approach Foucault had already endorsed in *The Will to Knowledge*, where the scope of nominalism was limited to power. Alternatively, the methodological nominalism introduced here confers an additional component to genealogical analysis by uncovering the content of universals as historically constituted. Foucault's genealogies, during this stage of his work, show that universals do not even exist in the mind as coherent entities, but are rather products of a multiplicity of relations that are discursively linked together. This does not merely commit him to the rejection of a Platonic understanding of universals, but also to rejecting conceptualism. Moreover, not only do universals not exist in the mind as concepts, but they are also not reducible to *verbal* associations as we find in Hobbes and Hume. Given Foucault's starting point, namely the analysis of practices rather than subjective experience, such universals are reduced to discursive formations that constitute bodies of knowledge and produce forms of subjectivity as power effects.

This aspect of Foucault's work enables us to recognize an empirical role for genealogies. Foucault, thus, begins with a nominalist presupposition that is supported by the explanatory force his local analysis of concrete phenomena provides. Though nonexistent, these universals come to be shaped or "mark[ed] ... out as reality," by a set of practices that are interlinked with a regime of truth (Foucault 2008: 19). This regime of truth, in turn, primarily consists of a set of rules that determine the truth or falsity of statements within a discourse (Foucault 2008: 35).

Consequently, if universals do not have any explanatory force independently of historical empirical content, Foucault is not concerned with mapping out a deductive historical narrative grounded in necessity. Instead, for Foucault, historical analysis will shed light on the conditions of possibility of these universals, or on how it became possible to speak of madness, sexuality, or even the state. If this analysis does not follow a deductive approach that deals with universals, and having disposed of the transcendental, it must be empirical in nature. Understood in these terms, and while recognizing that experience for Foucault is at least partly constituted by bodies of knowledge, we find a modified form of the Kantian project of accounting for the conditions that make experience possible. For Foucault, however, this experience is a *present* one, and its conditions are determined through historical analysis.

Yet undertaking the analysis of experience historically requires its own justification. Apart from referring to Nietzsche's genealogy, Foucault never explicitly provides a justification for the historical approach, which he presents as a strictly methodological commitment. Whereas his nominalism justifies recourse to an empirical analysis, the historical nature of such an analysis requires further warrant. The credit his early genealogical work gives to Nietzsche provides a good justification for moving towards a historical analysis that produces subjects through power relations. Yet, as I have just shown, in his later work, Foucault insists that invoking a historical account in relation to the ontology of ourselves also entails a debt to Kant. As Foucault maintains in "What is Enlightenment?," the positive aspect of critique will not be concerned with determining universal limits but with "separat[ing] out, from the contingency that has made us what we are [or from contingent conditions of possibility], the possibility of no longer being, doing, or thinking what we are, do or think" (Foucault 1998b: 315–16). The Kantian aspect of critique, then, is modified to identify what is contingent and arbitrary as opposed to what is universal and necessary. As Hendricks argues, Foucault locates this in Kant's reflection on a contemporary historical moment and his prescription for a political impetus to move beyond the state of immaturity towards a free public use of reason (Hendricks 2008: 362–3; Foucault 1998b: 309). But whereas Kant was concerned with marking out the legitimate use of reason within a historical moment following his critique of pure reason, Foucault locates conditions of possibility in terms of contingency. This opens up the space for moving beyond what has been identified as contingent through a historical critique as opposed to a transcendental one, an analysis that identifies the contingent elements thus offering the possibility for transforming them.[7] Foucault's genealogies, therefore, should be understood as *empirical verifications* of the historical conditions of possibility of what is said and known, which also allows for constituting ourselves differently through critique.

It is important to recognize that Foucault's historical nominalism does not attempt to grasp the reality that lurks beneath our delusions of stability. Thomas Lemke, for instance, argues that Foucault's historical nominalism entails a "negative" and a "positive" trait. The negative trait pertains to unpacking presupposed universal truths or, as Foucault puts it in "Questions of Method," it is a "breach of self-evidence" (Foucault 2001b: 226). The other function is a positive one that follows from introducing new links and relations, which present a phenomenon as universal and necessary (Lemke 2007: 47). For Lemke, what is primarily at stake in Foucault's view is whether the concept of the state we have is "identical to the 'state' itself" (Lemke 2007: 5). In other words, Lemke takes Foucault to give an accurate characterization of the state through invoking an analysis of historical processes that produce it as a dynamic entity. Though Lemke moves on to discuss the status of the state as a "transactional reality," to use the term Foucault introduces in *The Birth of Biopolitics*, the advantage he ascribes to Foucault's position suggests that there is a truly accurate account of the state that must be discovered through genealogical analysis. There is certainly a tendency in Foucault's work to identify the state as a process, but ultimately, for Foucault, understanding the state as a fixed entity or as a dynamic process that is the product of multiple arts of government must be recognized as a strategic move rather than an attempt to discover the underlying reality of political relations.[8]

Furthermore, whereas Lemke is correct in highlighting the negative and positive roles in Foucault's genealogical work, these are not to be *identified* with historical nominalism, but rather as results that *follow from* it. As I have maintained, Foucault's genealogical work on governmentality follows a method that is concerned with identifying historical conditions of possibility, and at least partly develops out of his reading of Kant. Consequently, in addition to justifying an empirical historical approach, the nominalism to which Foucault is committed also explains his refusal to provide a clear theory of power, while insisting on putting forward an analytics or mere methodological commitments. This leads to the other implication of nominalism for

Foucault, namely the concrete nature of the analysis invoked. Foucault insists on providing local content for analysis that is not limited to speculative conclusions derived from universals. Thus, even analyses that merely invoke power are insufficient, for Foucault maintains such analyses do not have any explanatory value. Therefore, an explanation will dispose of universals except as they appear to be "something" that is marked out in reality, and thus it will return to historical conditions of possibility. But for such an analysis to take place, one needs to invoke a concrete "analytical grid" for relations of power. Power relations on their own do not have explanatory force but require an empirical analytical grid as their principle of intelligibility. This grid is determined through an archaeological account that is produced by determining the historical limits of discourse, and a genealogical method that locates moments of contingency.[9]

This approach helps explain why Foucault switches to a different characterization of power in his later work. In "The Subject and Power," Foucault specifies that a power relation should be best understood in terms of government, or as the "conduct of conducts" (Foucault 2001d: 341). Foucault contrasts this with the warlike understanding of power he had identified in *Society Must Be Defended*, and argues that a power relation is "neither warlike nor juridical" (Foucault 2001d: 341). Recognizing a power relation in terms of governmentality enables us to offer content to a power relation. To understand a power relation in terms of government, then, or in terms of the conduct of conducts, is to invoke a grid of intelligibility that is not vacuous precisely because it depends on a historical analysis. This is why Foucault argues that the notion of governmentality becomes useful to "tr[y] out" in order to provide a "point of view" to the shifting history of government (Foucault 2008: 186). It is a principle of intelligibility, but qualifies only as a "transactional reality" as Foucault maintains. In other words, while abstract power relations, or abstract government, cannot offer an explanation by themselves, an analysis of the set of practices that are constituted by power relations provide the required "grid" in relation to a regime of truth determining truth and falsity.[10]

## Governmentality and Power—The New Conception of Power

Whereas Foucault initially situates his view of power in *Society Must Be Defended* as a counter-Hobbesian position, which promises to discover the rumbles of battle underneath any political account and thus reduce political analysis to war, Foucault relinquishes some of these elements as his work on governmentality crystallizes (Foucault 2003a: 34, 45, 47, 50–1, 79). This leads to the introduction of a more developed conception of power, a shift that Foucault does not clearly shed light on in his published work. But in his lectures *The Birth of Biopolitics*, Foucault develops crucial empirical elements for his account. This can be most clearly mapped out in the transformation he identifies in the form of government between *raison d'état* and the more recent modern form. In Foucault's view, the crucial shift occurring near the middle of the eighteenth century is that of the emergence of the economic sphere as a space that is beyond the grasp of the sovereign. This produces a crisis within juridical thought, for whereas the art of government under sovereignty is exercised over juridical subjects, it appears to be inhabited by subjects of interest, or subjects whose interest constitutes the core of economic analysis. Whereas juridical subjects can give up their rights in order to institute a transfer in power to a sovereign, economic subjects cannot relinquish their interests in favor of a ruler, for natural economic laws dictate that the economic realm must be beyond intelligibility, functioning according to laws that will ensure its own stability independently of interference, and thus lying outside the control of the sovereign (Foucault 2008: 282).

This new form of government that emerges out of the development of an independent economic space finally develops into a dichotomy between the state and civil society. Yet one significant implication of Foucault's analysis is that civil society is not an obstacle to the functioning of the state through its constant activity. It is, rather, a part of modern governmentality: a correlate body that is the object of governance. Foucault argues that whereas with early modern thinkers, such as Hobbes and Locke, the social body was reducible to a set of individuals that were linked together through a political bond, the social bond within civil society appears to develop spontaneously as a result of sentiments of benevolence within the social body that are constantly being challenged by an egoistic drive belonging to the economic individuals that constitute society (Foucault 2008: 297). Foucault attributes this view to Adam Ferguson, whose *Essays on the History of Civil Society* inaugurated a shift towards understanding social relations in terms of an inherent inequality. Under these conditions, it is pointless to consider what a prior condition to that of the state would be like, for such hypothetical claims have no bearing on history or on normativity. Thus, not only is the notion of a contract challenged historically, an argument which had already been articulated several times since Hobbes, but a contract is also not required to produce a unified social body. The social body is constituted out of social relations that are the product of sympathetic inclinations, a view that we also find among sentimentalists such as Hume and Adam Smith. In other words, no exchange of rights is necessary to produce a social body, for civil society already entails within it sufficient conditions to produce a unified society (Foucault 2008: 281–2, 302–03).

This notion of a civil society replaces contract in another sense, namely, that which Foucault discusses under the rubric of subjection. Whereas for both Hobbes and Locke, contract results from a condition of equality in the state of nature and leads to the appearance of hierarchy within a community, subjection under Ferguson's model of government is a natural process that arises within social relations due to the distribution of roles. Consequently, there is no need to transfer power from individuals in a state of equality to a sovereign thus establishing social differences as Hobbes had argued. These differences are spontaneous and give rise immediately to power relations (Foucault 2008: 304). Foucault suggests that under this model, "the fact of power precedes the right that establishes, justifies, limits, or intensifies it; power already exists before it is regulated, delegated or legally established" (Foucault 2008: 304).

Ferguson's conception of political power as prior to any agreement and coextensive with social relations should strike us as quite similar to the view Foucault endorses in "The Subject and Power." In *The Will to Knowledge*, Foucault had argued for understanding power relations in terms of forces and maintained that such relations can only arise out of inequality (Foucault 1990: 135). In his later work, Foucault retains the condition of inequality but appears to minimize references to power relations as material forces that act on bodies to constitute subjects. Hendricks's reading of Foucault's relation to Kant proves to be useful here. If Foucault's later project involves working on the present in order to uncover limits as contingent, then the starting point of any analysis must be recent views of power relations, and in this case partly that of Ferguson. The contemporary relevance of political analysis requires endorsing current social formations, or a view of power that arises out of unequal social relations.[11]

Two questions remain unanswered. First, how should we understand the different conception of power that emerges throughout Foucault's work on governmentality? Second, under this conception of power, what would it mean to retain the Kantian aspect of Foucault's critique?

Reconciling the two conceptions of power we find in Foucault presupposes the need to provide a coherent account for both. Yet one may argue that Foucault's commitment to nominalism rids us of such a necessity. Consequently, one way to understand the relation between these conceptions is to recognize that universals are only constituted discursively. In this case, there is no need to unify our account of power; instead, we can recognize that the material activity of power relations is only one form power can take. Similarly, power in terms of certain governmental practices is another form power can assume, in which Foucault finds the possibility of a degree of autonomy or freedom.

This response, however, remains inadequate, as it renders the use of "power" vacuous in the sense that it can refer to a multiplicity of unrelated phenomena. The excessive nominalism of this reading raises a problem for Foucault. Foucault sometimes appears to reduce everything to practices, which would thus eliminate the need to use universals. This would give further credence for his historical nominalism, which is itself based on the rejection of universals as real or conceptual entities. Foucault, however, very clearly does not reject the use of universals altogether. For instance, in "The Subject and Power," he introduces a general account of power relations. In *Discipline and Punish*, he had already focused on discipline and characterized it with some generality. Foucault's use of universals can, thus, be allotted an explanatory role without being committed to their metaphysical existence as real entities, nor to their conceptual existence in the mind. This, however, requires identifying some unifying component.

In order to render coherent Foucault's view, it may be useful to refer to his use of *dispositif* or apparatus. In a 1977 interview, Foucault states:

What I'm trying to pick out with this term is, firstly, a thoroughly heterogeneous ensemble consisting of discourses, institutions, architectural forms, regulatory decisions, laws, administrative measures, scientific statements, philosophical, moral and philanthropic propositions—in short, the said as much as the unsaid... The apparatus itself is the system of relations that can be established between these elements.

Foucault 1980: 194

Foucault continues to specify that an apparatus, in a specific historical moment, has a "dominant strategic function" (Foucault 1980: 195). The analysis of an apparatus, thus, must examine the relation between these different elements in order to determine an overarching strategy. This is why an apparatus is "essentially of a *strategic* nature," determining how forces are modified, blocked, or developed in order to achieve specific goals (Foucault 1980: 196). The material activity of forces, then, should be understood as part of the more encompassing apparatus Foucault identifies, or as means that allow for materializing the strategic goal. These force relations are, moreover, often supported by knowledge claims. Recognizing the heterogeneity of the elements involved in an apparatus, therefore, requires that we distinguish between practices that take the body as their target, such as disciplinary techniques, and the overall strategic functions they fulfill that are not reducible to the minute force relations. To understand a power relation in terms of governmentality, then, involves recognizing the sought-after strategic goal in any confrontation. In "The Subject and Power," Foucault maintains that a power relation always involves a strategy of struggle, given that it ultimately aims at triumph (Foucault 2001d: 346). This is why a power relation should be understood on the model of government, as it involves modifying forces for the sake of attaining an end. Understanding a power relation, therefore, involves recognizing the role of material forces, but it also invokes a wide array of mechanisms that regulate behavior, and identifies them in terms of an overarching, if momentary, strategy. The strategic element, however, can only have explanatory force when coupled with a historical analysis.

This view of power relations can also help us understand in what sense Foucault is a Kantian. I have argued that Foucault's view should be understood as entirely empirical and specifically historical, while disposing of any transcendental aspect. As I have maintained, since genealogy is concerned with uncovering contingency where necessity is presupposed, a genealogy of governmentality will be concerned with identifying contingent elements that can be transformed within the history of governmental practices which aim at the "conduct of conducts." This is further corroborated by Foucault's insistence in *The Birth of Biopolitics* that politics is nothing but the "interplay of ... different arts of government" (Foucault 2008: 313). The Kantian element in this approach, then, appears in locating, through an empirical inquiry, conditions of possibility that remain contingent and subject to transformation. Following Foucault's reading of Kant, this allows for identifying a moment in the present where critique can be effective.

Unlike Kant, Foucault's commitments are methodological and not transcendental. Consequently, Foucault is not concerned with metaphysics. Whereas universal and necessary conditions leave us with a metaphysical noumenal dependency in Kant to which we have no access, Foucault's employment of contingent and historical conditions does not lead to the introduction of the noumenal. Instead, we have conditions that can be transformed historically, not ones that are fixed and determined as they constitute preconditions for our experience. Foucault recognizes that the historical conditions certainly do influence our experience. Through discursively defining limits of intelligibility, our experience is constituted according to historical rules that can be transformed beginning with a genealogical analysis.[12] Changing discursive limits, however, does not occur through appealing to an ahistorical position, but by using tools that are already present within an existing discursive formation.[13] Consequently, Foucault's view can be regarded as Kantian in another way. Whereas

Hendricks had emphasized Foucault's concern with critiquing present limits, I suggest that Foucault's Kantian critique also has a bearing on the relation between politics and metaphysics. Foucault argues that since Kant, the political task has been "to keep watch over the excessive powers of political rationality" (Foucault 2001d: 328). Kant takes up this task by arguing that there are limits resulting from our active contribution to experience, a contribution that cannot be subtracted. By revealing those limits as contingent, Foucault does not open up the space to dogmatism by providing access to reality, but rather undermines to some degree the authority of all knowledge through emphasizing that historical shifts do not entail coming closer to a metaphysical ideal. These shifts are the products of power struggles, ones that constitute the social body in terms of inherent relations of inequality, while being masked by a "will to truth" that feigns progress towards reality.

This allows us to finally return to the divide that Foucault credits Kant with instituting, namely, that between an analytic of truth and the ontology of ourselves. If we recognize that Foucault is concerned with historicizing and undoing limits in order to retain a skeptical element with respect to all knowledge, we also should recognize that the question of the ontology of ourselves will have a bearing on the question of truth. The two are certainly not identical, but it is significant to recognize that offering a history of our constitution as subjects in relation to power and truth further credits the critique of metaphysics Kant had instituted. Uncovering limits as historical fulfills the task of destabilizing even the limits that Kant took as fixed. I have argued that Foucault's historical approach follows from endorsing Kant's critique of metaphysics and modifying the conditions that make knowledge possible by identifying contingent elements rather than necessary ones. If Kant had shown that the noumenal is inaccessible, Foucault develops a political account that, first, radicalizes that critique by promising to purge, on empirical grounds, all universal and necessary conditions, and, second, develops a post-Kantian view of politics. The question then becomes: How can we introduce a political account that does not presuppose metaphysical commitments and is nonetheless grounded? Foucault's answer is to return to a historical analysis.

## Conclusion

Recognizing Foucault's work in a Kantian vein as involving the problem of identifying conditions of possibility—though contingent ones—leads to a specific conception of political critique. For critique to be effective, it must offer a historical account of the political landscape, which allows for determining contingent conditions that can be changed. We must, therefore, begin by forming a conception of actual political practices. Only then are we able to put forward a normative evaluation with regards to what transformation should take place.

This paper has been concerned with putting forward a coherent reading of Foucault as following an empirical inquiry in order to justify the nominalist historicism he endorses. I have argued that Foucault's genealogical approach should be seen as one that broadly follows from Kant, by directing critique towards sufficient conditions of possibility that are identified from a historical analysis. Understanding such conditions as sufficient allows us to offer generalized descriptive accounts regarding the activity of power concerning problems that appear under different historical circumstances. Furthermore, historicizing these conditions allows Foucault to dispose of metaphysics and pursue a post-Kantian political view. Endorsing this reading emphasizes the role of genealogical analysis in terms of empirically verifying historical narratives. I have argued, however, that this raises a problem concerning the consistency of Foucault's view of power. Whereas in his earlier work Foucault insists that power relations are to be understood in terms of material forces that are best understood on the model of war, Foucault appears to recast the question of power in terms of governmentality in his later work. I, therefore, invoked the notion of apparatus or *dispositif* in order to bridge the gap between understanding force relations materially and through governmentality, by shedding light on long-term strategic goals. If the question of power is ultimately one of government, which invokes overarching apparatuses entailing different techniques and practices, then critique undertakes the task of highlighting the historical conditions that have rendered specific forms of government possible. This opens up the space to gradually unsettle and modify what we take to be problematic.

## Notes

1. The placement of his work within the Kantian tradition appears most clearly in the essay "What is Enlightenment?" as Foucault explicitly takes his project to involve a move that Kant had initiated, which involves "a reflection on history and a particular analysis of the specific moment at which he is writing" (Foucault 1998: 309). During the same year, Foucault wrote under the pen name Maurice Florence, "[i]f Foucault is indeed perfectly at home in the philosophical tradition it is within the *critical* tradition of Kant, and his undertaking could be called *A Critical History of Thought*" (Florence 1994: 314).
2. Foucault's Kantian view is certainly influenced by Canguilhem's critique of Kant. That influence, however, appears most clearly in Foucault's earlier work. My focus will be on Foucault's middle and later work in order to put forward a coherent reading of his treatment of Kant alongside Foucault's genealogical approach. I will, therefore, set aside the question of what mark Canguilhem's reading of Kant leaves on Foucault's work.
3. One instance of Foucault's rejection of transcendental conditions appears in "What is Enlightenment?" (Foucault 1998: 315–16). In addition, in a 1982 interview titled "Space, Knowledge, and Power," Foucault specifies Habermas' position in terms of "mak[ing] a transcendental mode of thought spring forth against any historicism," in contrast to Foucault's own position which is "far more historical and Nietzschean" (Foucault 2001c: 359). The opposition of his historical approach to a transcendental one also appears in a 1978 interview, where Foucault aligns his work with that of Nietzsche, Bataille, and Blanchot in their projects of desubjectivation which involves "wrenching the subject from itself" as opposed to the phenomenological tradition which locates a transcendental subject and assigns to it the role of constituting experience (Foucault 2001a: 241).
4. The necessity of those conditions can be questioned merely on the basis of the empirical nature of Foucault's work as I will be arguing later in the paper.

5   Recognizing that these conditions are sufficient does not conflict with Foucault's notion of a historical *a priori* that determines the limits of knowledge. These conditions are sufficient for certain possibilities within a given power-knowledge regime. Rendering my reading of Foucault's genealogical work compatible with his notion of the historical *a priori*, however, requires that we understand the historical *a priori* as empirically derived and serves primarily an explanatory or strategic function. If we accept this, it would follow that it is necessary to have historical conditions in order for problematizations to be possible, but *specific* historical conditions are contingent and only sufficient but not necessary to make a specific problematization possible. Whether we can justify arguing for the necessity of historical conditions from a Foucauldian point of view seems doubtful, especially if we accept his position as developing empirically. More importantly, for critique to be possible, we would have to recognize that an episteme is not internally consistent and can be transformed using resources within it. Though I consider this to be a sound reading of Foucault, it arguably involves a significant divergence from the view he endorses in *The Order of Things*, where identifying an episteme is characterized as a "pure experience of order and its modes of being" (Foucault 2005: xxiii).

6   Koopman's characterization of Hume's work in terms of identifying causes that render specific phenomena actual is problematic given Hume's critique of causation, which is itself a contentious matter in Hume scholarship. This, however, does not affect my argument of interpreting Foucault's work in terms of empirical conditions of possibility.

7   Endorsing a Foucauldian approach to the question of conditions of possibility does not necessarily preclude Kant's transcendental conditions. It is still possible to maintain that there could be necessary conditions for experience that are ahistorical, but these would have to be more limited than the ones Kant provides.

8   For Foucault's discussion of process, see "Questions of Method" (Foucault 2001b: 226–7).

9   For instance, in *The Birth of Biopolitics*, governmentality is presented as an "analytical grid" for power relations (Foucault 2008: 186).

10  In "What is Critique?," Foucault offers the following insight with regards to the connection between power and governmentality, contending that governmentality links together the exercise of power, the production of subjectivity, and the use of discourses of truth: "The core of critique is basically made of the bundle of relationships that are tied to one another ... power, truth, and the subject. And if governmentalization is indeed this movement through which individuals are subjugated in the reality of a social practice through mechanisms of power that adhere to a truth, well, then! I will say that critique is the movement by which the subject gives himself the right to question truth on its effects of power and question power on its discourses of truth ... Critique would essentially insure the desubjugation of the subject in the context of what we could call ... the politics of truth" (Foucault 2003b: 266).

11  Of course, Foucault need not recognize these social relations as naturally constituting social unity through benevolence, as in Ferguson. His very commitment to a historical approach precludes that.

12  The use of "discursive" in Foucault is ambiguous, as Oksala notes. Fully determining what discursivity means for Foucault is beyond the scope of this dissertation. See Oksala (2004: 109).

13  Even in his later ethical period, Foucault specifies that crafting oneself will depend on the resources available in one's culture. In "The Ethics of the Concern of the Self as a

Practice of Freedom," Foucault states that "these practices are nevertheless not something that the individual invents by himself. They are patterns that he finds in his culture and which are proposed, suggested and imposed on him by his culture, his society and his social group" (Foucault 1998: 291).

# References

Allen, A. (2007), *The Politics of Our Selves: Power, Autonomy, and Gender in Contemporary Critical Theory*, New York: Columbia University Press.

Florence, M. (1994), "Foucault, Michel, 1926–," in G. Gutting (ed.), *The Cambridge Companion to Foucault*, 314–19, Cambridge: Cambridge University Press.

Foucault, M. (1980), "The Confession of the Flesh," in C. Gordon (ed.), *Power/Knowledge: Selected Interviews and Other Writings, 1972–1977*, 194–228, New York: Harvester Wheatsheaf.

Foucault, M. (1990), *The History of Sexuality. Volume 1: An Introduction*, trans. R. Hurley, New York: Vintage.

Foucault, M. (1998), "The Ethics of the Concern of the Self as a Practice of Freedom," in P. Rabinow (ed.), *The Essential Works of Michel Foucault, 1954–1984, Vol. 1: Ethics, Subjectivity and Truth*, 281–301, New York: The New Press.

Foucault, M. (1998), "What is Enlightenment?," in P. Rabinow (ed.), *The Essential Works of Michel Foucault, 1954–1984, Vol. 1: Ethics, Subjectivity and Truth*, 303–20, New York: The New Press.

Foucault, M. (2001a), "Interview with Michel Foucault," in J. D. Faubion (ed.), *The Essential Works of Michel Foucault, 1954–1984, Vol. 3: Power*, 239–97, New York: The New Press.

Foucault, M. (2001b), "Questions of Method," in J. D. Faubion (ed.), *The Essential Works of Michel Foucault, 1954–1984, Vol. 3: Power*, 223–38, New York: The New Press.

Foucault, M. (2001c), "Space, Knowledge, and Power," in J. D. Faubion (ed.), *The Essential Works of Michel Foucault, 1954–1984, Vol. 3: Power*, 349–64, New York: The New Press.

Foucault, M. (2001d), "The Subject and Power," in J. D. Faubion (ed.), *The Essential Works of Michel Foucault, 1954–1984, Vol. 3: Power*, 326–48, New York: The New Press.

Foucault, M. (2003a), *"Society Must Be Defended": Lectures at the Collège de France, 1975–1976*, ed. M. Bertani and A. Fontana, trans. D. Macey, New York: Picador.

Foucault, M. (2003b), "What is Critique?," in P. Rabinow and N. Rose (eds), *The Essential Foucault: Selections from the Essential Works of Foucault, 1954–1984*, 263–78, New York: The New Press.

Foucault, M. (2005), *The Order of Things: An Archaeology of the Human Sciences*, London: Routledge.

Foucault, M. (2008), *The Birth of Biopolitics: Lectures at the Collège de France 1978–1979*, ed. M. Senellart, trans. G. Burchell, Basingstoke: Palgrave Macmillan.

Han, B. (2002), *Foucault's Critical Project: Between the Transcendental and the Historical*, trans. E. Pile, Stanford, CA: Stanford University Press.

Hendricks, C. (2008), "Foucault's Kantian Critique: Philosophy and the Present," *Philosophy & Social Criticism*, 34 (4): 357–82.

Kant, I. (1991), "An Answer to the Question: What is Enlightenment?," in H. S. Reiss (ed.), *Kant: Political Writings*, 2nd ed., 54–60, Cambridge: Cambridge University Press.

Koopman, C. (2010), "Historical Critique or Transcendental Critique in Foucault: Two Kantian Lineages," *Foucault Studies*, 8: 100–21.

Lemke, T. (2007), "An Indigestible Meal? Foucault, Governmentality and State Theory," *Distinktion: Journal of Social Theory*, 8 (2): 43-64.
McQuillan, C. (2010), "Transcendental Philosophy and Critical Philosophy in Kant and Foucault: Response to Colin Koopman," *Foucault Studies*, 9: 145-55.
Oksala, J. (2004), "Anarchic Bodies: Foucault and the Feminist Question of Experience," *Hypatia*, 19 (4): 99-121.

# 11

# On Authority: A Discussion Between Michel Foucault and Hannah Arendt

Edgar Straehle[1]

The concept of authority often tends to be oversimplified or discussed without prior definition. This can also occur in works that purportedly set out to analyze the notion, for example Bertrand Russell's *Authority and the Individual*. Authority is mainly understood in such cases as a simple negative concept, often mixed with other phenomena such as power, imposition, coercion, domination, authoritarianism, or even violence. This misinterpretation can be found not only in political thinkers but also in pedagogues who define themselves as antiauthoritarian and who consequently seek to abolish authority in society (Hardt and Negri 2004: 353). For these thinkers, authority can only be negative, and this explains why they pursue its complete eradication.

The problem in such cases is that the original and specific dimension of authority, a dimension which is often forgotten, can easily be overlooked. For this reason, in this chapter I set out to call this misconception into question and to approach the problem of authority in a distinct, heuristic way. To this end, I discuss the thought of Hannah Arendt, who vindicated the importance of authority and endeavored to rethink the concept. Subsequently, I reread Foucault's reflections on power and on *parrhēsia* from the standpoint of Arendt's interpretation of authority. While I argue that Foucault never developed his own theory of authority, I also contend that it is possible to use his account of *parrhēsia* to establish a discussion between him and Arendt and to shed light on the concept of authority as such.

To this purpose, I introduce first the problem of authority from Hannah Arendt's perspective and discuss how and why this concept should be disentangled from that of power. Second, I briefly outline Foucault's accounts of power, including that of governmentality, in order to show that they all differ from Arendt's account of authority. Third, I go into his remarks on *parrhēsia* and argue that in these reflections it is possible to find points in common with Arendt's concept of authority. In particular I underline the parallel between *parrhēsia* and ascendancy. Finally, I reread Foucault's reflections on the Cynics in order to examine how they can be deployed in rethinking authority. My purpose is not to affirm that Foucault had sketched out something similar to

Arendt's concept of authority but to use his remarks to enrich our understanding of what I call the problem of authority.

## Hannah Arendt and the Problem of Authority

Arendt argued that authority should be understood as a kind of power based on recognition and, consequently, not on the person who holds authority but on others; that is, on the people who acknowledge him or her and invest them with authority (Arendt 1970: 45). For this reason, power and authority can be similar (both "want" to obtain obedience from other people) but, from a certain point of view, they are also opposed. Whereas power is based on the people in power, authority rests on those who are not in authority. In other words, while power seeks to depend on itself and is compatible with imposition, force or violence, this is completely impossible for authority; it would be a contradiction in terms. According to Arendt, any authority based on imposition would immediately disappear and should rather be defined as authoritarianism (Arendt 1961: 93).

It is beyond the scope of this paper to explain in depth what authority was and how it was understood in the past.[2] How, for instance, authority was not always reducible to power, as in ancient Rome, or how it could even be linked with acts of resistance or what we currently call counter-power (Straehle 2016). In fact, for the ancient Romans power (*potestas*) and authority (*auctoritas*) were opposed concepts (Domingo 1999). In this context, Arendt recalls that "the most conspicuous characteristic of those in authority is that they do not have power" (Arendt 1961: 122). Besides, it must be said that the long, complicated and intricate history of this concept is full of semantic changes, confusions, interpretations, contradictions and political appropriations. Authority has often been an instrumentalized concept, suffering distortions related to particular political conflicts. Thus, it is impossible to give a single, exhaustive definition of the term. Fully aware of these issues, Arendt criticizes such "abuses" of the concept of power and attempts to rethink the concept of authority in its specificity. Her purpose is not to condemn authority generally but to rediscover its original meaning and to recapture its ancient political dimension (Arendt 1961: 15). To this end she vindicates some important aspects of authority which cannot be found amongst other political modern concepts.

She does not intend to essentialize "authority" (Arendt 1961: 92), however, and at no point does she idealize it. Neither did she seek to restore its lost ancient face. Despite what has been said about her (Friedman 1973), she never sought a kind of nostalgic return to ancient times and never stood for a kind of restoration of Roman *auctoritas*. This would contradict her understanding of politics. In her view, authority cannot be "made," "fabricated," or "designed" in advance (Arendt 1961: 111); it comes rather about as an unpredictable event that she repeatedly depicts as a kind of wonder or miracle (Arendt 1961: 125, 127). Accordingly, it must be explored, achieved, and "discovered" in political action. Her approach to authority, then, should be seen as one of her political exercises whose aim "is to gain experience in how to think; they do not contain prescriptions on what to think or which truths to hold. Least of all do they intend to retie the broken thread of tradition or to invent some newfangled surrogates with which to fill the gap between past and future" (Arendt 1961: 14).

First, Arendt admits that authority can be seen as a kind of asymmetrical relationship (Arendt 1961: 93). Yet she also argues that, ideally, authority precludes any use of external means of imposition, coercion or violence (Arendt 1961: 93). According to this view, authority is sustained by a combination of different, interrelated factors such as legitimacy, reputation, prestige, ascendancy, respect, trust, consent, or a recognition bestowed by others. In addition, Arendt stresses that, unlike power, this type of obedience cannot be forced or imposed and must be accepted or conceded by these others. In other words, authority depends ultimately not on itself but on others. Thus, it can be seen as a strange, abnormal type of power, since it does not depend on imposition or force but on a kind of concession and consent. From this point of view, authority is something that has to come from the outside, so to speak, and never from the inside, from itself.

Due to its dependence on the recognition of others, authority is a type of relationship that is also compatible with spontaneity and freedom (Arendt 1961: 106). For this reason, it always entails the possibility of being rejected or revoked. Authority is in fact defined by its constitutive frailty or precariousness. It is important to note that the others granting it are not only those who can undermine, limit, or invalidate someone's authority; in fact, they are also the condition of possibility for the existence of any kind of authority. This explains one of the paradoxes of authority: those who are the basis of its existence are also those who can suppress or revoke it: ultimately, it is others, and not the subject of authority itself, who always retain the power to institute it or, alternatively, to undermine and cancel it. Thus, authority is also defined by a certain powerlessness: apparently, it is not possible to do anything to attain this recognition and every act or strategy aimed at achieving it unravels and underlines its *de facto* lack or absence. According to Alexandre Kojève, authority is "the possibility that an agent has of acting on others (or on another) without these others reacting against him, despite being capable to do so" (Kojève 2014: 8). Authority therefore seems to be a kind of oxymoron or contradiction which can be succinctly described as a type of powerless power devoid of any imperative force. Further, the existence of authority reveals the indigent character and the incompleteness of power. If power is completely devoid of the endowment provided by authority, if it rests exclusively on itself or on violence, it is also destined to be questioned, disobeyed, contested, and deposed in the future. Insofar as it claims to be legitimate and seeks to avoid conflict, power cannot withdraw into itself, and thus needs the support of authority (Straehle 2016). Authority can reinforce, legitimate, or *authorize* power. In these cases, authority is linked to stability and permanence. In contrast, any lack of authority can discredit or disallow power. Without authority, it can be perceived as no more than naked, pure and violent power, as authoritarianism, despotism, tyranny or worse.

Arendt's account of authority is directed against the modern concept of sovereignty, defined by Jean Bodin (1967) and Thomas Hobbes (2012) as supreme, indivisible, indisputable, and absolute; in other words, a type of power which claims to authorize itself or seeks to incorporate the dimension of authority within itself. Under this new meaning, authority is no longer based on acknowledgment and turns into a different face of power, sometimes its worst. With this displacement, power attempts to usurp authority and emerges as a kind of conflation of power and authority that is compatible with violence or even based on it (Straehle 2017).

From that moment on power and authority became terms that, to this day, have been often used interchangeably. Also, both words have increasingly been claimed to be a monopoly of the state. Paraphrasing Max Weber (2004: 33), we could say that the modern state did not only vindicate the monopoly of legitimate violent power (*Gewalt*) but of legitimate authority, too. Thus, power, just because it is in power, seeks to be acknowledged as the sole authority and, conversely, the sole authority is by definition the sovereign power (Straehle 2017). As Arendt argues in *The Origins of Totalitarianism*, this is best epitomized by totalitarian regimes, which appear as the counter-face and the most radical, brutal, and violent negation of authority.[3] This shows that the identification of power with authority can be very dangerous and, at the same time, urges us to disentangle both concepts and to recapture the specific particularities of authority.

## Michel Foucault: From Power to Governmentality

It is very complicated to establish a philosophical dialogue between Hannah Arendt and Michel Foucault, since the two thinkers wrote from very different perspectives. In fact, Arendt never read Foucault's works and, as far as I know, the French philosopher mentioned her only once, in the interview "Politics and Ethics" (Foucault 1984: 362). Whatever the case, I do not intend to make a comparison between these authors here. My intention is rather to use their writings to shed light on the issue of authority and, in doing so, to reread part of Foucault's thought, above all his reflections on *parrhēsia*, from the standpoint of authority.

On the one hand, it must be said that Foucault pays no attention to the concept of authority in its specificity and that the terms "power" and "authority" are almost interchangeable in his work. In fact, he could be counted among the authors that have been unable to perceive the specific dimension of authority and go beyond the frame of power. Accordingly, it is understandable that Foucault criticizes Arendt's account of power by claiming that power and domination could not be dissociated.[4] It is also noteworthy that Foucault had previously stated in his lecture course *Psychiatric Power* that the concept of authority is a psycho-sociological question (Foucault 2006: 40). In contrast, Arendt rejected positions that reduce authority to a psychological phenomenon, as Theodor Adorno, Else Frenkel Brunswik, Daniel Levinson, and Nevitt Sanford had done in their study *The Authoritarian Personality* (1982). Contrary to these authors, she argues that authority had to be rethought from its original, political perspective. Furthermore, in my view Foucault's account of power is incompatible with Arendt's understanding of authority. As is well known, Foucault states that power is not an institution, structure or an individual capacity, but rather a complex arrangement of forces in society (Foucault 1990: 93). He conceives power as a multiple set of force relations, immanent processes through which these relations are transformed, systems or disjunctions that are constituted by the interplay of these force relations (Foucault 1990: 92). For this reason, Foucault also claims that power cannot be the exclusive property of a minority. It is omnipresent and can be found everywhere.

As in Arendt's understanding of authority, Foucault also contends that power is relational and that it is not possessed but exercised. Arendt's authority, then, would fit with the following sentence of Foucault: "power is not something that can be possessed, and it is not a form of might; power is never anything more than a relationship that can, and must, be studied only by looking at the interplay between the terms of that relationship" (Foucault 2003: 198). This explains the difficulty of finding an exhaustive definition of either concept: due to their relational dimension, both Foucault's power and Arendt's authority cannot be properly defined. Both are defined and redefined in every case and at every moment, depending on how the relationship between the two sides is developing.

Foucault also underscores that power is always accompanied by resistance (exerted by others). As he states, in relations of power, "there is necessarily the possibility of resistance, for if there were no possibility of resistance—of violent resistance, of escape, of ruse, of strategies that reverse the situation—there would be no relations of power" (Foucault 1987: 12). Both Arendt and Foucault coincide on this point: they call into question the illusion of sovereignty; that is, the existence or the pursuit of a unique, supreme, indivisible and indisputable power.[5] Nevertheless, whereas for Arendt resistance (or opposition and violence) entails the direct, immediate breakdown or disappearance of authority, Foucault's account of power is not only compatible with resistance: according to him, both power and counter-power are, in fact, interdependent and entwined; they are two sides of the same coin.

It is known that Foucault also pays attention to other kinds of power that are defined by the fact that they attempt to go beyond violence and in which the question of opposition, resistance and counter-power becomes subtler and less visible. These powers are "pastoral power" or, later, the modern "governmentality" and both can be seen as political and strategic efforts to rationalize the exercise of power (Foucault 2009: 138).[6] Both pastoral power and governmentality infiltrate deeply and persistently into the private lives of individuals and can be related to fields such as pedagogy, disciplines, normalization, biopower and knowledge.

However, regardless of their subtlety or lack of physical violence, these kinds of power reproduce anew a scheme that ultimately coincides with domination and cannot be defined as a concession by others. Although there is no physical violence, at least in a direct manner, both aim at establishing a strong relation of domination and subjection. Their purpose is to neutralize the dangers of freedom and the autonomy of the people who have to be dominated. From Arendt's perspective, instead, the philosophical and political challenge that is to be found behind the problem of authority is very different: how to think or articulate a kind of power which depends not on itself but, ideally speaking, on the consented, spontaneous, and free acknowledgment conferred by others. That is, Arendt's authority is not only based on these others but freely originated by them. Therefore, this is a kind of power that is different from the Foucauldian, that is not in the hands of the people in power and that cannot be sustained by force or coercion but above all—and even exclusively—by other factors such as acknowledgment, acceptance, reliability, and trust.

## Michel Foucault and the *Parrhēsia*

Although Foucault never developed his own concept of authority, it is possible to find some traces and remarks in his late work that share important traits with Arendt's account of authority. Here I focus on his interpretation of the concept of *parrhēsia*, which is surely the best example of this, and the remainder of the paper will be devoted to it.

As is well known, *parrhēsia*, translated into French as *franc parler*, means literally "to speak everything" and by extension "to speak freely" and "to speak frankly" (Foucault 2010: 188). Yet *parrhēsia* implies not only freedom of speech, but also the obligation to speak the truth for the common good, even at personal risk.[7] Telling the truth can be unpleasant at times, unwelcome to others, and even dangerous for the speaker. For this reason, the practice of *parrhēsia* is related to courage, frankness, political engagement, good citizenship, public freedom, and, quite often, dissidence. *Parrhēsia* therefore appears as a kind of democratic *ēthos* (Foucault 2001: 20). In this context, Foucault affirms that

> the *parrhesiastes* is always less powerful than the one with whom he speaks. The *parrhesia* comes from "below," as it were, and is directed towards "above". This is why an ancient Greek would not say that a teacher or father who criticizes a child uses *parrhesia*. But when a philosopher criticizes a tyrant, when a citizen criticizes the majority, when a pupil criticizes his teacher, then such speakers may be using *parrhesia*.
>
> Foucault 2001: 18

In ancient Greece, *parrhēsia* became an indispensable institution for the preservation and the proper functioning of Athenian democracy. *Parrhēsia* and democracy were closely intertwined and interdependent. The health of democracy partly depended on the citizens who dared to take the risk of expressing their opinions and denouncing the injustices, illegalities and errors they saw. The survival of democracy, then, could not solely be entrusted to the functioning of its own institutions. It had to remain open to its citizens' unforeseeable, hazardous, but also voluntary acts of freedom of speech. For this reason, Foucault contends that "generosity towards the other is at the very heart of the moral obligation of *parrhēsia*" (Foucault 2005: 385). Democracy needed the presence of *parrhēsia* in order to prevent its falling into tyranny. At the same time, however, it could become a major risk not only for parrhesiastic citizens but also for democracy itself, since the revelation of the truth can always lead to unpredictable consequences and turn into a political danger.

Foucault's account of *parrhēsia* is doubly related to the question of authority. Firstly, it is described as a kind of discursive practice that is trustworthy and that can tell the truth to political power. In doing so, *parrhēsia* does not appeal to any physical or violent power. On the contrary, it shows that the non-violent power of words may also be powerful and can challenge and undermine power's authority by denouncing its manipulations, injustices, repressions, or deceptions. In addition, the practice of *parrhēsia* can discredit, challenge, and call into question the government in power by unveiling, for instance, its lack of authority or even by causing it. In fact, Arendt also refers to this issue when she writes in *On Violence* that the "greatest enemy of authority" is contempt "and the surest way to undermine it is laughter" (Arendt 1961: 45). For this reason, she states that when authority leaves, power enters. A lack of authority easily leads to an increase in authoritarianism and violence. Further, *parrhēsia* is completely opposed to flattery and rhetoric (Foucault 2010: 302–05). In contrast to *parrhēsia*, which is defined by its spontaneity and openness, rhetoric is a kind of art and technique whose overriding purpose is to persuade or convince people. In addition, what is important in rhetoric is not the naked truth but the elaborate efficacy of the discourse. To this purpose, the orator can embellish his way of speaking, manipulate the audience or even lie. In contrast, Foucault claims that *parrhēsia* owes its strength to the fact that it springs from the very being which speaks through it (Foucault 2011: 327). For this reason, he also wrote that

> this is what is fundamental for rhetoric, its opposition precisely to philosophical discourse and to the technique peculiar to philosophical discourse, namely *parrhēsia*. There can only be truth in *parrhēsia*. Where there is no truth, there can be no speaking freely. *Parrhēsia* is the naked transmission, as it were, of truth itself. *Parrhēsia* ensures in the most direct way this *paradosis*, this transfer of true discourse from the person who already possesses it to the person who must receive it, must be impregnated by it, and who must be able to use it and subjectivize it. It is the instrument of this transfer that does nothing other than put to work the truth of true discourse in all its naked force, without adornment.
>
> Foucault 2005: 382

Finally, Foucault explains that the ancient *parrhēsia* was linked to the *isēgoria* and that both were the fundamental backbones of the true Greek democracy (Foucault 2010: 151). However, it must be said that although *parrhēsia* and democracy are certainly two sides of the same coin, they are also at odds with each other. As it is known, *isēgoria* was the statutory right to speak and meant that each citizen had the equal right to give his opinion and vote. However, *parrhēsia* both allowed for and favored a certain asymmetry and the ascendancy of some citizens over others. In fact, the word "ascendancy," constantly repeated throughout Foucault's course on *The Government of Self and Others*, can be considered one of the unnoticed key terms of this text. This ascendancy, which he depicts as legitimate, is obtained not by power or coercion but through an acknowledgment freely given by the people. Thus, *parrhēsia* can be understood as a kind of non-violent counter-power or, perhaps, counter-authority.

In one crucial passage Foucault summarizes the problem of *parrhēsia* in a few words:

> There can only be true discourse, the free play of true discourse, and access to true discourse for everybody where there is democracy. However, and this is where the relationship between true discourse and democracy becomes difficult and problematic, it has to be understood that true discourse is not and cannot be distributed equally in a democracy according to the form of *isēgoria*. Not everybody can tell the truth just because everybody may speak. True discourse introduces a difference or rather is linked, both in its conditions and in its effects, to a difference: only a few can tell the truth. And once only a few can tell the truth, once this truth-

telling has emerged into the field of democracy, a difference is produced which is that of the *ascendancy* exercised by some over others.

Foucault 2010: 158

Foucault is fully aware of this inherent conflict in Athenian democracy. There could only be true discourse through the egalitarian structure of democracy, but true discourse (*parrhēsia*) also introduced something that was completely different and irreducible to the egalitarian structure of democracy.[8] Democracy and *parrhēsia* depended on each other but their relationship could easily become tense and conflictive. Democracy, then, which is based on equality, depended on a practice (the *parrhēsia*) which favored and fostered the ascendancy of some citizens over others. The problem is that no one can predict the limits, the consequences or the future usage of this ascendancy. As authority, *parrhēsia* can be ambivalent. It was necessary to safeguard democracy but it could also threaten and endanger it. And, in fact, Foucault considers that democracy lives always in a perennial situation of conflict.[9]

We therefore find reformulated anew and expressed in other words, here in the historical context of Athenian democracy, what Arendt sees at the end of her book *On Revolution* as one of the most serious challenges in all modern politics (Arendt 1990: 278): the conflictive, but not incompatible, relationship between equality and the asymmetry of authority (ascendancy in Foucault)—in other words, the problem between the ideal horizontality and real asymmetry of democracy. The hidden issue in this context is the following: is it possible to reconcile horizontality with asymmetry within a democratic framework? If so, how?

Like Arendt, Foucault never answers this question. In fact, it could be said that this is not his purpose. He simply investigates the question of *parrhēsia* and explores its historical consequences. However, Foucault also separates the ascendancy inherent to *parrhēsia* from asymmetrical and oppressive types of government such as tyranny. To a large extent, this difference lies in the historical role played by *isēgoria*.

First, whereas *parrhēsia* allows (but does not force) citizens to speak freely, *isēgoria*, defined as all citizens' equal right to speak, merely establishes the constitutional and institutional framework in which *parrhēsia* can function (Foucault 2010: 158). Foucault stresses that all citizens can make use of this practice. *Parrhēsia* was supposed to be inclusive and not based on the status of the person but on his words, his courage and his personal integrity. Its superiority, thus, is not at all like to that of a tyrant, who exercises power without rivals, and can be revoked without appealing to violence (Foucault 2010: 156). In addition, the superiority connected to *parrhēsia* is of a type that is "shared with others, but shared in the form of competition, rivalry, conflict, and duel. It is an agonistic structure" (Foucault 2010: 156).

Secondly, *parrhesiastic utterances* are not authoritarian but persuasive or even authoritative.[10] No one is obliged to believe the content or the claims of the speakers. There is supposed to be a commitment of the *logos* to truth that the *demos* can consider trustworthy (*parrhesiastic*) or call into question. Ultimately, the effectiveness of *parrhēsia* rests on its reception among the listeners or spectators and their reaction to it. Like Arendt's authority, whether an utterance is considered parrhesiastic depends on a kind of recognition or acknowledgment that cannot be imposed on the audience. As

Foucault explains, although *parrhēsia* is a "discourse spoken from above", *parrhēsia* is "different from the pure and simple exercise of power" (Foucault 2010: 104).

Subsequently Foucault directs his attention to the decline of the good *parrhēsia* as a *logos alēthēs* (discourse of truth) and its replacement by flattery or manipulation, by a bad *parrhēsia* that did not remain true to its own principles. From this moment on, the purpose was no longer the quest for the truth or the safeguarding of democracy but the desire for success or the attainment of power. While the perversion of authority would lead to authoritarianism, the perversion of *parrhēsia* would turn democracy into a government dominated by demagoguery (Foucault 2010: 382), a form of rule that later became known as ochlocracy. In Thucydides' account, *parrhēsia* faded away gradually and its decline facilitated the initial success of the oligarchic coup of 411 BC.[11]

For Foucault, the trial of Socrates epitomized the defeat of both *parrhēsia* and truth in democratic politics. Although he embodied the union between *parrhēsia* and democracy and was the paradigm of *parrhēsiastēs*, and even though according to Plato he was Athens' finest citizen and philosopher, Socrates was condemned to death by a jury; and this verdict derived precisely from his parrhesiastic behavior. His death, then, symbolized the limits of democracy and contributed to the later transformation and resulting "de-democratization" of *parrhēsia*. After the death of Socrates the *parrhēsia* certainly survived, but in a new context and with a new meaning. Now, as in Plato, the place *par excellence* of *parrhēsia* was no longer the citizens' assembly; instead, it was displaced from the public square to the personal and private relationship between the counselor or the philosopher and the ruler, exemplified in Plato's relationships with the tyrants Dionysius and Dion of Syracuse. At this juncture, *parrhēsia* turned into a kind of private, dialogical *logos* and was related to *psychagogy*, the guidance and conduction of souls.[12] For this reason, Plato's redefinition of *parrhēsia* ran parallel to his criticism of democracy and to his argument that the philosopher should become the ruler of the *politeia*. While democratic *parrhēsia* was supposed to be open to every citizen and meant that no single person could own the truth, for Plato the philosopher is the person who knows the truth. Consequently, an institution such as the democratic *parrhēsia* becomes useless and even dangerous in his political project. According to Plato, politics should be subordinated to philosophy and ordinary citizens should lose their political *logos* and become subjects. In this way democratic *parrhēsia* was transformed, depoliticized, and converted into a philosophical *parrhēsia* (Foucault 2010: 354). Foucault also argues that the figure of Socrates appears as the ideal embodiment of a new form of *parrhēsia* enabling a new reconciliation between *parrhēsia* and truth. The word, in fact, becomes an ethical concept related to the *epimeleia heautou*, the care and the guidance of the self (Foucault 2011: 86). Thus, Socrates' *parrhēsia* is not only derived from his words and speeches, but also from his way of living and personal merits. The "reality of philosophy" (Foucault 2011: 239) is no longer the theoretical *logos* but its practice in the everyday life and in the work on oneself. *Parrhēsia* therefore becomes a kind of inner dialogue. Foucault explains that this courage "is not to be employed on the political stage where this mission cannot in fact be accomplished. This courage of the truth must be exercised in the form of a non-political *parrhēsia*, a *parrhēsia* which will take place through the test of the soul. It will be an ethical *parrhēsia*" (Foucault 2011: 90). For this reason, Foucault adds that the goal of this new *parrhēsia* is "not to persuade the Assembly, but to convince someone that he must take care of himself and of others; and this means that he must *change his life*" (Foucault 2001: 106).

## Authority and the Cynics

In his last lecture course at the Collège de France, *The Courage of Truth*, Foucault takes up the question of *parrhēsia* and develops it further. In the first half of the course, he continues his analysis of Socrates and what he calls the "aesthetics of existence" (Foucault 2011: 161). In the second half, however, he shifts his focus to the ancient Cynics: a group who lived apart from society and power and were famously characterized by their scandalous and provocative behavior. For Foucault, the question here is no longer the personal relationship between the philosopher and the ruler but the broader one between the outcast or *morosoph* (wise fool) and the rest of society. Furthermore, there are other important changes in this course that should be mentioned.

First, the word "ascendancy" disappears completely from the text and receives not a single mention in the whole course. I do not know whether this "disappearance" is intentional or not. There is no explanation for this omission and perhaps Foucault himself was not aware of it. Whatever the case, the change is highly symptomatic and of direct relevance to the issue we are discussing here. It may suggest the existence of a new kind of *parrhēsia* that could move beyond the asymmetric relationships of the previous types.

Second, amongst the Cynics the *parrhēsia* changed its meaning and was no longer tied to the personal, individual relationship with the ruler. Unlike Plato, the Cynics were determined to stay far away from power and challenged it through their transgressive lifestyle and insolent words towards the whole society. For this reason, there was no special place for *parrhēsia* amongst the Cynics and any space could serve its purpose. They pushed *parrhēsia* beyond the physical limits of the *agora* and, in doing so, implicitly declared that politics is everywhere. Through their example, they politicized private conduct and bore witness to the fact that politics is not restricted to the public sphere.

Third, the Cynics do not only or even principally challenge the power with their words. They model a transgressive way of life that, without doctrinal mediation, calls into question the society's costumes and beliefs. As Foucault states (Foucault 2011: 172), cynicism was not satisfied with establishing a kind of correspondence, a harmony or homophony between certain type of discourse and a way of life conforming to the principles declared in that discourse (an *alēthēs bios*). The Cynics linked lifestyle and the scandal of the truth in a much closer and more precise way, turning their mode of existence into a way of making truth itself visible in one's acts, one's body, the way one dresses, and in the way one conducts oneself and lives (Foucault 2011: 172). More than telling the truth, they witnessed and embodied it. In addition, they made possible the enunciation of a political and scandalous *logos* that at the same time could even remain silent.

Nevertheless, the Cynics do not eliminate the question of ascendancy (nor that of authority). Foucault does not take up this issue again and the word disappears in this course; but the problem remains, returning in the guise of tradition and transmission. Foucault shows that the Cynics, contrary to their contemporaries' claims and criticisms, did not renounce tradition either. Instead, they reformulated and reshaped the concept of tradition and, due to the rudimentary character of their theoretical assumptions, put forward another kind of traditionality, the so-called "traditionality of existence" (Foucault 2011: 209). This was very different from the traditionality of doctrine: it consisted not in theoretical statements but in memories of anecdotes and episodes of the "founding fathers," men like Crates and Diogenes (Foucault 2011: 209).

These stories, later recalled and propagated, became exemplary and authoritative and could be imitated and emulated by their disciples. However, for this tradition words were not as important as the traditionality of doctrine, and this enabled the Cynics to address a broader audience. One of their goals was to make philosophy popular. Foucault comments that their discourses and interventions "were addressed to a wide and consequently not very cultured public, and its recruits came from outside the educated elites who usually practiced philosophy" (Foucault 2011: 202). At the same time, then, this tradition underscores the priority of practice over theory. The function of their philosophical teaching was, above all else "to give both an intellectual and moral training to the individuals one formed" (Foucault 2011: 204). Foucault adds that "it was a matter of arming them for life so that they were thus able to confront events" (Foucault 2011: 204).

In some aspects, this traditionality of existence was similar to the practice of imitation and emulation that the ancient Romans called "*auctores habere*" and is related to the question of exemplarity. For the Romans, the words *auctor* (author) and *auctoritas* were closely interrelated. Both derived from the verb *augere*, whose meaning was linked to verbs such as "to expand" or "to make something grow" (Benveniste 2016: 428). An *auctor* was then a model whose life (*exemplum*) or reflections could help to guide or orient one's own. The *exemplum* of the past could inspire but never determine one's behavior. The link with tradition was indispensable but could also be contested and become in fact quite flexible. As I noted above, authority is sustained not by the person holding authority but by others: those who give or invest someone with authority; and these others can freely and willingly select a person (dead or alive) in order to learn and transform their lives and themselves. The transformation of the self is therefore achieved indirectly, by appealing to another's example. And this other becomes a mediation that does not block our personal development but helps us find words or ways to overcome our own limitations. Although Foucault does not use the word in *The Courage of Truth*, a certain ascendancy also persists amongst the Cynics. Like Arendt's authority, however, this ascendancy was based on acknowledgment, was compatible with freedom and could be revoked.

This is an aspect of the "aesthetics of existence" that Foucault never developed in detail and can serve us to rethink the meanings of autonomy and authority. For instance, this moral referent, the *auctor* of Roman tradition, is closely related to the figure invested with what we still call "moral authority." Normally the concept of autonomy is defined in opposition to dependence, as if it meant something like complete independence and "freedom from others." This image coincides for instance with the ideal of the self-made man, a person who does not owe anything to anyone. In my view, Foucault's account of the Cynics provides an alternative to this: they offered an example of an alternative tradition that could be based on freedom and could challenge not only the codes of the society's hegemonic tradition but also the concept of tradition as such. In this sense, I would claim that they provided us with a counter-tradition, and also became counter-authorities, opposing the *statu quo* and enabling the exploration of new paths of emancipation. Thus, this tradition can also become an incentive to criticism and a vehicle of transformation.

In conclusion, Foucault's reflections on *parrhēsia* can also help us understand his remarks on power in greater depth. Also, although Foucault never developed the concept of authority as such and considered it no more than a psycho-sociological question (Foucault 2006: 40), I would argue that when he addressed the issue of *parrhēsia* he depicted a kind of phenomenon with many similarities to Arendt's concept of authority. It is for this reason that I would like to end with a question: in his study of *parrhēsia*, didn't Foucault offer or outline an alternative kind of power that has largely been overlooked?

## Notes

1   This work has been written with the support of the research group "A transmisión desde el pensamiento filosófico femenino" (FFI2015-63828-P, MINECO/FEDER, UE) and the GRC "Creació i pensament de les dones" (2017 SGR 588) of the University of Barcelona.
2   For this question, see above all Furedi (2013) and Preterossi (2003).
3   For instance, she affirms in this book that "the principle of authority is in all important respects diametrically opposed to that of totalitarian domination" (Arendt 1979: 404).
4   He contends that "it seems to me that in many of the analyses that have been made by Arendt, or in any case from her perspective, the relation of domination has been constantly dissociated from the relation of power. Yet I wonder whether this distinction is not something of a verbal one; for we can recognize that certain power relations function in such a way as to constitute, globally, an effect of domination, but the network constituted by the power relations hardly allows for a decisive distinction" (Foucault 1984: 362).
5   As Foucault states in *Society Must Be Defended*: "Once we begin to talk about power relations, we are not talking about right, and we are not talking about sovereignty; we are talking about domination, about an infinitely dense and multiple domination that never comes to an end" (Foucault 2003: 111).
6   According to Foucault, "'Government' did not refer only to political structures or to the management of states; rather it designated the way in which the conduct of individuals or of groups might be directed: the government of children, of souls, of communities, of families, of the sick. It did not only cover the legitimately constituted forms of political or economic subjection, but also modes of action, more or less considered and calculated, which were destined to act upon the possibilities of action of other people. To govern, in this sense, is to structure the possible field of action of others. The relationship proper to power would not therefore be sought on the side of violence or of struggle, nor on that of voluntary linking (all of which can, at best, only be the

instruments of power), but rather in the area of the singular mode of action, neither warlike nor juridical, which is government" (Foucault 1982: 221).

7   According to Foucault, "*parrhesia* is a kind of verbal activity where the speaker has a specific relation to truth through frankness, a certain relationship to his own life through danger, a certain type of relation to himself or other people through criticism (self-criticism or criticism of other people), and a specific relation to moral law through freedom and duty. More precisely, *parrhesia* is a verbal activity in which a speaker expresses his personal relationship to truth, and risks his life because he recognizes truth-telling as a duty to improve or help other people (as well as himself)" (Foucault 2001: 19).

8   Foucault also states in *The Government of Self and Others* that "there can only be true discourse, the free play of true discourse, and access to true discourse for everybody where there is democracy. However, and this is where the relationship between true discourse and democracy becomes difficult and problematic, it has to be understood that true discourse is not and cannot be distributed equally in a democracy according to the form of *isēgoria*" (Foucault 2010: 183).

9   Foucault states for instance that "there is no democracy without true discourse, for without true discourse it would perish; but the death of true discourse, the possibility of its death or of its reduction to silence is inscribed in democracy" (Foucault 2010: 184). He adds later that "the peculiar characteristic of democratic *parrhēsia* was that it could only really function on condition that some citizens were distinguished from the others and, assuming ascendancy over the Assembly of the people, guided it in the right direction. In democratic equality *parrhēsia* was a principle of differentiation, a caesura" (Foucault 2010: 203).

10  I am aware that I am using a word that Foucault never used, since this ambiguous term, linked to the old meaning of authority, does not exist in French.

11  According to the Greek historian, the people of the Assembly "deliberated about nothing except what seemed best to the conspirators, and further those who spoke were from among them and what was to be said was first reviewed by them. And no one of the others still spoke against them, since they were fearful and saw the number of the conspirators. If anyone did speak against them, straight away in some convenient fashion, he was dead" (Thucydides, *cit. in* Saxonhouse 2005: 45).

12  It is noteworthy to remark the etymological link between *demagoguery* (*dēmagōgia*) and *psychagogy* (*psuchagōgia*).

## References

Adorno, T. et al. (1982), *The Authoritarian Personality*, New York: Norton.
Arendt, H. (1961), *Between Past and Future. Six Exercises in Political Thought*, New York: The Viking Press.
Arendt, H. (1970), *On Violence*, Orlando: Harcourt.
Arendt, H. (1979), *The Origins of Totalitarianism*, Orlando: Harcourt.
Arendt, H. (1990), *On Revolution*, London: Penguin.
Arendt, H. (1998), *Human Condition*, Chicago: Chicago University Press.
Benveniste, E. (2016), *Dictionary of Indo-European Concepts and Society*, Chicago: Hau Books.
Bodin, J. (1967), *Six Books of the Commonwealth*, Oxford: Basil Blackwell.
Domingo, R. (1999), *Auctoritas*, Barcelona: Ariel.

Foucault, M. (1982), "The Subject and Power," in H. L. Dreyfus and P. Rabinow (eds), *Michel Foucault: Beyond Structuralism and Hermeneutics*, 208–26, Chicago: The University of Chicago Press.

Foucault, M. (1984), *The Foucault Reader*, ed. P. Rabinow, New York: Pantheon Books.

Foucault, M. (1987), "The Ethic of Care for the Self as a Practice of Freedom," in J. Bernauer and D. Rasmussen (eds), *The Final Foucault*, 1–21, Cambridge and London: The MIT Press.

Foucault, M. (1990), *The History of Sexuality. Volume 1: An Introduction*, trans. R. Hurley, New York: Vintage.

Foucault, M. (2001), *Fearless Speech*, ed. J. Pearson, New York: Semiotext(e).

Foucault, M. (2003), *"Society Must Be Defended": Lectures at the Collège de France, 1975–1976*, ed. M. Bertani and A. Fontana, trans. D. Macey, New York: Picador.

Foucault, M. (2005), *The Hermeneutics of the Subject: Lectures at the Collège de France 1981–1982*, ed. F. Gros, trans. G. Burchell, New York: Palgrave Macmillan.

Foucault, M. (2006), *Psychiatric Power: Lectures at the Collège de France 1973–1974*, ed. J. Lagrange, trans. G. Burchell, Basingstoke: Palgrave Macmillan.

Foucault, M. (2009), *Security, Territory, Population: Lectures at the Collège de France 1977–1978*, ed. M. Senellart, trans. G. Burchell, Basingstoke: Palgrave Macmillan.

Foucault, M. (2010), *The Government of Self and Others: Lectures at the Collège de France, 1982–1983*, ed. F. Gros, trans. G. Burchell, Basingstoke: Palgrave Macmillan.

Foucault, M. (2011), *The Courage of Truth (The Government of Self and Others II): Lectures at the Collège de France 1983–1984*, ed. F. Gros, trans. G. Burchell, Basingstoke: Palgrave Macmillan.

Friedman, R. H. (1973), "On the Concept in Authority in Political Philosophy," in R. Flathman (ed.), *Concepts in Social and Political Philosophy*, 121–46, New York: MacMillan.

Furedi, F. (2013), *Authority: A Sociological History*, New York: Cambridge University Press.

Hardt, M. and T. Negri (2004), *Multitude: War and Democracy in the Age of the Empire*, New York: The Penguin Press.

Hobbes, T. (2012), *Leviathan*, Oxford: Clarendon Press.

Kojève, A. (2014), *The Notion of Authority*, London: Verso Books.

Preterossi, G. (2003), *Autoridad*, Buenos Aires: Nueva Visión.

Saxonhouse, A. W. (2005), *Free Speech and Democracy in Ancient Athens*, Cambridge: Cambridge University Press.

Straehle, E. (2016), "Between Power and Rebellion: Rethinking Authority," *Filosofia. Revista da Faculdade de Letras da Universidade do Porto*, 33: 273–85.

Straehle, E. (2017), "Thomas Hobbes and the Secularization of Authority," in A. Tomaszewska and H. Hämäläinen (eds), *The Sources of Secularism: Enlightenment and Beyond*, 101–20, London: Palgrave Macmillan.

Weber, M. (2004), *The Vocation Lectures*, Indianapolis and Cambridge: Hackett Publishing Company.

## 12

# Neoliberal Subjectivity at the Political Frontier

Matko Krce-Ivančić

In his lectures on neoliberalism at the Collège de France, better known as *The Birth of Biopolitics*,[1] Foucault introduced a novel conception of neoliberal subjectivity. In his words, the neoliberal subject is "an entrepreneur of himself" (Foucault 2008: 226), the embodiment of a particular social system, namely neoliberalism. Thus, we can explore distinctive characteristics of neoliberalism by analyzing neoliberal subjectivity. It is often neglected that an entrepreneur of himself reflects the differences between liberalism and neoliberalism explicated in Foucault's (2008) analysis of neoliberalism. This chapter argues for a return to Foucault's understanding of neoliberal subjectivity as a method of explaining the way neoliberalism operates nowadays. Considering that contemporary critical theory is focused on the subversion of neoliberalism and a radical change of neoliberal government, it remains unclear why these calls for subversion have not been met with an adequate response by neoliberal subjects. Why is neoliberalism functioning, whether we like it or not, without any major disturbances?

In order to explain current state of affairs, in which I argue that subversion is itself being subverted, this chapter develops aspects of Foucault's analysis of neoliberalism to critique one of the most influential models of emancipation in contemporary political theory as offered by Laclau and Mouffe (2001). Analyzing Laclau's model of emancipation, I examine why it has not realized its promise of emancipation or, in other words, why subversion is missing today. Introducing Foucault's understanding of the neoliberal subject as an entrepreneur of himself in the aforementioned model, I argue that Laclau overlooks the novelty of contemporary subjectivity. In order to explain why this type of subjectivity has become dominant in current society, I focus on some of the distinctive characteristics of neoliberalism identified by Foucault (2008) in his analysis of the German type of neoliberalism or, in other words, ordoliberalism. Emphasizing that contemporary neoliberalism operates as a radically *do-not-laissez-faire* system that rejects the idea of economism, in which the state is suppressed by big neoliberal government, I strive towards identifying how these characteristics are reflected in the notion of self-entrepreneurial subjectivity. The neoliberal subject is situated in Foucault's analysis of neoliberalism to explain the prominence of an entrepreneur of himself, who is self-governing and actively involved in producing and internalizing neoliberal discourse. Demonstrating that a productive character of power is not adequately acknowledged in Laclau's model of emancipation, I critically examine his notion of political frontier, arguing that such an external frontier has failed to form due to the emergence of self-entrepreneurial subjectivity.

## *Post*-Marxist Post-*Marxism*

Without any exaggeration, it could be said that Laclau and Mouffe stand as an unavoidable reference when contemporary political theory is considered, especially when post-Marxist perspectives are discussed.[2] Their analyses should be by no means understood as a simple disqualification of Marxist theoretical contributions. Quite on the contrary, they aimed to develop an improved theoretical standpoint based on the critique of Marxist concepts while acknowledging the significance of other theoretical legacies; most obviously, Laclau and Mouffe (2001) explicitly rely on Gramsci to articulate their theory of equivalence. Thus, their post-Marxism is in no way anti-Marxism, which is why they claim: "if our intellectual project in this book is *post*-Marxist, it is evidently also post-*Marxist*" (Laclau and Mouffe 2001: 4). However, they do reject orthodox Marxist belief in the objective determination of history which is to be completed by the revolutionary workers and their sympathizers. Laclau (2007) maps the parallels between the theological tradition of Christianity and Marxist belief in eschatological agents embodied in the revolutionary class of the proletariat, which is where he demonstrates that orthodox Marxism is essentially operating with beliefs and is yet another eschatological system, thereby challenging its explanatory power. Furthermore, Laclau and Mouffe reject economism, the belief that "from a successful economic strategy there necessarily follows a continuity of political effects which can be clearly specified" (Laclau and Mouffe 2001: 177). They highlight a deficiency of a shared, Marxist and liberal belief in the economy as a source of salvation. Here it is already possible to see the similarity with Foucault's understanding of the economy as embedded in broader social relations, and no longer operating as the infrastructural register.

In accordance with the rejection of economism, Laclau (2000a, 2000b) is dedicated to demystifying the category of class or, more precisely, its false primacy which continues to be a significant part of contemporary political theory. Class, as he argues, has lost its articulating potential due to the proliferation of particular identities, such as race, gender, age, etc. After this articulating dimension is lost, it remains unclear what class signifies in contemporary society. Laclau reminds us that, in Marx's theory, class is not just one among many struggles based on a particular identity but must have a strong potential for articulating various particular demands or, in his words, "the Marxist notion of 'class' cannot be incorporated into an enumerative chain of identities, simply because it is supposed to be the articulating core around which *all* identity is constituted" (Laclau 2000b: 297). He argues it is wrong to claim that class still has a primacy in society but that we just need to use a more open minded approach when establishing the criterion of what belongs to class and think of it as an enlarged community of people. Even if such an inflated concept of class is accepted, class politics is effectively made meaningless. Such fictional community is constituted on the basis of accumulating various characteristics while connections between the subjects of this alleged unity are far from being clear or, to put it in more orthodox Marxist terms, while class consciousness is missing. This is not to argue that the category of class should be completely abandoned or referred to only by using a code name, such as conflict theory, materiality or similar euphemisms. Simply, it is to acknowledge "that class struggle is just one species of identity politics, and one which is becoming less and less important in the world in which we live" (Laclau 2000a: 203). Thus, it is the matter of rethinking rather than rejecting Marx's concepts that characterizes Laclau's post-Marxism.

## The (Missing) Empty Signifier

Laclau (2000a, 2000b) insists that notions such as class and class struggle provide us with a false sense of confidence and duty. However, if the movements of the economic infrastructure are rejected as a myth, a void opens at the center of contemporary political theory. Acknowledging this, Laclau calls for rethinking the subject of contemporary politics:

> Someone who is confronted with Auschwitz and has the moral strength to admit the contingency of her own beliefs, instead of seeking refuge in religious or rationalistic myths is, I think, a profoundly heroic and tragic figure. This will be a hero of a new type who has still not been entirely created by our culture, but one whose creation is absolutely necessary if our time is going to live up to its most radical and exhilarating possibilities.
>
> Laclau 2007: 123

Thus, he is aware that theoretical work has come to a certain impasse, i.e. is unable to provide alternatives, leaving us once again confronted with the unresolved issue of emancipation. In his case, as we have seen, religion and rationalism cannot provide alternatives as they are seen as myths. The question that arises is, therefore, where should we look for the alternative? Confronted with the pressing issue of social change, Laclau and Mouffe (2001) propose their model of emancipation.

First, Laclau makes it clear that "if there is going to be the subject of a certain global emancipation, the subject antagonized by the general crime, it can be *politically constructed* only through the *equivalence* of a plurality of demands" (Laclau 2000c: 55). He does not stop at this point but provides a detailed explanation of how this chain of equivalences is formed, emphasizing the importance of an analytic distinction between the empty and the floating signifier. In Laclau's own words, "if I have called the general equivalent unifying an undisturbed equivalential chain the *empty signifier*, I will call the one whose emptiness results from the unfixity introduced by a plurality of discourses interrupting each other the *floating signifier*" (Laclau 2000b: 305). To illustrate this model using the feminist struggle as an example, Mouffe argues that the feminist movement, with the accompanying demands it poses, "should be understood not as a separate form of politics designed to pursue the interests of women *as* women, but rather as the pursuit of feminist goals and aims within the context of a wider articulation of demands" (Mouffe 1993: 87). In Laclau's model of emancipation, feminism is acting as always only one of many floating signifiers situated in a chain of equivalences. The empty signifier, on the other hand, occurs as a certain excess, something else that unifies and represents every demand without identifying with any in particular or being reducible to a sum of all demands in a chain of equivalences, thereby acting as "a signifier without a signified" (Laclau 2007: 36). Thus, the empty signifier does not need to be explicitly articulated in gendered terms, i.e. it can be labeled simply as "radical democracy," because "it is the empty character of these anchoring points that truly universalizes a discourse, making it the surface of inscription of a plurality of demands beyond their particularities" (Laclau 2000a: 210). In this way, it is ensured that the demands based on gender, ethnicity, class, age, etc. will not be mutually exclusive and exhaust themselves, intentionally or not, in overriding their different but equally valuable demands (Mouffe 1993). It could be said, firstly, that this model ensures that the call for anti-essentialism is taken seriously and consistently implemented in the emancipatory struggle. Second, it is a model of emancipation where a particular struggle always occupies a certain position in a chain of equivalences, without harming or being harmed by other social struggles. This is a very skillful way to resolve the tension between abandoning the essence on which so-called identity politics is based and the possibility of acting in a political manner.

However, having been impressed with this model and somewhat overwhelmed by its theoretical sophistication, one cannot fail to recognize that the empty signifier is nevertheless missing in contemporary society, in a way stopping Laclau's model in its tracks. Furthermore, it is far from clear what kind of demand could eventually occupy this structural position and successfully stand as "the general equivalent unifying an undisturbed equivalential chain" (Laclau 2000b: 305). The empty signifier cannot be simply ignored as less relevant because, according to Laclau, "there is no future for the Left if it is unable to create an expansive universal discourse, constructed out of, not against, the proliferation of particularisms of the last few decades" (Laclau 2000b: 306). In keeping with his post-Marxist view, Laclau (2000a, 2000b) acknowledges that the empty signifier will not inevitably occur and emphasizes the need for an active struggle that would lead to a set of emancipatory populist movements. However, the reasons why the empty signifier is effectively missing remain under-theorized as the priority is given to examining existing populist movements and reflecting on their emancipatory potential for the future actions of the Left. Rather than analyzing why the empty signifier is missing, Laclau is overwhelmed by the possibility of its creation. In a way, he acts according to Mannoni's well-known psychoanalytic formula "I know well, but all the same ..." (Mannoni 2003). Laclau knows well that the empty signifier will not inevitably arise, but all the same proceeds as it will and acts according to his belief. In that spirit he devises the model of emancipation and invests his further efforts in its potential. Consequently, the empty signifier is increasingly beginning to function as an eschatological resource in his model as there is the impression that it will eventually crystallize out of the multiple social struggles, thus bringing about emancipatory change in society. In the same manner, during her keynote speech ("In Defence of Left-Wing Populism") at a 2015 conference in London,[3] Mouffe stated that, while struggling for the populist movement to emerge and radical democracy to be established, it seems that we have lost democracy altogether. She recognizes this as an unintended consequence and hopes for a constitution of the populist movement on the level of the European Union. Even after democracy itself is lost, a more thorough reflection on why the empty signifier is not arising is far from something that would be seen as necessary. In contrast, I take a different approach, fully recognizing that the empty signifier is not an eschatological instance that will inevitably crystallize. This, in turn, enables me to take a less activist approach and focus on the reasons *why* the empty signifier is missing.

## An Entrepreneur of Himself at the Political Frontier

The answer can be found when Laclau's notion of political frontier is critically examined. In his late work, Laclau focused on populism, providing a conceptualization in which "populism is, quite simply, a way of constructing the political" (Laclau 2005: xi). The novelty of his position lies precisely in his re-evaluation of populism as he does not reject it from a well-known moralist standpoint but sees it as a necessary condition for a collective agency. Laclau elaborates the interconnection between his model and populism, arguing:

> So the destiny of populism is strictly related to the destiny of the political frontier ... Frontiers are the *sine qua non* of the emergence of the 'people': without them, the whole dialectic of partiality/universality would simply collapse. But the more extended the equivalential chain, the less 'natural' the articulation between its links, and the more unstable the identity of the enemy (located on the other side of the frontier).
>
> Laclau 2005: 89, 231

Laclau is aware that the enemy of global emancipation cannot be easily addressed and, in this respect, Laclau and Mouffe argue that the antagonisms provoked by a global capitalism should be used in order to "constitute new forms of radical subjectivity on the basis of discursively constructing as an external imposition—and therefore as forms of oppression—relations of subordination which until that moment had not been questioned" (Laclau and Mouffe 2001: 158). Parallel to this, the Left should actively work to prevent the fall into pure particularism of demands, always bearing in mind that neoliberalism has an immense capacity to absorb various struggles and resignify them to serve neoliberal ends. To illustrate his argument, Laclau provides an example of "in embryo, a populist configuration" in which

> there is an accumulation of unfulfilled demands and an increasing inability of the institutional system to absorb them and an *equivalential* relation is established between them. The result could easily be, if it is not circumvented by external factors, a widening chasm separating the institutional system from the people.
>
> Laclau 2005: 73–4

In his opinion, what might be born out of such a constellation of power relations, where the people are increasingly separated from the institutional system, is the global subject of emancipation.

This is where the crucial problem inherent in his model of emancipation is situated. The enemy is not just becoming increasingly unstable as the equivalential chain extends but the enemy that would make his model effective literally does not exist in neoliberal society. The main reason why the empty signifier is missing should be sought in the proliferation of neoliberal subjectivity. Foucault's (2008) understanding of neoliberal subjectivity follows his general idea of clearly distinguishing liberalism from neoliberalism. He sees the liberal subject as concerned mostly with the supply and demand of labor resources. This, for him, is the main characteristic of the *homo oeconomicus*. On the other hand, the neoliberal subject is not a passive one nor satisfied with a simple exchange, but rather takes an active role. She has a motivation to go further and make herself ever more competitive. For that reason, such a subject is, in Foucault's words, "an entrepreneur of himself" (Foucault 2008: 226). Understanding why this entrepreneurial subject has emerged is possible only if we remind ourselves that the neoliberals insist on using competition as a benchmark for all aspects of human behavior "and, thanks to this analytical schema or grid of intelligibility, it will be possible to reveal in non-economic processes, relations, and behavior a number of intelligible relations which otherwise would not have appeared as such—a sort of economic analysis of the non-economic" (Foucault 2008: 243). In other words, the neoliberal subject is personally pushing the boundaries of economic analysis, consequently auto-colonizing aspects of her life that were traditionally situated outside the competition playground. There is no person, such as a great totalitarian leader, institution, discourse or even emotion that could occupy such a position of the enemy external to neoliberal subjects that would contribute to the formation of political frontier as understood by Laclau. One is fully allowed to critique, disrespect, publicly talk against the logic of competition, etc. or can, on the other hand and in an equally free manner, peacefully and diligently keep on improving her capacities for competition, adapting to the vocabulary and norms that such processes require. However, the final consequence of the disobedience towards the principle of competition could easily lead to economic or other forms of isolation, a well-known fact among neoliberal subjects. Thus, neoliberal subjects are fully free to choose their preferred option and this is where Foucault (2008) identifies that freedom can be used to govern or, to be more precise, self-govern (Rose 2004). However, those who are using their freedom in order to increase their competitiveness are not the party apparatchiks but "ordinary," "everyday" people, which makes this governing logic at the same time omnipresent and impossible to attribute to a certain person or institution.

When a Foucaultian perspective is adopted, "the identification of an institutionalized 'other'" (Laclau 2005: 117) that subordinates and oppresses, necessary for establishing the political frontier, proves to be an increasingly obsolete task in the neoliberal era. This is not to say that the political frontier, essential for the functioning of Laclau's model of emancipation, does not exist anymore. The way I understand it, this frontier is primarily internal to subjects or, in other words, the enemy and the person who should resist the system are simultaneously embodied within the figure of neoliberal subject. Subversion is subverted by the lack of its addressee and, rather than confronting "an institutionalized 'other'" (Laclau 2005: 117), the political frontier manifests in self-confrontation. This is why, even though people are fully free to express their revolt and actively resist, it remains unclear against whom are they revolting. The neoliberal state does not operate as a separate body, but neoliberal subjects are perpetuating the system themselves, through their choices, embodying the productive character of power. If Laclau's aforementioned figure becomes tragic (and heroic) as it refuses to seek refuge in rationalist and religious narratives, Foucault's conception of the subject as an entrepreneur of himself, taking away the repressive instance of power that could be straightforwardly blamed for the suffering in contemporary society, is making the accompanying political void even more explicit and complex. It poses some uncomfortable questions about the heroic character of Laclau's figure as it examines the productive character of power, thereby challenging the innocence of the neoliberal subject, her role in the perpetuation of neoliberalism.

## Situating the Centrality of Neoliberal Subjectivity

In order to understand this political void, we should examine the governmentality under which the subject as an entrepreneur of himself has taken a dominant position. Otherwise, if Foucault's conceptualization of the subject is presented as an isolated point of interest, it might be misread as a subject suffering under radicalized liberal capitalism, being simply oppressed by neoliberal government. Laclau's model of emancipation suffers from such misreading as he is primarily concerned with producing the emancipatory subject while constructing his model of emancipation, relying on the notion of subjectivity which, in Foucault's theoretical framework, principally corresponds to the passive, liberal subject that is focused mostly on simple exchange: supply and demand. He largely overlooks the distinctive qualities of neoliberalism elaborated by Foucault (2008), primarily at the level of active, self-entrepreneurial subjectivity, which in turn allows him to establish the notion of political frontier as an instance external to neoliberal subjects. What seems to me as crucial to acknowledge, if the novelty of an entrepreneur of himself is to be fully recognized, is Foucault's emphasis on neoliberalism as a radically *do-not-laissez faire* society. According to his elaboration, the neoliberals reject the idea of economic reductionism, while the state in neoliberalism is being suppressed by big neoliberal government. These distinctive points are elaborated in Foucault's (2008) analysis of the German model of neoliberalism or, in more common terms, ordoliberalism. Ordoliberalism begins with the founding of the journal *Ordo* in 1936 and the economist Walter Eucken establishing the "Ordoliberal" or Freiburg School of economic thought. This school, which Foucault most often has in mind while referring to the neoliberals, emerged as a response to the collapse of Nazism and is primarily concerned with the reconstruction of the state.

## *Laissez-faire* Turned into *Do-not-laissez-faire*

Ordoliberals reject the liberal notion of *laissez-faire* and think of it as a naïve naturalism. They are well aware that there is no such thing as a biological human impulse to compete and, therefore, there is nothing *a priori* in human behavior that would, if exercised freely, be a sufficient condition to develop a proper capitalist society. The neoliberal subject is largely relieved of socio-biological presuppositions and the neoliberals indeed carefully avoid the pitfalls of essentialism. It should be made clear that the neoliberals have no intention to actively intervene in the internal logic of competition, but are seeking to change the structure of society in order to make it a more conducive environment for competition. This is why Foucault claims that "pure competition must and can only be an objective, an objective thus presupposing an indefinitely active policy. Competition is therefore an historical objective of governmental art and not a natural given that must be respected" (Foucault 2008: 120). It is primarily at this point that the transition from passive to active governmentality takes place. Neoliberal policies ensure that society is permanently perfecting its playground for inequalities between the individuals. Thus, "*laissez-faire* is turned into a *do-not-laissez-faire* government, in the name of a law of the market which will enable each of its activities to be measured and assessed ... It is a sort of permanent economic tribunal confronting government" (Foucault 2008: 247). This once again calls for a famous quote from the *Manifesto of the Communist Party*, "all that is solid melts into air, all that is holy is profaned" (Engels and Marx 1978: 476), as there is no such structure in society where the logic of the market fails to penetrate. This, however, is ultimately achieved not by repression but rather through a productive character of power, by a production and perpetuation of a new subjectivity obsessed with self-entrepreneurship. The neoliberal subject is, therefore, not standing in front of a permanent economic tribunal but is effectively acting under her own auspices, being her own harshest critic, relentlessly measuring and assessing the remaining space for her own improvement, always keeping one eye on how everybody else is performing compared to her self-discipline in the field of competition. What is essentially missing here in order for Laclau's political frontier, "*separating* the 'people' from power" (Laclau 2005: 74, *emphasis added*), to be established is a higher instance of power that imposes its requirements in a stronger and more aggressive manner than the neoliberal subject himself, thereby acting as an enemy. Laclau seems to ignore that

> what makes power hold good, what makes it accepted, is simply the fact that it doesn't only weigh on us as a force that says no, but that it traverses and produces things, it induces pleasure, forms knowledge, produces discourse. It needs to be considered as a productive network which runs through the whole social body, much more than as a negative instance whose function is repression.
> Foucault 1980: 119

After all, separation from power as a function of political frontier can be seen as something desirable only when power is equated with repression which, as Foucault (1980: 109–33) argues, fails to explain why the people are obeying power in the first place. In relying overly on a repressive character of power, we are left wondering how the people found themselves in a situation where they, according to Laclau, need to be separated from power.

## Abolishing Economic Reductionism

Returning to distinctive characteristics of neoliberalism, Marxist and liberal differentiation between the infrastructure and superstructure has also been re-evaluated by neoliberals. Bearing in mind that Weber (2005) used the example of the Protestant ethic to show how a certain cultural context enables capitalism, the aforementioned distinction between infrastructure and superstructure has been increasingly losing its theoretical value. Even though this distinction is usually used to provide a simplistic summary of Marxism, it is also one of the main characteristics of liberal economic theory. Thus, it is more appropriate to say that both Marxist and liberal conceptualizations of the economy have lost their explanatory power, indicating why Weber is a relevant author for both the neo-Marxist Frankfurt School and neoliberal Freiburg School. For Foucault this is so obvious that he even states: "the theoretical meaning, I am embarrassed to point it out, is that instead of distinguishing between an economic belonging to the infrastructure and a juridical-political belonging to the superstructure, we should in reality speak of an economic-juridical order" (Foucault 2008: 163). The neoliberals see that it is simply not possible, as in liberal theory, to maintain a strict boundary between the state on the one side and the economy on the other. The economy is enabled by the social context and cannot be isolated as a pure category on which it is subsequently possible to implement certain policy solutions. Quite on the contrary, they label such liberal approach as passive and are more than willing to intervene, once again, not in competition itself but in the conditions where competition is situated. From this perspective, of understanding society as an economic-juridical order, we can see what Röpke meant when he stated: "The free market requires an active and extremely vigilant policy" (Röpke, *cit. in* Foucault 2008: 133). This is why such type of neoliberalism is sometimes referred to as a "sociological liberalism" and "positive liberalism" (Röpke, *cit. in* Foucault 2008: 146, 133); sociological as it is trying to change social structures and positive to emphasize the need for an active governmental approach.

Subjectivity, in the perspective marked by the rejection of economism, is not something that belongs to the category of superstructure, being no more than an elusive reflection of the economy. It is a first-order issue, the engine power of neoliberalism, producing and perpetuating the system. This is not to say that institutions do not exist in neoliberal society or that they are completely purified of any sovereignty. Of course, neoliberal institutions do exist and are not simply relieved of acting in a coercive manner, which is illustrated by numerous studies.[4] It is simply to note that, as Foucault made it quite clear,

> in analyzing power relations from the standpoint of institutions, one lays oneself open to seeking the explanation and the origin of the former in the latter, that is to say, finally, to explain power to power ... This does not deny the importance of institutions on the establishment of power relations. Instead, I wish to suggest that one must analyze institutions from the standpoint of power relations, rather than vice versa, and that the fundamental point of anchorage of the relationships, even

if they are embodied and crystallized in an institution, is to be found outside the institution.

Foucault 1982: 791

Neoliberal institutions are not the final point of analysis and, accordingly, neoliberalism cannot be explained simply as the accumulation of micro-institutional settings. In Foucault's perspective, neoliberalism owes its strength (along with its institutions) to a particular form of self-entrepreneurial subjectivity. Discipline does not disappear but instead takes a new form, proliferating through the freedom of neoliberal subjects, paradoxically acting as a productive instance in the process of subjectification.

## The State is not a Special Organism

To gain a better understanding of neoliberalism, we need to change our perspective on the state and government. For Foucault, "the state is nothing else but the mobile effect of a regime of multiple governmentalities" (Foucault 2008: 77). When he is discussing Nazism and Stalinism, Foucault does not blame excess state power for the well-known atrocities, thereby challenging liberals' portrayal of the state as a kind of monster whose continuous growth of power finally culminated in these totalitarian regimes:

> I would also like to suggest that the characteristic feature of the state we call totalitarian is far from being the endogenous intensification and extension of the mechanisms of the state; it is not at all the exaltation but rather a limitation, a reduction, and a subordination of the autonomy of the state, of its specificity and specific functioning—but in relation to what? In relation to something else, which is the party.

Foucault 2008: 190

In this context, it is important to acknowledge that he sees the government not as an institution but as "the activity that consists in governing people's conduct within the framework of, and using the instruments of, a state" (Foucault 2008: 318). What such perspective implies, in its methodological consequences, is reconstructing macro-power issues, such as the state, starting with the analysis of micro-power "on the basis of men's actual practice, on the basis of what they do and how they think" (Foucault 2009: 358), thereby exposing the inextricable knot of power that goes beyond simple, clean and comforting micro-macro divisions. Thus, apart from distinguishing himself from liberals, it is quite obvious that Foucault also clearly distanced himself from the Marxist conception of the state and does not think of it as "a special organism separated from society" (Marx 1978: 539) or "a committee for managing the common affairs of the whole bourgeoisie" (Engels and Marx 1978: 475), to cite just a few quotes that portray the state as an instance merely external to its subjects.

Following Foucault's argumentation, it becomes clear that the distinction between harmful neoliberal government and innocent, "ordinary" people suffering under its impositions is an oversimplified one. Neoliberal subjects and neoliberal government cannot be simply delineated; these are not two distinct registers divided by a certain border. Indeed the lack of such a border is, as has been argued, what Laclau conceptualizes and implements in his model of emancipation as a political frontier. Fighting for the political frontier is a crucial part of what he sees as "the basic political dilemma of our age: will the proliferation of new social actors lead to the enlargement of the equivalential chains which will enable the emergence of stronger collective wills; or will they dissolve into mere particularism, making it easier for the system to integrate and subordinate them?" (Laclau 2000a: 210). It is in the context of this conundrum that Laclau emphasizes the role of the Left in identifying the enemy, as he is aware that the political frontier is not simply a line dividing the dichotomous but "without disappearing, is blurred as a result of the oppressive regime itself becoming hegemonic—that is trying to interrupt the equivalential chain of the popular camp by an alternative equivalential chain" (Laclau 2005: 131). However, this dilemma and the accompanying duty of the Left exists only if government is identified with a body that subordinates and integrates particular demands, acting coercively in relation to social actors. One can, without much effort, provide an example in which such constellation of power relations was radically present; those who doubt this should look no further than Ceauşescu[5] and the uprising that led to his execution. However, the exercise of power, even in such extreme cases, "is nevertheless always a way of acting upon an acting subject or acting subjects by virtue of their acting or being capable of action. A set of actions upon other actions" (Foucault 1982: 789). No matter how difficult this might be for us to comprehend, there would be no way for such instance of power to consolidate without relying on a particular network of already existing power *relations*. Of course, Laclau's model is more applicable in the cases where institutions act repressively and these are not simply relegated to the past but can be and are identified in contemporary society,[6] where we still often witness police violence, the denial of citizenship, the imprisonment of political activists, etc. The problem is that Laclau does not limit his model to particular contexts but applies it all the way from Plato's cave to the disintegration of Yugoslavia, thus striving to propose a grand narrative of emancipation. Certainly, at places, Laclau claims that *the* emancipation (note the singular) is an overly grandiose and naïve notion, arguing that "if all emancipation must constitute itself as power, there will be a plurality of powers—and, as a result, a plurality of contingent and partial emancipations" (Laclau 2005: 101). On the other hand, he explores "the subject of a certain global emancipation, the subject antagonized by the general crime" (Laclau 2000c: 55). Finally, with the title of his book *Emancipation(s)*, this tension gained its expression in a condensed form.

In any case, it seems that nowadays the suffering of neoliberal subjects is not predominantly marked by a repressive exercise of power, embodied in the figure of a totalitarian leader, which does not seem to offer us any relief. Returning to Foucault, we can see that, quite on the contrary, neoliberalism largely operates by dispersing and multiplying its governmental practices through individuals or, to be more precise, through their freedom. Understanding this, Rose asks:

> But what are the relations between these micro-practices and what "men call 'government' in great buildings and capitals?" ... Clearly a plan, policy or

programme is not merely 'realized' in each of these locales, nor is it a matter of an order issued centrally being executed locally. What is involved here is something more complex. I term this 'translation.'

Rose 2004: 48

This is a certain contribution to flattening the social (Latour 2005) in the field of governmentality studies but its applicability is limited to liberal governmentality, where both the government and subjects are understood as passive, while a respectful boundary is maintained between the state and the economy, thus requiring a translation process. Neoliberal governmentality, on the other hand, is characterized by a radical break with the idea of such delineation and is fundamentally active, indeed realizing itself almost immediately in neoliberal subjects. The metaphor of translation is simply not radical enough to accommodate the epistemological shift brought by neoliberalism, since it is still based on the understanding in which neoliberal subjects and neoliberalism are seen as two hierarchically separated levels in society. It is not quite the case that the microphysics of neoliberal government is dependent on the role that "small" people have in the system. Rather, neoliberal subjects are neoliberalism; or, to be more precise, neoliberalism is above all a form of subjectivity. This is the fundamental message of Foucault's work on this topic and is what makes Laclau's basic political dilemma head towards being obsolete in our age. What is essentially new in neoliberalism is a shift in subjectivity and this is what has turned it into a system that is immensely flexible and resistant to subversion.

## Conclusion

When Laclau's model of emancipation is contextualized using Foucault's understanding of neoliberal subjectivity, it becomes more obvious why "the subject of a certain global emancipation, the subject antagonized by the general crime" (Laclau 2000c: 55) is missing. Bearing in mind that we are facing "an entrepreneurial ethic that exhorts even the most powerless to take responsibility for their own lives without depending on anyone or anything else" (Butler 2015: 67), self-entrepreneurship was not presented as an embodiment of bourgeois in this article. It is in fact a form of subjectivity and not merely a class issue. Furthermore, it was argued that the political frontier is internal to contemporary subjects and, as it divides the neoliberal subject, is primarily expressed as a sort of self-confrontation. In this context, we should also recognize that, further down the road of self-entrepreneurship,

> the more one complies with the demand of 'responsibility' to become self-reliant, the more socially isolated one becomes and the more precarious one feels ... It involves an escalation of anxiety about one's future and those who may be dependent on one; it imposes a frame of individual responsibility on the person suffering that anxiety; and it redefines responsibility as the demand to become an entrepreneur of oneself under conditions that make that dubious vocation impossible.

Butler 2015: 15

This is why so many insights into the way neoliberal society operates are gained by emphasizing and analyzing the growth of anxiety in contemporary society (Salecl 2005, 2010). However, exploring anxiety, even though it is a rather pressing issue that follows my current argument, is beyond the scope of this chapter.[7] My aim here was to illuminate why, while there are many calls for subversion, it is essentially missing, and failing to identify its enemies. It was argued that the proliferation of a new, neoliberal subjectivity is the answer to why subversion is constantly being subverted by exactly those who are meant to be fighting it, namely unsatisfied neoliberal subjects.

Late Foucault, with whose legacy this collection engages, himself cherished a sort of indifferent stance towards subversion. As Sloterdijk reminds us, "When two journalists from *Les Nouvelles Litteraires* asked him in 1984, 'Does your return to the Greeks participate in a weakening of the ground on which we think and live? What did you want to destroy?', his laconic response to the subversion parrots was: 'I did not want to destroy anything!'" (Sloterdijk 2013: 158–9). Thus, instead of asking the famous question *What is to be done?* (Lenin 1990), he invites us to ask how have we done what we have done? How are we producing and perpetuating contemporary, neoliberal condition? The novelty of Foucault, according to Sloterdijk, lays precisely in his awareness "that one cannot subvert the 'existing'—only supervert it ... that human claims to freedom and self-determination are not suppressed by the disciplines, regimes and power games, but rather enabled" (Sloterdijk 2013: 152). In this respect, what Foucaultian analysis gives us is not yet another theory of subversion, but awareness that the notion of subversion operates with power as an oppressive instance and is fundamentally limited in its scope due to such reasoning.

This article does not offer a theory of the emancipatory subject. Understanding that subversion is subverted primarily due to the shift in neoliberal subjectivity is, rather, to remind of a contradictory character of emancipation. As a part of the debate concerned predominantly with Laclau's model of emancipation, Žižek (2000a, 2000b) criticized Laclau, claiming that class should still have a primacy in his model of emancipation. Laclau eventually summarized his reply: "Conclusion: Žižek cannot provide any theory of the emancipatory subject. Since, at the same time, his systemic totality, being a ground, is regulated exclusively by its own internal laws, the only option is to wait for these laws to produce the totality of its effects. *Ergo*: political nihilism" (Laclau 2005: 238). Whether class should or should not play a more prominent role in Laclau's model is not something that occupies my attention here. What is interesting is the criterion; is there any theory of the emancipatory subject?

Rather than providing an alternative model of emancipation, this chapter deployed Foucault's work on neoliberalism at the Collège de France in order to make it explicit that Laclau's political frontier, which leads the emancipatory subject to subversion of neoliberal order, largely ignores the productive character of power. At this point, we should also remember that social change is not something planned at academic conferences and carried out via academic publications. Analysis does contribute to social change as it works towards unraveling social relations that surround us, thus transforming our reality. However, social change is a significantly broader issue and is necessarily more of a collective effort. Confronted with theories that misleadingly—though undoubtedly in Laclau's and many other cases honestly—promise subversion, a return to Foucault's insights on neoliberal subjectivity makes us aware that subversion has already been subverted, reminding us of a contradictory character of emancipation. The solution, however, is not to abandon the notion of emancipation and use numerous euphemisms, the most famous example of which is probably "agency," instead. This would achieve little more than censoring this contradiction. One should, on the contrary, engage with the contradictory character of emancipation by recognizing subjectivity as a political category *par excellence*. This, rather than enthusiastically trying to avoid the label of political nihilism, contributes to a productive analysis of contemporary society.

## Notes

1 Chronologically, *The Birth of Biopolitics* (1979) is situated between Foucault's lectures *Security, Territory, Population* (1978) and *On the Government of the Living* (1980), all held at the Collège de France. Truth be told, the titles of his lectures do not really tell us much about their content, so one really has no other option but to read Foucault. However, a prospective reader might be surprised to see that these lectures are (relatively) easy to read.
2 See Critchley and Marchart (2004), Harrison (2014), Laclau (2005, 2007), Laclau and Mouffe (2001), and Marchart (2007).
3 *Socialism, Capitalism and the Alternatives*, organized by University College London (December 14–16, 2015).
4 For example, see Fraser (2013), Gill and Scharff (2011), Harvey (2007), Klein (2007), and Tyler (2013).
5 General Secretary of the Romanian Communist Party (1965–89).
6 For example, see Gill and Scharff (2011), Harvey (2007), Klein (2007), and Tyler (2013).
7 For my take on anxiety, see Krce-Ivančić (2018).

## References

Butler, J. (2015), *Notes Toward a Performative Theory of Assembly*, London: Harvard University Press.
Critchley, S. and O. Marchart, eds (2004), *Laclau: A Critical Reader*, New York: Routledge.
Engels, F. and K, Marx. (1978), "Manifesto of the Communist Party," in R. C. Tucker (ed.), *The Marx-Engels Reader*, 469–500, London: Norton.
Foucault, M. (1980), "Truth and Power," in C. Gordon (ed.), *Power/Knowledge: Selected Interviews and Other Writings, 1972-1977*, 109–33, New York: Pantheon Books.
Foucault, M. (1982), "The Subject and Power," *Critical Inquiry*, 8 (4): 777–95.
Foucault, M. (2008), *The Birth of Biopolitics: Lectures at the Collège de France 1978-1979*, ed. M. Senellart, trans. G. Burchell, Basingstoke: Palgrave Macmillan.
Foucault, M. (2009), *Security, Territory, Population: Lectures at the Collège de France 1977-1978*, ed. M. Senellart, trans. G. Burchell, Basingstoke: Palgrave Macmillan.
Fraser, N. (2013), *Fortunes of Feminism: From State-Managed Capitalism to Neoliberal Crisis and Beyond*, London: Verso.
Gill, R. and C. Scharff, eds (2011), *New Femininities: Postfeminism, Neoliberalism and Subjectivity*, Basingstoke: Palgrave Macmillan.

Harrison, O. (2014), *Revolutionary Subjectivity in Post-Marxist Thought. Laclau, Negri, Badiou*, Surrey: Ashgate.
Harvey, D. (2007), *A Brief History of Neoliberalism*, Oxford: Oxford University Press.
Klein, N. (2007), *The Shock Doctrine: The Rise of Disaster Capitalism*, New York: Metropolitan Books.
Krce-Ivančić, M. (2018), "Governing Through Anxiety," *Journal for Cultural Research*, 22 (3): 262–77.
Laclau, E. (2000a), "Structure, History and the Political," in J. Butler, E. Laclau, and S. Žižek (eds), *Contingency, Hegemony, Universality Contemporary Dialogues on the Left*, 182–212, London: Verso.
Laclau, E. (2000b), "Constructing Universality," in J. Butler, E. Laclau, and S. Žižek (eds), *Contingency, Hegemony, Universality Contemporary Dialogues on the Left*, 281–307, London: Verso.
Laclau, E. (2000c), "Identity and Hegemony: The Role of Universality in the Constitution of Political Logics," in J. Butler, E. Laclau, and S. Žižek (eds), *Contingency, Hegemony, Universality Contemporary Dialogues on the Left*, 44–89, London: Verso.
Laclau, E. (2005), *On Populist Reason*, London: Verso.
Laclau, E. (2007), *Emancipation(s)*, London: Verso.
Laclau, E. and C. Mouffe (2001), *Hegemony and Socialist Strategy. Towards a Radical Democratic Politics*, London: Verso.
Latour, B. (2005), *Reassembling the Social: An Introduction to Actor-Network-Theory*, Oxford: Oxford University Press.
Lenin, V. I. (1990), *What Is To Be Done?*, London: Penguin.
Mannoni, O. (2003), "I Know Well, but All the Same . . .," in D. Foster, M. A. Rothenber, and S. Žižek (eds), *Perversion and the Social Relation*, 68–92, Durham, NC: Duke University Press.
Marchart, O. (2007), *Post-Foundational Political Thought: Political Difference in Nancy, Lefort, Badiou and Laclau*, Edinburgh: Edinburgh University Press.
Marx, K. (1978), "Critique of the Gotha Program," in R. C. Tucker (ed.), *The Marx-Engels Reader*, 525–41, London: Norton.
Mouffe, C. (1993), *The Return of the Political*, New York: Verso.
Rose, N. (2004), *Powers of Freedom Reframing Political Thought*, Cambridge: Cambridge University Press.
Salecl, R. (2005), *On Anxiety*, London: Routledge.
Salecl, R. (2010), *Choice*, London: Profile Books.
Sloterdijk, P. (2013), *You Must Change Your Life: On Anthropotechnics*, trans. W. Hoban, Cambridge: Polity.
Tyler, I. (2013), *Revolting Subjects: Social Abjection and Resistance in Neoliberal Britain*, London: Zed Books.
Weber, M. (2005), *The Protestant Ethic and the Spirit of Capitalism*, trans. T. Parsons, London: Routledge.
Žižek, S. (2000a), "Class Struggle or Postmodernism? Yes, please!," in J. Butler, E. Laclau, and S. Žižek (eds), *Contingency, Hegemony, Universality: Contemporary Dialogues on the Left*, 90–135, London: Verso.
Žižek, S. (2000b), "Holding the Place," in J. Butler, E. Laclau and S. Žižek (eds), *Contingency, Hegemony, Universality: Contemporary Dialogues on the Left*, 308–29, London: Verso.

Part Five

# Truth-Telling, Truth-Living

13

# Rethinking Confession

Andrea Teti[1]

In Hurley's translation of *History of Sexuality, vol. 1*, Foucault famously states: "Western man has become a confessing animal [*bête d'aveu*]" (Foucault 1978: 59). This translation epitomizes the way *confession* and *aveu* are usually understood as semantically and analytically interchangeable in Foucault's work: both are taken to index a form of power in which the self is asked to continuously scrutinize and speak a hidden truth about itself (e.g. Dreyfus and Rabinow 1983). This conflation of *aveu* and *confession* results from a combination of Foucault's own, sometimes ambiguous, usage: for example, in the Dartmouth lectures he uses "confession" in English in a way that is reminiscent of his use of *aveu* in the Louvain lectures on the avowal, rather in than the way he uses *confession* in *Government of the Living*. This approach makes possible a rich vein of research, including Burchell's (2009) analysis of subjection/subjectivation and resistance and Elden's (2005) important reconstruction of the problem confession posed for Foucault in the genealogy of his work. Echoes of this conflation can be found in a wide range of subfields, including Philosophy (Taylor 2008), Political Theory (Bevir 1999), Education (Fejes and Dahlstedt 2013; Fejes and Nicoll 2015), Legal Studies (Tadros 1998), Nursing and Psychiatry (Roberts 2005), International Relations (Salter 2007), and Anthropology (Van Maanen 1988; cf. Webster 2008). However, current scholarship provides no systematic analyses of these concepts or of their evolution in Foucault's work.

By contrast, this chapter argues that a close examination of Foucault's work shows that this conflation, while found in Foucault's own writing, is not analytically justifiable, that grounds for distinguishing between *aveu* and *confession* emerge in his texts, and that it is analytically useful to make this distinction rather than treat the concepts as interchangeable. To do so, drawing from all published English and French sources, the chapter traces the evolution in Foucault's use of confession (*confession*) and avowal (*aveu*) throughout his work, first briefly summarizing Foucault's early usage, and then focusing in particular on his "last decade," since currently available material suggests it is only after 1974 that Foucault starts more frequently, explicitly, and systematically using those terms.[2] In particular, the chapter focuses on traces of the elements of a confessional dispositive provided in the first volume of *History of Sexuality*, which remains the most complete in Foucault's published work on confession. The chapter then focuses on Foucault's late works, particularly two resources which have recently become available: the *Wrong-Doing, Truth-Telling* lectures in Louvain, and the fourth volume of Foucault's *History of Sexuality, Les aveux de la chair*. It concludes by outlining core characteristics of confessional relations of power based on elements available in Foucault's texts.

The chapter therefore notes when and how Foucault's own usage varies, indicating when *aveu* and *confession* are being used in the sense of admission as in the more common English usage; when *confession* is used to index a broader economy of power; and what conceptual and analytical value Foucault's texts give beyond common usage. Accordingly, French terms have been bracketed in order to better reflect the original and bring to light the distinction between confession (*confession*) and avowal (*aveu*).

Based on this analysis, the chapter makes two claims. First, save sparse references to *confession* in his later texts, in Foucault's usage, *aveu* and *confession* broadly occupy the same semantic field as "admission," being linked primarily to quasi-judicial procedures (e.g. in secular and religious justice, psychiatry, etc.).

Second, Foucault's work during this period nonetheless displays discernible conceptual differentiation between *aveu* and *confession* which will emerge with some greater clarity in his later work. These differences are embryonic in his early work but become increasingly pronounced throughout the 1970s until they culminate in the analyses outlined in the 1981 Louvain (Foucault 2012b, 2014b), 1980 Dartmouth (Foucault 1993), and 1980 *Government of the Living* (Foucault 2012a, 2014a) lectures, and the recently-published *Les aveux de la chair* (Foucault 2018).

The chapter concludes by arguing that it is possible to discern something Foucault sometimes calls "sacramental confession" in his late work, a specific configuration of power relations rooted in a particular articulation of confession with the avowal in which the avowing subject's normalization is undermined by a subjectivity already and necessarily marked by deviant, stained nature—i.e. a figure in which the other remains trapped by its ontological distinctiveness, undermining the putatively emancipatory transformation enjoined upon it by the listening subject who demands the avowal.

## Avowal and Confession in Foucault's "Early Years," 1954–74

References to either *aveu* or *confession* in Foucault's early texts are either sparse (Foucault 1961) or entirely absent (e.g. Foucault 1954). Mostly, *confession* designates the Roman Catholic ritual, but elsewhere both it and *aveu* are used interchangeably as "admission." Later 1960s monographs (Foucault 1963, 1970, 2002a) make no reference to either term, and while his Introduction to Rousseau's *Rousseau Juge de Jean-Jacques* mentions *aveu, confession* does not appear.

The Collège de France lectures on the *Will to Know* (1970–1) (Foucault 2013b) contain sparse references to both words. Neither is central to Foucault's analysis, and while they each denote forms of truth-telling (in a judicial context), they are linked strictly to the semantic field of admission, and at no point is the *nature* of the speaking self in question, as will be shown to be in confession proper. In *Théories et institutions pénales* (1971–2), mentions of *confession* are rare and strictly refer to admission (e.g. Foucault 2015: 139). Foucault offers no explicit definition of *aveu*, but comments on "the idea that ... justice passes through or rests upon the enunciation of the truth" (Foucault 2015: 116).

In *Société Punitive* (1972–3), Foucault uses *aveu* several times, although never meaning admission, but rather being *sans aveu*—i.e. being placeless, vagabond, etc. *Confession*, however, is linked to an economy of power: Foucault's first reference links it to a "punitive sector [a core part of which was] the Church and its confessional-penitential system" (Foucault 2013a: 199), while the second reference provides an embryonic explicit definition of confession as an economy of power: "catholic confession is one of the ways in which [individual behavior] is made to enter into a kind of discursivity. But it is characterized by the fact that it is the subject himself who speaks [about himself]" (Foucault 2013a: 220–1). However, these terms are never linked, suggesting that Foucault is not thinking systematically about these concepts, whether singly or in their articulation.

In the 1973–4 *Psychiatric Power* lectures (Foucault 2006b), Foucault never mentions *confession*, and while his usage of *aveu* covers a semantic field roughly coinciding with "admission," he is also refining his thinking about the *aveu* into a "costly avowal regarding the self," and is clearly aware too of the difference between the avowal and its operation in the broader power relations psychiatry is built upon: in "the organization of the central confession (*aveu central*)" (Foucault 2006b: 273) the avowal is crucial to the possibility of therapeutic intervention, and thus to the way psychiatry (re)produces hierarchies of power between doctor and patient.

## The Avowal and its Economies of Power: From *The Will to Know* to the Stanford Lectures

Foucault's concern with avowal is present in his research on the asylum, in which the subject's avowal acts as a bridge between reason and madness, between normal and pathological, as well as in his analysis of the question of justice and its relation to police power, particularly in creating a "demand for torture": "by assigning such a privilege to confession [as a form of evidence], the judicial system is partly accomplice of this police practice of extracting it at any price" (Foucault, Bojunga and Lobo 1975: 13, *my translation*). By the first half of the 1970s, those two concerns converge in the study of Greek justice and the emergence of Christian forms of avowal and self-examination, which will influence his work on sacramental confession and its later percolation into a variety of other sites.

From 1973–5 onward, Foucault's references to *aveu* and *confession* increased markedly. He mentioned them more frequently in interviews, and the 1975 *Abnormal* Collège de France lectures sketch an analysis of the diffusion of the "Christian avowal"—confession-like dispositives articulated around an avowal—in different forms across Europe. In a 1975 interview, Foucault offered the first formal definition of the avowal, namely: "the avowal consists in the subject's discourse on himself in a situation of power in which that subject is dominated, constrained, and which [situation] that avowal modifies" (Foucault, Bojunga and Lobo 1975: 12).[3] Albeit refined over time until the most complex and detailed definition provided in Louvain, this definition would remain essentially the one Foucault works with until his death.

## *History of Sexuality*, vol. 1: *The Will to Know*

In 1976, Foucault published the first volume of the *History of Sexuality*, which contains the most systematic analysis he produced of confession. Along with the Louvain lectures and *Les aveux de la chair*, it remains the richest outline of confession available. As Elden (2005, 2017) has shown, Foucault certainly changed tack in his analysis of confession after publishing this volume, realizing that his genealogy of avowal and of the "Christian confession" needed to reach far further back than the Counter-Reformation. However, the first volume of the *History of Sexuality* is still the only text which explicitly and systematically analyses the characteristics of the avowal linking it to a confessional economy of power, within which it is deployed.

This sketch of a confessional dispositive remains very useful. First, Foucault begins by noting that confession proper—beyond the avowal, in order to make that avowal "function" in a given way—requires a particular "specification of individuals." The presence of an imperative to scrutinize the self and return its truth into discourse to an interlocutor is necessary but not sufficient to establish a confessional relation: it is also necessary for two subject positions to be established, the "sinner" (stained by original sin, ontologically bound to a pathological alterity) and the "confessor," the subject position of the pure and the normal. Second, pathological deviance, the ontological stain marking the sinner's alterity, translates into a "general and diffuse causality" and an "inextinguishable and polymorphous causal power"—a force which by the sinner's own nature drives it towards transgression against the norm. For Christian confession, this constant and constantly mutable deviant force is rooted in the Evil's influence on a constantly mobile mind, the most significant and powerful example of this being sex.

The implications of a dispositive with such characteristics are first, a "constant, endless and ubiquitous surveillance" of the sinner's deviant alterity: the completeness and constancy of this surveillance was necessary because, given the pathological nature of the deviance affecting the sinner, "the most discrete event—whether an accident or a deviation, a deficit or an excess—was deemed capable of entailing the most varied consequences" (Foucault 1978: 65). The second implication is apparently paradoxical, namely the fact that precisely this surveillance which is intended to neutralize the threat of pathological deviance provokes an "excitement of alterity." Foucault's analysis of the "repressive hypothesis" shows how it is precisely the strict codification, examination, and surveillance of sexuality which elicits the very deviance it sought to neutralize. Third, having drawn out pathological alterity, a confessional framework legitimizes "disciplinary intervention" against it. The final implication Foucault notes is that in a confessional dispositive, truth is produced through a "method of interpretation" which both disenfranchises the sinner in the production of truth about itself (Foucault, 1978: 66) and demands that this deviant Other confirm the truth about the *confessor* which that normal self already held (Foucault 1978: 69).

This outline is indicative of the kind of systematic analysis of the properties of a confessional dispositive as such which are notably missing from the bulk of Foucault's production. Even in *Will to Know*, Foucault's attention seems more focused on sex and "the uses of pleasure" than on the "strategic" characteristics of the dispositive within which these are deployed.

## The Government of the Living

The 1980 *Government of the Living* lectures do not systematically theorize *confession*, but they do present in a nutshell the analysis of *aveu* which Foucault would present in Louvain the following year. Like much of his production during this "late" period, this text shows an awareness of the importance of the broader level of the economies of power within which the avowal is put to work. Foucault's analysis in 1975–80 moves to general political mechanisms (governmentality, etc.), but between avowal and confession his primary focus remains on the avowal, the definition, and configuration of which Foucault continues to refine all the way up until the Louvain lectures.

In relation to avowal and confession, Foucault's focus in *Government of the Living* oscillates between the avowal as a singular act of admission, and acknowledging its location in broader mechanisms. On the one hand, throughout the lectures, Foucault's focus appears to remain on the avowal, and while he is aware of the distinction between the two and comments ways in which the former can be articulated, he does not develop an analysis of confessional dispositives. This is clear from the definition he provides of the "reflexive truth act:"

> I will call the truth act (*acte de vérité*) the part that falls to a subject in the production of alethurgy, the part that may be defined (1) by the subject's role as operator of the alethurgy, (2) by the subject's role as spectator of it, and (3) by the subject's role as the object itself of the alethurgy...
>
> Foucault 2014a: 81

> [T]he purest and also historically most important form of this reflexive form of the truth act is what we call confession (*l'aveu*)... a truth act in which the subject is at once actor of the alethurgy,... witness [and] its object.
>
> Foucault 2014a: 82

On the other hand, the general problem in which the question of the avowal is being formulated is to understand "why and how does the exercise of power in our society,... demand... truth acts in which individuals who are subjects in the power relationship are also subjects as actors, spectator witnesses, or objects in manifestation of truth procedures?" (Foucault 2014a: 82). Here, Foucault is clearly focusing on the role of the avowal in an economy of power. Indeed, Foucault specifies he wishes to analyze

> a regime of truth... defined by the obligation for individuals to have a continuous relationship to themselves of knowledge, their obligation to discover, deep within themselves, secrets that elude them, their obligation, finally, to manifest these secret and individual truths by acts that have specific, liberating effects that go well beyond the effects of knowledge.
>
> Foucault 2014a: 83

Foucault also refers to the macro-properties of confession as a "regime." For example, he notes the differences between Christianity as a "regime of faith" (avowal as profession of "adherence to an inviolable and revealed truth") and as a "regime of confession" (avowal as "exploring individual secrets, and of exploring them endlessly" (Foucault 2014a: 83–4)). He also traces the genealogy of modern confession, from "someone who is prepared to make the profession of faith ... to the point of risking death" to confession "in the sense of confession [*aveu*] of self" (Foucault, 2014a: 84) i.e. of a costly admission through which broader relations of power are articulated (see also Foucault 2014a: 85).

That said, Foucault's distinction between avowal and confession is never explicit or systematic. For example, in *The Government of the Living*, Foucault also specifies that this regime of truth "is not so much organized around the truth act as act of faith, but around the truth act as *act of confession*" (Foucault 2014a: 83–4, *emphasis added*). This presents *confession* as an act, the moment of the admission/statement of the self on the self, *not* as the economy of power within which that admission is located. Indeed, this confusion is again evident in the six times in under two pages—precisely the ones where he notes the genealogy of confession—that Foucault calls "*aveu*" the "confession of self," thus portraying *confession* as the speech act and *aveu* as the dispositive in which it is located.

In sum, on the one hand, by the late 1970s there are clearly two levels in Foucault's analysis: the admission (of a hidden, costly truth rendered into discourse) and the economy of power which demands it, articulates and deploys it, and within which its effects play out. On the other hand, first, it is equally clear that there is still considerable overlap and contradiction in the way Foucault actually uses *aveu* and *confession*, and second, while he has explicitly worked on the definition of the avowal as a concept, he never formulates a similarly systematic analysis of confession.

## Pastoral Power in the Stanford Lectures

The notable feature of the 1979 *Omnes et Singulatim* lectures at Stanford is that they were given in English, and thus might have provided evidence of how Foucault himself would translate *aveu* and *confession*, or whether he would find enough conceptual distinction to explicitly distinguish between the two. Unfortunately, Foucault did not mention *aveu*/avowal at all, and *confession*/confession only twice, both in the same passage of the first lecture, claiming first that early Christian texts "delineate the emergence of a very strange phenomenon in Greco-Roman civilization, that is, the organization of a link between total obedience, knowledge of oneself, and confession [*confession*] to someone else" and immediately following, that "[t]here is another transformation—maybe the most important. All those Christian techniques of examination, confession [*confession*], guidance, obedience, have an aim: to get individuals to work at their own "mortification" in this world.... A death which is supposed to provide life in another world" the novelty of which lay in the fact that "Christian mortification is a kind of relation from oneself to oneself. It is a part, a constitutive part of the Christian self-identity ... a game that neither the Greeks nor the Hebrews imagined" (Foucault 2002b: 310–11).

The text presents an important tension: on the one hand, in both the instances in which he uses "confession," the semantic fields seem to be related to "admission," and while the second instance is ambiguous, either case would suggest that still at this stage Foucault was not systematically distinguishing between *aveu* and *confession*. On the other hand, his analysis centers on the relationship between the shepherd's management of the flock and the expectation placed upon each member of that flock that they would yield up the truth about themselves to the shepherd. Thus, while Foucault's analysis of pastoral power does involve a form of "direction of conscience"—i.e. an economy of power within which the avowal is inserted—the absence of a clear semantic and conceptual distinction between the avowal and that broader dispositive seems to confirm that he was not thinking in a manner which explicitly, rigorously distinguished between the avowal and confession as concepts. As Foucault states explicitly at the start of the lecture, he is interested in analyzing the point at which and the manner in which broad technologies of populations become individual(ized): "my 'ligne de conduite' in my previous work [was to] analyse the relations between experiences like madness, death, crime, sexuality, and several technologies of power. What I am working on now is the problem of individuality—or ... self-identity as referred to the problem of 'individualising power'" (Foucault 2002b: 300).

In doing so, his first lecture on pastoral power returns to the question of the genealogy of modern sacramental confession (Elden 2005, 2017) and covers similar territory to the final section of *Les aveux de la chair*, including examination of first Plato, then ancient Christian literature (Chrysostom, Cyprian, Ambrose, Jerome, Cassian, and Benedict). Foucault then traces a genealogy of pastoral power, differentiating between pastorality in the ancient world, in early Christianity, and noting its ancient Jewish origins (Foucault 2002b: 300–01). He also outlines a series of analytical characteristics of a pastoral dispositive: the imperative that the shepherd's action be continuous (Foucault 2002b: 302); the shepherd's responsibility to "give account" for every sheep and his actions, as well as for the flock as a whole (Foucault 2002b: 308); the play of care, kindness, and generosity involved in the justification/exercise of pastoral power—"It's not only a matter of saving them all, all together, when danger comes nigh. It's a matter of constant, individualized, and final kindness" (Foucault 2002b: 302)—as well as the construction of duty which responsibilizes the individual to contribute to the shepherd's knowing every aspect of its life (Foucault 2002b: 301–03).

## Defining the Avowal: *Wrong-Doing, Truth-Telling*

In the *Wrong-Doing, Truth-Telling* lectures given in Louvain, Foucault provides the most systematic and detailed definition of the avowal (*aveu*) available in his published work, but not only does he mention *confession* rarely, but beyond the specifics of the juridical context he pays virtually no attention to the general properties of the dispositives within which the avowal can be located.

The definition of the avowal is set out in the lectures' Preliminary Meeting of April 2, 1981. Here Foucault elaborates on the specific meaning which he attaches to *aveu*, initially outlined in 1975, showing the distinctiveness of the avowal by considering a number of types of statements which display elements which are necessary but not sufficient to define the avowal. First, Foucault distinguishes the avowal from a simple declaration: an avowal must certainly be *declarative*, but "to declare, even solemnly or ritually, that one did or said something is not sufficient to constitute an avowal" (Foucault 2014b: 15). Second, he notes that an avowal cannot be a statement which simply brings to light a *hidden* truth: "What separates an avowal from a declaration is not what separates the unknown from the know, the visible from the invisible" (Foucault 2014b: 15). Then, he proceeds to identify further necessary characteristics for a statement to be an avowal: *freedom*, i.e. the avowal must be at least nominally freely made, "voluntary" such as in the case of Doctor Leuret insisting that the "madman" "recognize in full liberty that [he is] mad" (Foucault 2014b); *commitment*, inasmuch as the avowal "implies that he who speaks promises to be what he affirms to be" (Foucault 2014b: 16); and *costliness*: not unlike *parrhēsia*, the avowal entails "a certain cost of enunciation. [The] Avowal consists of passing from the untold to the told, given that the told has ... a great value" (Foucault 2014b: 15): a statement "is an avowal if this declaration runs the risk of being costly" (Foucault 2014b: 16), opening up the speaker to the *possibility* of having to pay a price. It is in this particular way—by making a costly, revealing, verbalized performance—that the avowal "modifies the subject's position in relation to power."

Foucault also identifies several key characteristics of the judicial economy of power within which the avowal thus understood is inserted, particularly in relation to the entanglement of the avowal with a surrounding economy of power and truth. For example, first, Foucault reprises the definition given in 1975, stating that the "avowal is a verbal act through which the subject affirms who he is, binds himself to this truth, places himself in a relationship of dependence with regard to another, and modifies at the same time his relationship to himself" (Foucault 2014b: 17). Second, Foucault notes that, as such, "avowal can only exist within a power relation [*dans un relation de pouvoir*] and the avowal enables the exercise of that power relation over the one who avows" (Foucault 2014b: 17). Third, Foucault notes a *performative* dimension of the avowal which affects the speakers' position within that economy of power: "While the avowal ties the subject to that which he affirms, it also qualifies him differently with regard to what he says" (Foucault 2014b: 17)—for example, one might be a criminal, but hopeful of repentance and reform, or mad but with the desire to heal.

More generally, Foucault seems aware of the need to differentiate between the avowal itself and the economies of power within which it could be inserted—despite not theorizing these explicitly, much less labeling them "confessional." For example, in the third lecture (April 29, 1981), Foucault traces elements of a relation between the avowal and a changing hermeneutics of the self: contemporary forms of subjectivation have their roots in the "Christian avowal," but that avowal in its contemporary form "hardly existed before Christianity" (Foucault 2014b: 91). The "Christian avowal" in its contemporary form "was invented relatively recently, dating more or less from the twelfth century. [Before this] Penance was not a sacrament; it did not require avowal, nor was it obligatory" (Foucault 2014b: 104). On the contrary, as he emphasizes in *Government of the Living*, in *Dire-vrai sur soi-même* and later in *Les aveux de la chair*, early Christianity displays two distinct practices: *exagoreusis*, which involved an avowal either of the status of sinner or—mostly privately—of specific sins, and *exomologesis*, which entailed the public manifestation/recognition of the status of sinner as a general condition, not linked *in that performance* to specific violations, so much so that "there is no avowal, nor is there any verbal formulation, nor is there any verbal enunciation of sins" (Foucault, 2014b: 106). The "translation of the self into discourse" found in modern forms of confession and contemporary forms of subjectivation takes a different route: "in the monastic practices that began to develop in the fourth and fifth centuries, self-mortification was still tied to veridiction, but through . . . language. It was through a continuous verbalization of oneself that the monk was to generate, himself, the link between veridiction and mortification" (Foucault 2014b: 112–13).

From those early beginnings, "Christianity" is increasingly linked to an economy of power articulated around the manifestation/performance, recognition and production of truth—not just dogmas that must be adhered to, but also "another kind of obligation to truth that is situated in an entirely different dimension . . . the obligation to search within himself for the truth of what he is. Christianity has bound the individual to the obligation to search for a certain secret deep within himself and in spite of everything that might hide this truth" because "when brought into the light of day and manifested" this secret truth will "play a decisive role in his path towards salvation" (Foucault 2014b: 92). The avowal is the lynchpin of this economy of power inasmuch as the imperative behind it entails nothing short of "the obligation to a hermeneutics of the self" (Foucault 2014b: 93).

## Avowal and Pastoral Power: *Les aveux de la chair*

In *Les aveux de la chair*, avowal and confession are mentioned nearly exclusively in two parts: Paper 1, *The Creation of a New Experience*, on baptism and purification from sin (Papers 2 and 3 on virginity and marriage focus on how to maintain such pure states), and Annex 2 which focuses on avowal first and then on pastoral power, an economy of power which entails the obligation of the avowal. Throughout *Les aveux de la chair*, *aveu* and *confession* are used more or less interchangeably to refer to the "admission of sins." The peculiarity of this text in relation to the question of avowal and confession considered here is that while Foucault analyzes early Christian practices noting their differences with modern confession, he never explicitly defines the avowal—in this sense, *Les aveux de la chair* can be read as a complement to *Wrong-Doing, Truth-Telling*—nor does he explicitly attempt to sketch the general characteristics of a confessional economy of power as he had done in *Wrong-Doing, Truth-Telling* and in the first volume of *History of Sexuality*. For example, when Foucault describes "confession" of sins/thoughts (e.g. Foucault 2018: 70–2, 80, 89–91), *confession* used as a synonym for admission, not as describing a particular political technology or economy of power. This being said, *Les aveux de la chair* provides an innovative analysis of several elements which are relevant to the development of an explicit theorization of confessional economies of power.

### The Formation of a New Experience

The first section of the book, *The Formation of a New Experience*, concentrates on baptism, the "second penitence," and the "art of arts," all of which are concerned with the operations involved in an individual's attempts to clear itself of a fault/sin. It is also clear that in this section—and throughout *Les aveux de la chair*—there are elements which run through Foucault's entire production (e.g. *publicatio sui*, translation of self into discourse), elements conventionally identified with the "late Foucault" (e.g. work on the self and the issue of truth-telling, formation of normality and deviance, the juridical procedures of the classical period, such as truth, veridiction, test, and trial) but also innovative elements, particularly the coupling of "truth-telling" (*dire vrai*) and "truth-doing" (*faire vrai*) and the emphasis Foucault places on the performative and "non-discursive" aspects of truth-production, which are dealt with in more detail than they were in his outline of "alethurgy" in the *Government of the Living* lectures.

In addition, while Foucault may not have focused explicitly on confession as a distinct form of power relations, his analyses of baptism, of the "second penitence," of direction of conscience, and of pastorality present all the key elements of a confessional economy of power. For example, Foucault spends a considerable amount of time outlining the question of baptism and the remission of sins: in his reading of Tertullian, his concern is to show first and foremost that through baptism sins can be remitted, wiped clean, and second that this remission can only ever be temporary because the imprint of original sin/the nature of human beings is ever to fall.

> penitential discipline since the second half of the second century, and monastic ascetism since the end of the third ... did not produce merely a reinforcement of prohibitions ... they defined and developed a specific mode of the relation of the self to the self and a specific relation between evil and truth ... between the remission of sins, the purification of the heart, and the manifestation of hidden transgressions (*fautes*), of secrets, and of the *arcana* of the individual within the examination of the self, within the avowal, within the direction of conscience or different forms of penitential "confession."
>
> Foucault 2018: 50[4]

> The practice of penitence and the exercises of ascetic life organise relations between "wrong-doing" and "truth-telling," it binds together the relation to the self, to evil and to truth, in a way that is without doubt much more innovative and crucial than this or that degree of severity added or lessened in the code [of conduct]. This [innovation] is in effect the form of subjectivity: the exercise of the self on the self, knowledge of the self by the self, constitution of oneself as object of investigation and discourse, liberation, purification of oneself by means of operations which bring light to the deepest parts of the self, and which lead the deepest secrets [back] to the light of a redemptive manifestation.
>
> Foucault 2018: 50

Foucault also shows awareness of the mutability across time of the dispositives built around the "Christian avowal." In the first section of the book (*Formations*), Foucault's analysis of modern confession leads him to note the difference between this construct and its early antecedents, addressing the genealogical issues which had led him to change the historical focus of his original project on confession. Baptism, for example, is an early practice entailing absolution from sin, as confession does later: indeed, it is the first sacrament granting absolution of sins, i.e. purification, making possible the emancipatory trajectory from a pathological state to a normalized one.[5] However, Foucault shows that baptism and modern confession are distinct: for the Patristic Church, baptism entailed a (public) avowal of sinfulness rather than an identification and manifestation of specific sins. Foucault argues that its public nature and physical and emotional intensity, and the fact that this display was "alethurgically" intended to publicly demonstrate that a fundamental turn towards truth (*metanoia*) had taken place, suggest that early "baptismal confession" displays the structure of trial/test (*épreuve*), not the recitation of specific sins characteristic of modern confession along with the introspective examination and *publicatio* this entailed (see Foucault 2018: 57).

Baptism does display a particular property which will later become central to the "Christian avowal," to confession specifically, and to confessional economies of power generally, namely an ethic of suspicion towards one's own thoughts. Foucault suggests that Tertullian epitomizes this ethic insofar as he not only first theorizes "original sin," but that it is he who first folds such suspicion of the self by the self into practices of direction of conscience. It is this novel union which turns them into relations of subjection and domination rather than the emancipatory and contingent form they possessed in pre-Christian Hellenism. Foucault observes that Tertullian argues that "those who submit to the procedure of salvation (*rachat*) must never be entirely sure of their selves" (Foucault 2018: 61) and that in saying this Tertullian points to "both the fear of God and the fear of oneself—namely the fear of one's own weakness (*faiblesse*), of the mistakes (*défaillances*) one is capable of, of the insinuation of the enemy within the soul, of the blindness or the complacency which will make it possible for him to surprise us" (Foucault 2018: 61). For Tertullian, baptism "is also the time at which one acquires this feeling of "fear" (*metus*), that is to say the awareness that one is never entirely the master of oneself, that one never knows oneself fully, and that given the impossibility of knowing of what slips (*chute*) one is capable, the undertaking one makes is commensurately more difficult, commensurately more dangerous" (Foucault 2018: 61).

However, Foucault does not believe that baptismal procedures betray an early form of "confession," primarily because this confession was a public proclamation/recognition of sinfulness (*exomologesis*) rather than a recitation of specific sins (Foucault 2018: 89–91). It is instead in penitential discipline that Foucault locates two crucial elements of the modern confessional dispositive: first, the role of the avowal in direction of conscience and in "penitential confession;" and second, the relation of the self to the self, work/operation of the self on the self.

## Avowal and Pastoral Power

In a sense, rather than a supposed turn "away" from politics and "toward" ethics in the "late Foucault," one can read Foucault's entire production in this period as an attempt on the one hand to describe a microphysics (Deleuze 2018: 41–2) of the forms of power in operation in "modern" societies (sovereign power, disciplinary power, biopower, etc.), and on the other to describe the forms which individual interventions in the (re)production or disruption of those forms of power took (avowal, *parrhēsia*, etc.). Clearly, the forms of power Foucault's texts are primarily concerned with are the ones which had an avowal of some sort at their core. These texts dedicate considerable attention to the avowal and to biopower separately, but focus less attention on the interplay between these two "levels," particularly with regard to the way the avowing subject's failures *sustain* rather than undermine confessional economies. As noted above, the exception in this regard is the first volume of *History of Sexuality*, in which the foundations of that linkage are sketched, while subsequent studies are weaker, probably preliminary studies in the context of the revision of his broader project in his later years. *Les aveux de la chair* is emblematic in this regard, insofar as it analyses explicitly both the avowal (primarily Paper 1) and pastoral power (primarily Paper 4), but does not return to elaborating on the link between avowal and pastorality beyond simply stating in various ways that the avowal is a technique central to the production of knowledge, subjectivity, and the overall economy of pastoral power. He never, for example, returns to *Abnormal*, to that genealogy of the "percolation" of the avowal into various socio-political technologies in the eighteenth and nineteenth centuries. Instead, in *Government of the Living*, for example, he speaks rarely and fleetingly of the relation of the avowal to the "regime of confession." In *Les aveux de la chair*, Annex 2, he does speak of these two elements *in sequence*—first avowal (examination in direction of conscience), *then* pastoral power—but the latter remains disjoined from avowal.

The analytical sequence avowal–confession–pastorality is significant both as a clue to Foucault's possible thinking and—more importantly—to retrieve tools from Foucault's texts for the expansion of his embryonic analysis.

Having realized that modern confession's genealogy reached far further back than the Counter-Reformation, Foucault traces its origins to early Christianity, and specifically to two separate contexts, one lay and the other monastic, and in two different institutions: baptism among the laity; and the direction of conscience in monasteries. Broadly speaking, baptism involved *exomologesis*, an admission of one's condition as a sinner which, unlike modern confession, was both public and generic, while monastic direction of conscience instead involved *exagoreusis*, a recounting of one's sins but also one's very thoughts which was addressed to a master and carried out in private rather than publicly. Foucault then explicitly argues that the fact that modern forms of confession which he identified in the first volume of the *History of Sexuality* are described as rooted in a convergence between *exagoreusis* and *exomologesis*, in reality demonstrates the degree to which the former won out over the latter (Foucault 2018: 369). The modern confessional dispositive Foucault sketches there is rooted in this emergence of *exagoreusis* and *exomologesis* and in their later articulation: it is from this monastic context that "these regular examinations of conscience which the *devotio moderna* [have been] disseminated into lay milieus" (Foucault 2018: 369) such as those described in *Abnormal* described as percolating throughout various social domains (medical, judicial, psychiatric, etc.).

Another way of looking at Foucault's analysis is to note that he identifies two axes along which early Christianity articulates answers to the problem of Evil—the examination of conscience, and the nullification of one's will—both of which remain central characteristics of confessional economies of power. Foucault shows that "the goal [of the examination of conscience] is to bring upon oneself a continuous attention, as detailed and as in depth as possible. Not, however, [in order] to know what one is at root (*au fond*), not to establish the authentic, pure and original form of a subjectivity, but in order to decipher in the deepest arcana of the soul the trickery of the Evil One" (Foucault 2018: 368). The examination of conscience—at least in this new guise it is given by the Christian Fathers, so significantly different from their Greco-Roman antecedents—aims to sift thoughts based on their origin, detecting the influence of Evil even when it presents itself under the guise of apparently pure thoughts. But given the shadow of radical doubt that Early Christianity casts over the self's will, since it is one's very self which is the object of doubt at the level of one's consciousness, early monastic Christianity proposes that the logical and safest way to avoid Evil is the neutralization of that will itself: "the examination-avowal in monastic life aims to 'no longer will' which, at the root of the soul, expels the other through the formulation of the true" (Foucault 2018: 368). The examination of one's self recounted to a Master, the doubt over the origins and nature of one's very thoughts, and the nullification of one's will sacrificed to one's master's are all traits that are present not only in modern confession but in all confessional dispositives which Foucault earlier described in *Abnormal* as propagating through society: they remain central characteristics of any fully confessional dispositive, such as forms of pastoral power.

This final section of the book devotes considerable attention precisely to this third term in the avowal-confession-pastorality sequence, specifically focusing on pastoral power as a power over a flock which must prosper (i.e. as a form of biopower). Here Foucault's text focuses on the bond between individual and pastoral leader, particularly on the manner in which within a pastoral logic of power the shepherd's fate is tied to the flock's under the sign of an enforceable but generous and obligatory care for each individual as much as for the whole flock (*omnes et singulatim*). The text brings its discussion to a close by noting the simultaneity of the production of truth by individuals and the search for truth by the shepherd/confessor: one requires and is conducted through the other. Perhaps oddly, however, this part of the text never speaks of the avowal's role in that production of truth. Foucault hints at the link between avowal-pastorality only once, but does so—significantly—in the context of a discussion of the reciprocal roles of shepherd and sheep:

> once attacked by temptation, the weak [i.e. all human beings] must seek asylum in their shepherd, "as children in the breast of their mothers." But the shepherd must also discover [in each sheep]—even despite themselves—that which they hide or hide from themselves (*ce qu'ils dissimulent ou se dissimulent à eux-mêmes*) ... that is to say "examine external conduct" of sinners with the aim of "discovering through this that which they hide in their heart which is most criminal and detestable."
> Foucault 2018: 394

It seems plausible to think that for Foucault the link between avowal and pastoral power was clear, but even without systematic treatment this interconnection can be readily recognized today.

It is worth noting that this power which "hides itself" is described in precisely the same way as the deviant power of sexuality to produce sin is described in the first volume of *History of Sexuality*: "If it was necessary to extract the truth of sex through the technique of confession (*aveu*), this was not simply because it was difficult to tell, or stricken by the taboos of decency, but because the ways of sex were obscure; it was elusive by nature; its energy and its mechanisms escaped observation, and its causal power was partly clandestine" (Foucault, 1978: 66).

Pastoral power—an economy of power similar to confession—is rooted in precisely this type of intrinsically, inescapably deviant, pathological alterity. This subjectivity in turn permits the articulation of a complex series of moral relations—including care, obligations, gift, emancipation, failure, guilt, discipline, attractions, evasions, circular incitements, the "method of interpretation" in which the production of truth is embedded, the "perpetual spirals of power and pleasure" Foucault hints at in *History of Sexuality I*, and of course the Patristic approach to the "work of the self on the self" which is so starkly innovative compared to Classical Antiquity—establishing and binding the shepherd of the norm to the flock of deviant sinners.

## Conclusion

A close reading of Foucault's usage of *aveu* and *confession* permits several conclusions. First, while all the elements of the avowal and the confession—of the transformation into discourse of a truth about the self by the self, and of a particular dispositive within which that avowal is located—are embryonically present in Foucault's early work, it is only in his late lectures that he offers definitions of the avowal. His late work also confirms he never sought to provide a definition or systematic analysis of *confession*, much less of the possible articulation(s) of avowal and confession. Indeed, a specific epistemology of confession is virtually absent in his early work, and even in his late writings, with the partial exception of *History of Sexuality I* and sparse references elsewhere, *confession* remains underdeveloped. Instead, there is a considerable overlap in Foucault's usage, with *aveu* and *confession* mostly occupying the same semantic field as "admission."

However, whether or not Foucault might have developed a more systematic analysis of confession and the avowal's articulation therein, his texts do provide a jumping off point to do this. For a start, certain core elements of this differentiation are present throughout his work, albeit emerging more clearly later. For example, while *confession* appears in both judicial and sacramental contexts, *aveu* nearly always refers to the subject's utterance of a truth about itself and quite rarely designates the broader sacramental practice. Additionally, *aveu* is more closely associated with different kinds of judicial procedures, while *confession* appears primarily in sacramental contexts and in domains such as psychiatry structured by ontological oppositions between "normal" and "pathological" states (e.g. in *Abnormal*, *History of Sexuality I*, *Government of the Living* and *Les aveux de la chair*). Finally, Foucault's texts do display a concern—however unsystematic—with the articulation of the avowal across different economies of power at least in the sense that while the avowal is a component of confessional dispositives, it can also be found in other types of dispositives (e.g. *Abnormal, History of Sexuality I, Omnes et Singulatim*).

What, then, might a properly confessional economy of power look like? The following characteristics can be identified: first, a discursive framework which distinguishes between two subject positions, the Self (pure, normal) and the Other (stained, pathological); second, an imperative placed on the latter to emancipate, normalize; third, the failure of that emancipatory effort—a double failure, of both shepherd and flock—made inevitable precisely by the emancipating Other's stained, impure alterity; and finally, fourth, the responsibilization of that Other for these failures, thus allowing the failure generated by this dispositive to paradoxically reproduce the dispositive itself, rather than undermine it. Within the parameters of that framework, and so long as its internal cohesiveness and strategic function remain unchanged, such a "failure" actively supports the confessional dispositive itself by attributing responsibility for that failure precisely to a deviant alterity (Teti 2014). While the avowal lies at the heart of such a confessional dispositive, it is only nominally capable of affecting the subject's emancipation: the avowing subject's normalization is undermined by a subjectivity already and necessarily stained, trapped by its own alterity (original sin, the delinquent, the degenerate, etc.).

With the qualified exception of *History of Madness*, Foucault's early texts do not point to a source of pathology as cause behind a fault/defect ingrained in the figure enjoined upon to avow/admit. Only since the emergence of the figure of the delinquent does the judicial context focus on deviance inscribed into the nature of the self rather than mere violations of the law (analogously for the mad, the sinner, etc.). Only in the texts from his "last decade"—in a line that goes quite clearly from *Abnormal* and *History of Sexuality I* to *Government of the Living* and *Les aveux de la chair*—is the self both obscure to itself and its source of deviance located precisely at that point of inscrutability, thus requiring constant scrutiny. In *History of Madness*, it is possible to see the beginning of what will be the defining trait of a confessional economy of power: the emergence of the permanence of the demand for avowal rooted in an inescapably deviant alterity. Here, Foucault focuses on a shift towards a pathologization of difference in which forms of social marginality—poverty, laziness, vice, madness, unemployment, sin, etc.—become increasingly both sign and result of a deeper deviance (Foucault 2006a). This shift is what sets confession aside from the avowal.

It is precisely here that the significance of Foucault's "late lectures" can be located: through Tertullian and monastic practices, Christianity comes to place sin at the heart of the individual, and indeed Foucault's overriding concern in *Les aveux de la chair* is precisely to trace—through the Christian Fathers' re-elaboration of Stoicism—the roots of this shift in "Western thought" from error to fault and stain. Indeed, the problem of the transition from error to stain could be thought of as the central theme of all Foucault's later work, from madness, delinquency, normalization, and biopolitics, all the way to the subjectivation, avowal and *parrhēsia*.

## Notes

1   The author is grateful to the editors for their meticulous and insightful feedback, as well as to Eddie Campbell, Chris Fynsk, Andrea Mura, Iain Munro, and Graham Burchell for

comments on earlier versions of this paper. I am also grateful to the universities of Ghent and Cagliari for allowing me to develop these ideas as Visiting Fellow in 2017–18 and 2018 respectively.
2   His final lecture in the 1971–2 cycle offers important reflections on the avowal, but Foucault offers no explicit definition of avowal, nor does he relate it to confession. By contrast, by 1973, he offers a definition of the avowal, and in the 1974–5 *Abnormal* lectures he distinguishes between avowal and confession, and begins to reflect on their articulation(s).
3   The Portuguese text reads: "a confissão consiste no discurso do sujeito sobre ele mesmo, numa situação de poder na qual ele é dominado, constrangido, e que por essa confissão modifica" (Foucault et al. 1975: 12; *my translation*). The French translation from Portuguese in *Dits et Écrits*, reads: "L'aveu consiste dans le discours du sujet sur lui-même, dans une situation de pouvoir où il est dominé, contrait, et que, par l'aveu, il modifie" (Foucault, 1994: 809).
4   This translation and all subsequent English translations from *Les aveux de la chair* are the author's own.
5   Foucault also considers the later development of the *paenitentia secunda*, another practice which entailed the remission of sins: this will not be considered here in detail for reasons of space but also because its characteristics relevant to the neutralization of pathological deviance (remission of sins) are already present in penitential discipline and in baptism (see Foucault 2018: esp. 80–5).

# References

Bevir, M. (1999), "Foucault and Critique: Deploying Agency against Autonomy," *Political Theory*, 27 (1): 65–84.
Burchell, G. (2009), "Confession, Resistance, Subjectivity," *Journal for Cultural Research*, 13 (2): 159–77.
Deleuze, G. (2018), *Il Potere: Corso su Michel Foucault (1985–1986), vol. 2*, Verona: Ombre Corte.
Dreyfus, H. H., and P. Rabinow, eds (1983), *Michel Foucault: Beyond Structuralism and Hermeneutics*, 2nd ed., Chicago: The University of Chicago Press.
Elden, S. (2005), "The Problem of Confession: The Productive Failure of Foucault's *History of Sexuality*," *Journal for Cultural Research*, 9 (1): 23–41.
Elden, S. (2017), *Foucault's Last Decade*, Cambridge: Polity Press.
Fejes, A. and M. Dahlstedt (2013), *The Confessing Society: Foucault, Confession and Practices of Lifelong Learning*, London: Routledge.
Fejes, A. and K. Nicoll (2015), *Foucault and a Politics of Confession in Education*, London: Routledge.
Foucault, M. (1954), *Maladie mentale et personnalité*, Paris: PUF.
Foucault, M. (1961), *Folie et déraison: Histoire de la folie à l'âge classique*, Paris: Plon.
Foucault, M. (1963), *Raymond Roussel*, Paris: Gallimard.
Foucault, M. (1970), *The Order of Things: An Archaeology of the Human Sciences*, New York: Pantheon.
Foucault, M. (1978), *The Will to Knowledge: The History of Sexuality, Volume 1*, trans. R. Hurley, London: Penguin.
Foucault, M. (1993), "About the Beginning of the Hermeneutics of the Self: Two Lectures at Dartmouth," *Political Theory*, 21 (2): 198–227.

Foucault, M. (1994), "Michel Foucault: El filósofo responde ('Michel Foucault. Les réponses du Philosophe')," in D. Defert and F. Ewald (eds), *Dits et écrits: 1954–1988, vol. 2/4: 1970–1975*, Paris: Gallimard.

Foucault, M. (2002a), *The Archaeology of Knowledge*, trans. A. M. Sheridan Smith, London: Routledge.

Foucault, M. (2002b), "Omnes et Singulatim: Towards a Critique of Governmental Reason," in J. D. Faubion (ed.), *The Essential Works of Michel Foucault, 1954–1984, Vol. 3: Power*, 298–325, London: Penguin.

Foucault, M. (2006a), *History of Madness*, ed. J. Khalfa, trans. J. Murphy and J. Khalfa, London: Routledge.

Foucault, M. (2006b), *Psychiatric Power: Lectures at the Collège de France 1973–1974*, ed. J. Lagrange, trans. G. Burchell, Basingstoke: Palgrave Macmillan.

Foucault, M. (2012a), *Du gouvernement des vivants: Cours au Collège de France. 1979–1980*, ed. M. Senellart, Paris: Gallimard/Seuil.

Foucault, M. (2012b), *Mal faire, dire vrai: Fonction de l'aveu en justice*, ed. F. Brion and B. E. Harcourt, Louvain: Presses Universitaires de Louvain.

Foucault, M. (2013a), *La société punitive: Cours au Collège de France, 1972–1973*, Paris: Gallimard/Seuil.

Foucault, M. (2013b), *Lectures on the Will to Know: Lectures at the Collège de France 1970–1971*, ed. D. Defert, trans. G. Burchell, Basingstoke: Palgrave Macmillan.

Foucault, M. (2014a), *On the Government of the Living: Lectures at the Collège de France 1979–1980*, ed. M. Senellart, trans. G. Burchell, Basingstoke: Palgrave Macmillan.

Foucault, M. (2014b), *Wrong-Doing, Truth-Telling: The Function of Avowal in Justice*, ed. F. Brion and B. Harcourt, trans. S. W. Sawyer, Chicago: University of Chicago Press.

Foucault, M. (2015), *Théories et institutions pénales: Cours au Collège de France: 1971–1972*, Paris: Gallimard/Seuil.

Foucault, M. (2018), *Histoire de la sexualité 4: Les aveux de la chair*, Paris: Gallimard.

Foucault, M., C. Bojunga and R. Lobo (1975), "As respostas do filósofo," *Jornal da Tarde*, 1 November: 12–13.

Roberts, M. (2005), "The Production of the Psychiatric Subject," *Nursing Philosophy*, 6 (1): 33–42.

Salter, M. B. (2007), "Governmentalities of an Airport: Heterotopia and Confession," *International Political Sociology*, 1 (1): 49–66.

Tadros, V. (1998), "Between Governance and Discipline: The Law and Michel Foucault," *Oxford Journal of Legal Studies*, 18 (1): 75–103.

Taylor, C. (2008), *The Culture of Confession from Augustine to Foucault: A Genealogy of the "Confessing Animal,"* London: Routledge.

Teti, A. (2014), "Orientalism as a Form of Confession," *Foucault Studies*, 17: 193–212.

Van Maanen, J. (1988), "Confessional Tales," in J. van Maanen, *Tales of the Field: On Writing Ethnography*, Chicago: University of Chicago Press.

Webster, J. (2008), "Establishing the 'Truth' of the Matter: Confessional Reflexivity as Introspection and Avowal," *Psychology & Society*, 1 (1): 65–76.

14

# Truth-Telling as Therapeutic Practice: On the Tension Between Psychiatric Subjectivation and Parrhesiastic Self-Cultivation[1]

Marta Faustino

The practice of telling the truth about oneself has been an integral part of most therapeutic configurations in the Western tradition. It can be found in the practices of self-examination in ancient philosophy, in Christian confession, where it became the very means of curing or saving the soul, and in the processes of self-exposure and self-disclosure that constitute the basis of psychiatric and psychoanalytic treatments. This continuity does not preclude but rather anticipates the fact that the practice has gone through an extremely complex evolution and transformation, such that the distance between the practices of self-examination in ancient philosophy and the confessional dispositive we find in Christianity and in the first psychiatric and psychoanalytic approaches is very wide indeed. Given the practice's centrality to each of these therapeutic configurations, its transformation also contributed in a decisive way to the transmutation of the type of therapy in question, both in its conception and practice and in terms of its historical, social, political and cultural effects on "patients." It therefore played a pivotal role in Foucault's studies on the relation between subjectivity and truth, and especially on the impact of different truth games and truth regimes on the constitution of subjectivity.

When combined with his work on psychiatric power in the 1970s (especially the first volume of the *History of Sexuality* and the 1973–4 lecture course on the topic), Foucault's late writings on what he called the hermeneutics of the self (Foucault 1993), together with his lecture courses in ancient philosophy—most notably *The Hermeneutics of the Subject* and *The Courage of Truth*—offer a powerful and illuminating genealogical account of how the practice of discovering the truth about oneself and communicating it to others developed in the therapeutic context from the first centuries of our era to the last decades of the twentieth century. Foucault's negative and pessimistic evaluation of this development is well known: the development of the hermeneutics of the self through Christian ascetic and confessional practices led to a progressive renunciation and sacrifice of the self that, when appropriated by the discourse of psychiatric and psychoanalytic sciences, became increasingly subjected to the controlling, normalizing, and totalizing power of our modern disciplinary societies. This concerning outcome, together with the stark differences between it and the truth-telling practices of antiquity and their corresponding ethics of self-cultivation, led Foucault to recommend, at the end of his Dartmouth lectures, a thorough transformation of the hermeneutics of the self altogether in favor of a more positive politics of ourselves (Foucault 1993: 222–3).

I have reconstructed and tracked Foucault's genealogy of this development and have discussed his pessimistic evaluation of this process elsewhere (see Faustino 2020). Almost forty years have passed since Foucault's last pronouncements on the subject, however, and the complex evolution that the psychological sciences have undergone ever since is remarkable and worthy of attention.[2] As a result of strong internal criticism (in many senses similar to Foucault's), the psy-sciences today are more aware of the dangers involved in their practices and have undergone a notable development, eliminating or at least softening crucial aspects of Foucault's criticism (see Taylor 2008: 154–5). One of the most evident outcomes of this has been the development and proliferation of psychotherapies that are built precisely on the basis of this awareness and, to a great extent, as a form of resistance to the totalizing and normalizing power of former approaches in psychiatry and psychoanalysis. A particularly interesting trend in this context is the attempt to connect modern psychotherapies with ancient philosophical schools, showing both how therapeutic philosophies in antiquity fulfilled the role and purposes of modern psychotherapies and how modern psychotherapies are indebted to ancient thought and can enrich their practice by turning their attention to ancient wisdom, techniques and therapeutic exercises.[3]

This article aims to evaluate, from a Foucauldian point of view, part of these recent developments in psychotherapy by focusing on one of its most widely known and used branches, which claims to have a philosophical provenance, namely cognitive behavioral therapy (CBT). For this purpose, I will rely mainly on the work of the psychotherapist Donald Robertson, who in his recently published *The Philosophy of Cognitive-Behavioural Therapy* not only offers a comprehensive and illuminating account of the philosophical background of CBT's theory and practice but also draws on Pierre Hadot's and the late Foucault's readings of ancient philosophical therapies. In order to evaluate the sense in which modern CBT comes closer to the model of therapy we find in ancient philosophy—and thus the extent to which it overcomes, at least in part, the limits and dangers that Foucault ascribed to psychiatric discourses and practices—I will first outline the main features that, according to Foucault, radically distinguish ancient therapeutic practices from early psychiatric and psychoanalytic ones. I will then bring to the fore the main arguments that lead Robertson to conclude that CBT equates to a modern rediscovery and revival of ancient Stoicism. I will conclude by discussing, from a Foucauldian perspective, both the innovation and the improvement that this approach to psychotherapy represents when compared to previous psychiatric approaches and the limits and shortcomings that it must nonetheless overcome if it is to promote the true politics of ourselves that Foucault recommended.

## Truth-Telling as a Therapeutic Practice in Philosophy and Psychiatry

According to Foucault, the origin of truth-telling practices for therapeutic purposes in Western culture can be found in ancient philosophy, most notably in the Hellenistic schools, the "golden age of the culture of the self, of the cultivation of oneself, of the care of oneself" (Foucault 2005: 30), when philosophy was conceived as an art of living and, more specifically, as a therapy of the soul, designed to lead individuals from their sick (ignorant) condition to one of health, flourishing and fulfillment (see Foucault 2005: 81–100).[4] Due to its very specific orientation and the broad swathe of people it addressed, philosophy at the time did not consist of complex and abstract theoretical paradigms; to the contrary, it was based on a set of concrete, practical techniques and exercises, which Foucault calls "technologies of the self" (Foucault 2000c: 207). These permitted individuals

> to effect, by their own means or with the help of others, a certain number of operations on their own bodies and souls, thoughts, conduct and way of being, so as to transform themselves in order to attain a certain state of happiness, purity, wisdom, perfection, or immortality.
> 
> Foucault 2000c: 225

The main goal of these technologies was thus to provide the individual with a set of principles, techniques, and strategies that would enable her to acquire self-mastery and tranquility of mind in all possible circumstances and situations (see Foucault 1993: 205). In this sense, taken together, these practices reflected a "universal code" of conduct for one's entire life and therefore constructed what can be called a form or way of life.

One of the most important technologies of the self in this context was precisely the discovery and formulation of the truth about oneself, be it in the form of self-examination (the examination of one's conscience) or confession (Foucault 1993: 204). In this early form, these practices were very different in content and scope from those we find in the context of Christian rituals, or later in the context of psychiatric practice. As Foucault stresses, self-examination in this period was not aimed at discovering every detail about oneself, all of one's hidden secrets, in order to obtain and communicate a revelation concerning one's "true self" (Foucault 1993: 207). It was also not concerned with discovering all of one's moral faults or sins, with a view to self-criticism and self-punishment, not to mention redemption or salvation. On the contrary, the aim of self-examination was basically and simply to recall the main events of the day and one's reactions to them in an effort to determine which actions had been worthy of praise and which, on the other hand, deserved further reflection and future correction. As a means of helping individuals to determine the extent to which their conduct conformed to the rules of behavior to which they had committed, the sole function of these forms of evaluation and self-examination was to detect any mistakes (with a view to their correction in future action) and to make rational principles of behavior as permanent, active, and stable as possible in one's life (Foucault 1993: 207).[5]

Self-analysis was thus essentially a tool to reactivate, assimilate, and commit to memory proper rules and precepts of behavior, or, in Foucault's words, a way "to give a place to truth as a force" (Foucault 1993: 209; Foucault 2000b: 208–09). In this sense, the examination of conscience, together with writing about oneself, confession and correspondence, had an *ethopoietic* function—that is, it functioned as "an agent of the transformation of truth into *ethos*" (Foucault 2000b: 209)—which means that, far from intending to uncover or decipher a hidden and mysterious self, these practices aimed to constitute, create, and shape that self (Foucault 1993: 210). Foucault thus stresses how the obligation to tell the truth about oneself was actually peripheral in antiquity, functioning as a means of transforming the self in the direction of the happy life rather than as an end in itself.

Foucault emphasizes that what was really fundamental at this time was not the obligation to tell the truth to somebody else, but rather the imperative to tell the truth to oneself: to reflect on oneself and to learn from that self-reflection, "constituting oneself as an 'inspector of oneself'... and reactivating the rules of behavior that one must always bear in mind" (see Foucault 2000b: 219). It is in this context that Foucault mentions ancient self-examination and self-scrutiny as a parrhesiastic game, where what is at stake is essentially the courage to be truthful to oneself—rather than to another—with the aim of achieving self-mastery or self-sovereignty (see Foucault 2001: 142–5).

For this reason, confession—that truth game in which one seeks to report truths about oneself in the presence of another (at the time typically the master, the "physician of the soul")—was actually rare, occasional and provisional. It occurred only in given moments, or at certain stages of life, when the individual needed specific help or advice. The content of these confessions would generally be the same as that of his self-examinations,[6] and the role of the master was not to judge, condemn, save, interpret or decipher the hidden meaning of his words but to temporarily guide him through recollection of the main philosophical principles of the school. As a consequence, the master would actually verbalize much more than the disciple (Foucault 1993: 205). Since the ultimate aim of this cultivation and guidance was the absolute autonomy of the disciple, no relationship of eternal dependence or obedience was established. The connection between master and disciple was temporary and provisory, the role of occasional or temporary confession simply being the orientation of the disciple towards a happy and autonomous life (Foucault 1993: 216).

When one contrasts this parrhesiastic model of telling the truth about oneself in ancient philosophy with the confessional dispositive of psychiatric practice identified by Foucault in the 1970s, we quickly realize that even though the roots of truth-telling practices in psychiatry and psychoanalysis can in some way be traced to the ancient practices of self-examination, there is a tremendous gulf that inevitably separates the former from the latter and renders them completely different therapeutic configurations. Abstracting from the long and complex evolution of these practices, through Christianity up to the emergence of psychiatry, it is possible to identify the key transformations of the practice in the psychiatric and psychoanalytic context that justify Foucault's strong criticism and concern.

One of the most relevant and decisive differences in this context is that, contrary to ancient philosophical practices, where the self was not primarily given in any possible form, psychiatric sciences presuppose, in strict continuity with Christianity, that there is a hidden self that is truer and more essential than the self that is immediately given, which in turn determines its most diverse manifestations at the level of behavior, action and thought. As a consequence, unveiling and deciphering this obscure and hidden self becomes the fundamental object of therapy and the very means of being cured (see

Foucault 1978: 67). The therapeutic process is thus no longer based on an active cultivation of a self that is still to be created or shaped but on deep scrutiny and interpretation of a secret, mysterious and to some extent suspicious and unhealthy self that must be uncovered and deciphered in order to be cured.

This different understanding of the self and the means of handling it in therapy has important consequences both in terms of the content of the truth that must be told and in terms of the relationship that is established between the one who tells the truth and the one who listens to the confessions. For if what is at stake in healing is unveiling and deciphering one's hidden self, the truth-telling practice that is demanded of the patient no longer involves a simple act of parrhesiastic self-examination or recollection of crucial moments of daily life, but rather a deep excavation of the most obscure depths of the self, associated with the belief that the simple act of exposing this hidden self through confession in a doctor's office is itself curative or therapeutic. In Foucault's formulation, "spoken in time, to the proper party, and by the person who was both the bearer of it and the one responsible for it, the truth healed" (Foucault 1978: 67).[7]

Furthermore, since what the patient now needs to confess is not only his daily routine—or even intimate and shameful secrets that he would prefer to hide (as in Christianity)—but what tends to be hidden even from himself, this process of excavation and scrutiny of the unconscious requires the expertise of a therapist, who is fundamental not only to guiding the patient through this process but also to providing a specialized interpretation of his confessions, thus producing a truth—*the* truth—about who the individual *is*. It is in this sense that the therapist became "not simply the forgiving master, the judge who condemned or acquitted ... [but] the master of truth" (Foucault 1978: 66-7; see also 2016: 159 ff.). The relationship between therapist and patient has thus become absolutely crucial to healing, which means that the patient is no longer self-sufficient with regard to the healing process and is dependent on the one who, due to his qualified knowledge and expertise, knows who he is and holds the key to his healing. This "dependence on and submission to the doctor as someone who, for the patient, holds an inescapable power" is a problem that, according to Foucault, "stubbornly recur[s] throughout the history of psychiatry" (Foucault 2006: 177). Such a dependency is particularly worrying inasmuch as mental health and well-being—the aim of the psy-sciences—are based on a certain socially and culturally defined standard of normality, which is necessarily reproduced and conveyed in the doctor's practice. Since part of the doctor's job is indeed to diagnose and cure individuals of possible deviations from this standard of normality, psychiatry, and psychoanalysis, due to their clinical authority, also have a dangerous controlling, totalizing, and normalizing effect on the population (see Foucault 1988, 2006). This power tends to be internalized in unnoticed and unconscious ways, influencing individuals without their being aware of it.

Foucault views psychiatric and psychoanalytic practices as the culmination of the hermeneutics of the self that, with its roots in ancient practices of self-examination, truly only began with Christianity and ultimately led to what he calls the "confessing animal" in modern societies (see Foucault 1978: 59).[8] He considers this development and its outcome problematic inasmuch as they imply ignorance of the ways in which power is exercised over individuals, contributing to the progressive subjection of the individual to the disciplinary power of modern social institutions, together with the renunciation or sacrifice of the self that ultimately resulted in the abandonment of a true relation between the self and itself. As Foucault observes at the end of his lectures *About the Beginning of the Hermeneutics of the Self*, psychiatric practices are part of the failed and misguided attempt of the last two centuries to found the hermeneutics of the self on the positive emergence, rather than the sacrifice, of the self (Foucault 1993: 222). For Foucault, however, the real challenge today is not to discover a positive self or the positive foundation of the self but to change the very technologies of the self that have been developing over the past few centuries and to engage in what he calls "the politics of ourselves" (Foucault 1993: 222–3). This has a strong resonance with Foucault's praise of the ancient ethics of care in *The Hermeneutics of the Subject* and the related urge, despite his considerable skepticism and pessimism, to reconnect the self to itself and to reconstitute an ethics of the self as an "urgent, fundamental, and politically indispensable task" (Foucault 2005: 252).

## The Philosophy of Cognitive Behavioral Therapy

Let us now turn to one of the most significant branches of contemporary psychotherapy in order to evaluate its relation both to the ancient practices of the Hellenistic schools and the psychiatric model identified by Foucault, with an eye to evaluating its relation to the different technologies of the self and what Foucault called the politics of ourselves. CBT is particularly interesting in this context. First, despite some critical discourse surrounding it,[9] it is still one of the most widespread and used branches of psychotherapy today and thus serves as a touchstone for at least one of the main trends in the evolution of psychotherapy over the past decades. Second, it is a form of verbal therapy and therefore equally involves a certain form of truth-telling, which allows us to compare it to the different forms analyzed by Foucault. Finally, it explicitly claims to have roots in, and derive inspiration from, the therapeutic practice of ancient philosophy outlined above. Especially relevant in this context and pivotal to this study is Donald Robertson's *The Philosophy of Cognitive-Behavioural Therapy*, which explains, in a clear and illuminating way, both the "philosophical origins" of CBT and the similarities between modern CBT practices and ancient Stoic therapeutic techniques and exercises. As the book aims to demonstrate, "the modern phenomenon of psychotherapy, originating within the nineteenth century medical field, has led to an indirect and gradual rediscovery of practical Stoic exercises in the guise of cognitive-behavioural therapy" (Robertson 2010: 47–8).

CBT is a short-term, goal-oriented psychotherapeutic treatment which is meant to address a variety of emotional problems and psychological disorders, including depression, anxiety, insomnia, and drug and alcohol abuse. In its contemporary form, CBT encompasses many different approaches, the most important of which are Albert Ellis's rational emotive behavior therapy and Aaron Beck's cognitive therapy. The basic premise that unites these different approaches is that thoughts, beliefs and in general the way one conceives of, understands and gives meaning to the world have a direct impact on one's feelings and emotions and that, while the latter are difficult to change directly, they can be transformed by changing one's patterns of thinking, behaving and relating to the world.

As Robertson emphatically emphasizes, this principle was one of the most important tenets of several Hellenistic therapies, most notably Stoicism, which, according to Robertson, should be seen as the real precursor of modern CBT (Robertson 2010: 4–5).[10] Indeed, both CBT and Stoicism base their therapeutic practices on the assumption that most suffering and emotional distress is caused not by facts or events, but by the individual's evaluation and judgment of those events and her consequent relation and reactions to them. Since one's cognitive activity can be monitored and changed, desired behavior and emotional stability can be achieved through cognitive change, which both Stoicism and CBT encourage the patient to undergo with the help of a therapist (Robertson 2010: 4–7). As such, both Stoicism and CBT "embody a cognitive *theory* and *therapy* of emotional disturbance: cognitions are central to both the *cause* and *cure* of emotional disturbance" (Robertson 2010: 73).

Strongly resembling Stoic practices, in the cognitive behavioral therapeutic process the patient is encouraged to take responsibility for her own thoughts, ideas, and judgments, with a view to helping her to understand that her behavior and emotional responses are "subjective attitudes rather than objective facts" and that strong emotions are ultimately "self-inflicted disturbances, and not primarily the result of external events, which merely serve as the occasion, or vehicle, for them" (Robertson 2010: 12). Taking responsibility for our own thoughts and maintaining strict awareness of them is expected to provide us with the means to change them, and thus to "change the way we think about life, review the value we attribute to things, and gain control over our emotions" (Robertson 2010: 13).

Since emotional disturbance and instability is seen as the main obstacle to *eudaimonia* or happiness, in the case of Stoicism, and to mental health and well-being, in the case of CBT, the two therapeutic configurations also come considerably close when it comes to defining the purpose or goal of therapy: whereas the Stoics called this (together with "living in accordance with nature" and "living according to reason") *apatheia* (freedom from irrational and unhealthy passions) and conceived of a set of strategies and techniques to help individuals to achieve this form of self-mastery and self-discipline, CBT "is concerned with helping clients to deal with irrational or disturbing emotions, and to cultivate rational, healthy, and proportionate ones in their stead" (Robertson 2010: 3; see also Robertson 2016: 374).[11]

As impressive as the similarities between the theoretical background of CBT and Stoicism may be, the most interesting and more relevant part of Robertson's study for our current purposes is related not so much to the theoretical resemblance between the premises of both therapeutic forms as to the similarities between their practices and therapeutic techniques and exercises. According to Robertson, in addition to sharing the same theoretical background and therapeutic goal, CBT and Stoicism arrive at "similar conclusions regarding the best strategies for achieving therapeutic change" (Robertson 2016: 375). In particular, Robertson emphasizes that

> the Stoics do not merely present abstract philosophical theories loosely related to the clinical applications of cognitive therapy ... Their writings contain many specific psychological techniques or exercises, most of which are consistent with

modern CBT, and some of which have been forgotten or neglected by modern psychotherapists, though still relevant today.

Robertson 2010: 8

Robertson provides a variety of examples from CBT practice, which indeed bring to mind what Foucault called "technologies of the self" in Greco-Roman philosophy. These include, among others, the use of "short 'coping statements,' brief phrases which can easily be committed to memory and made ready to hand during future adversities" (Robertson 2010: 54, 193–206); making use of a mental "role model" (which in the case of the Hellenistic schools was the ideal sage and in the context of CBT is often but not necessarily the therapist) against which irrational patterns of thought and behavior are to be challenged (Robertson 2010: 135–50); a range of interventions based on "mindfulness" or "attention to oneself" designed to purify the mind and "heighten self-awareness of one's body, feelings, and thoughts, through periods of meditative contemplation and ongoing practice of self-awareness throughout the day" (Robertson 2010: 151); a variety of mental imagery techniques meant to prepare oneself to cope with adversity by anticipating difficult situations in imagination and training one's emotional response to them (similar to the classic *praemeditatio malorum*), such as "cognitive rehearsal," "stress-inoculation," and "repeated review" (Roberston 2010: 207–25); the adoption of a deterministic perspective that favors tolerance, empathy, and acceptance (Robertson 2010: 227–47); and the practice of visualizing a particular disturbing event or situation from a broader, more distant and less attached perspective, "as if seen from very high above" (Robertson 2010: 249–59).

Given our purposes here, it is worth taking a closer look at what Robertson views as CBT's parallel to the Stoic practice of self-examination, which Foucault so emphatically contrasted to the practice of confessional self-disclosure in psychiatry and psychoanalysis, and which Robertson describes as the very core of CBT practice: self-analysis and dispute. According to Robertson, "the central method of cognitive therapy consists of monitoring one's thoughts and challenging those ones that are irrational or unhelpful and the beliefs that underlie them" (Robertson 2010: 169). Robertson views this method as clearly mirroring the practice of constantly examining and questioning one's thoughts and impressions (like a "night watchman") recommended by Epictetus, or the close monitoring of one's judgments for error and their vigorous disputation during morning or evening examination prescribed by Seneca in his *Letters to Lucilius*. Even though Robertson does not speak of *parrhēsia*, it is interesting to recall that Seneca's evening examination and Epictetus' control of representations are two of the techniques of the parrhesiastic games that Foucault highlights in his Berkeley lectures on *parrhēsia* (Foucault 2001: 142 ff.). The permanent surveillance and "constant putting on trial of all our representations" (Foucault 2001: 160) that Foucault ascribes to Epictetus in particular seems very similar to CBT's practice of self-monitoring and respective guiding principle according to which "negative judgements and bad habits of thinking should be repeatedly counteracted by means of direct disputation and the cultivation of alternative, more realistic and helpful thoughts and attitudes" (Robertson 2010: 172).

Robertson stresses that in ancient philosophy, psychological self-examination was also encouraged via dialogue with a philosophical teacher, and he further implies that a similar role is assumed by the modern cognitive behavioral therapist. More concretely, Robertson compares the relationship established in individual psychotherapy sessions to that which existed between master and disciple in Roman Stoicism, especially as portrayed in Seneca's *Letters to Lucilius* (Robertson 2010: 48; 2016: 375). In the same sense, the expressions "Socratic disputation" and "Socratic questioning" are often used in CBT manuals to describe the method of cognitive disputation employed in CBT and the specific role played by the therapist in it (see Robertson 2010: 180–1). As the behaviorist B. F. Skinner explains,

> The patient is not to be told how to behave more effectively or given directions for solving his problems; a solution is already within him and has only to be drawn out with the help of the midwife therapist.
>
> Skinner, *cit. in* Robertson 2010: 181[12]

Robertson adds that "the notion of helping others to achieve deep personal insight by encouraging them to think for themselves is clearly one shared by modern psychotherapy" (Robertson 2010: 183),[13] and indeed, it is often emphasized that CBT involves what is essentially collaborative work between therapist and client towards a common goal—a practice which the literature generally refers to as "collaborative empiricism" (see e.g. Kirk 2005; Dattilio and Hanna 2012). This means that the client is ideally involved in an active way both in the diagnosis of his problems and their cognitive sources and in the therapeutic process and corresponding means and aims.

The therapist will typically approach individuals as singular human beings with equally singular needs and will offer a set of principles and techniques—including self-analysis, the disputation of dysfunctional cognitions, and versions of the exercises mentioned above—that the client is advised to test and experiment with in her own life, either when dealing with present difficulties or on future occasions (see Martin 2019; Robertson 2010: 3). The client is supposed to learn these strategies and exercises and to progressively become more independent in the process, until she acquires full autonomy. The fact that CBT has "an educational and skills training orientation" distinguishes it from other approaches to psychotherapy, especially psychoanalytic ones (Robertson 2010: 58). Since CBT is a problem-solving approach, focused on difficulties that any individual may face in life, it does not pathologize the client's condition and tends to be short in length, the therapy being completed as soon as the client has changed her negative patterns of cognition and has acquired the set of precepts, techniques and exercises that will enable her to cope with her difficulties, both present and future. According to Robertson, this was roughly already the structure of Stoic therapy, the success of which depended "upon the complete internalization of certain key ideas, or rules of living, and their future recall in the face of stressful situations" (Robertson 2010: 52).

## Modern Psychotherapy Revisited: A Foucauldian Approach

When treating Robertson's compelling account of CBT's theory and practice as being exemplary of at least some of the trends in the development of contemporary psychotherapy, three aspects must be taken into account. First, the field of modern psychotherapy includes a wide variety of approaches, of which CBT is only one—even if one of the oldest and most widely used in the Western world (see Norcross, Freedheim and Vandenbos 2010: 744–5). Second, psychotherapy is increasingly becoming a hybrid and idiosyncratic practice in which therapists draw on techniques and therapeutic strategies from different branches, regardless of their own specific orientation, such that in actual practice a pure paradigm is hard to find (see Norcross, Freedheim and Vandenbos 2010: 745). Finally, CBT is itself a pluralistic orientation in psychotherapy (see Hollon and DiGiuseppe 2010: 230–1). What Robertson describes is his own understanding and clinical practice of CBT, and his philosophical academic background and personal sympathy for Stoicism likely imply that his approach is slightly different from those of other CBT practitioners.

This notwithstanding, Robertson's account provides us with a solid theoretical background on the basis of which to evaluate, from a Foucauldian point of view, the fundamental traits of modern psychotherapeutic practice in contrast both to ancient therapeutic philosophy and to the psychiatric model outlined and criticized by Foucault. The fact that CBT is one of the oldest and perhaps most conservative branches of psychotherapy makes it particularly fitting for this purpose, as the fundamental traits that already sharply distinguish CBT from earlier psychiatric and psychoanalytic practices tend to be even more deeply pronounced in other approaches.

In the face of Foucault's analysis, two features of modern psychotherapy are particularly deserving of attention. The first concerns the therapeutic relation, that is, the relationship that is established between therapist and client as a condition and means of therapeutic success. As we have seen in the case of CBT, there is an increasing tendency to depathologize common problems and difficulties that lead individuals to consult a psychotherapist and to establish a relationship that is essentially one of mutual cooperation toward a common goal, rather than a strongly asymmetric one between a sick patient and a doctor who has expertise in mental health and the authority to tell the patient what to do. In modern versions of psychotherapy, the word "patient" is even avoided (with "client" generally being adopted in its stead), and, at least in CBT, the therapist explicitly assumes the role of a Socratic midwife, whereby the client is not simply instructed but rather guided to the source of her problems and the means to cope with them both in the present and in future situations. In other versions of psychotherapy (especially narrative therapy and humanistic approaches, such as existential, person-centered and gestalt psychotherapies), the autonomy of individuals, as well as their capacity to affirm their individuality against socially and culturally fixed norms and preconceptions, is even more strongly encouraged (see White and Epston 1990; Rice and Greenberg 1992). Even though some degree of psychological dependency on the part of the client may result, therapists are increasingly aware of this risk and struggle against it (see Storr 1990: 63). Their aim is thus to make the individual progressively independent in the therapeutic process until she reaches a condition of complete autonomy (see Storr 1990: 17), in a way that effectively resembles the practice of ancient physicians of the soul.

The second distinguishing mark of contemporary psychotherapy worth mentioning is directly related to the hermeneutics of the self and the use of truth-telling practices in the therapeutic context. Contrary to the confessional dispositive that characterizes psychiatric and psychoanalytic practices, most modern psychotherapies are clearly no longer equally concerned with the total scrutiny and deciphering of a hidden, secret and suspicious self as a means of healing (see Rice and Greenberg 1992). The problem-solving approach that characterizes many branches of modern psychotherapy makes it clear that the client is led to speak frankly and to reflect on particular situations that cause distress rather than talking about whatever comes to mind or digging into the depths of her unconscious (Martin 2019). In the case of CBT, where the source of individual problems is identified in cognition, the therapeutic approach is clearly no longer based on hermeneutics and interpretation but rather on specific cognitive change and behavior modification. The emphasis on practice, training, and education on the basis of a set of techniques and practical exercises, common to several branches of modern psychotherapy, clearly shows that the therapeutic process is focused not on self-disclosure but rather on self-transformation and the cultivation of individual skills for coping with everyday situations (see Arnkoff and Glass 1992). In some versions of modern psychotherapy, it is common to approach the self as a never-ending work in progress, similarly to what was practiced in the ethics of self-cultivation that was characteristic of ancient philosophical therapies. It is also noteworthy that even though most modern psychotherapeutic practices still rely on conversation and the openness of the individual to being truthful, many are no longer based exclusively on truth-telling practices or even verbal communication and instead focus on other forms of communication such as dance, drama, art, music, and writing (see Malchiodi 2005).

These are significant distinguishing marks of modern psychotherapy, which separate it from the model of psychiatric practice identified and criticized by Foucault. Does this mean that modern psychotherapy, as exemplified by CBT, has completely overcome the limits and dangers involved in the psychological sciences and has neutralized the normalizing and totalizing power that underlay their practice, as diagnosed by Foucault? Can one in any way compare modern psychotherapy to the therapeutic endeavor at stake in ancient philosophical practices? Are truth-telling practices in the modern psychotherapeutic context indeed able to promote the kind of parrhesiastic self-cultivation that was found in ancient philosophy, to the detriment of the psychiatric subjectivation that characterized the early development of the psy-sciences? As much as modern psychotherapy can be seen as an important improvement on early psychiatric and psychoanalytic practices in the clinical handling of mental health, our answer must be no, and this for essentially one reason—one with multiple ramifications, which we can only briefly outline here.

Indeed, most psychotherapeutic approaches still evidently claim to be a scientific and empirically-based form of knowledge, whereas ancient philosophical therapies obviously did not. Even though Robertson presents this as something of an advantage that gives CBT a kind of evidence-based superiority over philosophical therapies (see Robertson 2010: xvii–xviii), this factor also evidently makes it liable to the dangerous controlling and normalizing power dynamic that is generally established between doctor and patient. Several studies show that CBT is in fact, despite its claims to the contrary, particularly prone to the establishment of strongly asymmetric and abusive relations (see e.g. Proctor 2008; Heaton 2006). This can occur not only due to the scientific authority of the therapist—which is particularly emphasized in CBT—but also as a result of the specific object of CBT practice: cognition. Basing his practice on research evidence, the therapist knows the best way to think and has the power to change the client's cognitive activity—or dismiss his judgments and beliefs as irrational—accordingly, on the basis of his supposedly objective, neutral and scientific perspective. If, on the contrary, this perspective is not neutral but rather culturally, socially and politically informed—as it probably is—the therapist is likely to continue to exert a normalizing power over his clients, in which case even notions such as "guidance" and "collaboration" would be deeply distorted, dangerous and misleading. Taking all these aspects into account, Proctor is thus led to the conclusion that, "from a Foucauldian perspective, traditional CBT ... is rife with 'regimes of truth,' normalizing principles on which the 'right' or 'helpful' way to think are based" (Proctor 2008: 233).

It is plausible that this risk is inherent not only to CBT but, to a greater or lesser degree, to all psychotherapeutic practices that base their authority in science. Even though the power dynamic established in therapy is ultimately a matter of individual responsibility on the part of the therapist, who can indeed take measures to prevent abuses of power (see Proctor 2008: 232), it is nevertheless important to realize that wherever a therapy claims to be a science, an asymmetrical power relation between therapist and patient will always, to a greater or lesser degree, be present and prone to abuse. Given that this risk can hardly be avoided in the context of (scientific) psychotherapy, it may be pertinent to recall Foucault's pronouncement in one of his last interviews concerning pedagogical institutions, which is also certainly applicable to psychotherapeutic practices in all their possible forms:

> I see nothing wrong in the practice of a person who, knowing more than others in a specific game of truth, tells those others what to do, teaches them, and transmits knowledge and techniques to them. The problem in such practices where power—which is not in itself a bad thing—must inevitably come into play is knowing how to avoid ... domination effects.
>
> Foucault 2000d: 298–9

It is perhaps in this context that ancient philosophy has something to teach present and future psychotherapeutic endeavors, as its practice effectively revealed a form of power (which to a certain degree also existed between master and student) that was able to do without any form of domination or normalizing effects. Contrary to most psychotherapeutic configurations, philosophy conceived as an art of living or therapy of the soul was practiced in total independence of—and often even in deep opposition to—all institutionalized forms of external authority, whether science, knowledge or even theory, without being viewed as less efficacious or persuasive because of it. On the contrary, although the ways of life that the different schools proposed were based on complex philosophical systems, their persuasive force was related not to the scientific authority of those systems but to the lives of those who lived in accordance with them and were able to completely align their thoughts, words and deeds. It was precisely because they were exemplary of a perfect correspondence between theory and practice, *logos* and *bios*, and because their lives were exemplary of an ideal, happy human life, that ancient philosophers such as Socrates, Epicurus, and Epictetus functioned as role models and had a parrhesiastic function as touchstones for other people's lives and behavior (see Foucault 2001: 101 ff.; cf. Heaton 2006). Moreover, since the philosopher's life did not fit into any cultural standard of normality, corresponding more to an eccentric exception than the rule, the therapeutic impact of their philosophies was far from being totalizing or normalizing, instead implying, in contrast to most psychotherapeutic endeavors, the courage to lead a "paradoxical" or "abnormal" way of life (see Hadot 2019: 299).

This courage to take care of oneself and to choose one's way of life in total independence of—and ideally, in deep contrast and resistance to—all institutionalized forms of authority or power can be said to be the condition of possibility of the constitution of a true relationship of the self to itself. In this sense, it is probable that a true ethic of the self can ultimately only emerge in absolute solitude and freedom, outside of the therapist's office. And yet, the current tendency in modern psychotherapy (as exemplified by Robertson's book) to take informal recourse to and inspiration from Hellenistic philosophical therapies is a good sign and likely a good direction at which to aim (see Hadot 2019: 300). Even though no institutionalized form of psychotherapy can ever equate to the therapeutic endeavor and corresponding ethics of self-cultivation that was found in antiquity,[14] modern psychotherapeutic approaches can nevertheless fulfil the role of bringing individuals closer to themselves, leading them to take responsibility for their own lives and promoting practices of self-cultivation and self-mastery that ultimately clash with socially, culturally and politically established conventions regarding human life and human flourishing rather than reproducing them. This, however, can be achieved only *if* their practice is effectively consistent with their theoretical aims and propositions. In this context, modern psychotherapy would perhaps profit more from philosophical reflection than from further scientific trials and confirmations, leaving behind "the epistemological underpinnings and the methodological validity of the 'evidence-based' ideology" (House and Loewenthal 2008: iii) in favor of a more encompassing and enriching perspective on how to ground and pursue their practice. This would widen the relevance of Foucault's work to the psychological sciences beyond the scope of mere criticism and self-awareness. His late work on ancient *parrhēsia*, care of the self, and the related ethics of self-cultivation in particular, could help therapists to reshape their practices and function as a positive foundation for a more flourishing-based and liberating version of therapy,[15] in the context of which Foucault's "politics of ourselves" could eventually be promoted rather than hindered. While there has already been a tendency in this direction, this possible use of the late Foucault is certainly deserving of further attention.

## Notes

1  This work is funded by national funds through the FCT—Fundação para a Ciência e a Tecnologia, I.P., under the Norma Transitória—DL 57/2016/CP1453/CT0042.
2  On this evolution, see Freedheim (1992) and Norcross et al. (2010).

3   See Montgomery (1993), Reiss (2003), McGlinchey (2004), Brookshire (2007), Still and Dreyden (2012), and Robertson (2016). For more critical approaches, see Gill (1985) and Herbert (2004). Another interesting trend is the development of humanistic therapies on the basis of existential philosophy, such as existential psychotherapy (see Rice and Greenberg 1992). Narrative therapy is also worth exploring in this context, as its founders claim to have been deeply influenced by Foucault's work (see White and Epston 1990). Discussing these other approaches is beyond the scope of this article, however.
4   On the therapeutic character of the Hellenistic schools, see especially Hadot (1995) and Nussbaum (1994).
5   See also Foucault (2001: 165-6): "In all these different exercises, what is at stake is not the disclosure of a secret which has to be excavated from out of the depths of the soul. What is at stake is the *relation* of the self to truth or to some rational principles ... [T]he problem of memory is at the heart of these techniques, but in the form of an attempt to remind ourselves of what we have done, thought, or felt so that we may reactivate our rational principles, thus making them as permanent and as effective as possible in our life." Foucault stresses the difference between Christian confession and this form of self-examination: "In the Christian confession the penitent has to memorize the law in order to discover his own sins, but in the Stoic exercise the sage has to memorize acts in order to reactivate the fundamental rules" (Foucault 1993: 207).
6   "Confession" would often follow self-examination in the form of a letter written the next day to the teacher or friend. It is thus presented as a derivative form of self-examination (see Foucault 2000b: 220).
7   In another formulation, "The fact alone of saying something that is the truth has a function in itself; a confession, even when constrained, is more effective in the therapy than a correct idea, or an idea with exact perception, which remains silent. So, the statement of the truth has a performative character in the game of the cure" (Foucault 2006: 159). See also Foucault (2006: 274-5).
8   For a thorough and comprehensive reconstruction of this genealogy, see especially Taylor (2008).
9   See House and Loewenthal (2008) for a complete overview of the current debate on the advantages and disadvantages of CBT. Taking a position in this debate is beyond the scope of this article. The argument proposed here is based on Robertson's account, which, even though it reflects an individual practice, is representative of significant trends in modern psychotherapy, especially but not exclusively in CBT.
10  This affinity is acknowledged by the main pioneers of CBT, Albert Ellis and Aaron Beck, who frequently quote one of Epictetus' most famous sayings—"Men are disturbed not by things, but by the views which they take of them"—to support their theory and to reveal the philosophical origins of their therapeutic practice (see Robertson 2010: 5-7). See the first chapter of Robertson (2010) for a complete account of the references to Stoic authors and precepts made by the most influential authors in the field of CBT, including (in addition to Ellis and Beck) Hans Eysenck and Donald Meichenbaum. See also Still and Dreyden (2012), especially for Epictetus' influence on Albert Ellis and rational-emotive behavior therapy, the branch of psychotherapy that was most directly influenced by Stoicism and that bears the strongest resemblance to its main principles and exercises.
11  Contrary to Stoicism, however, CBT does not function on the basis of an ideal of human flourishing. According to Robertson, "if asked to point to a specific human being who embodies the principles of CBT in their life, most therapists would be at a loss for

words" (Robertson 2010: 137). The lack of an encompassing "art of living" is, for Robertson, CBT's greatest deficiency when compared to ancient philosophical therapies (see Robertson 2010: xx, 262).

12 Cf. Foucault's description of Seneca's evening examination: "this examination, it's not at all a question of discovering the truth hidden in the subject. It is rather a question of recalling the truth forgotten by the subject" (Foucault 1993: 207).

13 According to Robertson, CBT also comes close to Stoicism regarding the tactics it employs to dispute irrational cognitions and cultivate alternative, healthier cognitive patterns, even if in the case of the Stoics these tactics were "elevated from the field of therapy to the level of a, comparatively extreme, philosophy of life" (Robertson 2010: 189). These tactics include daily records of negative emotions or behavioral habits and one's rational response to them (similar to the ancient *hupomnēmata*), counter rhetorical exercises, contemplation of the consequences of different courses of action or different mental attitudes, and the double standards method (see Roberston 2010: 169–91).

14 As Robertson rightly acknowledges (see Robertson 2010: 262), philosophy in Antiquity was an art of living, a way of life, its therapy encompassing not only regional problems or particularly difficult situations in one's life, but rather one's entire being, one's entire life and even the whole world, the reason why it implied a form of conversion to a completely different way of living and inhabiting the world (see Foucault 2005: 178 ff.; Hadot 1995: 265). It would therefore be wrong to reduce philosophical therapies to a set of methods, precepts and prescriptions, that can easily be replicated and reinvented in a totally different environment and context: in a certain sense they can, of course, but the absence of an encompassing worldview behind them, that integrates them and makes them meaningful, makes it a radically different endeavor (see Hadot 2019: 299–300).

15 As Foucault claims in a late interview, "My idea is that it's not at all necessary to relate ethical problems to scientific knowledge. Among the cultural inventions of mankind there is a treasury of devices, techniques, ideas, procedures and so on, that cannot exactly be reactivated but at least constitute, or help to constitute, a certain point of view which can be very useful as a tool for analyzing what's going on now—and to change it" (Foucault 2000a: 261). On possible uses of the late Foucault for further reflection and change in modern psychotherapy, see e.g. Matey (2002), O'Grady (2004), Heaton (2006), and House (2012).

# References

Arnkoff, D. and C. Glass (1992), "Cognitive Therapy and Psychotherapy Integration," in D. Freedheim (ed.), *History of Psychotherapy: A Century of Change*, 657–94, Washington, DC: American Psychological Association.

Brookshire, S. (2007), "Utilizing Stoic Philosophy to Improve Cognitive Behavioral Therapy," *NC Perspectives*, 1 (1): 30–6.

Dattilio, F. and M. Hannah (2012), "Collaboration in Cognitive-Behavioral Therapy," *Journal of Clinical Psychology*, 68 (2): 146–58.

Faustino, M. (2020), "Therapy, Care, and the Hermeneutics of the Self: A Foucauldian Approach," *International Journal of Philosophy and Theology*, 81 (3): 260–74.

Foucault, M. (1978), *The History of Sexuality. Volume 1: An Introduction*, trans. R. Hurley, New York: Random House.

Foucault, M. (1988), *Madness and Civilization: A History of Insanity in the Age of Reason*, trans. R. Howard, New York: Vintage Books.

Foucault, M. (1993), "About the Beginning of the Hermeneutics of the Self: Two Lectures at Dartmouth," *Political Theory*, 21 (2): 198–227.
Foucault, M. (2000a), "On the Genealogy of Ethics: an Overview of Work in Progress," in P. Rabinow (ed.), *The Essential Works of Michel Foucault, 1954–1984, Vol. 1: Ethics, Subjectivity and Truth*, 253–80, London: Penguin Books.
Foucault, M. (2000b), "Self Writing," in P. Rabinow (ed.), *The Essential Works of Michel Foucault, 1954–1984, Vol. 1: Ethics, Subjectivity and Truth*, 207–22, London: Penguin Books.
Foucault, M. (2000c), "Technologies of the Self," in P. Rabinow (ed.), *The Essential Works of Michel Foucault, 1954–1984, Vol. 1: Ethics, Subjectivity and Truth*, 223–51, London: Penguin Books.
Foucault, M. (2000d), "The Ethics of the Concern of the Self as a Practice of Freedom," in P. Rabinow (ed.), *The Essential Works of Michel Foucault, 1954–1984, Vol. 1: Ethics, Subjectivity and Truth*, 281–301, London: Penguin Books.
Foucault, M. (2001), *Fearless Speech*, ed. J. Pearson, New York: Semiotext(e).
Foucault, M. (2005), *The Hermeneutics of the Subject: Lectures at the Collège de France 1981–1982*, ed. F. Gros, trans. G. Burchell, New York: Palgrave Macmillan.
Foucault, M. (2006), *Psychiatric Power: Lectures at the Collège de France 1973–1974*, ed. J. Lagrange, trans. G. Burchell, Basingstoke: Palgrave Macmillan.
Foucault, M. (2011), *The Courage of Truth (The Government of Self and Others II): Lectures at the Collège de France 1983–1984*, ed. F. Gros, trans. G. Burchell, Basingstoke: Palgrave Macmillan.
Freedheim, D., ed. (1992), *History of Psychotherapy: A Century of Change*, Washington: American Psychological Association.
Gill, C. (1985), "Ancient Psychotherapy," *Journal of the History of Ideas*, 46 (3): 307–25.
Hadot, P. (1995), *Philosophy as a Way of Life*, ed. A. Davidson, trans. M. Chase. Oxford: Blackwell.
Hadot, P. (2019), *La philosophie comme éducation des adultes. Textes, perspectives, entretiens*, ed. A. Davidson and D. Lorenzini, Paris: Vrin.
Heaton, J. (2006), "From Anti-Psychiatry to Critical Psychiatry," in D. B. Double (ed.), *Critical Psychiatry: The Limits of Madness*, 41–59, New York: Palgrave Macmillan.
Herbert, J. (2004), "Connections Between Ancient Philosophies and Modern Psychotherapies: Correlation Doesn't Necessarily Prove Causation," *The Behavior Therapist*, 27 (3): 53–4.
Hollon, S. and R. DiGiuseppe, (2010), "Cognitive Theories of Psychotherapy," in J. Norcross et al. (eds), *History of Psychotherapy: Continuity and Change*, 203–41, Washington, DC: American Psychological Association.
House, R., and D. Loewenthal, eds (2008), *Against and For CBT: Towards a Constructive Dialogue?*, Gateshead: Athenaeum Press.
House, R. (2012), "Psychotherapy, Politics and the 'Common Factor' of Power," *Psychotherapy and Politics International*, 10 (2): 157–60.
Kirk, J. (2005), "Cognitive-behavioural assessment," in K. Hawton, P. Salkovskis, J. Kirk, and D.M. Clark (eds), *Cognitive Behaviour Therapy for Psychiatric Problems*, 13–51, Oxford: Oxford University Press.
Malchiodi, C., ed. (2005), *Expressive Therapies*, New York: The Guilford Press.
Martin, B. (2019), "In-Depth: Cognitive Behavioral Therapy," *Psych Central*, June 19. Available online: https://psychcentral.com/lib/in-depth-cognitive-behavioral-therapy/ (accessed November 21, 2019).
Matey, J. (2002), "Review of *Fearless Speech*," *Metapsychology Online Reviews*, 6 (3). Available online: https://metapsychology.mentalhelp.net/poc/view_doc.php?type=book&id=924&cn=394 (accessed November 25, 2019).

McGlinchey, J. (2004), "On Hellenistic Philosophy and Its Relevance to Contemporary CBT," *The Behavior Therapist*, 27 (3): 51–2.

Montgomery, R. (1993), "The Ancient Origins of Cognitive Therapy: The Reemergence of Stoicism," *Journal of Cognitive Psychotherapy*, 7 (1): 5–19.

Norcross, J. et al., eds (2010), *History of Psychotherapy: Continuity and Change*, Washington, DC: American Psychological Association.

Norcross, J., D. Freedheim, and G. Vandenbos (2010), "Into the Future: Retrospect and Prospect in Psychotherapy," in J. Norcross et al. (eds), *History of Psychotherapy: Continuity and Change*, 743–60, Washington: American Psychological Association.

Nussbaum, M. (1994), *The Therapy of Desire: Theory and Practice in Hellenistic Ethics*, Princeton, NJ: Princeton University Press.

O'Grady, H. (2004), "An Ethics of the Self," in D. Taylor and K. Vintges (eds), *Feminism and the Final Foucault*, 91–117, Urbana and Chicago: University of Illinois Press.

Proctor, G. (2008), "CBT: The Obscuring of Power in the Name of Science," *European Journal of Psychotherapy & Counseling*, 10 (3): 231–45.

Reiss, S. (2003), "Epicurus: The First Rational-Emotive Therapist," *The Behavior Therapist*, 26 (8): 405–06.

Rice, L. and L. Greenberg, "Humanistic Approaches to Psychotherapy," in D. Freedheim (ed.), *History of Psychotherapy: A Century of Change*, 197–224, Washington: American Psychological Association.

Robertson, D. (2010), *The Philosophy of Cognitive-Behavioural Therapy (CBT): Stoic Philosophy as Rational and Cognitive Psychotherapy*, London: Karnac.

Robertson, D. (2016), "The Stoic Influence on Modern Psychotherapy," in J. Sellars (ed.), *The Routledge Handbook of the Stoic Tradition*, 374–88, London and New York: Routledge.

Still, A. and W. Dryden (2012), *The Historical and Philosophical Context of Rational Psychotherapy. The Legacy of Epictetus*, London: Karnac.

Storr, A. (1990), *The Art of Psychotherapy*, New York and Oxon: Routledge.

Taylor, C. (2008), *The Culture of Confession from Augustine to Foucault. A Genealogy of the "Confessing Animal,"* New York: Routledge.

White, M. and D. Epston, *Narrative Means to Therapeutic Ends*, New York and London: W.W. Norton & Company.

15

# Foucault, the Politics of Ourselves, and the Subversive Truth-Telling of Trauma: Survivors as Parrhesiasts

Kurt Borg

Foucault concluded his Dartmouth lectures in 1980 by saying that "one of the main political problems would be nowadays, in the strict sense of the word, the politics of ourselves" (Foucault 2016: 76). Despite the insistence of some, Foucault, the archaeologist of knowledge and the genealogist of power relations, held that his main concern had always been the question of subjectivity or, as he put it, "to create a history of the different modes by which, in our culture, human beings are made subjects" (Foucault 1983: 208). He claims to have dealt with this objective through three ways: first, by analyzing scientific discourses of inquiry that objectify individuals as speaking, living and laboring subjects; second, by looking at dividing practices that define normality at the exclusion of other subjects; and third, by studying ways in which humans turns themselves into a subject. Elsewhere (Foucault 1997a: 262) he describes this as the "three axes" or "domains of genealogy"—truth, power, and ethics—with which he engaged with differing emphasis in different moments in his work.

Among the various practices analyzed by Foucault in order to get to the heart of the issue of subjectivity, he considered the seemingly mundane practices of self-narration; or practices of telling the truth about oneself. His analysis of self-narration begins implicitly in his early works on discourse and the archaeology of knowledge, and continues in the middle works on power relations, sexuality, and confession. Even Foucault's "side projects" on the "lives of infamous men" (Foucault 2000b), "dangerous individuals" (Foucault 2000a), and "parallel lives" are especially concerned with practices of self-narration, from his fascination with "marginal characters" such as Raymond Roussell (Foucault 2007), Pierre Rivière (Foucault 1982), and Herculine Barbin (Foucault 2013) to his interest in *lettres de cachet* (Foucault and Farge 2016). Foucault's engagement with self-narration becomes more pronounced in his later work, as attested by his interest in the historical development of "the obligation to speak, the obligation to tell, the obligation to tell the truth, to produce a true discourse on oneself" (Foucault 2014: 311). This concern is also at the heart of the problematic of confession that spans Foucault's work from *The Will to Knowledge* to his study of governmentality to its eventual transformation into an engagement with the hermeneutics of the subject (Foucault 2005, 2016), technologies of the self (Foucault 1988), self-writing (Foucault 1997b), and, ultimately, *parrhēsia* (Foucault 2010, 2011).

This chapter uses material from both the "middle" and "late" Foucault since the insights in his earlier work have to be understood in light of the later work, while also acknowledging that any insights in his later work build upon and cannot be distanced from his earlier influential work on power.[1] Yet this chapter is not exclusively a contribution to Foucault studies, but also an application of his work on self-narration that extends it beyond its original aims and theoretical confines. The area of application of Foucault's ideas in this chapter is the realm of the narration of trauma by survivors, and the ethical and political questions raised by trauma narratives, showing how Foucault's work, particularly his later work on *parrhēsia*, can shed critical light upon these questions. Thus, not any form of self-narration is considered but, specifically, this chapter focuses on how trauma is narrated by survivors, that is, *traumatic self-narration*. There are various contexts in which trauma can be narrated: in autobiographies or fiction, to significant others, in clinical or psychotherapeutic settings, and in legal or institutional contexts. This chapter focuses on traumatic self-narration insofar as it is, to a great extent, a public or social narration. This does not mean that only public narrations of trauma will be analyzed. Rather, it means that there is a necessarily public or social dimension to any narration of trauma; once they are uttered, narratives of trauma are discursively channeled and transmitted through a publicly given medium that exceeds any individual grasp. This sphere in which trauma is narrated is the realm of discourses, power relations and subject-formation.

The main argument of this chapter is that survivors' narrations of trauma can function as instances of *parrhēsia*. Foucault's account of *parrhēsia* as risky, courageous, and possibly subversive truth-telling will be outlined in order to show how acts of traumatic self-narration can manifest characteristics of *parrhēsia*, namely the tendency to function as acts of critique that destabilize norms that are taken as given, and to gnaw at attempts to account for and categorize subjects into regulated categories. The other face of this argument is that, like *parrhēsia*, traumatic self-narration is a risky and precarious activity. This is because one of the ways in which power functions is by transforming the subversive destabilizing potential of *parrhēsia* into normalized, docile, and individualized confessional truth-telling that reinforces dominant discourses that regulate the domain of self-narration. Traumatic self-narration is precariously positioned in a tense relation between critical subversion on the one hand, and attempted normalization on the other. It is only by acknowledging this tension between subversion and normalization that the activity of traumatic self-narration can be understood in its complexity. This complexity refuses to be reduced to interpretations that unilaterally and uncritically regard self-narration as absolutely transgressive or, contrarily, as inevitably individualizing and confessional.

This chapter is divided into four sections. The first section provides an overview of Foucault's different approaches to the practice of self-narration in his work prior to the 1980s. This will involve viewing self-narration through the lens of discourses and power relations by outlining Foucault's intentions in publishing the medico-legal dossier of Pierre Rivière. This section then turns to the case of Herculine Barbin to highlight how Foucault also approached the practice of self-narration through the problematic of the confessional will to truth.

The second section outlines Foucault's approach to practices of self-narration in his work in the 1980s, particularly on the hermeneutics of the self and self-writing. This section considers his work on *parrhēsia* as an extension of his lifelong engagement with the relation between the power of truth and subjectivity, and looks closely at Foucault's account of Cynic *parrhēsia*. It is with this form of *parrhēsia* that traumatic self-narration is eventually compared to.

The third section considers a feminist application of Foucault's ideas on self-narration. In the spirit of "the personal is political,"[2] it is not surprising that feminists influenced by Foucault's work have elaborated further on how practices of self-narration are imbued with power relations, and that in the same way that power impacts practices of self-narration, so too can such practices trouble hegemonic exercises of power and subvert some of its effects. This section explores the uneasy tension between what Ewick and Silbey (1995) term "subversive stories" and "hegemonic tales" in their proposed sociology of narratives.

The fourth and final section of the chapter builds upon these applications of Foucault's ideas to highlight how traumatic self-narration is caught up in a similar tension since narratives of trauma can be co-opted by power so that preferred conceptions of trauma narratives are reinforced, but they can also resist such co-option and depoliticization by positively functioning as subversive acts. In this latter way, narrations of trauma can function as a form of *parrhēsia* by, at a risk to the speaker, courageously uttering truth.

## Foucault on Rivière and Barbin: Discourse, Power, Confession

Foucault's use of the notion of discourse highlights how discourse is not only or primarily controlled negatively, that is, through censorship or prohibition, but also positively or productively by influencing how the individual speaks and what the individual speaks about (Foucault 1981). The power of discourses does not only repress: "it incites, it induces, it seduces, it makes easier or more difficult; it releases or contrives, makes more probable or less" (Foucault 1983: 220). Discussing the anonymously authored voluminous book of a Victorian man's sexual encounters, titled *My Secret Life*, Foucault (1998: 21–3) shows how the book reveals the anonymity of discourses, in this case of sexuality. Discourses precede and exceed the self in such a way that *My Secret Life* is more a work on how desires were problematized and spoken about in the nineteenth century than on the specificity of the anonymous author's desires.

The relation between discourse and power, and how they bear on the practice of self-narration, is further illustrated by Foucault's work on the memoir of Pierre Rivière. In 1835, Rivière murdered his mother, sister, and brother, and in the weeks leading up to his trial, wrote a memoir detailing his actions and motivations. The memoir was written with unexpected eloquence, and this confused the authorities and the public who took Rivière for a "village idiot" (Foucault 1982: 25). Foucault published Rivière's memoir in 1973, alongside a dossier made up of medical, legal, journalistic, and administrative documents outlining Rivière's case. The memoir was the object of intense discussion by various authorities. Doctors, lawyers, judges, as well as the general public, all tried to give their interpretation of the truth about Rivière's identity that the memoir supposedly revealed; his sanity or insanity, his guilt or innocence. Foucault insists that his aim in publishing the dossier was not to establish a definitive truth about Rivière which the medico-legal institutions of the 1830s could not determine. Rather, he wanted to show how the discourses employed by the different institutions were caught up in a site of conflict and plurality, and functioned as "weapons of attack and defense in the relations of power and knowledge" (Foucault 1982: xi). Whereas some discourses may manage to achieve the desired order and regulation, sometimes these aims are frustrated or resisted. Foucault's presentation of Rivière's case is intended to manifest these possible productive failures of discourse. As he put it in an interview:

> the book was a trap ... [T]o publish this book was for me a way of saying to the shrinks in general (psychiatrists, psychoanalysts, psychologists): well, you've been around for 150 years, and here is a case contemporary with your birth. What do you have to say about it? Are you better prepared to discuss it than your 19th century colleagues? ... [T]hey were literally reduced to silence: not a single one spoke up and said: "Here is what Rivière was in reality. And I can tell you now what couldn't be said in the 19th century."
>
> Foucault 1989: 131

The practice of self-narration can furthermore be considered as a form of confession. In *The Will to Knowledge*, Foucault discusses the central role of confession in practices of subjectification, and recognizes how practices of confession function as exercises of power by instilling in individuals a supposedly inherent truth which is the object of study and interpretation by disciplines of power/knowledge (Foucault 1998). Similar to the Rivière dossier, Foucault (2013) published Herculine Barbin's memoir alongside and in tension with authoritative discourses presenting their interpretation of the case. Barbin was a nineteenth-century French "hermaphrodite" (intersex person) whose memoir Foucault published in 1978 alongside her medico-legal dossier. Herculine was assigned the sex of female at birth but in her early twenties, after a series of "revelations," was legally compelled to change her sex to male, resulting in complications and imposed expectations on her social life, love life, and self-understanding. Rather than a quest for truth and knowledge, Barbin's case highlighted the violence and exclusion inherent in the will to knowledge which poses as innocent and neutral: "it can hardly come as a surprise that, eight years later, his-her corpse was discovered, a suicide, or rather, to Foucault's mind, the victim of a new passion for the truth of sexual identity" (Bernauer 1990: 165). It is true that the case of Barbin was a tragic one; like Rivière, Barbin killed herself before her thirtieth birthday. For Foucault, her memoir—which she composed before her death in 1868—is proof of the intrusive and violent will to knowledge that dictated how individuals should understand themselves. Yet, there is an important sense in which both memoirs functioned in a *different* way; a possibly subversive way which revealed the contingency of power relations and discourses. The eloquence of Rivière's memoir defied the easy categorizations of the institutions that attempted to pin him to a decipherable identity. The poignancy of Barbin's memoir highlighted the unsuitability of the obsessive will to truth. In their moment of subversion, these tragic individuals open up a space in which selves and identities can be otherwise. This is the realm of the non-confessional, of creativity and innovation, and of the risky truth-telling of *parrhēsia*.[3]

## Beyond Confession: Self-Writing and the Risky Truth-Telling of *Parrhēsia*

Foucault's later works on classical antiquity present another approach to practices of self-narration that complements the analysis of such practices in terms of discourse and power. His motivation in considering antiquity in his later works was not to search for solutions to contemporary problems: "I am not looking for an alternative; you can't find the solution of a problem in the solution of another problem raised at another moment by other people" (Foucault 1997a: 256). Rather, Foucault turned to antiquity insofar that "their example can be an inspiration to our own efforts" (O'Leary 2002: 84) to create practices of the self that did not conform to the predominant confessional model whose primary aim is to decipher an inherent truth about the self. His analyses of Stoic practices of self-examination and confession (Foucault 2005, 2016) and self-writing (Foucault 1997b) are a step in this direction.

Foucault argues that although practices of self-writing are associated with an increase in modern autobiographical and confessional writing, they can be traced back, albeit in different configurations, to pre-Christian literature concerning the philosophical cultivation of the self. Seneca and Epictetus, for example, emphasized that besides practices of reading (which should not be extensive and excessive, lest they have a scattering and agitating effect on the soul), meditating and physical training, the art of living must also involve practices of writing. The central aim of such practices was self-transformation and cultivation by writing down ethical principles or sayings in order for the individual to memorize them and actively take them up as one's guiding principles. Writing, thus, had an *ethopoietic* function; it implied "the fashioning of accepted discourses, recognized as true, into rational principles of action" (Foucault 1997b: 209). This was the function of the *hupomnēmata*, which were individual notebooks kept by "cultivated" individuals as memory aids. The wisdom from the *hupomnēmata* was also used in personal correspondence among friends who consulted each other for life advice. Foucault describes the *hupomnēmata* as follows:

> One wrote down quotes in them, extracts from books, examples, and actions that one had witnessed or read about, reflections or reasonings that one had heard or that had come to mind. They constituted a material record of things read, heard, or thought, thus offering them up as a kind of accumulated treasure for subsequent rereading and meditation.
>
> Foucault 1997b: 209

Foucault contrasts the function of such writing practices of the self with the early Christian writings of the first centuries, characterized by tropes of temptations, struggles, and downfalls, aimed at constituting a confessional narrative of oneself to reveal that which is hidden in the unspeakable depths of one's soul. This also demanded work of decipherment by an external authority that castigates the self and bears witness to the defects of the individual.

It is within this context that Foucault's discussion of *parrhēsia*, commencing in his 1982 lecture course must be approached.[4] His late works on *parrhēsia* can be read as separate studies in themselves but, more fruitfully, one can follow Foucault in reading almost all of his work in terms of the question of the relation between subjectivity and truth (Foucault 1997d: 281–2). Foucault analyzes *parrhēsia* within the context of techniques of the self that characterized the ancient ethics of care of the self, and that are not reducible to the later confessional model. *Parrhēsia*, he says in his final lecture course, is "a certain way of speaking" (Foucault 2011: 6), "telling all" (Foucault 2011: 9), "free-spokenness" (Foucault 2011: 2), "saying everything" (Foucault 2011: 9) without concealing anything. The parrhesiast commits to one's speech, "he binds himself to this truth" (Foucault 2011: 11). Furthermore, for the speech to qualify as *parrhēsia*, it must present some kind of risk to the speaker. That is, in speaking what and how he does, the speaker is at risk. The receiver of the speech of *parrhēsia*, usually a person in a position of power that is higher to that of the speaker, will feel confronted or insulted by what is being said. The parrhesiasts' speech is consequential and exposes the speaker to danger, if not violence (Foucault 2011: 11).

A defining feature of *parrhēsia* is symphony of discourse and action; it manifests harmony between *logos* and *bios*, and this has bearing upon the individual's ethical conduct. In fact, Foucault notes that *parrhēsia* was "originally rooted in political practice and the problematization of democracy, then later diverging towards the sphere of personal ethics and the formation of the moral subject" (Foucault 2011: 8). Analyzing Socratic *parrhēsia*, Foucault maintains that *parrhēsia* concerns the way in which one lives. It is an attitude, an *ēthos*, the style one gives to one's life; in other words, it is a component of the care of the self, the beautiful existence, and the true life, all crucial notions in classical ethics. Foucault turns to Cynicism as a model of a philosophical practice that radicalized the Socratic notion of ethics and the Platonic notion of truth as unconcealed and incorruptible. The Cynic pushes the practice of truth-telling "to the point that it becomes intolerable insolence" (Foucault 2011: 165); the Cynic's life is "scandalous, unbearable, ugly, dependent, and humiliated poverty" (Foucault 2011: 259). The Cynic bears witness to the truth in its crude and scandalous extreme by embodying a disregard for the codes of propriety and conventions with which the Platonic true life was associated. For example, Diogenes broke the distinction between activities that are conventionally done in private, such as satisfying basic needs, and other public ones. Doing so implied disregard for the Platonic injunction to live in a balanced and organized way with regard to nature and customs. The Cynics transgressed this organization and conformism by basing their behavior only on the domain of nature, to the point of destitution and dishonor; they promoted practices that were otherwise unheard of in ancient Greek society and its moral economy.

These normative reversals embodied by the Cynics complement the advice that the Delphic oracle gave to Diogenes the Cynic: change the value of the currency. This advice was generally understood as referring to the Cynics' tendency to challenge customs and break conventions. In view of this injunction, Cynic *parrhēsia* implies a change in the way in which people generally lead their lives. The Cynic ethic implies a life lived *otherwise*; "an *other* life, not simply as the choice of a different, happy, and sovereign life, but as the practice of a combativeness on the horizon of which is an *other* world" (Foucault 2011: 287). Rather than an ethics of self-renunciation and obedient submission to an authority which deciphers the truth of one's soul, the Cynic *ēthos* creates a transformative rupture in standard conventions and points to the possibility of selves and worlds being otherwise. Cynics defy; Cynics reveal the artificiality of norms and "explode the hypocrisy of accepted values" (Gros 2011: 354).

The two approaches Foucault adopts to practices of self-narration discussed in this and the previous section—namely, self-narration as caught up with subjugating effects of power/knowledge, and self-narration as a possible instance of ethical self-constitution with parrhesiastic potential—must be seen in tandem and not exclusive of one another. The next section explores how feminist uses of Foucault's ideas have drawn upon his work to highlight this inherent tension in practices of self-narration, whereby they can possess a trace of *parrhēsia* while also facing the risk of having this critical potential neutralized.

## Self-Narration Between/Beyond the Personal and the Political

Feminist theory has been particularly receptive to Foucault's late work, and some feminist thinkers have turned to his late work to locate conceptual resources that complement or extend feminist aims. Margaret A. McLaren uses Foucault's work to identify feminist technologies of the self, particularly practices of self-narration, that can destabilize current configurations of power relations and can result in the development of creative practices of the self imbued with the potential for *parrhēsia*. McLaren highlights how confessional self-narration occupies a dual space:"[c]onfession, Foucault says, has a *double* sense of subjection; one is *compelled to tell the truth* about oneself by institutionalized religious norms, but at the same time the speaking subject *constitutes herself* through this articulation. Confession is, at least in part, about the subject's participation in her own self-construction" (McLaren 2002: 146, *emphasis added*). Despite contrary interpretations, Foucault did not deny this latter active possibility, arguably not even in his earlier work, as seen in the cases of Rivière and Barbin. Confessional practices thus ambivalently position the subject "both as producer of and as produced through her discourse" (McLaren 2002: 149). If self-narration aims solely or predominantly at discovering an inherent truth about oneself, then it qualifies as an example of normalizing confession. On the contrary, self-narration can function as a critical practice of active subject-formation (or active subjectification, as opposed to passive processes of subjection or, worse, subjugation) if it aims at critically examining how one came to be as one is with reference to normalizing discourses, or seeks to reveal the discursive conditions and practices of power that enable a particular self-characterization over another.

Except for occasional references in interviews to practices of friendship or sexual pleasure (Foucault 1997c), Foucault did not dwell much on how contemporary practices of the self can function critically rather than hegemonically. McLaren's work is fruitful in that she identifies a series of feminist practices of autobiography and consciousness-raising that can go beyond normalizing confessional power and have the potential for subversive *parrhēsia*.[5] Although criticized by some (McLaren 2002: 157–9; Alcoff and Gray 1993: 282–3) as depoliticizing due to their insistence on the personal at the expense of the political, or by assuming a false homogeneity among women, proponents of practices of consciousness-raising argued that the strength of these practices lay in how women were empowered by realizing that some of their daily struggles were shared by other individuals too and, as such, "were not personal pathologies, but reflected a larger pattern of social and political discrimination" (McLaren 2002: 155). Through such practices, one's experiences of discrimination are not seen as referring back to an inherent truth about the individual's identity; instead, experiences are *connected* to broader social realities that perpetuate these discriminations. The shareability of concerns among women, although surely subject to individual differences, could have an empowering function that motivates social change. Importantly, such practices did not have any individual therapeutic aims: "Consciousness-raising is many things, but one thing it is not is psychotherapy, or any other kind of therapy. Therapeutic processes have been employed mostly to encourage participants to adjust to the social order. Consciousness-raising seeks to invite rebellion" (Dreifus, *cit. in* McLaren 2002: 156); "[t]he total group process is not therapy because we try to find *the social causes for our experiences* and the possible programs for changing these" (Allen, *cit. in* McLaren 2002: 157, *emphasis added*). This point invites further consideration of the social situatedness of individual narratives.

Ewick and Silbey (1995) too regard consciousness-raising groups as a good example of how counter-hegemonic and possibly subversive narratives can be developed, both as a form of resistance against dominant narratives as well as a creative and politically transformative practice. Ewick and Silbey analyze the possibility of counter-hegemonic narratives by referring to a dual function of narrative: an *epistemological* role through which narratives reveal social and cultural meanings, and a *political* role whereby narratives can be invoked with subversive or transformative aims to counter culturally dominant ways of organizing and interpreting social realities. This countering gesture is not to be understood as mere opposition: it is not clear where, when and how a narrative becomes a counter-narrative. "Narratives," Ewick and Silbey argue, "can function to sustain hegemony or, alternatively, subvert power" (Ewick and Silbey 1995: 200). It is not easy to neatly delineate where hegemony ends and subversion begins; indeed, the two phenomena are, by their complex nature, not clearly demarcated in any convenient way.

To unpack this difficult tension, Ewick and Silbey analyze what they call the social organization of narrative by suggesting that "narratives are told for a variety of reasons, to a variety of audiences, with a variety of effects" (Ewick and Silbey 1995: 205). They highlight that narratives are not told in a random manner; there are contexts that regulate (by eliciting as well as by discouraging) *when* a narrative is given. Even if it is determined that it is a right context for narration, social norms and conventions govern the narrative content, that is, *what* gets narrated. Not any type of content is expected and treated favorably. Ewick and Silbey cite an example from the courts whereby narratives that defy the court's definitions of a coherent and persuasive account tend to be treated "as filled with irrelevancies and inappropriate information" (Ewick and Silbey 1995: 207). This also raises questions on whether narratives need to fulfil certain performative conditions in order to be treated as credible (see Borg 2018). Ewick and Silbey note that, especially in court contexts, true accounts are disbelieved simply because they do not satisfy the implicit presentation requirements. From a critical theory perspective that seeks to reveal how power relations function, it is crucial to analyze how a subject's credibility is tied to specific discursive norms, who has access to such knowledge of norms, and what kind of narratives these norms are precluding from the start. Thus, "[t]he social organization of narrative or storytelling regulates not only when and what kinds of stories can be told, it also governs ... *how* stories are told" (Ewick and Silbey 1995: 208). Lastly, alongside the *when* (context), the *what* (content) and the *how* (presentation), narratives are also socially organized with regard to their intention, that is, with regard to their *why*: "storytelling is strategic. Narrators tell tales in order to achieve some goal or advance some interest. ... We tell stories to entertain or persuade, to exonerate or indict, to enlighten or instruct" (Ewick and Silbey 1995: 208).

These different dimensions of narratives operate simultaneously. To some degree, narratives must satisfy some narrative and social expectations if they wish to be intelligible and efficacious; otherwise, they are condemned to unintelligibility or triviality. Inevitably, narratives rely on a social conventionality, which means that "[b]ecause of the conventionalized character of narrative, then, our stories are likely to express ideological effects and hegemonic assumptions" (Ewick and Silbey 1995: 212). The hegemonic contribution of narratives happens through various means, for example when they reproduce existing structures of meaning and power, or when narratives stifle and preclude alternative narratives by presenting themselves as the only viable or credible narratives. Narratives also function hegemonically when "they conceal the social organization of their production" (Ewick and Silbey 1995: 214) and hide the fact that their significance and pervasion are cultural phenomena, and thus are not unquestionable.

Importantly, Ewick and Silbey emphasize that narratives contribute to existing hegemonies "by effacing the connections between the particular and the general" (Ewick and Silbey 1995: 215). This ties back to McLaren's characterization of feminist consciousness-raising groups as possibly embodying *parrhēsia* by resisting what Foucault calls "individualizing power" (Foucault 2000c: 300). Foucault highlights how power does not only act in a *totalizing* manner by aspiring to give, despite cracks and resistance, an exhaustive account of the individual; power is also *individualizing*, that is, it uses the notion of individuality as a vehicle for normalization and subjection. As he explains, "the state's power (and that's one of the reasons for its strength) is both an individualizing and a totalizing form of power" (Foucault 1983: 213). Narratives can be studied in a similar way. Besides offering totalizing schemes of interpretation, power functions hegemonically on narratives by individualizing. Ewick and Silbey argue that this happens, for example, in the legal system:

> In fact, given the ideological commitment to individualized justice and case-by-case processing that characterizes our legal system, narrative, relying as it often does on the language of the particular and subjective, may more often operate to sustain, rather than subvert, inequality and injustice. The law's insistent demand for personal narratives achieves a kind of radical individuation that disempowers the teller by effacing the connections among persons and the social organization of their experiences.
>
> Ewick and Silbey 1995: 217

This point suggests that what constitutes a counter-hegemonic or subversive narrative is not its being the absolute opposite of hegemonic narratives; it might be the case, as Foucault after all suggests, that there is no "outside" to power relations, and that counter-narratives work through the same logic of power relations and "merely" thwart or frustrate the intended outcomes of power (Foucault 1998: 94–102). Ewick and Silbey characterize narratives as subversive insofar that they emplot a connection between "biography and history" (Ewick and Silbey 1995: 218). This does not amount to reducing an individual's narrative to the broader socio-historical conditions that give rise to it, or to generalizing an individual's narrative, but encourages a consideration of particular experiences as socially, culturally, and politically rooted. Ewick and Silbey characterize such subversive or counter-hegemonic narratives as follows:

> [S]ubversive stories are those that break the silence. Stories that are capable of countering the hegemonic are those which bridge, without denying, the particularities of experience and subjectivities and those which bear witness to what is unimagined and unexpressed ... Subversive stories are narratives that employ the connection between the particular and the general by *locating the individual within social organization*.
>
> Ewick and Silbey 1995: 220

This, however, is not a straightforward matter; narratives can sway and be swayed between hegemonic normalization and subversive parrhesiastic truth-telling, despite the aims of the speakers. The next section situates narratives of trauma within this tension that characterizes practices of self-narration. Despite—or perhaps because of—the risks entailed in attempting to do so, traumatic self-narration can function as *parrhēsia* by revealing the artificiality of hegemonic norms and subverting them.

## Survivors as Parrhesiasts: The Subversive Truth-Telling of Trauma

In their Foucauldian analysis of survivor discourse, Linda Alcoff and Laura Gray locate this tension that surrounds and haunts trauma narratives. On the one hand, narratives of trauma can function critically and subversively by revealing and disrupting hegemonic discourses and practices. But equally, on the other hand, the flexibility of power relations can neutralize this subversive potential by transforming it into another technique by which power functions. Reflecting on the constantly emerging narratives of rape, incest and sexual assault, they ask: "Is this proliferation and dissemination of survivor discourse having a subversive effect on patriarchal violence? Or is it being co-opted: taken up and used but in a manner that diminishes its subversive impact?" (Alcoff and Gray 1993: 261) Alcoff and Gray recognize that practices of "speaking out" and "breaking the silence" have great critical potential in calling for and effecting political transformation, but they also recognize that such practices must be analyzed as discursive acts that are subject to entanglement with and co-option by power relations that can sterilize and commodify them (Alcoff and Gray 1993: 261). Drawing on Foucault's accounts of discourse and confession as power, they show how, beyond the conscious intentions of speakers, power functions through:

> multiple and subtle mechanisms by which dominant discourses have co-opted our collective speech and whether this tendency toward co-optation can be effectively resisted. One of our central concerns will be how the tendency of the confessional structure to disempower the confessor can be overcome.
> 
> Alcoff and Gray 1993: 263

Alcoff and Gray "explore the transgressive character of survivors' speech" (Alcoff and Gray 1993: 263) not to conclude that survivors' narratives are unilaterally powerful, but to show how survivors' discourse constitutes a site of unstable conflict. Despite efforts—be they systemic, structural, or not—to silence and discredit survivors, their discourse persists in, echoing Cynic *parrhēsia*, "disgusting and disturbing ... the listeners' constructed sensibilities" (Alcoff and Gray 1993: 266). Survivor speech intervenes at a discursive level by introducing in the realm of the thinkable categories such as "'rapist father' or 'rapist boyfriend' as an object of discussion or analysis" (Alcoff and Gray 1993: 266). Survivors' discourse posits itself as demanding to be heard while critically foregrounding "conventional speaking arrangements: arrangements in which women and children are not authoritative" (Alcoff and Gray 1993: 267).

However, although survivors' narratives of trauma can rattle and disconcert, "the speaking out of survivors has been sensationalized and exploited by the mass media, in fictional dramatizations as well as 'journalistic' formats such as ... television talk shows" (Alcoff and Gray 1993: 262). These techniques amount to the silencing of the subversive potential of trauma narratives, or "to channel it into nonthreatening outlets" (Alcoff and Gray 1993: 268). Such nonthreatening outlets include an excessive focus on the individualizing facet of the narrative which places the prime emphasis on the individual narrative while failing to regard how the trauma suffered connects to wider structural issues. To connect the narrative in this way does not amount to obscuring the individual out of the narrative, but shows how individual experiences are made possible by broader social conditions, and that a therapeutic emphasis on experience may fail to capture the role of social constitution. Another nonthreatening outlet is to transform the survivor into "docile, self-monitoring bodies who willingly submit themselves to (and thus help to create and legitimate) the authority of experts" (Alcoff and Gray 1993: 260), whereby such experts coolly position themselves as possessors of universal truths. In such circumstances, "[i]t is the expert rather than the survivor who will determine under what conditions the survivor speaks and whether the survivor's speech is true or acceptable within the dominant discourse's codes of normality" (Alcoff and Gray 1993: 271).

It is amid this unstable terrain that survivors' narratives of trauma exist, with their potential to subvert continuously subject to intricate recuperation tactics. Speaking out as a political tactic loses its critical efficacy if, or when, it amounts to passing everything having to do with trauma "through the endless mill of speech" (Foucault 1998: 21). While recognizing that there is no one clear answer to their questions, Alcoff and Gray ask:

> has it [the growth of the phenomenon of speaking out] simply replayed confessional modes which recuperate dominant patriarchal discourses without subversive effect, or has it been able to create new spaces within these discourses and to begin to develop an autonomous counterdiscourse, one capable of empowering survivors? Given that power operates not simply or primarily through exclusion and repression but through the very production and proliferation of discourses, should we not be more than a little wary of contributing to the recent proliferation of survivor discourse?
>
> Alcoff and Gray 1993: 275

This wariness complements Foucault's own hesitance in uncritically regarding any seeming practice of resistance as obvious, unilateral and actual resistance, without acknowledging that this presumption of subversion would, in fact, be mistaking power for its ruse and rashly confusing the cure with its lure. As he cautions at the end of *The Will to Knowledge*: "The irony of this deployment [of sexuality] is in having us believe that our 'liberation' is in the balance" (Foucault 1998: 159). By thinking that one is placing oneself outside the ruse of power could mean that one might be contributing to the solidification of power relations, despite one's best intentions.

Alcoff and Gray's analysis does not seek to pour cold water on any attempt to subvert the grip of hegemonic power. Rather, they speak from the position of survivors motivated by concerns of justice and empowerment who also recognize that human experience is imbued with theory and discourses, and thus "always already political" (Alcoff and Gray 1993: 283). In conclusion to their charged analysis, they highlight how "[a]s survivors, we must develop and identify methods and forums in which emotional expression can activate the subversive potential of our rage" (Alcoff and Gray: 286), amid attempts to discredit survivors' narratives on the basis of their emotional presentation displaying either "too much emotion" (and thus manipulative) or "too little emotion" (and thus not as credible) (Alcoff and Gray 1993: 285). Ultimately, the subversive potential of survivors' narratives of trauma can be unleashed if the depoliticizing and silencing strategies of power that channel the narratives through the authoritative and familiar discourses is overridden. Managing to do so elevates trauma narratives from the realm of the subjugated confessional to the status of *critical witnessing*: "to speak out, to name the unnameable, to turn and face it down" (Ziegenmeyer, *cit. in* Alcoff and Gray 1993: 287). Alcoff and Gray conclude that this empowered and empowering use of trauma narratives is a way "to make survivor discourse public in such a way as to minimize the dangers of speaking out for survivors yet maximize the disruptive potential of survivor outrage" (Alcoff and Gray 1993: 286). This critical use of outrage, which is not within any individual's sole grasp and which can have effects that transcend individual subjectivity, is echoed by Judith Butler's remarks on the state of ec-stasy which she defines as follows:

> To be ec-static means, literally, to be outside oneself, and thus can have several meanings: to be transported beyond oneself by a passion, but also to be *beside oneself* with rage or grief. I think that if I can still address a "we," or include myself within its terms, I am speaking to those of us who are living in certain ways *beside ourselves*, whether in sexual passion, or emotional grief, or political rage.
> 
> Butler 2004: 24

The central question that this chapter is asking is: can certain narrations of trauma by survivors function as instances of *parrhēsia* and, if so, how? Nowadays, the authoritative currency which gives meaning to narratives of trauma is that of the psychological sciences, psychotherapy, discourses of resilience, recovery, well-being, integration, and therapies aimed at restoring the individual's control and mastery over his or her own life story. This has implications on which narratives of trauma are privileged, which are normalized, and which testimonies are silenced. Hence, the valence of these discourses must be kept in mind when critically evaluating how and why trauma is narrated, and how such narrations can function subversively. Survivors of trauma often report a powerful need to testify, to bear witness to the horror they suffered. Survivors feel it as their duty to remember what they and others, especially those who died, have been through. Auschwitz survivor Primo Levi recalls how, after his release from the concentration camps, he felt an unrestrainable need to narrate the trauma—"Every situation was an occasion to tell my story to anyone and everyone" (Levi, *cit. in* Agamben 1999: 16)—leading him to resort to writing in an almost obsessive way. Testimonies can be a coping mechanism for survivors, an opportunity to finally render in words that which has haunted the survivor. Trauma testimonies persist; as Terrence Des Pres puts it, they are "given in memory, told in pain and often clumsily, with little thought for style or rhetorical device" (Des Pres 1976: 29). Trauma narratives are told with hesitance, urgency, and brutality. Trauma is also narrated amid the risk of being subject to the possibly normalizing discourses of well-being, and particular forms of trauma narratives—homogenized, pathologized, commodified, if not aestheticized—are encouraged at the expense of other narratives.

Beyond the feeling of utter powerlessness, trauma is so catastrophic because it involves a betrayal of trust in what is supposed to sustain and secure the comfort of one's life. This, Jenny Edkins writes, "can be devastating because who we are, or who we think we may be, depends very closely on the social context in which we place and find ourselves ... If that order betrays us in some way, we may survive ... but the meaning of our existence is changed" (Edkins 2003: 4). Auschwitz survivor Jean Améry echoes this sense of betrayal which trauma brings with it in his poignant remark: "Every morning when I get up I can read the Auschwitz number on my forearm ... Every day anew I lose my trust in the world" (Améry, *cit. in* Edkins 2003: 8). For the trauma survivor, something significant about oneself and the society one inhabits loses its meaning. What before the traumatic incident felt more or less fixed and secure now becomes an appearance. Yet survivors are in a way trapped within that same linguistic and social context, and their suffering is made sense of through the current predominant schemes of intelligibility: "This is the dilemma survivors face. The only words they have are the words of the very political community that is the source of their suffering" (Edkins 2003: 8). In the face of the seemingly unquestionable contemporary regimes of truth, the survivors' statements jar and disturb. The affective dimensions of survivors' voices too—their anger, bitterness, and urgency—have a critical value. As Edkins notes, referring to a remark by a U.S. Marine veteran: "Their anger was not new. It was 'old, atavistic. We were angry as all civilized men who have ever been sent to make murder in the name of virtue were angry'" (Edkins 2003: 7, *cit. in* Herman 1992: 27).

Survivors' narratives can have a politically subversive role that challenges structures of power and authority (Edkins 2003; Jensen 2013). Terrence Des Pres locates the subversive trace within survivors' testimonies when he writes that "[t]he survivor, then, is a disturber of the peace. He is a runner of the blockade men erect against knowledge of "unspeakable" things. About these he aims to speak, and in so doing he undermines, without intending to, the validity of existing norms. He is a genuine transgressor" (Des Pres 1976: 42–3). By foregrounding the lack of fixity of technologies of power that uphold the appearance of social order, survivors' testimonies appear as untimely, unusual, irregular and unwanted because of their untamed character. Testimonies of trauma may subvert in a parrhesiastic vein when they challenge a nation-state's version of events, or a state's defense of violent practices it may employ to, paradoxically, prevent violence. Narratives of trauma may uncover instances when legal apparata do not function as empowering tools that secure and protect the vulnerable. Trauma narrations may shatter the brashness, solidity and presumptuous certainty with which certain policies are implemented, condemnations are made, and commemorations are performed. Non-conforming testimonies may reveal a potentially violent will to truth lurking beneath speech, transforming it to confessional discourse rather than critical *parrhēsia*. The risky truth-telling of traumatized individuals may present a critique to the model of subjectivity upon which political practices and discourses of psychology are based—the resilient and free subject of self-mastery—enabling care of the self to mean something other than depoliticizing therapeutic care. It is in these senses that the narrative interventions of trauma survivors can function politically as socially engaged practices of *parrhēsia*, pointing to *other* ways in which subjectivity and social life can be organized.

## Conclusion: Narrating Otherwise

This chapter analyzed traumatic self-narration through a theoretical lens informed by Foucault's varied approaches to practices of self-narration, arguing that the truth-telling of survivors' narratives of trauma can be compared to the courageous truth-telling of *parrhēsia* by virtue of its subversive potential. However, trauma narratives at large *may not* achieve such an aim, since narrations of trauma can be veered by normalized confessional discourses rather than the courageous subversion associated with *parrhēsia*. Foucault's work on Rivière and Barbin exemplifies his ideas on discourse and power, which can be read in dialogue with the ethical and political questions raised by the late Foucault. His work enables the development of critical conceptual resources with which to study practices of self-narration. Further research prospects are now opened up in this area by the recent publication of *Les aveux de la chair* (Foucault 2018).

This chapter follows Foucault's claim on the centrality of the politics of ourselves by analyzing micro-practices of self-narration to highlight how, despite their seeming mundaneness, they are a gateway to the study of processes of subject-formation and the government of the self in contemporary times. Such an analysis shows how power functions intricately and intimately through practices of narrating oneself, but also shows how such "small practices" harbor a possibility of resistance. Exploring the theoretical stakes of practices of self-narration means asking questions about what experiences are being enabled, and what modes of relating to oneself, to others, and to the world are being hindered by dominant discourses and practices. The stories we tell about ourselves can be swayed by the hard grip of normalizing power, but stories can also reveal the fallibility of power, its finitude, and can present new and creative opportunities which might disclose, as Foucault puts it, "the possibility of no longer being, doing, or thinking what we are, do, or think [. . . by giving] new impetus, as far and wide as possible, to the undefined work of freedom" (Foucault 1997e: 316). Adopting a critical outlook to the activity of self-narration foregrounds its ethical and political stakes; what can be called the political ethics of self-narration. The late Foucault, indeed his entire work, can enrich this endeavor.[6]

## Notes

1 "Middle" Foucault is generally regarded as being his 1970s works. This "period" is typically associated with his genealogical "phase," during which he studied connections between discourse and power relations as they manifest themselves, for example, in disciplinary practices and in conceptualizations of modern sexuality. "Late" Foucault refers to his 1980s works, which are often said to have undergone a so-called "ethical turn" to an engagement with Greco-Roman antiquity. While there are notable shifts in Foucault's later work, it is less correct to speak of "breaks" or "turns" than of fruitful developments. I discuss how the relation between Foucault's work on power and ethics can be understood in terms of a continuity in his engagement with the question of the subject and *assujettisement* in Borg (2015).
2 This refers to a second-wave feminist slogan, made popular in the 1960s, that emphasizes that the personal or subjective is always (if not always already) tied to the social or political. Thus, problems which women might have thought were their personal problems—such as domestic violence or sexual abuse—are, in fact, a reflection of wider socio-political structures.

3   For more on Foucault's analyses of Rivière and Barbin, including critiques of his approach, see Butler (1990), Gilmore (2001), Lafrance (2005), Pereira Andrade (2007), Repo (2014), and Taylor (2009).
4   For further studies on the notion of *parrhēsia* in Foucault's work, see Flynn (1991), Dyrberg (2014), Folkers (2016), Lawlor (2016), Ross (2008), and Simpson (2012).
5   For further works that highlight how consciousness-raising groups, and strands of narrative therapy, can entail the potential of *parrhēsia*, see also Taylor (2009) and Valverde (2004).
6   Different parts of this chapter were presented in a more preliminary form in conferences and seminars in Lisbon, Malta, and Granada. I sincerely thank all those who helped me improve this work with their feedback, particularly Raylene Abdilla, Aaron Aquilina, Keith Pisani, and Kathrin Schödel.

# References

Agamben, G. (1999), *Remnants of Auschwitz: The Witness and the Archive*, trans. D. Heller-Roazen, New York: Zone Books.

Alcoff, L. and L. Gray (1993), "Survivor Discourse: Transgression or Recuperation?," *Signs: Journal of Women in Culture and Society*, 18 (2): 260–90.

Allen, P. (1970), *Free Space: A Perspective on the Small Group in Women's Liberation*, New York: Times Change Press.

Améry, J. (1999), *At the Mind's Limits: Contemplations by a Survivor on Auschwitz and its Realities*, trans. S. Rosenfeld and S. P. Rosenfeld, London: Granta.

Bernauer, J. W. (1990), *Michel Foucault's Force of Flight: Toward an Ethics for Thought*, New York: Humanity Books.

Borg, K. (2015), "Conducting Critique: Reconsidering Foucault's Engagement with the Question of the Subject," *Symposia Melitensia*, 11: 1–15.

Borg, K. (2018), "Narrating Trauma: Judith Butler on Narrative Coherence and the Politics of Self-Narration," *Life Writing*, 15 (3): 447–65.

Butler, J. (1990), *Gender Trouble: Feminism and the Subversion of Identity*, New York: Routledge.

Butler, J. (2004), *Precarious Life: The Powers of Mourning and Violence*, New York: Verso.

Des Pres, T. (1976), *The Survivor: An Anatomy of Life in the Death Camps*, New York: Oxford University Press.

Dreifus, C. (1973), *Women's Fate: Raps From a Feminist Consciousness-Raising Group*, New York: Bantam Books.

Dyrberg, T. B. (2014), *Foucault on the Politics of* Parrhesia, New York: Palgrave Macmillan.

Edkins, J. (2003), *Trauma and the Memory of Politics*, Cambridge: Cambridge University Press.

Ewick, P. and S. S. Silbey (1995), "Subversive Stories and Hegemonic Tales: Toward a Sociology of Narrative," *Law & Society Review*, 29 (2): 197–226.

Flynn, T. (1991), "Foucault as Parrhesiast: His Last Course at the Collège de France (1984)," in J. Bernauer and D. Rasmussen (eds), *The Final Foucault*, 102–18, Cambridge, MA: The MIT Press.

Folkers, A. (2016), "Daring the Truth: Foucault, Parrhesia and the Genealogy of Critique," *Theory, Culture & Society*, 33 (1): 3–28.

Foucault, M. (1981), "The Order of Discourse," trans. I. McLeod, in R. Young (ed.), *Untying the Text: A Post-Structuralist Reader*, 48–78, Boston, London and Henley: Routledge & Kegan Paul.

Foucault, M., ed. (1982), *I, Pierre Rivière, Having Slaughtered My Mother, My Sister, and My Brother: A Case of Parricide in the 19th Century*, trans. F. Jellinek, Lincoln: University of Nebraska Press.

Foucault, M. (1983), "The Subject and Power," in H. L. Dreyfus and P. Rabinow (eds), *Michel Foucault: Beyond Structuralism and Hermeneutics*, 2nd ed., 208–26, Chicago: The University of Chicago Press.

Foucault, M. (1988), "Technologies of the Self," in L. H. Martin, H. Gutman, and P. H. Hutton (eds), *Technologies of the Self: A Seminar with Michel Foucault*, 16–49, London: Tavistock Publications.

Foucault, M. (1989), "I, Pierre Rivière," in S. Lotringer (ed.), *Foucault Live: Interviews 1966–84*, 131–6, New York: Semiotex(e).

Foucault, M. (1997a), "On the Genealogy of Ethics: an Overview of Work in Progress," in P. Rabinow (ed.), *The Essential Works of Michel Foucault, 1954–1984, Vol. 1: Ethics, Subjectivity and Truth*, 253–80, New York: The New Press.

Foucault, M. (1997b), "Self Writing," in P. Rabinow (ed.), *The Essential Works of Michel Foucault, 1954–1984, Vol. 1: Ethics, Subjectivity and Truth*, 207–22, New York: The New Press.

Foucault, M. (1997c), "Sex, Power, and the Politics of Identity," in P. Rabinow (ed.), *The Essential Works of Michel Foucault, 1954–1984, Vol. 1: Ethics, Subjectivity and Truth*, 163–73, New York: The New Press.

Foucault, M. (1997d), "The Ethics of the Concern of the Self as a Practice of Freedom," in P. Rabinow (ed.), *The Essential Works of Michel Foucault, 1954–1984, Vol. 1: Ethics. Subjectivity and Truth*, 281–301, New York: The New Press.

Foucault, M. (1997e), "What is Enlightenment?," in P. Rabinow (ed.), *The Essential Works of Michel Foucault, 1954–1984, Vol. 1: Ethics, Subjectivity and Truth*, 303–19, New York: The New Press.

Foucault, M. (1998), *The Will to Knowledge: The History of Sexuality, Volume 1*, trans. R. Hurley, London: Penguin Books.

Foucault, M. (2000a), "About the Concept of the 'Dangerous Individual' in Nineteenth-Century Legal Psychiatry," in J. D. Faubion (ed.), *The Essential Works of Michel Foucault, 1954–1984, Vol. 3: Power*, 176–200, New York: The New Press.

Foucault, M. (2000b), "Lives of Infamous Men," in J. D. Faubion (ed.), *The Essential Works of Michel Foucault, 1954–1984, Vol. 3: Power*, 157–75, New York: The New Press.

Foucault, M. (2000c), "Omnes et Singulatim: Towards a Critique of Governmental Reason," in J. D. Faubion (ed.), *The Essential Works of Michel Foucault, 1954–1984, Vol. 3: Power*, 298–325, London: Penguin.

Foucault, M. (2005), *The Hermeneutics of the Subject: Lectures at the Collège de France 1981–1982*, ed. F. Gros, trans. G. Burchell, New York: Picador.

Foucault, M. (2007), *Death and Labyrinth: The World of Raymond Roussell*, trans. C. Ruas, London: Continuum.

Foucault, M. (2010), *The Government of Self and Others: Lectures at the Collège de France, 1982–1983*, ed. F. Gros, trans. G. Burchell, Basingstoke: Palgrave Macmillan.

Foucault, M. (2011), *The Courage of Truth (The Government of Self and Others II): Lectures at the Collège de France 1983–1984*, ed. F. Gros, trans. G. Burchell, Basingstoke: Palgrave Macmillan.

Foucault, M. (2013), *Herculine Barbin: Being the Recently Discovered Memoirs of a Nineteenth-Century French Hermaphrodite*, trans. R. McDougall, New York: Vintage Books.

Foucault, M. (2014), *On the Government of the Living: Lectures at the Collège de France 1979–1980*, ed. M. Senellart, trans. G. Burchell, Basingstoke: Palgrave Macmillan.

Foucault, M. (2016), *About the Beginning of the Hermeneutics of the Self: Lectures at Dartmouth College, 1980*, ed. H.-P. Fruchaud and D. Lorenzini, trans. G. Burchell, Chicago: The University of Chicago Press.

Foucault, M. (2018), *Histoire de la sexualité 4: Les aveux de la chair*, Paris: Gallimard.

Foucault, M. and A. Farge (2016), *Disorderly Families: Infamous Letters from the Bastille Archives*, ed. N. Luxon, trans. T. Scott-Railton, Minnesota: University of Minnesota Press.

Gilmore, L. (2001), *The Limits of Autobiography: Trauma and Testimony*, Ithaca, NJ: Cornell University Press.

Gros, F. (2011), "Course Context," in M. Foucault, *The Courage of Truth (The Government of Self and Others II): Lectures at the Collège de France 1983–1984*, ed. F. Gros, trans. G. Burchell, 343–58, Basingstoke: Palgrave Macmillan.

Herman, J. L. (1992), *Trauma and Recovery: The Aftermath of Violence—From Domestic Abuse to Political Terror*, London: Pandora.

Jensen, M. (2013), "Post-Traumatic Memory Projects: Autobiographical Fiction and Counter-Monuments," *Textual Practice*, 28 (4): 701–25.

Lafrance, M. (2005), "The Struggle for True Sex: Herculine Barbin dite Alexina B and the Work of Michel Foucault," *Canadian Review of Comparative Literature*, 32 (2): 161–82.

Lawlor, L. (2016), *From Violence to Speaking Out: Apocalypse and Expression in Foucault, Derrida and Deleuze*, Edinburgh: Edinburgh University Press.

Levi, P. (1997), *Conversazioni e interviste*, Turin: Einaudi.

McLaren, M. A., (2002), *Feminism, Foucault, and Embodied Subjectivity*, New York: State University of New York Press.

O'Leary, T. (2002), *Foucault and the Art of Ethics*, New York: Continuum.

Pereira Andrade, D. (2007), "Parallel lives: Foucault, Pierre Rivière and Herculine Barbin," *Tempo Social*, 19 (2): 233–52.

Repo, J. (2014), "*Herculine Barbin* and the Omission of Biopolitics from Judith Butler's Gender Genealogy," *Feminist Theory*, 15 (1): 73–88.

Ross, A. (2008), "Why is 'Speaking the Truth' Fearless? 'Danger' and 'Truth' in Foucault's Discussion of *Parrhesia*," *Parrhesia*, 4: 62–75.

Simpson, Z. (2012), "The Truths We Tell Ourselves: Foucault on *Parrhesia*," *Foucault Studies*, 13: 99–115.

Taylor, C. (2009), *The Culture of Confession from Augustine to Foucault: A Genealogy of the "Confessing Animal,"* New York: Routledge.

Valverde, M. (2004), "Experience and Truth Telling in a Post-Humanist World: A Foucauldian Contribution to Feminist Ethical Reflections," in D. Taylor and K. Vintges (eds), *Feminism and the Final Foucault*, 67–90, Chicago: University of Illinois Press.

Ziegenmeyer, N. (1992), *Taking Back My Life*, New York: Simon & Schuster.

# List of Contributors

**Karim Barakat** is a lecturer at the American University of Beirut, Lebanon. His research focuses on non-ideal theory and in particular on the problem of deriving evaluative dictates beginning from an analysis of history. His research interests additionally include contemporary Arabic political philosophy. He has also published on Rawls, Hobbes, and Foucault.

**Laurence Barry** is a researcher at the Chaire PARI (ENSAE/Sciences Po Paris). Her thesis, "Foucault and Postmodern Conceptions of Reason," deals with the intertwinement of knowledge and power in a historical perspective. Her research interests include the digital knowledge/power nexus, current trends of neoliberalism, and the impact of big data technologies on our conception of risk and the practice of insurance.

**Amélie Berger-Soraruff** is a fellow of the Scottish Centre for Continental Philosophy and teaches at the University of Dundee, UK. She has also lectured at the Melbourne School of Continental Philosophy. Recently, she co-translated Bernard Stiegler's first article, "Technologies of Memory and Imagination," for the journal *Parrhesia*. Her research focuses on technologies and their psycho-political significance. Her areas of interest include French philosophy, media theory, phenomenology, and aesthetics.

**Kurt Borg** completed a PhD in Philosophy at Staffordshire University, UK, with a thesis on the ethics and politics of narrating trauma in institutional contexts, drawing particularly on the work of Michel Foucault and Judith Butler. He obtained a BA and MA in Philosophy from the University of Malta, the latter with a dissertation on the relation between Foucault's work on power and ethics. He lectures at the University of Malta on Foucault, ethics, medical sociology, and philosophy of disability. He has published articles and book chapters on Foucault, Butler, trauma theory, and disability studies.

**Élise Escalle** is a PhD student in aesthetics, who teaches in the Department of Philosophy at Paris Nanterre University, France. Her dissertation topic is located at the intersection of cultural history, feminist music criticism, and transgender studies. A research assistant for the COMUE Paris Lumières project "Gender and Transmission" (2016–19), she has contributed to several publications, workshops, and conferences on Music and Gender.

**Marta Faustino** is a research fellow at the Nova Institute of Philosophy (IFILNOVA), in Lisbon, Portugal, where she currently coordinates the Art of Living Research Group.

Her main research focus is the relationship between philosophy and therapeutic and self-cultivating practices. She is the author of several articles on Nietzsche, Hadot, Foucault, and the Hellenistic philosophers as well as co-editor of *Nietzsche e Pessoa: Ensaios* (Tinta-da-China, 2016) and *Rostos do Si* (Vendaval, 2018).

**Gianfranco Ferraro** is a post-doctoral researcher at the Nova Institute of Philosophy (IFILNOVA), in Lisbon, Portugal. His research focuses on philosophical forms of conversion, particularly concerning Foucault, Nietzsche, and the history of utopian thought. Recent publications on this topic include "Da vocação" (2019), "From Merleau-Ponty to Foucault (and Beyond): Towards a Contemporary Ontology of Immanence" (2019), "Exercícios de inactualidade" (2019), and "La conversione del quotidiano: Foucault e l'utopia come tecnica di vita" (2019). He is a member of the Red Iberoamericana Foucault and director of the international journal *Thomas Project: A Border Journal for Utopian Thoughts*.

**Matko Krce-Ivančić** has a PhD in Sociology from the University of Manchester, UK. His primary interest is in exploring the relation of subjectivity and politics, where power is understood to be constitutive for our subjectivity. His PhD project was concerned with the interconnection of neoliberal governmentality and gendered subjectification process. He has published on anxiety and neoliberalism.

**Luca Lupo** is professor at the University of Calabria (Italy) in the Department of Humanities. His research interests focus on moral philosophy, especially on Friedrich Nietzsche's thought and on the relationships between ethics and psychoanalysis. He has published articles on several authors (Schopenhauer, Wittgenstein, Freud, and Jung). His most recent book is *Forme ed etica del tempo in Nietzsche* (2018).

**Antonio Moretti** is a member of Centro di Ricerca Interdisciplinare di Storia delle Idee (CRISI) at San Raffaele University, Milan, Italy. His research interests focus on contemporary French philosophy in its relationship with both political and ethical practices of *critique*, particularly in the work of Gilles Deleuze and Michel Foucault. He obtained his PhD with a thesis on *Governamentalità e verità. Uno studio sul problema del governo in Michel Foucault* (Governmentality and truth. A study of Michel Foucault's relationship of government). He has edited Italian translations of works by Pierre-Joseph Proudhon and Jacques Rancière.

**John Sellars** is a Reader in Philosophy at Royal Holloway, University of London, UK. He is also a Visiting Research Fellow at King's College London and a member of Wolfson College, Oxford. He is the author of *The Art of Living: The Stoics on the Nature and Function of Philosophy* (2003; 2nd ed. 2009), *Stoicism* (2006), and *Hellenistic Philosophy* (2018). In 2016 he edited *The Routledge Handbook of the Stoic Tradition*.

**Edgar Straehle** is professor at the Universitat de Barcelona and a researcher at the Seminar Philosophy and Gender / ADHUC—Research Center for Theory, Gender, Sexuality at the University of Barcelona. His research interests focus on contemporary political philosophy and philosophy of history. His most recent book is *Claude Lefort. La inquietud de la política* (2017).

**Federico Testa** is an IAS Early Career Fellow at the University of Warwick, UK, where he teaches philosophy and sociology. His current research focuses on the notions of life and norms in Michel Foucault and Georges Canguilhem, contemporary French thought, and the revival of Hellenistic tradition in modern and contemporary philosophy. He is the co-editor and translator of Pierre Hadot's *Selected Writings. Philosophy as Practice* and Jean-Marie Guyau's *The Ethics of Epicurus*.

**Andrea Teti** is Senior Lecturer at the University of Aberdeen (Scotland) and Associate Editor of *Middle East Critique*. His research focuses on the politics of democracy promotion, democratization, and authoritarianism in the Middle East, and political theory. He is co-author of the forthcoming *Democratization against Democracy*.

**Michael Ure** is a Senior Lecturer in the School of Social Sciences, Monash University, Australia. His research interests focus on modern European philosophy, the history of political thought, and the politics of emotions. His most recent book is *Nietzsche's The Gay Science: An Introduction* (2019).

# Index

action 7, 19, 45, 56, 67, 79, 102–5, 109, 117, 124, 126, 136, 138, 140–1, 145, 152–6, 184, 194n.6, 200, 207, 221, 235–6, 247n.13, 253, 255–6
Adorno, Theodor 186
aesthetics 10, 39, 40, 41, 44, 62, 62n.30, 74, 80, 83, 89
    of existence 23, 26, 40–3, 54–5, 57, 192–3
Agamben, Giorgio 4, 43–4, 48nn.1,8, 65
Alcibiades 68n.9, 95, 120
Alcoff, Linda 260–3
*alethurgy* 22, 140, 219, 224
Améry, Jean 263–4
antiquity 3, 9–10, 19, 20, 24, 30, 38–9, 43, 55, 63, 75, 89, 110, 115, 123, 126, 129n.19, 133–5, 141, 144, 159, 228, 233, 234, 236, 245, 247n.14, 255, 265n.1
archaeological 3, 7, 10, 89, 115–19, 123–6, 129n.11, 133, 135, 167, 170, 171, 173
archaeology 5, 7, 75, 82, 115–16, 118, 120–7, 129n.14, 134, 160n.3, 167, 170, 251
Arendt, Hannah 11, 183–94, 194n.4
Aristotle 6, 22, 95, 133–7, 145n.2
Aristoxenus 94, 96
art 6, 8, 34n.8, 39–40, 42–4, 48n.9, 58–9, 73, 85, 89–90, 92, 94–5, 113, 119, 122, 133, 150, 159, 161n.11, 74, 176, 189, 204, 223, 235
    of government 58, 59, 122, 156, 159, 174
    of living 23, 26, 34n.8, 43, 68n.14, 73, 79, 85, 235, 244, 247nn.11,14, 255
    of the self 85
ascetic 25, 42, 224, 233
asceticism 25
*askēsis* 26–32, 34n.10, 39, 79, 91, 119, 128n.8, 159
attitude 6–7, 38, 53, 60, 97, 102–3, 115–19, 125–7

Augustine, Saint 134
Aurelius, Marcus 39, 45, 47, 49n.18, 64
authoritarian 183–6, 190
authoritarianism 183–9, 194
authority 11, 64, 152, 177, 183–94, 194n.3, 195n.10, 237, 242, 244–5, 256–7, 262, 264
autobiography 128n.8, 258
*aveu/aveux* 12, 38, 215–21, 223, 228
avowal 12, 157–60, 161n.14, 215–9, 230n.2

Barbin, Herculine 251–5, 257, 265, 266n.3
Baudelaire, Charles 118
Beck, Aaron 238, 246n.10
biopower 79, 84, 187, 225–7
biopolitics 5, 123, 229
*bios* 22, 126, 192, 244, 256
body 6, 22, 38, 40, 56, 76, 79, 84, 92, 153, 154, 156, 174–7, 192, 203, 204, 207, 240
Butler, Judith 4, 82, 160n.2, 161n.10, 208, 263, 266n.3

capitalism/capitalist 201, 203–5
care 3, 7, 9, 10, 31, 45, 53, 55, 56, 58, 59, 68nn.9,14, 73, 74, 79, 82–5, 97, 104, 115, 119–27, 129n.13, 221, 227–8, 234, 263
    ethics of 3, 7, 10, 73, 238, 256
    of others 9, 45, 120, 123, 125
    of the self 8–10, 23, 31, 38, 40–7, 48n.4, 53, 55–9, 64–7, 79, 103–4, 115, 119–21, 123–7, 129n.13, 133–4, 149, 245, 256, 264
Carlier, Jeannie 40, 44, 53–4
Christian/Christianity 6–7, 10, 29, 38–9, 42, 44, 57–8, 66, 97, 111n.9, 122, 125–7, 129nn.10,13, 141, 156, 159, 198, 217–27, 220–5, 229, 233, 235–7, 246n.5, 255–6

Cicero 92
cognitive behavioral therapy (CBT) 234, 238–44, 246nn.9,10,11, 247n.13
conduct 43–4, 79–80, 82, 91, 96–7, 101, 122, 140, 149, 152, 154, 157, 159, 160n.6, 161n.11, 173, 176, 192, 194n.6, 206, 224, 227, 235, 256
   of conducts 140, 154, 157, 159, 173, 176
confession 12, 38, 97, 121, 122, 129n.10, 140, 156, 157, 160, 161n.8, 170, 215–29, 230n.2, 233, 235–7, 246nn.5,7, 251, 254–7, 261
control 11, 55, 76, 83, 85, 90, 93, 96, 103, 105, 107, 109, 115, 122, 151, 174, 239, 244, 263
conversion 21–2, 25, 27, 30, 42, 54, 58–60, 63–7, 119, 123, 247n.14
Council of Trent 140
courage 64, 123, 144, 188, 190–2, 236, 245
   of truth 144
Crates 33n.6, 193
critical theory 83, 197, 259
critical experience 120
critical witnessing 262–3
criticism 1, 9, 37, 40, 43, 45, 46, 49n.13, 53–6, 69n.30, 75, 78, 84, 110, 117, 120, 129n.10, 158, 167, 191, 193–4, 195n.7, 234, 236, 245
critique 6, 7, 11, 25, 31–2, 53–4, 59, 66, 81, 93, 116–19, 121, 123, 125, 128n.5, 134–8, 140, 145n.4, 167–72, 175–8, 178n.2, 179nn.5,6,10, 197–8, 202, 252, 264, 266n.3
culture 21–7, 30, 39, 42, 55, 59, 85, 120, 129n.13, 160, 179n.13, 180, 199, 234–5, 251
Cynicism/Cynics 19–24, 31, 33n.6,8, 119, 183, 192–4, 253, 256–7, 261

Damon of Athens 92
dandyism 40, 42–4, 47, 55, 68n.7
Davidson, Arnold 33n.4, 34n.9, 37, 40, 44, 53–4, 160n.8
death 1–3, 5, 23, 38, 40–1, 62, 107–9, 110n.3, 112n.14, 127, 133, 149, 159, 191, 195n.9, 217, 210–11, 254
Defert, Daniel 13n.1, 160nn.4,5
Delattre, Daniel 89–92, 94–6, 97nn.1,2

Deleuze, Gilles 4, 13n.5, 74, 77, 81–2, 124, 129n.11, 139, 225
democracy/democratic 84, 153, 188–91, 195nn.8,9, 200, 200, 201, 256
democratization 191
Derrida, Jacques 81
Descartes, René 24–5, 34n.9, 48n.10, 137, 142
   "*cogito ergo sum*" 142
desire 23, 24, 28, 29, 32, 66, 68n.11, 84, 95, 136–8, 145n.5, 155, 160, 161n.9, 191, 222, 239, 253–4
Diogenes of Babylon 90–7, 98n.3, 193
Diogenes the Cynic 24, 34n.8, 256–7
Diogenes Laertius 49nn.17,20, 94
Dion of Syracuse 191
disciplinary 3–4, 10, 74, 76, 78, 83–5, 89, 133, 156–7, 168, 176, 218, 225, 233, 238, 265n.1
discipline/disciplines 26, 69n.26, 75, 78, 83–4, 120, 149, 154–6, 159, 161n.11, 175, 187, 204, 206, 209, 224–5, 228, 230n.5, 254
dispositive 133, 215, 217–21, 224–9, 236, 243
Dreyfus, Hubert 76, 111n.7,8, 112n.14, 215
Dumézil, Georges 12n.1, 157

economic reductionism 203, 205–6
economy 153–5, 198, 205, 216–29
education 90–4, 243
Elden, Stuart 8, 13nn.1,2,4, 14nn.14,16, 48n.3, 129nn.10,14, 215, 218, 221
Eliot, T. S. 107
Ellis, Albert 238, 246n.10
emancipation 11, 12, 32, 121, 151, 194, 197–203, 207–10, 228–9
empirical 30, 74–5, 78–85, 167, 170–3, 176–9
empiricism 167, 170, 241
Epictetus 45, 49n.16, 240, 245, 246n.10, 255
Epicurus/Epicurean 10, 27, 31, 33n.3, 41, 60–1, 64, 69n.23, 89–96, 102, 105–9, 240, 245
*epimeleia heautou* (care of the self) 9–10, 120, 123–4, 191
*epithalamia* 95
Erato 94–5

Eribon, Didier 12, 13nn.3,5,9, 14n.13, 128n.8, 135
ethics 9, 14n.15, 19, 21, 26, 28, 32, 42, 44, 53, 55, 60, 76, 79, 81, 96, 127, 159, 225, 256
  ancient 3, 9–10, 20, 28, 32, 33n.2, 39, 47, 54, 59, 62, 238, 256
  of care 3, 7, 10, 73, 238, 256
  modern 9, 19–21
  notion of 124, 256
  and pleasure 48n.10, 54–5
  and politics 10, 58, 124, 186
  and power 251, 265n.1
  of self-completion 9, 20
  of self-cultivation 234, 243, 245
  of self-dissolution 9, 20, 30
  of self-formation 74, 77
  of self-narration 265
  of self-renunciation 257
  Stoic 37, 46–7, 54, 65
  of subjectivation 73
  and truth 134, 251
ethos/*ēthos* 6–7, 20, 26–7, 31, 64, 117–18, 125–7, 141, 188, 235, 256–7
Ewald, François 4, 6, 13n.2, 152
example/exemplar/exemplary 25, 42, 43, 49n.19, 54, 110n.3, 120, 140, 188, 193, 194, 205, 218, 243, 244
exercise/exercises 9–11, 25–33, 37, 39, 41, 54, 59–61, 66, 74, 80, 101–2, 105–9, 110n.5, 123, 184, 224, 234–5, 238–9, 241, 243, 246nn.5,10, 247n.13
  of power 11, 140, 149, 151–3, 155–6, 159, 179n.10, 187, 191, 207, 219, 253–4
  of the self 31, 111, 126, 224
  spiritual 9, 20–4, 26–7, 29, 31–2, 33nn.4,5, 37, 39, 41–2, 44, 53, 55. 60–2, 65, 67, 105, 109, 111n.12
experience 10, 20, 25, 31, 41, 44, 53, 59–64, 67, 69nn.33,34, 80, 82, 89–90, 105, 109, 111n.9, 120–1, 128n.8, 171, 178–9, 260–2
experiment 6, 32, 60, 126, 241
experimentation 30, 60, 126

Ferguson, Adam 55, 174–5, 179n.11
Fontana, Alessandro 4, 6, 13n.1, 141

Foucault, Michel (works)
  *Abnormal: Lectures at the Collège de France, 1974-1975* [*Les Anormaux: Cours au Collège de France, 1974-1975*] 140, 217, 226–9, 230n.2
  *About the Beginning of the Hermeneutics of the Self: Two Lectures at Dartmouth, 1980* [*L'origine de l'hermenéutique de soi. Conférences prononcées à Dartmouth College, 1980*] 135, 238
  *Dits et écrits* 3, 135, 230n.3
  *Discipline and Punish* [*Surveiller et punir*] 57, 84, 133, 154, 156, 160n.7, 175
  *Discourse and Truth: The Problematization of Parrhesia* [*Discours et vérité* précédé de *La parrêsia*] 2
  *History of Madness* [*Histoire de la folie à l'âge classique*] 2, 134, 229
  *History of Sexuality 1: The Will to Know* [*Histoire de la sexualité 1: La volonté de savoir*] 3, 29, 38, 56, 75, 89, 96, 123, 149, 152, 156, 160n.8, 215, 218, 223, 226, 228, 229, 233
  *History of Sexuality 2: The Use of Pleasure* [*Histoire de la sexualité 2: L'usage des plaisirs*] 3, 8, 9, 13n.10, 29, 38, 39, 43, 75, 96, 133, 135
  *History of Sexuality 3: The Care of the Self* [*Histoire de la sexualité 3: Le souci de soi*] 3, 8, 9, 29, 38, 39, 40, 44, 75, 76, 96, 120, 133, 135
  *History of Sexuality 4: The Confessions of the Flesh* [*Histoire de la sexualité 4: Les aveux de la chair*] 2, 3, 8, 12n1, 29, 38, 44, 75, 96, 216
  "I, Pierre Rivière, having slaughtered my mother, my sister, and my brother: A Case of Parricide in the 19th Century" ["Moi, Pierre Rivière, ayant égorgé ma mère, ma sœur et mon frère... Un cas de parricide au XIXe siècle"] 134, 251–3
  *Lectures on the Will to Know: Lectures at the Collège de France, 1970-1971* [*Leçons sur la volonté de savoir:*

*Cours au Collège de France (1970–1971)]* 11, 135, 136, 139, 141, 142n.2, 149, 216

"Nietzsche, Genealogy, History" ["Nietzsche, la généalogie, l'histoire"] 27, 134

"Omnes et singulatim" 122, 125, 220, 227, 229

*On the Government of the Living: Lectures at the Collège de France, 1979–1980 [Du gouvernement des vivants: Cours au Collège de France (1979–1980)]* 3, 8, 48n.5, 136, 140, 146n.6, 215, 216, 219, 220, 222, 224, 226, 228, 229

*Penal Theories and Institutions: Lectures at the Collège de France, 1971–1972 [Théories et institutions pénales: Cours au Collège de France (1971–1972)]* 2, 216

"Politics and Ethics" ["Politique et éthique"] 186

"Questions of Method" ["Table ronde du 20 mai 1978"] 172, 179n.9

*Security, Territory, Population: Lectures at the Collège de France 1977–1978 [Securité, territoire, population: Cours au Collège de France (1977–1978)]* 140, 210n.1

"Self Writing" ["L'écriture de soi"] 92, 252, 253, 255

"Society Must Be Defended": Lectures at the Collège de France, 1975–1976 ["Il faut defendre la société": Cours au Collège de France (1975–1976)] 2, 173, 194n.5

"Space, Knowledge, and Power" ["Espace, savoir et pouvoir"] 178n.3

*Speaking the Truth about Oneself: Lectures at Victoria University, Toronto, 1982 [Dire vrai sur soi-même: conférences prononcées à l'Université Victoria de Toronto, 1982]* 145

Subjectivity and Truth: Lectures at the Collège de France, 1980–1981 [*Subjectivité et vérité: Cours au Collège de France (1980–1981)*] 4, 8, 120, 121, 233, 256

*The Archaeology of Knowledge* [*L'archéologie du savoir*] 134, 160n.3, 251

*The Birth of Biopolitics: Lectures at the Collège de France, 1978–1979 [La naissance de la biopolitique: Cours au Collège de France (1978–1979)]* 161n.11, 171–3, 176, 179n.9, 197, 210n.1

*The Courage of Truth (The Government of the Self and of Others II): Lectures at the Collège de France, 1983–1984 [Le courage de la vérité. Le gouvernement de soi et des autres II: Cours au Collège de France (1984)]* 3, 8, 12, 22, 120, 124, 144, 145n.2, 192, 193, 233

"The Ethics of the Concern of the Self as a Practice of Freedom" ["L'éthique du souci de soi comme pratique de la liberté"] 179n.13

*The Hermeneutics of the Subject: Lectures at the Collège de France, 1981–1982 [L'herméneutique du sujet: Cours au Collège de France (1981–1982)]* 4, 8–10, 21, 33n.4, 43, 46, 48n.2, 53, 115, 119–25, 133, 233, 238, 252

*The Order of Things: An Archaeology of the Human Sciences [Les mots et les choses: Une archéologie des sciences humaines]* 134, 179n.5

*The Punitive Society: Lectures at the Collège de France, 1972–1973 [La société punitive: Cours au Collège de France (1972–1973)]* 217

"The Subject and Power" ["Le sujet et le pouvoir"] 173–6

"Truth and Juridical Forms" ["La vérité et les formes juridiques"] 135

"What is an Author?" ["Qu'est-ce qu'un auteur?"] 1

"What is Critique?" ["Qu'est-ce que la critique?"] 179n.10

"What is Enlightenment?" ["Qu'est-ce que les Lumières?"] 117–18, 169, 178nn.1,3

*Wrong-Doing, Truth-Telling: The Function of Avowal in Justice [Mal faire, dire vrai: Fonction de l'aveu en justice]* 11, 216, 221, 223–4

*franc parler* 188, *see also parrhēsia*
freedom 6–7, 30–1, 33, 65, 74, 76, 78, 82,
    102, 115, 117–19, 121, 127–9, 138,
    142, 153, 175, 180, 185, 187–8,
    193–5, 202, 203–7, 209, 222, 239,
    245, 248, 265

genealogical 3, 6, 7, 10, 20, 27, 30–1, 73, 77,
    115–19, 125, 133–5, 156, 167, 171–3,
    176–8, 224
genealogy 5, 9–10, 20, 33, 38, 59, 68n.11,
    79, 83, 120, 129n.10, 134, 136, 139,
    160n.5, 170–1, 176, 215, 218, 226,
    234, 246n.8, 251
  archaeo-genealogy 73
  and archaeology 116, 118, 120, 124,
    134
  and confession 220–1, 224
  and government 140, 146n.6, 170, 172
  and ontology 116–17
  and philosophy 20, 136
  and power 172
  self-genealogy 117–18
  as a spiritual exercise 26–32
  and truth 144–5
Gernet, Louis 151
government 56–9, 68n.14, 124, 133–44,
    146n.6, 153–7, 161n.11, 167–81
governmentality 8, 11, 53, 56–9, 76, 78,
    118–24, 140, 149, 152–3, 157, 160,
    161n.9, 167–77, 186–7
Gray, Laura 258, 260–3
Greek 2, 12, 19, 23–4, 39, 79, 90, 92, 95,
    122, 135, 159, 188, 217
Greece (ancient) 135–6, 151, 157, 160n.4,
    188
Gros, Frédéric 2, 4, 13n.7, 101, 103, 110,
    110nn.1,4, 129n.10, 257

Habermas, Jürgen 68n.8, 118, 158, 178n.3
Hadot, Ilsetraut 21–2
Hadot, Pierre 4, 9, 19–22, 31, 33nn.1,4,5,
    34n.9, 37–51, 48nn.1,2,6,8,10,
    49nn.14,19, 53–68, 68nn.2–6,11,
    69nn.22–8,30,31, 111n.12, 234, 245,
    246n.4, 247n.14, 270
Halperin, David 90
Han-Pile, Beatrice 32, 167
Hegel, Georg Wilhelm 33n.6, 118, 126

Heidegger, Martin 76, 110, 112n.14, 118,
    127–8, 129n.14, 137
Heraclides Ponticus 96
hermeneutics 29, 123–4, 235, 243
  of the self 89, 91, 97, 119, 144, 222–3,
    233–4, 237–8, 242–3, 252–3
  of the subject 10, 115, 119, 124, 252
historical 6–7, 10, 31, 42, 54, 57–60, 65, 68,
    73–7, 89, 906, 115, 134, 167, 168,
    170, 171, 172, 176–7, 179n.5
history 20, 144, 172, 177, 190, 251
Hobbes, Thomas 171, 173–4, 185
Homer 23, 34n.8, 150–1, 157–9, 161n.12
Hume, David 170–1, 174, 179n.6
*hupomnēmata* 79, 83, 91–3, 96, 255
Husserl, Edmund 73, 75, 79–80, 82, 118

Ignatius of Loyola 39
individual 1, 3, 6, 21, 25, 34n.8, 39, 46, 54,
    56, 60–8, 74, 76–80, 84, 119, 141,
    155–6, 180, 208, 221, 235, 238, 242,
    252, 256, 260, 263
individualism 3, 227, 259
individuation 84, 260
institution/institutions 3, 83–5, 120, 128,
    135, 140, 154, 175, 186, 188, 202,
    205–7, 254
interpretation 1, 4, 5, 8, 9, 12, 13n.4, 29,
    41–2, 44, 54, 56, 60–1, 77, 81, 90,
    129n.11, 135, 139, 144, 157–60, 167,
    169, 183–4, 188, 218, 228, 237, 243,
    252, 254

Kafka, Franz 2–3
Kant, Immanuel, 11, 73–4, 79, 82, 117–18,
    129n.14, 137, 167–72, 175–8,
    178nn.1–2, 179n.7
knowledge 43, 58, 62, 68, 76, 93, 110n.3,
    111n.10, 117, 120–2, 140, 144,
    154–5, 160n.2, 167, 176, 177, 204,
    220, 237, 243–4, 251, 259, 264
  bodies of 171
  conditions of possibility of 74, 169
  as *connaissance* 117, 126, 149–52,
    160n.3
  effects of 219
  limits of 169, 179n.5
  of nature 47, 53, 59, 61, 64–7
  passion for 27–9, 34n.11

and power 11, 74, 136, 150, 152, 158, 170, 178n.3, 179n.5, 187, 254, 257
production of 226
scientific 247n.15
of the self 47, 224
subject of 30, 126
systems of 134
and truth 21, 136–9, 254
and veridiction 11, 149–61, 161n.14, 170, 223–4
and will 136
Kojève, Alexandre 185

Laclau, Ernesto 11–12, 197–204, 207–9, 210n.2
Lemke, Thomas 172
Levi, Primo 263
liberalism 152–5, 197–8, 202, 205–6
 neoliberalism 3, 197–210
 ordoliberalism 197, 203
liberation 65–6, 111, 224, 262
life 1, 5–7, 12, 21–3, 31, 41, 56, 64, 107–9, 120, 193, 235, 257, 263
 way of 9, 19–33, 49n.21, 60–1, 79, 104, 107, 192, 235, 245, 247n.14
limit 6, 7, 12, 25, 31–2, 34n.9, 61, 78, 91, 111n.13, 118, 152–4, 168–70, 185, 190, 207, 234, 243
 limit-attitude 7, 31
Locke, John 174
Lorenzini, Daniele 14n.15, 48n.1, 49n.13, 143, 145n.4, 150, 160n.1
Lucius Calpurnius Piso Caesonius 92
Lucretius 62
Luhmann, Niklas 106

McLaren, Margaret A. 257–9
madness 120, 170–1, 217, 221, 229
Marx, Karl 198–9, 204
Marxism/Marxist 20, 198–9, 205–6
 post-Marxism 198–9
meditation/meditations 107, 123, 134, 255
 *meditatio mortis* 10, 102, 107–9
 *praemeditatio malorum* 10, 102, 105–7, 109, 240
 premeditation 105, 107
*melete* 123
Morris, Phyllis Sutton 74, 78, 81
Mouffe, Chantal 197–201, 210n.2

music/musical 10, 89–97, 97n.1, 98, n.3, 243
musicality 89–90

Negri, Antonio 4, 183
Neoplatonism 9, 39, 44–5, 47, 49n.14
Nietzsche, Friedrich 6, 13n.5, 23–30, 33, 34nn.10–12, 78, 101, 104, 118, 125, 134, 136–9, 145n.4, 146n.5, 150, 171, 178n.3
 Nietzschean 9, 20, 26, 29–31, 136, 139, 151, 158, 160n.5, 161n.10, 178n.3
nominalism 167, 170–3, 175
Nora, Pierre 12n.1
norm/norms 31, 57, 82, 152, 157, 159, 202, 218, 228, 242, 252, 257, 259–60, 271
normal/normality 19, 33, 120, 155, 217–18, 224, 228–9, 237, 245, 251, 262
normalization 83, 187, 216, 229, 251–2, 259, 260

*ontogenesis* 81
ontology 78, 115–28, 129n.14, 169
 critical ontology of ourselves 6, 7, 10, 115–19, 123, 125–6, 134
 of freedom 118, 128
 historical 115–16, 129n.14, 134
 of subjectivity 124
 of the present 6, 7, 10, 116–19, 124–5, 127, 169

*paideia* 23, 90, 95
pain 105, 263
Pareyson, Luigi 128, 129n.15
*parrhēsia* 8, 11–12, 98n.5, 119–21, 124, 144–5, 183–94, 195nn.7, 9, 222, 229, 236, 240, 245, 252–64
parrhesiastic 97, 110, 188, 190–1, 236, 237, 240, 243, 247, 253, 260, 264
Pasquino, Pasquale 141
pastoral/pastorality 6, 57, 120, 122–3, 125, 140–1, 156, 187, 221, 223–8
Philo of Alexandria 61
Philodemus of Gadara 10, 89–97, 97nn.1, 2, 98n.5
philosophy 6, 8, 48n.10, 49n.14, 74, 83, 96, 102, 117, 124, 126, 136–9, 168–9, 191, 193, 215, 242

ancient 9, 19–31, 33nn.1,3,5, 37, 39–41, 54–5, 58–64, 67, 133–5, 233–6, 238, 240, 243–5
  as an art of living 43, 235
  history of 20, 60
  modern 25, 117–19
  as a way of life 19, 22, 24–32, 60
Pindar 23, 93–4
Plato 22, 27, 31, 34n.8, 68nn.9,20, 90, 92, 94–6, 97n.3, 98n.4, 111n.9, 134, 191–2, 207, 221
  Platonic 33n.1, 43, 46, 58, 66, 77, 171, 256
  Platonism/Neoplatonism 9, 31, 39, 44–5, 47, 49n.14, 76
pleasure 10, 38, 42, 48n.10, 54–5, 62, 65–6, 89–97, 155
Plotinus 39, 44
Plutarch 91, 103–4
politics 10–12, 14n.15, 53, 56–9, 83–5, 124–5, 129n.13, 134, 141, 167, 172, 176–7, 179nn.9,10, 184, 190–2, 198–201, 225, 234, 238, 245, 251–65
population 56, 122, 133, 221, 237
power, 9–11, 28, 55–8, 61, 62, 78–80, 92–6, 120–3, 128n.9, 135–45, 149–60, 183–92, 194, 197, 198, 202–10, 215–29, 233, 234, 237, 238, 243–5, 251–65
  and authority 184–8
  and avowal 222–3, 226, 229
  and genealogy 172
  and governmentality 53, 76, 173–8, 179n.10, 187
  and knowledge 11, 74, 136, 158, 257
  metaphysics of 78
  non-violent 188
  pastoral 125, 140–1, 156, 187, 220–1, 223, 225–8
  productive 11, 136, 140
  psychopower 79, 84–5
  relations 11, 57–8, 77–9, 85, 116, 151, 171–8, 179n.9, 194nn.4,5, 202, 216, 217, 224, 251–4, 257, 259–62, 265n.1
  repressive 84, 203, 204, 207
  systems of 134, 145
  and truth 136, 142–4, 159, 177, 222
practice/practices 6–10, 19–24, 43–4, 53–4, 57–60, 75, 77, 79, 82, 84–5, 89–97, 105, 108–9, 111nn.12,13, 115–122, 124–8, 134, 136, 139, 141, 143–5, 151, 154–7, 159–60, 171, 173, 176–8, 179n.10, 190–1, 193, 206–7, 217, 222–5, 228–9, 230n.5, 233–5, 246nn.9,10, 251–8, 260–2, 265n.1
  ancient 10, 20, 26–7, 30–2, 34n.9, 37, 39–40, 43, 47–8, 48n.10, 64, 119, 125, 236, 237–8
  Christian 223
  discursive 8, 188
  ethical 26, 41, 44
  governmental 175–6, 207
  of government 57, 154
  pagan 38–9
  philosophical 6–7, 9–10, 20–1, 26, 53, 57, 60, 115, 117–18, 128n.8, 236, 243, 256
  political 145, 177, 256, 264
  of self-transformation 7, 24, 26, 37, 39, 43
  of subjectivation 85
  of the self 10, 19–20, 26–7, 29–32, 34n.9, 37–8, 40–1, 47, 48n.10, 54, 59, 64, 101–3, 109, 111n.13, 159, 255–8
  therapeutic 234, 239
psychiatry 133, 155, 216–17, 228, 234–7, 240
psychoanalysis 170, 234, 236–7, 240
psychology 64, 84, 154, 155, 170, 264
psychotherapy 12, 234, 238, 241–5, 252
Pythagoras 92, 93, 95, 98n.3

rational 45, 93, 95, 120, 153, 155, 158, 168, 238
rationality 66, 103–4, 140–1, 177
reason 13n.9, 20, 21, 30–1, 40, 42, 45–7, 60, 62, 66, 75, 83, 94–6, 102–3, 111n.12, 121, 127, 128n.3, 136, 140, 155, 157, 168–9, 171–2, 183–91, 200–2, 217, 230n.5
recognition 11, 73, 76–7, 133, 158, 184–5, 190, 222–3, 225
religion 151, 159, 199
resistance 56, 80, 126, 184, 187, 215, 234, 245, 258–9, 262
Revel, Judith 14nn.11,14, 116, 128n.2
revolution/revolutionary 122, 198

Robertson, Donald 234, 238–42, 245, 246nn.3,9–11, 246nn.13,14
Rolland, Romain 63, 69n.33
Roman 19, 22, 30–2, 38–49, 46, 69n.29, 90, 92–4, 97, 97n.1, 122, 133–4, 184, 193, 241
Rome (ancient), 19, 23, 30–1, 46, 54–6, 90, 93–4, 97, 133, 134–5, 159, 184, 193, 220, 241
Rousseau, Jean-Jacques 216
Roussell, Raymond 251
Russell, Bertrand 183

salvation 125–7, 198, 223, 225, 235
Schopenhauer, Arthur 25–6, 109
science/scientific 19, 26, 64, 77, 92, 116, 122, 142, 155–6, 158, 233, 27, 243–5, 263
self 9, 19–21, 25, 29–32, 37–47, 49n.13, 53–63, 65–7, 69nn.30,31, 73–82, 85, 90–1, 93, 96–7, 103, 109–10, 110n.6, 111n.12, 119, 121, 123, 126–7, 129n.13, 140, 156–60, 161n.11, 215–18, 220, 224–9, 235–8, 243, 245, 246n.5, 253, 255–6, 265
  care of the 8–10, 23, 31, 38, 40–7, 48n.4, 53, 55–9, 64–7, 79, 103–4, 115, 119–21, 123–7, 129n.13, 133–4, 149, 245, 256, 264
  conversion of the 21, 27, 30, 59
  ethic of the 56, 245
  hermeneutics of the 89, 91, 97, 119, 144, 222–3, 233–4, 237–8, 242–3, 252–3
  practice(s) of the 10, 19–20, 26–7, 29–32, 34n.9, 37–8, 40–1, 47, 48n.10, 54, 59, 64, 101–3, 109, 111n.13, 159, 255–8
  technics of the 73–85
  technologies of the 3, 7, 9, 11, 21, 33n.5, 37–9, 41, 43, 48n.4, 55, 79, 80, 83, 85, 90, 101, 112n.14, 121, 129n.13, 235, 238, 240, 252, 257
  transformation of the 27, 31, 38, 193
self-analysis 235, 240–1
self-awareness 107, 240, 245
self-completion 9, 20, 31, 33
self-construction 257
self-creation 40, 48n.4, 81, 83
self-cultivation 21, 32, 46, 48, 48n.4, 234, 243, 245
self-dehiscence 32
self-dissolution 9, 20, 31, 33
self-entrepreneurship 204, 208
self-examination 38–9, 217, 233–7, 240, 246nn.5,6, 255
self-monitoring 240, 261
self-narration 12, 251–4, 256–5
self-sufficiency 21, 31–2, 34n.8
self-transformation 7, 24, 26–7, 37, 39, 43, 48, 48n.4, 243, 255
self-writing 92–3, 97, 252–3, 255
Seneca, 22, 31, 38–41, 45–7, 48n.3, 53, 62, 64–7, 69nn.29,36,37, 106–7, 240–1, 247n.12, 255
sex/sexual 6, 8, 10, 38, 75, 89–91, 96–7, 155, 161n.8, 218, 228, 253–4, 258, 261, 263, 265n.2
sexuality 38, 68n.11, 89–91, 96, 129n.10, 133, 160, 161n.8, 168, 171, 218, 221, 228, 251, 253, 261, 265n.1
Sloterdijk, Peter 4, 209
Smith, Adam 127, 174
society 1, 34n.8, 39, 54, 121–2, 125, 141, 144, 156, 174, 192, 197, 202, 204, 206, 209–10, 227
soul 21–2, 39–40, 61, 64, 92–3, 134, 191, 225, 233–6
sovereign/sovereignty 19–20, 22–4, 31, 34n.8, 79, 110, 111n.13, 122, 126, 152–4, 157, 159, 160n.7, 173–4, 185–7, 194n.5, 205, 225, 236, 257
Spinoza, Baruch 29, 145n.5
spiritual/spirituality 9, 20–7, 29, 31–3, 33nn.4,5, 37, 39, 41–2, 44, 53, 55, 60–2, 64–5, 67, 105, 109, 110n.3, 111n.12, 140
Stesichorus 93–4
Stiegler, Bernard 10, 73–85
Stoic/Stoicism 10, 19, 20, 22, 27, 31–2, 33n.3, 34n.7, 37–9, 41–7, 48n.10, 49n.14, 53–4, 60–2, 64–6, 69n.23, 89–97, 102, 105, 107, 125, 126, 229, 234, 238–42, 240–1, 246nn.5,10,11, 247n.13, 255
struggle 5, 6, 26, 65, 78, 83, 110, 115, 133, 134, 144, 194, 199–201, 242, 256, 258

subject 1, 7, 10–11, 19–26, 29–32, 34n.9, 38, 47, 56–8, 60, 64, 68, 68n.11, 73–9, 82–3, 89, 101–4, 109, 111n.13, 112n.14, 118–27, 134, 137–44, 149, 152–60, 161n.8, 168–71, 174–7, 178n.3, 179n.10, 185, 191, 197–9, 202–9, 216–22
subjection 74–8, 94, 96, 144, 147, 161n.11, 174, 187, 194n.6, 215, 225, 237, 257, 259
subjectivation, 73–85, 93, 144, 149–50, 156–9, 206, 253
subjectivity, 9–11, 20–1, 25, 28, 34n.9, 57, 73, 120, 121, 136, 140, 149–60, 197–210, 208, 226–7, 229, 251

techniques 11, 23, 25, 58, 60, 77–80, 83, 119–20
*technogenesis* 81
technology/technologies 3, 7, 9–12, 21, 33n.5, 37–9, 41, 43, 55–6, 74, 78–85, 90, 101, 109, 112n.14, 121–2, 124–5, 129, 129nn.10,13, 221, 226, 233, 235, 238, 240, 252, 257, 264
    of power 221, 264
    of the self 3, 7, 9, 11, 21, 33n.5, 37–9, 41, 43, 55–8, 79–80, 83, 85, 90, 101, 109–10, 112, 121, 124, 129n.13, 235, 238–40, 252, 257
    of time 109–10, 111n.14, 112, 125
*tekhnē* 23, 39, 43–4, 49n.11, 79, 126
Tertullian 224–5, 229
therapy 12, 31, 233–44, 246nn.3,7,10, 247nn.13,14, 258, 266n.4
therapeutic/therapeutics 31, 40, 61, 217, 233–4, 236–9, 241–5, 246nn.4,10, 258, 261, 264
thinker/thinkers 174, 183, 186, 257
thought 3–12, 13n.1,4,9,10, 19, 23, 26, 27, 38–44, 47, 49n.13, 56, 61, 67, 80, 85, 101–10, 112n.14, 117, 121–4, 128n.8, 129n.14, 133–4, 139, 145, 149, 168, 173, 178, 183, 186, 203, 223–30, 233–4, 236, 239–40, 244, 255, 265
Thucydides 191, 195n.11
time 10, 101, 103–7, 110, 110n.5, 112n.14
transcendentalism 74, 76, 116
transformation 7, 21–7, 30–1, 37–9, 58, 63, 126–7, 176–7, 228
trauma/traumatic 12, 252–3, 260, 263
truth 5, 10, 30, 38, 46, 57, 68, 77, 94, 96, 101, 102, 105, 109, 110, 121–4, 126, 133, 155–60, 172, 184, 192, 215, 217
    about oneself 39, 123, 233, 235–7, 251, 257
    agonistic 133–45
    analytics of 169, 177
    in antiquity 24–5, 141, 157–9
    discourse of 11, 89, 93, 149, 151, 191
    games of 20, 26, 27, 75–6, 141, 144
    history of 136, 139
    and *parrhēsia* 97, 191, 236–7, 255–7, 260
    production of 139, 218, 223, 227–8
    reflexive truth act 156, 219
    regime of 141–4, 171, 173, 219–20
    and subjectivity 20–3, 25, 28, 155, 253
    telling 12, 23, 58, 91, 93, 119, 145, 146n.7, 149, 155–7, 189–90, 195n.7, 224, 233–45, 251–65
    will to 34n.12, 89, 135–6, 177, 253, 255, 264

Vegetti, Mario 133–5
veridiction, 11, 149–50, 152, 154–9, 160n.1, 161n.14, 170, 223
Victorinus, Marius 39
Villa of the Papyri, Herculaneum 91

Weber, Max 118, 186, 205
wisdom 54, 59–62, 80, 101, 234–5, 255
writing 1, 4, 9–11, 13n.5, 41–3, 91–3, 96–7, 255–6

Zeno of Sidon 91
Žižek, Slavoj 209

www.ingramcontent.com/pod-product-compliance
Lightning Source LLC
Chambersburg PA
CBHW072128290426
44111CB00012B/1822